Mastery of the Financial Accounting Research System (FARS) Through Cases

Second Edition

THE WILEY BICENTENNIAL–KNOWLEDGE FOR GENERATIONS

*E*ach generation has its unique needs and aspirations. When Charles Wiley first opened his small printing shop in lower Manhattan in 1807, it was a generation of boundless potential searching for an identity. And we were there, helping to define a new American literary tradition. Over half a century later, in the midst of the Second Industrial Revolution, it was a generation focused on building the future. Once again, we were there, supplying the critical scientific, technical, and engineering knowledge that helped frame the world. Throughout the 20th Century, and into the new millennium, nations began to reach out beyond their own borders and a new international community was born. Wiley was there, expanding its operations around the world to enable a global exchange of ideas, opinions, and know-how.

For 200 years, Wiley has been an integral part of each generation's journey, enabling the flow of information and understanding necessary to meet their needs and fulfill their aspirations. Today, bold new technologies are changing the way we live and learn. Wiley will be there, providing you the must-have knowledge you need to imagine new worlds, new possibilities, and new opportunities.

Generations come and go, but you can always count on Wiley to provide you the knowledge you need, when and where you need it!

WILLIAM J. PESCE
PRESIDENT AND CHIEF EXECUTIVE OFFICER

PETER BOOTH WILEY
CHAIRMAN OF THE BOARD

Mastery of the Financial Accounting Research System (FARS) Through Cases

Second Edition

Wanda A. Wallace, Ph.D.
The John N. Dalton Professor of Business, *Emerita*
College of William and Mary

JOHN WILEY & SONS, INC.

VICE PRESIDENT AND PUBLISHER	Don Fowley
EXECUTIVE EDITOR	Christopher DeJohn
ACQUISITIONS EDITOR	Mark Bonadeo
PRODUCTION EDITOR	Nicole Repasky
SENIOR MARKETING MANAGER	Clay Stone
DESIGNER	Hope Miller
SENIOR MEDIA EDITOR	Allie K. Morris
EDITORIAL ASSISTANT	Karolina Zarychta
PRODUCTION MANAGEMENT SERVICES	Aptara, Inc.
COVER PHOTO	Steve Rawlings/Digital Vision
WILEY 200TH ANNIVERSARY LOGO	Richard J. Pacifico

This book contains citations from various FASB pronouncements. Copyright by Financial Accounting Standards Board, 401 Merritt 7, P.O. Box 5116, Norwalk, CT 06856.

This book was set in Times New Roman by Aptara, Inc. and printed and bound by Hamilton Printing. The cover was printed by Phoenix Color.

This book is printed on acid free paper. ∞

To order books or for customer service, please call 1-800-CALL WILEY (225-5945).

Library of Congress Cataloging in Publication Data:
Wallace, Wanda A.,
    Mastery of the Financial Accounting Research System (FARS) Through Cases /
Wanda A. Wallace. — 2nd ed.
       p. cm.
   ISBN-13:   978-0-471-74161-9 (paper/cd-rom)

  1.   Financial accounting research system. 2.   Accounting—Data processing
  3.   Accounting—Problems, exercises, etc.   I. Title.
   HF5679.W293 2008
   657.0285′53—dc22

2006101039

Dedicated to
Alan Peterson

An avid reader, believer in lifelong learning,
and true investor in human capital

*All who have meditated on the art of governing mankind have been
convinced that the fate of empires depends on the education of youth.*
—Aristotle (384–322 BC)

About the Author

Wanda A. Wallace, Ph.D., completed her doctorate at the University of Florida, with an Accounting Major, Finance Minor, and Statistics Research Skill. Professor Wallace has been a member of the faculty at the University of Rochester, Southern Methodist University (as The Marilyn R. and Leo F. Corrigan, Jr. Trustee Professor), and Texas A & M University (as The Deborah D. Shelton Systems Professor of Accounting) before joining the College of William and Mary as The John N. Dalton Professor of Business Administration and the Associate Dean for Academic Affairs at the School of Business. Dr. Wallace retired from academe in 2005, at which time the Board of Visitors awarded recognition as The John N. Dalton Professor of Business, *Emerita.* Dr. Wallace consults with national and international firms, ensuring up-to-date appreciation of current practice problems. She has consulted with such companies as Navigant Consulting and DuPont-Conoco. She was the Regression (Analysis) Consultant to the national office and world firm of Price Waterhouse (now PricewaterhouseCoopers) for over a decade. Previous expert testimony has involved a number of areas including: statistical sampling; statistical analysis; surveys; research methods; auditing; market competition; modeling and econometrics; systems and control processes; accounting; finance and valuation; distribution systems; intellectual property; economics; and business operations.

Dr. Wallace joined the Financial Accounting Standards Advisory Council (FASAC) which advises the Financial Accounting Standards Board (FASB) in 1991 and served through 1995. At the invitation of Charles A. Bowsher, then Comptroller General of the United States, Dr. Wallace served on the Government Auditing Standards Advisory Council from 1991 through 1996.

Dr. Wallace has received the Wildman Gold Medal, awarded to the most significant literary contribution to the advancement of public accounting over a three-year period by the American Accounting Association (AAA) and Deloitte and was a co-author of a chapter in the winning title of a second Wildman Gold Medal. She has received two AWSCPA Literary Awards. In 1998, a monograph containing a co-authored chapter on "Analytical Procedures" was awarded the Joint American Institute of Certified Public Accountants (AICPA)/AAA Collaboration Award. In September 2005, Dr. Wallace was highlighted in an article appearing in *Journal of Accountancy*, "Profiles in Success — Advice from Trailblazers and Rising Stars." She has been awarded a Certificate of Distinguished Performance on the Certified Management Accounting Examination and the Highest Achievement Award (Gold Medal) on the international Certified Internal Auditor Examination. She was issued her license as a Certified Public Accountant by the Texas State Board of Public Accountancy in 1974 and maintained the license throughout her academic career. Prior to her Ph.D., she was in public accounting. Dr. Wallace was selected in 1998 to receive the Virginia Society of CPAs Outstanding Accounting Educator Award in recognition of excellence in classroom teaching and for active involvement in the accounting profession. She was selected as the recipient of the Association of Government Accountants' 2002 Cornelius Tierney/Ernst & Young Research Award for outstanding research accomplishments over her career; the award "recognizes financial management professionals whose visionary leadership, outstanding accomplishments and exceptional service have significantly advanced our profession, strengthened our Association and improved our communities."

Dr. Wallace was extremely active in the academic profession, serving on over a dozen editorial boards for national and/or international journals, as well as having served as past editor of two academic journals. She served as the AAA Vice President, an officer in the AAA's Auditing Section, Chair of the AAA's Government and Nonprofit section, a member of the Board of Regents of the Institute of Internal Auditors (IIA), and Visiting Distinguished Faculty member of the Doctoral

Consortium, New Faculty Consortium, and Senior Faculty Consortium of the AAA. Professor Wallace was selected as an External Referee by the Research Grants Council of Hong Kong in 1998, which continued through 2005 to involve assessment of research proposals analogous to the domestic evaluation of proposals to the National Science Foundation. Among past activities, she has screened applicants for Fulbright Scholar awards. While in academics, she was a member of the American Statistical Association, AICPA, IIA, AAA, and the Institute of Management Accountants, among a number of other organizations. Dr. Wallace has been a visiting scholar at domestic and international universities, including The University of Manchester in England and the Norwegian School of Economics and Business Administration in Bergen, Norway.

Dr. Wallace has authored over 50 books and monographs (including *Internal Controls Guide* (3rd ed.), published by CCH Incorporated, A WoltersKluwer Company), and over 250 articles in such journals as the *Harvard Business Review, European Management Journal, Accounting Review, Journal of Accounting Research, Contemporary Accounting Research, CPA Journal, Government Finance Review, Journal of Government Financial Management, Financial Executive, Journal of Accounting, Auditing & Finance, Scandinavian Journal of Management, China Accounting and Finance Review, California Management Review, Auditing: A Journal of Practice & Theory, Corporate Governance: An International Review, Accounting Today, Business Horizons*, and the *Wall Street Journal*. In 1990, she was identified as the "Most Prolific Author in the Past Decade (1979–88) in 24 academic accounting journals" in the *International Journal of Accounting*. In 2003, she was identified as achieving the highest composite measure of articles from 1967 to 2001, adjusted for both co-authorship and quality of the journal among doctoral graduates in 1978 in a research study appearing in *Advances in Accounting*. Dr. Wallace's research has been supported by 28 different grants from a number of foundations including the National Science Foundation. Translations of her work include publications in Japanese, Chinese, and French.

Dr. Wallace's research, teaching, lecturing to professional audiences, and associated writings in academic journals, textbooks, and professional books have involved the application and development of extensive statistical, econometric, and analytical tools in diverse practice settings. She has presented seminars at over 30 universities domestically and internationally, including Columbia, Cornell, University of Chicago, University of British Columbia, Wharton, Northwestern, University of Alabama, University of Arizona, University of Texas (Austin), University of Arkansas, University of Connecticut, Boston University, Florida State University, Georgia Institute of Technology, University of Illinois, University of Iowa, Ohio State University, Texas Tech University, Washington University, University of Lancaster in England, and the Copenhagen School of Economics and Business Administration in Denmark.

PREFACE

The Financial Accounting Research System (FARS) is a powerful tool for gaining an understanding of generally accepted accounting principles (GAAP). FARS can be accessed in a variety of ways, including use of a CD-ROM, Intranet, or Internet. The academic version of FARS is updated once a year. The use of FARS is a formal part of the CPA Exam. See http://www.cpa-exam.org, where you can access the American Institute of Certified Public Accountants (AICPA) tutorial and related information.

You need to develop your ability to search the standards and associated guidance using Boolean logic. This second edition of *Mastery of the Financial Accounting Research System (FARS) through Cases* permits you to learn through a series of exercises, problems, and cases. Numerous self-study questions and answers, as well as completed examples of assignments and their solutions, provide you with guidance and quick feedback to facilitate your development of information search skills.

First you will learn to navigate in FARS. You will gain an understanding of the mechanics of navigation, as well as the nature of each of the infobases within FARS. Then you will build an essential competency of learning to reason through indices, becoming adept at determining where certain types of questions might be addressed. Chapter 1 begins with a Quick-Start and then provides a step-by-step detailed explanation on the use of FARS and its numerous search capabilities. It is a very functional primer that shows not only how to search, but what you can do with the results. Informative tables will prove to be handy references as you increasingly apply FARS in problem-solving and research activities.

You will want to refer to this book in a variety of courses throughout the curriculum. As you address a topic in your coursework and professional reading, you can turn to related coverage in exercises, problems, and cases.

Chapter 1 has Self-Review and Cross-Check sections that permit you to test whether you have gained an understanding of key dimensions of FARS. By revisiting Chapter 1 periodically, you can refresh your knowledge of FARS, including researchers' common pitfalls. Among topics highlighted within Chapter 1 are: (1) how the Financial Accounting Standards Board (FASB) Web site can be used for updating information not yet integrated into FARS but why that site and pulling up .PDF files cannot substitute for FARS; (2) the power of searches using the Topical Index; (3) the nature of the GAAP Hierarchy; and (4) why looking at dissents to the standards that have been issued can be helpful to your understanding of GAAP.

Chapter 2 shows how FARS can be complemented to explore specific facts and circumstances in which accounting principles are being applied. Its coverage includes handy reference materials on Internet resources, interactive databases, and professional literature. First an overview of these resources is presented, then a Case Study focuses on a 2005 event involving a small public company. The Case Study exercises apply the diverse resources to exploring revenue recognition issues, regulatory process, and developments associated with restatements. Exercise F addresses "Acronym Acumen." Remember as you use the Web that you need to carefully review the reputation of each site before using its material. In particular, watch out for outdated or incorrect information, and be sensitive to the distinction between fact and opinion.

Chapter 3 has categorized key vocabulary related to subject matter that is usually addressed in the common body of knowledge in accounting. Demarcation into three columns of basic, intermediate, and advanced helps to guide your construction of a personal dictionary for reference, as you shift from introductory topics to more advanced studies. All of the Vocabulary table entries are easily located in the Terminology section of the Topical Index of FARS. The Vocabulary tables organize key terms by subject matter, providing quick access to the professional literature's glossary definitions.

By phrasing a sentence that uses each term, you will demonstrate your understanding of the core meaning of terms and phrases.

Chapter 3 also includes complete-the-table exercises that describe searches to infer the meaning of various terms and concepts. The problems in Chapter 3 draw on the same subject matter as each of the tables.

Chapter 3 problems include Self-Study Q&A. These self-help, handholding types of problems permit you to walk through searches and provide immediate feedback on your performance. You are encouraged to work through all self-study problems associated with the subject matter of interest. It is excellent practice and will remind you of the diverse approaches you can take to searching FARS.

Chapter 3 has an Example of Assignments and Solution that will be a useful reference on how to proceed to solve each section of potential assignments from the three types of materials organized by subject matter. In addition, since that example includes a definition of the GAAP Hierarchy, it will be a ready resource to which to turn when analyzing the results of a search and considering the prioritization among citations.

Brain Teasers in Chapter 4 use an active dialogue approach of individuals discussing a conceptual or practice problem that needs to be analyzed. Search phrases must be designed to identify the resources that can shed light on the issue at hand. In addition, you are asked to explore a number of resources beyond FARS. Responding to such requests is facilitated through referencing the resource materials in Chapter 2 (and solving the five-part case that draws upon interactive databases, including resources for searching the literature, Internet, Web sites, public filings, legal cases, and both financial statement and financial markets information).

Chapter 4 Brain Teasers all have a narrow, directed Bonus Question that tends to be a bit more difficult than the Self-Study Q&A in Chapter 3. That facet of Chapter 4 permits you to build on your mastery of the self-study component in Chapters 1 and 3. The Bonus Question that appears for each Brain Teaser tends to be a straightforward, directed question that facilitates enhancement of FARS search skills. Depending on the topic within the Brain Teaser, you will find additional questions in varied subject matter from across the accounting curriculum, including Accounting Theory, Auditing, Tax, Not-for-Profit, Advanced Accounting, and International.

Chapter 4 includes an introduction with an Example of Brain Teaser with Solution that addresses the topic "What Has Changed in the Conceptual Framework?" In addition to its self-study advantages, the example will be a useful reference on how to proceed to solve assignments from among the Brain Teasers.

GAAP are filled with areas of judgment that require a clear understanding of context in order to analyze the alternative reporting practices that are acceptable and their consequences. FARS is a powerful tool for gaining an understanding of how GAAP apply to a particular case setting. Cases in Chapter 5 draw on actual financial statements and events involving real companies and not-for-profit entities, to provide realistic applications of FARS. Particular case settings integrate requirements that call upon expertise in FARS, the Internet, and the general literature. Analytical abilities and reasoning processes are honed through consideration of real company events and reporting practices, as well as debates in the media.

By mastering the use of FARS, you will be better equipped to address the challenges that will arise in the course of your careers. All professions are affected by standard setting and regulations and call on individuals to exercise judgment in their interpretation and application. An increasing number of databases are becoming available that use Boolean logic—the search infrastructure found in FARS. You can hone your ability to properly identify the scope of relevant guidance, the differences between a particular setting and the circumstances that may be illustrated in available guidance, and implied directions for "uncharted territories."

These resources in combination offer you the opportunity to be introduced to FARS in an effective and productive manner at the introductory level and then build on those skills to achieve mastery. Education in business is committed to building reasoning skills that facilitate the exercise of effective judgment when addressing unstructured problems. FARS provides a particularly appropriate resource for such use. Professionals in business are increasingly accessing multiple information bases using Boolean logic and coping with ever-changing guidance in regulation and business practices. The development of an appreciation of how to access, analyze, apply, and discern why contradictions might arise and only later be resolved will be an invaluable competency upon which to draw in the course of your professional career.

Dissents by standard setters provide insight into core conceptual issues on which decision makers disagreed. FARS facilitates access to such perspectives, enhancing one's understanding of continuing disagreements by particular standard setters with the guidance that was issued. Among the lessons learned will be an appreciation for (1) the variety of pronouncements that speak to even basic accounting concepts and issues, just in different contexts; (2) the diversity of business transactions that must be accounted for in business settings; and (3) the nature of changes over time in guidance (highlighted as gray sections or superseded guidance within the FARS materials, including integration in the FASB-OP [amended] infobase).

Many cases have discussions of related issues that span a variety of business topics associated with economics, finance, management, marketing, and analytical applications. Strategy and financial reporting issues arise in business measurement and management decision making. Those interested in not-for-profit entities will find the comparison of Universal Health Services to St. Jude Children's Research Hospital/ALSAC to be an effective vehicle to consider distinctions in types of organizations, including comparing sources of capital accessible to organizations of differing legal form. As you develop an interest in tax, explore the United Parcel Service case, integrating the actual tax court case findings. Other topics of likely interest are Internet-specific considerations such as the growing role of barter transactions, e-commerce, and valuation as it relates to practice issues common in acquisitions.

This second edition of *Mastery of the Financial Accounting Research System (FARS) through Cases* retains the structure of the first edition, emphasizing the content of the FARS resource and how to use it, rather than the particular interface by the user. In other words, whether the user accesses a CD version of FARS or the Internet version of FARS, the core content of FARS is retained. It is that content to which this resource is directed. This second edition adapts to the evolving FARS product, the new standards and regulations issued, as well as media events and recent literature.

Chapter 1 has been expanded to include a Quick-Start, an overview of standards in accounting, reference to the GAAP Hierarchy, and a discussion of how the database evolves as new pronouncements emerge and its effect on searches. In addition, a "general approach" primer discussion of which InfoBase is more likely to address which types of questions is integrated in the expanded Self-Review.

Chapter 2 uses a 2005 event to focus attention on accounting, regulation, and technology. Internet resources such as blogs and Wikipedia are discussed, advising caution in their use, and alternative search approaches with "tagosphere" have been added. Attention is particularly directed to accounting literature that involves trends and techniques, as well as restatements. A crossword puzzle must be solved "backwards" to define a variety of accounting and business related acronyms, using resources identified in Chapter 2.

Chapter 3, recognizing that FARS now has a terminology section within its topical index, organizes two types of vocabulary assignments. The first uses the terminology resource, separating concepts into basic, intermediate, and advanced. The second is an approach used in the first edition of this book. Then, problems are augmented to include numerous Self-Study Q&A, permitting readers to develop their own skills with immediate feedback, beyond assigned materials. Added tables and problems directed to regulation and industry considerations are reflected. A Completed Example and Solution at the start of Chapter 3 can serve as a prototype on how to complete the three distinct types of assignments associated with the 40 topics addressed.

Chapter 4 has increased the number of Brain Teasers to 33, incorporating topics that have received attention in the media and in the standards since the first edition. All Brain Teasers now have additional assignments, including a straightforward, directed Bonus Question, as well as questions that tie to subject matter across the curricula. At the start of Chapter 4 is a Completed Example of a Brain Teaser with a Suggested Solution. Such a resource is intended both for self-review and to act as a prototype on how to solve a Brain Teaser.

Chapter 5 retains the same core cases as the previous edition but calls on readers to identify for themselves the resources that used to be included in Cases 6, 11, and 12. This change has permitted the increased coverage in Chapters 1 through 4, without lengthening the publication. All cases have been updated, integrating 2005 and 2006 developments. In addition, each case has a Directed Self-Study Assignment.

The support of the staff of John Wiley & Sons for the first edition of this book was greatly appreciated. Mark Bonadeo and David Kear worked toward the effective integration of the hard copy of the casebook with Internet capabilities. Cheryl Ferguson as copy editor made a number of creative suggestions. For this second edition, Mark Bonadeo has continued as Acquisitions Editor. I thank Nicole Repasky and Karolina Zarychta of Wiley and Dennis Free of Aptara, Inc. for their help in bringing this second edition to fruition. I appreciate the helpful suggestions for this edition from Edward W. Adams of Rider University, Christina Gehrke of City University, Janet Jamieson of University of Dubuque, and Jay S. Rich of Illinois State University. The cooperation of the FASB has permitted the development of this educational resource that is expressly designed to support the use of FARS.

My partner in life, James J. Wallace, has been, as usual, indispensable. A sounding board for ideas, first drafts, and multiple iterations, Jim has encouraged, improved upon, and selflessly contributed to this book.

Wanda A. Wallace, Ph.D.
Williamsburg, Virginia
February 14, 2007

CONTENTS

Chapter 3 — Building Your Business Vocabulary   3-1
Defining Terms and Solving Problems through The Financial Accounting Research System (FARS)

Chapter 4 — Brain Teasers

4-1

Using the Financial Accounting Research System (FARS) to Untangle the Mystery

CHAPTER 1 – THE FINANCIAL ACCOUNTING RESEARCH SYSTEM (FARS) PRIMER

Getting Started with FARS: The Basics

Quick-Start

Local Installation

1. Insert the FARS CD-ROM into your CD-ROM drive.
2. If the setup program does not start automatically, click on Start, Run, and type D:SETUP (where D is the drive letter of your CD-ROM drive).

3. Follow the prompts on your screen.

Run FARS from the CD-ROM or from a CD Tower/Jukebox

1. Insert the FARS CD-ROM into your CD-ROM drive.
2. Open Windows, click on Start, Run and type D:\cdrom\cdsetup (where D is the drive letter of your CD-ROM).

Note: This procedure will only install an icon on your workstation. The FARS for Windows CD-ROM must be in your CD-ROM drive to run the program.

Using Individual Workstations in Network Environment

1. Attach to your network and start Windows.
2. Open Explorer (Windows 95/98 or NT) or My Computer (2000 or XP) and locate the drive and directory in which FARS is installed.
3. A FARS for Windows or a FARS for Windows folder in the Start Programs Menu, along with appropriate icons should be accessible.

   FARS frequently asked questions (FAQs) are accessible from the FARS menu by selecting "FARS Reference Guide." FAQs are also accessible at http://www.fasb.org/fars/farsfaq.shtml.

Starting FARS

1. Double-click on the FARS icon in Start, Programs, FARS, FARS.
2. The opening menu screen in FARS is depicted in Figure 1.1.

Financial Accounting Research System

Welcome to the FASB Financial Accounting Research System (FARS) which is current through
February 15, 2006.
Click on your desired selection below.

What's new this update

- Original Pronouncements, as amended, including Implementation Guides and FASB Staff Positions
- Original Pronouncements
- Current Text
- EITF Abstracts
- Derivative Instruments and Hedging Activities
- Topical Index
- FARS Reference Guide

Figure 1.1 Opening Menu Screen in FARS

FARS is made up of six major databases known as infobases, each of which is designed to resemble the printed version of the original documents as much as possible:

Original Pronouncements	(FASB-OP)
Original Pronouncements, as amended, including Implementation Guides and FASB Staff Positions	(AMENDED)
Current Text	(FASB-CT)
EITF Abstracts	(EITF)
Comprehensive Topical Index	(FASINDEX)
Derivative Instruments and Hedging Activities	(DERIVCOD)

Opening Infobases

The first step in using FARS is opening an infobase. To open one infobase:

1. Move your mouse pointer over your choice and click on the infobase of your choice at the bottom of the FARS menu screen (below the FASB logo, shown in Figure 1.1, are six infobase choices). The title bar identifies in which infobase you are at any point.
2. FASB-OP infobase contains all American Institute of Certified Public Accountants (AICPA) and Financial Accounting Standards Board (FASB) pronouncements in chronological order, including totally superseded pronouncements. See Figure 1.2 for opening screen.

 **Original Pronouncements**

Copyright 2006 Financial Accounting Standards Board

> *To search the entire infobase, click the **Query** button on the **Toolbar** or to search using a predefined query template, choose from the list in the **Search** menu. To directly access a segment of the infobase, click on any link token () in the menu below.*

- ◆ **Committee on Accounting Procedure Accounting Research Bulletins (ARB)**
- ◆ **Accounting Principles Board Opinions (APB)**
- ◆ **AICPA Accounting Interpretations (AIN)**
- ◆ **Accounting Principles Board Statements (APS)**
- ◆ **Accounting Terminology Bulletins (ATB)**

Financial Accounting Standards Board:

- ◆ **Statements of Financial Accounting Standards (FAS)**
- ◆ **Interpretations (FIN)**
- ◆ **Technical Bulletins (FTB)**
- ◆ **Statements of Financial Accounting Concepts (CON)**

Figure 1.2 Opening Screen in FARS Original Pronouncements, as Amended

> *Note:* Alternatively, click on **F**ile at the top of the toolbar and access infobases to "open."

Drilling Down into an Infobase

Click on the diamond icon to the left of the entry in Figure 1.2 to proceed. For example, a listing of all Statements of Financial Accounting Standards can be accessed by clicking on the first diamond icon under FASB. The screen that follows will begin that listing, as shown in Figure 1.3. A click on the diamond icon to the left of any one of the FASB Statements listed allows you to drill down further and see the entire document.

FASB Statements

◆ FAS 1:   Disclosure of Foreign Currency Translation Information
◆ FAS 2:   Accounting for Research and Development Costs
◆ FAS 3:   Reporting Accounting Changes in Interim Financial Statements…

   Figure 1.3 Listing of FASB Statements

Table of Contents

The Table of Contents is quite useful for browsing an infobase. It includes a complete listing, in outline format, of all the infobase's records. A click on any heading of interest will take you directly to that section. To use the Table of Contents window:

1. Click on the Contents tab (see Figure 1.4) on the bottom of the Views application.
2. Use the arrow keys or the vertical scroll bar to browse the listings.
3. To expand or contract a section of the Table of Contents, click the + and − signs, respectively. (A click on FASB Statements will result in a list of all FASs. By opening Original Pronouncements, as amended, shifting from document to contents, then clicking the right button on the mouse and clicking Expand All, related lists such as ARBs are provided.)
4. Once you have found a subject of interest, click on it to jump directly to that location in the document window (or select the subject and click Contents tab again).

   Figure 1.4 Tabs to Change Views of Infobase Data

Viewing an Infobase

An infobase can be viewed in several ways, with the default being Document (Figure 1.4). It shows the document reference and the results corresponding to the hit list. Clicking on the Contents/Document tab shows the document reference, table of contents, and hit list, to see all related information at one time. The Contents tab shows the table of contents. The Hit List shows the search results or hit list. The Object tab displays any linked objects.

Closing an Infobase

To close any infobase, select Close from the File menu or click on the document window's control-menu box (the X button at the top right-hand corner of your screen).

Use of the Topical Index

1. Click on the Topical Index infobase at the opening menu screen.
2. Click on a letter to go to a segment of the Index.
3. Scroll through the listings to find a topic of interest or use the Contents button to see a concise list of topics. (See "Table of Contents.")
4. Click on any reference.
5. To return to the Topical Index, click on the Go Back button:

> *Note:* A Search such as a Query is another useful way of locating references in the Index. Perform a query on a term, document title, and so forth, to find applicable Index references. (See "How Do I Search?" in Chapter 1.)

Exiting FARS

To exit FARS, click on the main window's control-menu box (the X at the very top right-hand corner of your screen). The remaining materials in Chapter 1 elaborate and build upon this Quick-Start.

Where Am I Going to Look?

The Financial Accounting Standards Board's (FASB's) Financial Accounting Research System (FARS) originally was a PC-based tool for accounting research that used software for efficient and effective access to databases (infobases) of FASB literature. Now it is also accessible as an Internet-based research tool. FARS, regardless of whether it is accessed on a CD, a network, or the Internet, is a research tool commonly used to identify guidance regarding how transactions and events are to be reported in order for financial presentations to be in conformance with generally accepted accounting principles (GAAP).

The first question to answer as you access this tool is where should you look? Within the Financial Accounting Research System (FARS) are six major information bases from which to choose. These may differ over time, depending on the development of new types of guidance and the stage of completion at the point in time that a new version of FARS becomes available. In addition, the FARS Reference Guide contains an Overview, alongside files named Getting Started, FARS Basics, FARS FAQ (frequently asked questions requiring access to the Internet), Searching the Infobases, Printing and Exporting Text, and Glossary. A machine-readable resource, available by clicking on the menu of FARS, provides the basis for this description of FARS, complementing this primer chapter as you use the software. The FARS main menu acronyms for each of the six major information bases, with a description of the content of each follows:

FASB-OP   *Original Pronouncements*—All AICPA and FASB pronouncements, even if superseded (i.e., replaced by newer rulings): Accounting Research Bulletins (ARB), Accounting Principles Board Opinions (APB), AICPA Accounting Interpretations (AIN), Accounting Principles Board Statements (APS), Accounting Terminology Bulletins (ATB), FASB Statements (FAS), FASB Interpretations (FIN), FASB Technical Bulletins (FTB), and FASB Concepts Statements (CON). Note that superseded materials are shaded, with red diamonds that when clicked link to an explanation of what material applies in lieu of the superseded sections. For users who need to determine the content of a pronouncement at a particular point in time, the original pronouncements as originally issued, are indispensable. (Note that .PDF files of original pronouncements are available at the http://www.fasb.org Web site. It is prudent to check the site for developments subsequent to the version of FARS in use. However, .PDF files are no substitute for FARS, since they do not have the powerful search capabilities, do not integrate later developments as does the amended file within FARS, and cannot build the competency required to be demonstrated on the CPA exam. See http://www.cpa-exam.org where you can access the AICPA tutorial and related information.)

AMENDED   *Original Pronouncements, as Amended*—Contains all currently effective AICPA and FASB pronouncements, as they have been amended by subsequent pronouncements, including Implementation Guides and FASB Staff Positions, staff Special Reports and other published implementation guidance on various FASB Statements, and Emerging Issues Task Force (EITF) Issues. There are no shading, sidebars, or links to amending language except for pronouncements that have been superseded but are still applicable for some entities due to delayed effective dates of the superseding pronouncement or due to scope exceptions. Those pronouncements have been updated for any amendments and are shaded to indicate that they have been superseded. A status page is retained for those pronouncements that are omitted because they have been completely superseded. Such status pages for this information base likewise identify which pronouncement (and paragraph within it) created the amendment(s) reflected. The pronouncement creating the amendment must be reviewed to see the amendment as it was originally issued and, if applicable, subsequently amended (i.e., see infobase FASB-OP).

FASB-CT   *Current Text*—General Standards, Industry Standards, and the Current Text sections that have been superseded but are still applicable due to delays in effective dates. An appendix lists current AICPA Practice Bulletins, Audit and Accounting Guides, and Statements of Position (SOPs), excluding specialized accounting relating to governmental units (which is the responsibility of the Governmental Accounting Standards Board, or GASB). Shaded sections indicate superseded materials.

EITF   *EITF Abstracts*—The Emerging Issues Task Force infobase includes the full text of each abstract for every issue discussed by the EITF since its inception in 1984, the introduction to EITF Abstracts, a list of task force members (Appendix A), announcements of general and administrative matters (Appendix C), discussions of other technical matters (Appendix D), and the EITF topical index, as well as a Topical Table of Contents.

FASINDEX   Comprehensive *Topical Index*—This is the combined topical index for AMENDED, FASB-CT, and EITF infobases. Each reference in the index is linked to the appropriate paragraph(s), EITF issue, or questions in the relevant infobase. All "See" references (e.g., See Income Taxes) are linked to that section within the index. In the Topical Index, under the word "terminology", you will find core glossary terms. Since the table of contents of all three infobases are concurrently browsed when searches are performed on Topical Index, it is a powerful tool.

DERIVCOD   *Derivative Instruments and Hedging Activities*—This is an aid to implementing FASB Statement 133 (Accounting for Derivative Instruments and Hedging Activities), as amended through May 2003, including amendments from Statements 137 (Deferral of the Effective Date of FASB Statement No. 133), 138 (Accounting for Certain Derivative Instruments and Certain Hedging Activities, an amendment of FASB Statement No. 133), and 149 (Amendment of FASB Statement No. 133 on Derivative and Hedging Activities). It also includes the full text of issues related to the implementation of Statement 133 that was discussed by the Derivatives Implementation Group and cleared by the FASB prior to February 10, 2004.

FARS is updated approximately five times a year, as appropriate, to ensure that the infobases contain the latest FASB pronouncements and abstracts of EITF issues. The AMENDED infobase (FASB-OP [amended]) does not identify additions or deletions as a result of amendments unless a complete paragraph or footnote has been deleted or added. The numerical sequence of the original paragraphs and footnotes has not been changed as a result of any amendments, but instead bear the message: "[This paragraph (footnote) has been deleted. See Status page.]" or add a capital letter to the preceding paragraph's numbers to identify additional paragraphs (e.g., 15A), or a lower-case letter to the preceding footnote number (e.g., 4a). If an adjustment was needed to make a sentence read more smoothly, brackets are used to show such effective amendments or editorial changes; these are relatively rare.

Although you can look in multiple infobases, it is probably preferable to learn FARS by accessing one infobase at a time (probably using AMENDED) and proceeding with your analysis. As you become more adept with the system, you can open multiple databases and apply your search to all of them at one time. However, you will find that a number of the FARS capabilities (such as *query templates* and *clear query*) are not applicable to multiple infobases and that the Hits button affects only the current view. Also, the tag function must be applied to each infobase separately. Given the cluttered display that can result from multiple open infobases (as well as system crashes tied to RAM constraints), you may well find it more effective to work on a single infobase at a time. Yet, remember, you can browse the table of contents of all infobases at the same time by opening the Topical Index from the opening FARS menu (Figure 1.1), then performing a search either by first letter or using the *query* function. Drilling down by clicking on the links provided within the Topical Index permits access to multiple database resources.

Before proceeding to using FARS, consider the fact that accounting standards encompass a broader set of guidance than that found within this database. reminds us of the diverse standard setters and organizations that have developed guidance for varied sectors of the economy. In September 2004, the FASB announced it would prepare a codification to integrate the guidance from FASB, AICPA, EITF, and the Securities and Exchange Commission (SEC), but this codification is not expected until 2007, and then it will be subject to a lengthy verification process. Eventually it is expected to become the authoritative source of GAAP in the United States, superseding all existing domestic standards in the nongovernmental sector. The expectation is that a searchable codification will eventually become available that will permit the types of research described herein to be performed on an even larger set of documents.

Table 1.1   Overview of Accounting Standards

Organization or Standard-Setting Body	When Issued	Acronyms—Cumulative, with Some Superseded or Revised
Committee on Accounting Procedure (CAP)	1939–1953	Accounting Research Bulletins (ARBs)
Committee on Accounting Terminology	1956–1957	Accounting Terminology Bulletins (ATBs)
American Institute of Certified Public Accountants (AICPA) Accounting Principles Board (APB)	1959–1973	Accounting Principles Board Opinions (APBOs or APBs) AICPA Accounting Interpretations (AINs) [APB Statements (APS)]
Financial Accounting Standards Board (FASB)	1973 to date	Statements of Financial Accounting Standards (SFASs or FASs) FASB Interpretations (FINs) FASB Staff Positions (FSPs) FASB Technical Bulletins (FTBs) Staff Implementation Guides (Q&As)
AICPA Accounting Standards Executive Committee (AcSEC)	1975–2002	Statements of Position (SOPs)
Emerging Issues Task Force (EITF)	1984 to date	Emerging Issues Task Force Abstracts— discussions and consensus positions (EITFs)
Governmental Accounting Standards Board (GASB)	1984 to date	Governmental Accounting Standards Board Statements (GASBSs) GASB Interpretations (GASBIs) GASB Staff Technical Bulletins (GASBTBs)
Other Examples: International Accounting Standards Committee (IASC) International Accounting Standards Board (IASB) Federal Accounting Standards Advisory Board (FASAB)	1973–2001 2001 to date 1990 to date	International Accounting Standards (IASs) International Financial Reporting Standards (IFRSs) International Financial Reporting Interpretations Committee (IFRIC) Statement of Federal Financial Accounting Standards (SFFASs) FASAB Interpretations and Technical Bulletins
United States Securities and Exchange Commission (SEC)	1975 to date	Staff Accounting Bulletins (SABs) provide administrative interpretations and practices of the Commission's staff [codified in SAB 103 in 2003]

Many firms develop their own proprietary databases that encompass the Financial Accounting Research System (FARS) documents, alongside those of the AICPA, their own firm materials directed at additional guidance in accounting and auditing applications, and a number of other standards associated with activities of the GASB, FASAB, the SEC, the Public Company Accounting Oversight Board, the General Accounting Office, and the International Accounting Standards Board. Various other groups and resources offering guidance may likewise be included. Search capabilities allow use of key words and phrases to identify relevant materials. Subject organization is common, with acronyms internal to each system that identify the source of each publication. Your skills with FARS will likewise be helpful as you use other research tools.

Navigating in FARS

When you begin the FARS program (on a PC select FARS from the <u>Start</u> menu), you should see a screen with the icon at the top and buttons corresponding to the infobases linked to the FARS menu as shown in Figure 1.1. Internet versions of the software and Intranet access may have diverse approaches to starting the program. The provider of such software should have a user guide or tutorial for gaining access. Depending on the platform, some capabilities will vary.

Note that these buttons correspond to each of the infobases already described. If you click on any of the buttons, you will be connected with the respective infobase. For example, you can click the button beside <u>Original Pronouncements, as amended, including Implementation Guides and FASB Staff Positions</u> and the introductory screen in Figure 1.5 will appear.

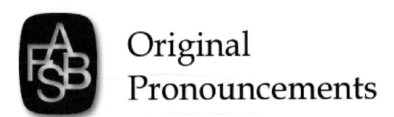

Original Pronouncements

AS AMENDED, including Implementation

Guides and FASB Staff Positions   [more information]

Copyright 2006 Financial Accounting Standards Board

> *To search the entire infobase, click the **Query** button on the **Toolbar** or to search using a predefined query template, choose from the list in the **Search** menu. To directly access a segment of the infobase, click on any link token () in the menu below.*

Figure 1.5 Icon for the Original Pronouncements, as Amended

If you click on <u>Window</u> at the top menu bar, you should see an indication that you are looking at the FASB-OP (amended) infobase. The toolbar for FARS (which can vary across versions) is depicted in Figure 1.6. To the right of the Clear Query box, an open book with a magnifying glass overlay represents: "Find Infobases (Ctrl+F)."

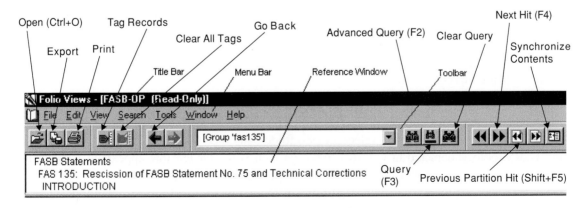

Figure 1.6 FARS Toolbar

Any infobase can be opened by clicking your choice at the bottom of the FARS menu screen in Figure 1.1 and then clicking Go Back on the toolbar or using the F6 key to permit clicking on more than a single infobase. Alternatively, to open the infobases on which you wish to search, click on the menu bar File, which will provide a pull-down menu, and click on Open. (In some settings, if FARS is on a network, you may need to click on Programs and FARS to reach the choice that presents Nfo.) Then click on the folder Nfo, and choose the infobase of interest by clicking on it. You can repeat the sequence to open multiple infobases. To check which are open, click Window on the menu bar and see what open infobases are listed.

Linkages

Keep in mind that as you access an infobase, a number of embedded links are of interest. Specifically, you begin with *query* links from the FARS menu to the infobases connecting menu items, document references, and topical index references to the related information in the appropriate infobase. **A Query is a search for information within an infobase. The words *Search* and *Query* are used interchangeably. Within the software, the main toolbar has Search, with a pulldown menu that distinguishes Query and Advanced Query.** Within infobases, you will find diamonds at the start of any superseded material (indicated by gray shading) that will link to explanations of what guidance applies in place of that material.

In other words, in FASB-OP links connect superseded or amended material in one document with the superseding or amending language in another document. At times you will find that materials you locate through a diamond will likewise include diamonds. That is because with the passage of time, amendments themselves may be amended or superseded. That is the nature of standard-setting activities. Within the text of both FASB-OP and FASB-CT, you will also notice diamonds to the left side of certain words; these will link glossary terms with their definitions. When footnotes appear, you can click on the number (the cursor will change to a hand image) and a pop-up screen will appear with the content of that footnote. This is known as a *pop-up link*. If you export text, remember that links may not be easily interpreted by word-processing applications selected. You may need to reformat, and symbols relating to links may be deleted.

How Do I Search?

You can search the infobases using any of three general techniques. One approach is to use the index, much as you would in a printed book. The second approach is to use a *query template*. The third is to query for particular words or phrases using either Query or Advanced Query capabilities.

Search Alternatives

To access the index, you may go to the FARS menu and click on *Topical Index*, which will link to the screen depicted in Figure 1.7. Alternatively, you can go to the menu bar and click File, select from the pull-down menu Open, select the Nfo folder, and then Open FASINDEX. Also note that the FARS toolbar, depicted in Figure 1.6, has an icon at the far left that appears as a folder and can be used to open a folder and infobase. A particularly handy attribute of the *Topical Index* is provided under the letter *T*, specifically the entry "Terminology." Within that section of the index is an alphabetized listing of terms defined within FARS (a mini glossary).

 # Topical Index

Copyright 2006 Financial Accounting Standards Board

---

*To search the entire infobase, click the **Query** button on the **Toolbar**. To directly access a segment of the infobase, click on any letter below. Links to referenced material are indicated with text which is colored according to the type of reference as follows:* See Amortization, FAS19, ¶30, Oi5.121, and EITF.93-1. To follow a link, click with the mouse on the text of the reference.

A B C D E F G H I J K L M N O P Q R S T U V W

XYZ

Figure 1.7 Icon for the Topical Index Infobase

If clicked, the letter will take you to an index of topics that begin with that letter of the alphabet. You will note that the citations appear in three columns, incorporating (1) the original pronouncements, amended, (2) the current text, and (3) the EITF/Other infobases. The third column would include EITF abstracts, as well as the Staff Implementation Guides. By clicking on the citation, the link will be made to the underlying pronouncement listed.

Topical Index Example

The Topical Index has references to material contained in all of the FARS infobases. Each reference in the Topical Index is linked with the appropriate paragraph(s), EITF issue, or question(s) in the relevant infobase. All "See" references (for example, See Income Taxes) are linked with that section within the index. From the main menu, click on Topical Index to view the screen with segmentation into alphabetical groups.

Click on the first letter of the term of interest, and that will link to a listing of terms that begin with the letter chosen, with detailed links to underlying cites. Within topics, references are sorted into three columns, as in the following example accessed under the letter G:

	OP	CT	EITF/Other
GOODWILL (FAS 142) ...			
Amortization			
.. Prohibition	FAS142, ¶18	G40.116	EITF.85-42

In this example, FAS142, ¶18 indicates paragraph 18 of FASB Statement No. 142, *Goodwill and Other Intangible Assets*. G40.116 indicates paragraph .116 of the Current Text Section G40, "Goodwill and Other Intangible Assets." EITF.85-42 indicates EITF Issue No. 85-42, "Amortization of Goodwill Resulting from Recording Time Savings Deposits at Fair Values." An alternative means to identify this citation is to use a *query template*. First you must open an infobase. This can be accomplished by selecting one of the buttons on the FARS menu (recall Figure 1.1). Alternatively, you can go to the menu bar and click on File, select Open from the pull-down menu, choose the folder Nfo, and then open an infobase. Either approach will have an open infobase on which you can search. **If you open the Topical Index, you are able to search across the table of contents of all the infobases at the same time.** Simply click on Search, select *query* and type in the search word or phrase – in this example, *goodwill fas 142*. (Alternatively, *advanced query* can be selected.) Click on a link in the Topical Index results, such as FAS142, ¶18, and the Search pull-down menu will offer additional choices.

Search Menu Alternatives

Proceed to click on Search at the menu bar and select from among the *query template* alternatives in that pull-down menu: search by issue date; search FSP documents only; search only current documents; search within a single OP document title; or search within a single OP document type. The boxes that will be displayed guide you in requesting that you specify a date or range of dates, that you select from among a menu of titles or documents, and that you then proceed to specify your search in terms of words or phrases. If you select the *query template* to search within a single OP title, scroll through the choices in the Heading window and click to place the result in the document title. Then move to the Query window and type the search term and click OK. If you merely wanted to locate the document and not perform a search, then after selecting the document title, click OK and move to the Document pane.

To perform a search of a given infobase, once you click on File, Open, Nfo, and an infobase, you can click on Search and then select Query from the pull-down menu and enter a command. Query can be accessed by pressing F3, and Advanced Query can be accessed by pressing F2. Alternatively, you can click on the Query button on the toolbar, which is a set of binoculars icon (the smaller binoculars icon with the underscore is the simple query, whereas the larger binoculars on the icon represents the advanced query; the binoculars with a large red X through it is the Clear Query button). Figure 1.6 has these three icons shown to the right.

Words or phrases you type will be searched on the open infobase. If instead you choose to click on Advanced Query, you will obtain information on word counts that can assist your search. In addition, you will have the option of using the Apply to All capability that will search all open infobases, permitting multiple infobases to be concurrently searched. Note that when multiple infobases are opened they can be viewed by pressing Ctrl+Tab (in other words, hold the control key down and press the tab key to cycle through the views). Do not forget to clear the query when you are finished, before proceeding to the next search. Just click Search on the toolbar and then select Clear Query from the pull-down menu; this must be done per infobase. Figures 1.8 and 1.9 show

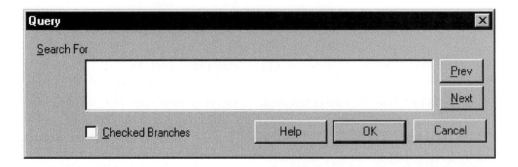

Figure 1.8 Query Screen

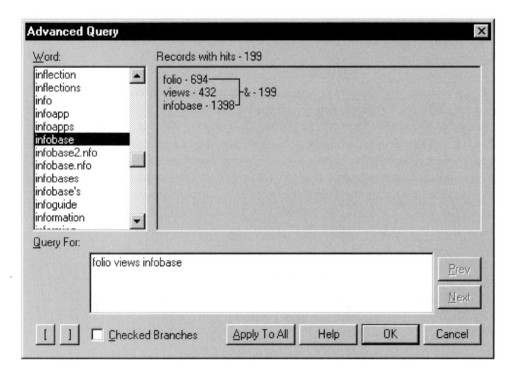

Figure 1.9 Advanced Query Screen

examples of the screens that appear when you click on Search and select Query or Advanced Query from the pull-down menu. Merely type the search word or phrase and click OK.

Boolean Logic

There are many ways to conduct a search. A *keyword search* finds all records that contain the word(s) you want to specify. If you search for more than one word, separate the words with a space. A *phrase search* finds all records that contain an exact phrase. This phrase must be enclosed in quotes. These two searches are the building blocks for all other types of searches. (at the end of this section) is a summary table that lists search options available under Boolean logic. They are described in more detail in the following paragraphs. Note that the *query* search is different from that of the *advanced query* search in its power to use such Boolean logic. In particular, the proximity searches will not operate as described in except in the *advanced query* mode. In the *query* mode, the inclusion of a proximity command merely brings the number specified into the search process. Similarly, the Boolean operators work as word searches with *query* and only follow the use described in within the *advanced query* mode or *query template* options accessible through the search screen (such as Search FSP documents only or Search within a single OP document title or Search within a single OP document type).

Search phrasing can be a precise quote, which means you enter the command in quotes and that is the exact phrasing to be identified. It does not matter whether something is capitalized or lower case. Alternatively, within Advanced Query you can apply what are termed *proximity searches*. This requires that the search phrase be in quotes and then be followed by some symbols that instruct the software as to the distance between words and the order of the words required for a match to occur. Specifically, if you follow the quoted phrase with a forward slash and a number, then the words can appear anywhere within the specified number of words of each other but must be in the order you have indicated. Or you could follow the quoted words with @ and a number instead of a forward slash, and the words would have to appear within that specified number of word distance from one another, but they could appear in any order. The terms of /5 or @5 as examples are referred to as proximity conditions whereby the words are within five words of one another, with the first word in the quotes counting as number one and the other words having to appear before the sixth word. For example, you might specify "current assets"/5, which would mean these two words are within five words of one another in the order stated. Alternatively, if you indicated "current assets"@7, it would mean that the words *current* and *assets* appear within seven words of one another but may be in either order—*current assets* or *assets current*.

The search in the absence of a proximity indicator tends to be record based, which typically is defined as a paragraph. At times, you may wish the search process to consider more than a single record as the scope for the search. This can be accomplished by following the quotes of the *advanced query* search phrase with a # and a number representing the number of records you wish to consider as sufficient proximity. For example, "big business" on the FASB-OP infobase results in no hits. By adjusting the command to "big business"#3, it is possible to generate matches. Hence, rather than requiring two terms to be in the same record, one can tailor the search to finding the two terms within a certain number of records. Instead of constraining the space within a record as the scope of the search, this actually extends the search across records.

In addition to proximity conditions, Boolean logic permits the use of what are called *wildcards*, which facilitate more robust search phrasing. Specifically, if you were uncertain as to spelling, a question mark (?) could be inserted for any given letter. Then any word that has the letters you specified, along with any substitution of a letter for the question mark, would be selected. Multiple question marks for multiple letters can be used, but they must map one-to-one in terms of their number relative to the letters omitted. For example, if you were searching the word *uncollectible* and you were uncertain whether it should be spelled *uncollectable*, you could specify *uncollect?ble* and either spelling would be captured by the search.

A second wildcard capability is the percent sign, or % wildcard. This finds all forms of a specified root word. For example, if you are interested in variations of the root word purchase, such as *purchases*, *purchaser*, *purchasing*, and *purchased*, the search specification of *purchase%* would pick up all of these forms of that root word.

An alternative that is broader than the root word concept moves from guiding the search based on a root word to guiding the search based on the pattern of letters. Specifically, any multiple character substitution is captured by an asterisk. Note that if you specified *purchase** you would again obtain the *purchases*, *purchaser*, and *purchased*, but you would fail to access *purchasing* because the *e* is not found in the spelling and the asterisk only covers those letters omitted in the search. If instead you specified *purchas**, then the *purchasing* alternative spelling would be located. It should be apparent that you need to determine whether the better direction to your search can be gathered through root word guidance, or the pattern of letters. Then you can choose whether to use a % or an *.

One other wildcard capability can be particularly useful, and it is the synonym $. For example, you may wish to find any reference to synonyms of *purchase*. By using the command *purchase$* you will likewise find words such as *acquisition* and *buy* among the search results—both synonyms for your specification. Wildcards are effective within both <u>Query</u> and <u>Advanced Query</u>.

Beyond direct quotes, proximity and ordering variation (within <u>Advanced Query</u>), and wild-cards, Boolean logic permits the association among key words. These are referred to as *Boolean operators* that are effective within <u>Advanced Query</u>. The term *and* can also be specified as &. This operator means that both terms must be contained in a record in order for it to be identified as a match. If two words appear side by side without typing any word in between, it will be presumed that the search is intended to be equivalent to inserting & in between the two words. The word *or* can also be specified as |. It means that all records containing any of the words will be matches. The term *not* can be specified as a caret, ^. It means that the first word would be included but the latter would not be included in the record. The *exclusive or* operator is abbreviated *xor* and can be specified as a tilde, ~. This is interpreted as either the first term or another but not both terms within a record.

Combinations of Boolean searches are helpful. When performing such a search, you can use parentheses. These define the order of operation similar to basic mathematics. In other words, the search within the parentheses is performed first and then the order of operations is from left to right. If no parentheses are used, then the order of operations is just left to right. Keep in mind that wildcards cannot be used with proximity searches available in <u>Advanced Query</u> mode because exact characters within the quotes are their focus. Hence, at times, you will need to perform multiple proximity searches if different word forms are of interest.

Remember to clear previous queries before beginning a new query. Click the <u>Clear Query</u> button to do this. As an example of the manner in which Boolean search operators can be combined, consider the following search phrasing entered after opening the FASB-OP infobase, clicking on the menu bar search, selecting <u>Advanced Query</u> from the pull-down menu, and then resulting in two matches, one of which is superseded, within the infobase:

current&assets$~liabilities^cash^(securities|investments)uncollect?ble

The term *assets*$ includes the synonyms of property, capital, wealth, holdings, and liquid. Another example of a narrowing search phrase with a single match follows:

qualif*&securitization$&special&purpose&entit*&wash&sale*

An example of a broadened search within FASB-OP using <u>Advanced Query</u> would be a change from *wash transaction* which has two matches, to *wash transaction*$ having six matches. Such examples clearly reflect how Boolean operators and wildcards can either narrow or broaden a search of FARS, depending on their use.

What Results Can I Expect?

When you have completed a search, your results will be reported as *hits*. A match to a query is a hit and will appear in the infobase as highlighted text. Hits are usually reported as the number of records in the infobase that meet the search criteria (or it is the default number set, e.g., 50 hits, if that is a lower number than the actual matches). There are a variety of ways in which you can view these findings. The <u>Reference Window</u> pane is always connected to the top of the <u>Document</u> pane and is shown in Figure 1.6. This is the portion of the infobase window that displays the parent headings for a particular location within the infobase. It also appears with the <u>Contents/Document</u>

pane. It identifies the document being viewed—both its title and paragraph. To change views of the infobase data, click on the tabs at the bottom of the infobase window, as is shown in Figure 1.4.

Views Available

After you do a search, five panes are accessible through clicking on tabs at the bottom of the infobase window. A pane is that region within a window that displays specific information, while a view is the current display of information in the infobase. Moving from left to right in Figure 1.4, the first pane is <u>Contents/Document</u>, the second is <u>Document</u>, the third is <u>Contents</u>, the fourth is <u>HitList</u>, and the fifth is <u>Object</u>. Note that multiple windows of the same infobase can be viewed by pressing Ctrl+Tab.

Contents/Documents   The first pane at the left identifies how many hits appear in each of the document types. By clicking on the + you are able to identify more details, such as in which *Accounting Research Bulletin* the hit was found. Another click on the + will identify the paragraph and subheads within the documents. The display of <u>Contents</u>, <u>Document</u>, and <u>Reference Window</u> panes permits browsing of the infobase for information related to the table of contents.

Documents   The <u>Document</u> pane is the actual document in FARS in which the hit appears. The <u>Document</u> pane is the primary pane for working with an infobase; all other panes provide navigational assistance or display other ancillary information. If you click on the bottom tab and open document, you will see both that display and the <u>Reference Window</u> pane. Keep in mind that FARS defaults to an "on" setting for those records with hits. As a result, the view is narrowed to those records with matches to your search and the text is seen out of the context of the original document. This should be apparent as you scroll down the screen, because the <u>Reference Window</u> pane will list different document titles and paragraphs as you scroll from hit to hit. If you wish to see the hits in context, select <u>All Records</u> from the view menu bar and choose the <u>HitList</u> tab.

Contents   The <u>Contents</u> pane displays the table of contents from the first pane. It permits a clear view for scanning the contents and full names that are headings in the table of contents. By double-clicking on a heading in the <u>Contents</u> pane, you will be taken to the appropriate section in the <u>Document</u> view. The table of contents may be expanded or collapsed by double-clicking on the plus or minus signs to the left of the headings. The toolbar icon for *synchronize contents* (see Figure 1.6 toward the far right) allows you to automatically expand the table of contents to the same location that you are at in the Document pane.

HitList   The <u>HitList</u> pane permits the search results to be viewed. By double-clicking on a reference in the HitList, you are taken to the <u>Document</u> view of that

Table 1.2   Search Options Using Boolean Logic

Option	Symbol	Example	Use
Precise quote	"*n*"	"current assets"	Find the exact phrase.
Proximity search			
Distance between words, order specific	/*n*	"current assets"/*n*	Find the word *assets* within *n* words of *current*, in order.
Distance between words, order not specific	@*n*	"current assets"@*n*	Find the word *assets* before or after *current*, within *n* words.
Across records	#*n*	"current assets"#*n*	Find the word assets within *n* records of current.
Wildcards			
Uncertain character	?	purch?se	Find any words that are spelled purch?se, with ? representing any letter.
Root word search	%	purchase%	Find words with the root word of *purchase*: purchasing, purchaser, purchased, purchases.
Letter pattern	*	purchas*	Find words that begin with the letters *purchas*: purchasing, purchaser, purchased. (Note that if purchase* were used, the word p*urchasing* would not be a hit.)
Synonym	$	purchase$	Find synonyms: *buy, acquire*.
Boolean operators			
and	&	current&assets	Find records that contain both words.
		current and assets	Find records that contain both words.
or	|	current|assets	Find records that contain either word.
		current or assets	Find records that contain either word.
not	^	current^assets	Find records that contain the first word but not the second word.
		current not assets	Find records that contain the first word but not the second word.
exclusive or (xor)	~	current~assets	Find records that contain either word but not both.
		current xor assets	Find records that contain either word but not both.

section. If you have FARS set to its default, the hits are listed in order of relevancy.

Objects

The <u>Object</u> pane will display very large tables and exhibits too large to be displayed in line with the document text. These are displayed as objects when you follow an object link in the Document pane. To return to the <u>Document</u> pane, click the tab at the bottom of the infobase view.

Tailoring Your Search and Considering Dissents

In your search, the first 50 hits are displayed by default, unless there are fewer hits. If you want to consider means of tailoring the search, review the Boolean logic options. You can use the advanced query to review the counts of various searching approaches to better tailor the results. If you want to narrow the focus to a specific infobase, particular documents, or dates, consider using the *query template* options.

To move quickly between views and panes, try these shortcut keys:

Action	Shortcut Key
Next pane	F8
Next view	F7
Previous pane	SHIFT+F8
Previous view	SHIFT+F7

As you perform the word search, you will likely want to have your current view clicked onto the <u>Document</u> pane, since it will display the text and will provide a three-line source reference, the last of which is the important information necessary for definition of the full reference (e.g., CON6, Par. 234). To explore lower prioritized search results, you can click onto the <u>HitList</u> and peruse the sources, then click on the highlighted term and return to the <u>Document</u> screen to review further details.

Keep in mind that dissents are helpful in explaining key points of contention and promoting understanding as to the content of final pronouncements. They are easily identified by using the key word *dissent*, within the original pronouncement infobase, or by narrowing the search to a particular pronouncement of interest (i.e., by selecting one of the last three options on the Search menu). As an example, presume you are interested in whether a dissent was registered to FIN46(R). Click <u>S</u>earch, then select Search within a single OP document title from the pull-down menu. In the screen that appears, type under Document Title to the left FIN46(R) and double click in the Heading box to the right so that the full title appears in the Document Title Box. In the Query Box type the word *dissent*, and two results will be returned, with the first related to FIN 46(R) and the second related to its predecessor FIN 46. Click the Document tab (recall Figure 1.4) to read these results.

<u>What Can I Do with the Results?</u>

As you click the <u>HitList</u> items and review the document, you will see the search terms highlighted. Then the <u>Next Partition Hit</u> and <u>Previous Partition Hit</u> buttons can assist you in navigating through the hits. *Partitions* are logical divisions of the infobase used to report hits. The default partition is called a *record* and, as mentioned earlier, is usually a numbered paragraph. (In FASINDEX, each reference is generally a record.) Partition icons are double arrowheads, as depicted to the right side of the toolbar shown in Figure 1.6—note that screens may differ as to icons' location (e.g., they may appear as a second row to the left).

If you judge the record to be of use for your research purposes, a variety of options exist for marking and then exporting or printing those sections. The exporting can be to a file that is then retrievable by other software programs. Another alternative is to copy materials and paste them into a word-processing document. However, since the pasting is unformatted by default, italic and bold type will be lost. If the passage contains footnotes, you will need to click on the pop-up screen, select all, and copy and paste it into your document for completeness. For these reasons, the tagging process with the exporting capability has advantages to the researcher.

Tagging

Select a hit that appears to be of use in your research, and that will bring you to the underlying document, click on the menu bar, and select the command Edit and then from the pull-down menu, select Tag in order to tag the record. The Tag Record function allows you to mark random records and collect them for subsequent actions. You can proceed through multiple hits, view the related document, and tag records as you analyze on the screen. The tagging will continue until you choose to clear the tags previously placed. The toolbar depicted in Figure 1.6 has an icon fourth from the far left that looks like a tag. By pressing that button, a record can be tagged. To the right of that icon is a Clear All Tags icon, which shows a tag with a large red X over it.

To collect all tagged records into a single view, tag the records you wish to collect. Then choose Tagged Records from the View menu. From here, they may be viewed, printed, exported, or formatted.

Exporting

Once you have tagged records of interest, you can export the collection of records to a separate file. Select File from the menu bar, select Export from the pull-down menu, and then type in the file name and select the type of file saved. For example, you can select such formats as a text file output, a Word or WordPerfect file, or a rich text format. The toolbar depicted in Figure 1.6 contains an icon, second from the left, that looks like a piece of paper linked to a disk, and it can be clicked to export.

Follow these steps to Export records or text:

1. Select or tag the records you wish to export, choose the branches in the Contents pane that you wish to export, or narrow the view of the infobase to display what you wish to export.
    *   To narrow the view, you may search the infobase and view records with hits, tag records and view tagged records, or select branches in the Contents pane and view selected branches.
    *   If you are exporting the entire infobase, make sure that no text is selected.
    *   Note that the entire record containing the selection is exported.
2. Choose Export from the File menu. The Export dialog box appears.
3. Choose Save as type and select the file format to which you want to export the infobase.
4. Type in the name of the new file. Change the drives and directories as needed.

5. Select the <u>Export range</u>. You may export the entire infobase (regardless of the current view), the current view, tagged records, selected text, or checked branches.
6. Choose <u>Options</u> and set any necessary options for the filter.
   - Not all filters have options for you to set.
   - Setting filter options is *not* supported on Windows 3.x.
7. Click <u>OK</u>.

Remember that links may not be interpretable by the word-processing application into which text is exported. Moreover, due to differences in font size, the numeric data in lists and tables might not appear as it did within FARS, requiring some reformatting. Generally, within a word processor, if you select the text in the table or listing and apply a Courier font that is either eight point or ten point, it will help you in aligning such lists and tables. If you export a table in text format, you may choose to import it into Excel, which will often achieve alignment and permit copying and pasting into a word-processing document with ease.

If the delimited importing approach within Excel does not effectively achieve alignment, try the fixed-width alternative and then click to create or delete the lines that separate the columns in the importing process. In this manner, it is often possible to achieve alignment of tabular information from text files.

Links contained in exported text may not be easily interpreted by your word-processing application. For example, some versions of Word will display a question mark inside a yellow circle anywhere a link token appeared in the FARS document. Simply delete these "links" from your document. Additionally, some reformatting may be required for numeric data (lists and tables), and fonts may change, depending on your application's default settings.

To save your search results:

1. Perform your query on the infobase.
2. Verify that <u>All Records</u> is on. (To save only selected records within your search results, use the tag function.)
3. From the <u>File</u> menu, choose <u>Export</u>.
4. Pick a destination directory from the directory tree.
5. From the <u>List Files of Type:</u> window, choose the file format in which you would like to save your data. A number of word-processing programs are listed, along with ASCII and generic text.
6. Type a file name in the appropriate window.
7. Click <u>OK</u>.

Printing

If you wish to print the results of a search, click <u>File</u> on the menu bar and then click <u>Print</u>. The screen will permit you to choose among different panes that alternatively will print <u>Document</u>, <u>Contents</u>, <u>HitList</u>, or <u>Object</u>. If you are printing the table of contents, expand the table to show the branches you wish to print. To print a single branch, select that branch. You can specify that the printer prints tagged records, specific records, sections, or all. The toolbar in Figure 1.6 has an icon on which a picture of a printer appears (it is the third icon from the left). When clicked, it will generate a <u>Print</u> command.

Before printing, consider clicking on Tools from the menu bar and selecting Options from the pull-down menu, then clicking on Print to consider other choices. You may wish for your results to use inline headings, thereby ensuring citations to the full source name, section, and paragraph reference. Note that interspersing of complete cites between records can be cumbersome in large excerpts, but they can be very useful for focused excerpts. If you want to highlight the words that were hit through your query, you may select Integrate Query. This results in words that were hit being boldfaced and underscored. In the absence of selecting this option, the text prints in regular format, without highlighting hits. After accessing Tools on the menu bar, click on Options. On the Print pane, click on the box beside Inline Headings and/or Query Results to print these options onto materials you generate. (Access page setup to specify preferences as to paper options, orientation, margins, and header or footer.)

Follow these steps to print:

1. Select the information you wish to print.
2. Choose Print from the File menu.
3. Verify your printer interface is set correctly.
4. Select the appropriate tab for the type of information to be printed: Document, Contents, HitList, or Object.
5. Set the print range for the job. The print range options depend on the tab you use. Possible choices may include:
    *   Choose All to print all of the records in the current view. (The current view of the Document control may be narrowed to only those records or partitions with search hits or tagged records. Otherwise, All prints the entire infobase.)
    *   Choose Records: to print a specific range of records (you must also enter the first and last record to print).
    *   Choose Selection to only print the selected portion of the infobase.
    *   Choose Tagged Records to only print the tagged records in the infobase.
    *   Choose Section to specify a section of the infobase to print based on the table of contents headings.
6. Specify the number of copies to make.
7. Specify the starting page number, if desired. Page specifies the starting page number to be printed in the header or footer for the print job (provided that the header or footer uses the Page # code). Use this when you do not want the first page to be numbered 1.
8. Specify the number of columns to print, if desired.
    *   Folio Views can print information in one to five equal columns on a page. The columns flow like newspaper columns (top-to-bottom and left-to-right).
    *   The default number of columns for all print jobs is set in the Print tab of the Options dialog box.
9. Choose OK.

Copying and Pasting

Rather than exporting or printing, the user can concurrently open the FARS program and another word-processing program and then mark the selections of interest and copy and paste the section onto the word processor's file. The advantage of this approach is its ease of integrating direct quotes from the FARS resources into formal reports or articles that are being prepared. The disadvantage is that gray coloring, formatting, links, and footnotes will probably be lost. If this information is important, you will have to make the restorations individually afterward.

Follow these steps to paste text directly into other applications:

1. Block the FARS text you want to paste (use <u>Shift-arrow</u> keys).
2. Press <u>Ctrl-C</u> to copy the text or select <u>Copy</u> from the <u>Edit</u> menu.
3. Open the application you want to paste into. (Use <u>Alt-Tab</u> keys to toggle between applications.)
4. Position your insertion point where you want to paste the text and press <u>Ctrl-V</u>, or select <u>Paste</u> from your application's <u>Edit</u> menu.

Where Can I Go for Additional Direction?

This FARS primer is intended to provide an overview to get you started. However, additional direction is provided within the FARS program. You can press the F1 key and use Query to access help on any specific topic. A tutorial is likewise available online.

Help Capability: Online User's Guide

As you use FARS and have a question, access the Online User's Guide for assistance. If you click on <u>Help</u>, a menu appears. If you click on <u>Overview</u>, a brief introduction to the software used in FARS, reinforcing points discussed herein, will be accessed. If you click on <u>How Do I?</u>, you will see the following message:

> For more information, click a topic below.
> Folio Views Topics
> Find Information
> Annotate Infobases
> Print & Export Information
> Format Text
> Incorporate Images
> Edit Infobases
> Organize Infobases
> Customize Folio Views
> Advanced Topics
> Use Help

If you click on <u>Use Help</u> the following instructions appear:

Accessing Help
There are four primary methods for accessing <u>Folio Help</u>:
1. Press F1. Help on the current dialog or menu item appears.

- Use this method for quick help on a specific item or to open Help before performing a search.
2. Choose Contents from the Help menu. The contents listing for Help appears.
   - Use this method to browse for the information you need.
3. Choose How Do I? from the Help menu. The How Do I? list appears.
   - Use this method when you want a topical listing of tasks that you can perform in Folio Views.
4. Open the FOLIOHLP.NFO infobase in Folio Views. Click on the Contents button to go to the contents listing, search this infobase using the *query templates*, or browse the infobase using the Contents pane.
   - Use this method when you want to take full advantage of the Folio Views interface while using the Help file.

FARS Reference Guide

When accessing FARS, click on File on the menu bar, and select Open from the pull-down menu, then click on Nfo folder and select the FARS Reference Guide. The result will be access to the online guide, which will detail materials that reinforce the discussion herein. Alternatively, use the FARS menu screen and click the button for the FARS Reference Guide.

Folio Views 4 Getting Started

Another approach to accessing guidance, besides through the Help menu bar already described, is through the file option. You can access File on the menu bar, select Open from the pull-down menu, and then select the Nfo folder and click Open, select Getstrt4, and click Open (Folio Views 4 Getting Started file will then open for use). Alternatively, the last selection could be made, clicking on Foliohlp and then a click on Open (Folio 4 Help Infobase will then open for use). Approaches to help screens will vary by platform.

Advanced Search Capabilities of FARS

The following materials describe how the advanced search options can be accessed and applied with the Financial Accounting Research System (FARS). The advanced capabilities can be helpful in crafting searches. For example, the frequency count for each of the words included in a search command can help tailor the Boolean logic to better address the issue of interest. This resource is available within FARS, elaborating upon how to go beyond simple queries.

Advanced Query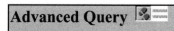

Search, Advanced Query

Purpose

Use the advanced query to unleash the full power of the Folio Views query syntax. This syntax helps you focus and refine your searches through the use of Boolean operators, wildcards, proximity operators, and scope limitations.

> *Note:* See at the end of this section for a summary chart of the query syntax.

Steps

The following procedures are detailed in this section:

- Searching the infobase
- Searching a subset of the infobase
- Performing a relevancy ranked search
- Performing a heading search
- Changing the view of your search results

Searching the Infobase

To search all text in the infobase:

1. Choose **Advanced Query** from the **Search** menu. (Recall the Figure 1.9 dialog box.)
2. Type the words you wish to search for, separated by a space or the appropriate operator.
   - You may search by keyword (not using any specific operators). For example:
     specialized industry guidance
   - You may search for an exact phrase. Enclose the phrase in quotation marks. For example:
     "impairment of goodwill"
   - You may use Boolean operators (and, or, not, exclusive or). For example:
     research and development
     research or development
     research not development
     research xor development
   - You may use wildcards (single character, multiple character, word form, synonym). For example:
     taxe?
     tax*
     tax%
     tax$
   - You may use proximity operators to specify how close terms must be. For example:
     "intangible asset" /7
   - If you wish to modify a previous query, click the **Prev** button next to the **Query For** box to display the previous query.
   - Note that as you type, the Query dialog attempts to complete the word you are typing with a word contained in the infobase. If the word is correct, press the Enter key and type the next term.
   - Queries may be up to 2048 characters in length.

3. If desired, choose **Checked Branches** at the bottom of the dialog to search only the checked branches of the table of contents.
    *   If you have not selected any branches in the <u>Contents</u> pane, do not select this option. Doing so will result in zero hits (you will be searching an empty set).
    *   To select branches in the <u>Contents</u> pane, click in the <u>Contents</u> pane, choose <u>Show Check Boxes</u> from the <u>View</u> menu, and then click in the check boxes next to the headings in the <u>Contents</u> pane.
4. Choose **OK** to apply the search to the current infobase. Choose **Apply to All** to apply the search to all open infobases.

For more information on selecting branches in the **Contents** pane, see **Show Check Boxes**.

Note: Depending on how the infobase was created, a simple search may or may not search in pop-ups and notes within the infobase. The infobase author may specify whether pop-ups and notes are searched by default. See New for additional information on setting the options for infobase creation. See the <u>Misc</u> tab in the <u>Properties</u> dialog for the settings for the infobase.

Searching a Subset of the Infobase

Changing the scope of your search allows you to focus on a particular subset of the infobase. <u>Views</u> defaults to searching the entire infobase unless a specific scope is selected. You may limit the scope of your search to a particular contents heading, level, field, highlighter, note, group, or pop-up. To set the scope of your search:

1. Choose **Advanced Query** from the **Search** menu.
2. Click the left bracket ▐ at the bottom of the dialog (or type in a left square bracket). The Word list changes to display the general search Scopes in the infobase.
3. Select the general scope you wish to search (contents, field, group, headings, highlighter, level, note, partition, or pop-up).
    *   The Scope list changes to display the names of the available specific scopes (the names of the levels, fields, highlighters, or groups, etc.)
    *   Notes and pop-ups are not named for searching purposes. Skip to step 5 if searching in notes or pop-ups.
    *   Some query options are not displayed in the dialog but are still valid (such as rank and heading). See Advanced Query Constructions for more information.
4. Double-click the specific scope you wish to search.
    *   You can also scroll to the name using the up and down arrows and then press CTRL+Enter.
5. Select the **Query For** box and move the insertion point after the colon or the right bracket ▐. Type the words, phrases, or patterns you wish to search for.
    *   Field, Headings, Highlighter, and Level searches require the search terms to follow a colon.
    *   Contents and Group searches require the search terms to follow the right bracket; no colon is used. Skip step 6 for these scope searches.
    *   You may use Boolean operators (and, or, not, exclusive or), wildcards, and proximity operators, and may perform phrase searches.

6. Click the right bracket ▮ (or type a right square bracket), if you did not in step 5. This closes the current scope.
7. If desired, choose **Checked Branches** at the bottom of the dialog to search only the checked branches of the table of contents.
   • If you have not selected any branches in the Contents pane, do not select this option. Doing so will result in zero hits (you will be searching an empty set).
   • To select branches in the Contents, click in the Contents pane, choose Show Check Boxes from the View menu, and then click in the check boxes next to the headings in the Contents pane.
8. Choose **OK** or **Apply to All**.
   • **OK** applies the query to the current infobase.
   • **Apply to All** applies the query to all open infobases.

For more information on selecting branches in the **Contents** pane, see Show Check Boxes.

Performing a Relevancy Ranked Search

The simplest way to perform a relevancy ranked search is to use the Query dialog or the Query toolbar. However, you also may construct a ranked query in the Advanced Query dialog or use this syntax to create a ranked search in a custom query template. (The Query Template Editor is included with the Folio Builder product.) To find a specified number of records most relevant to your search topic (rather than all records having anything at all to do with your search topic):

1. Choose Advanced Query from the Search menu. The Advanced Query dialog appears.
2. Type
        [Rank
3. Enter the number of items you want ranked, followed by a closing bracket.
        [Rank 10]
   • Think of this as the top ten list. If you want to the see the ten most relevant items, enter 10. If you want to see the one hundred most relevant items, enter 100.
   • You must enter a whole number (no fractions or decimal values permitted).
4. Enter the query you wish to perform.
   • *Note:* If you wish to specify a partition, you must do so before the rank. For example:
        [Partition Chapter][Rank 15]
5. Choose **OK** to apply the query to the infobase.
   • See Query for information on how Folio Views determines relevance.
   • See Ranking Queries for additional ranking options.

Performing a Heading Search

Heading searches allow you to specify a subsection of the infobase to search without having to specify the entire heading structure (as is required with the Contents search).

Note: This option is not available for all infobases. A special index must be created when the infobase is built for heading searches to work. This option may be set in the New dialog (choose Options).

To perform a heading search:

1. Choose <u>Advanced Query</u> from the <u>Search</u> menu. The Advanced Query dialog appears.
2. Type
    [Headings
    *   Note that this option is not available for all infobases. The infobase must have a special option set when it is created for this to work.
3. Enter the level name for the headings you wish to search.
    *   The level name must be one of the levels in the infobase. Usually, it is not the first level.
    *   For example:
        [Headings Primary Level
4. If desired, enter the specific heading name you wish to search. End the scope with a closed bracket, ▮.
    *   The heading name corresponds to an actual heading in the infobase, such as Purpose and Scope of FASB Technical Bulletins and Procedures for Issuance.
    *   The level name and heading name must be separated by commas.
    *   Subheadings may also be listed. Separate subheadings by commas.
    *   For example:
        [Headings Primary Level, Purpose and Scope of FASB Technical Bulletins and Procedures for Issuance]
        [Headings Third Level, question*]
        [Headings Fifth Level, assumptions]
5. After the closing bracket, enter any terms or other query constructs that you wish to search for. You may enter any other query constructs except partition or rank.

See Headings for more information.

Changing the View of Your Search Results

After performing a query, you may wish to view the search hits in a variety of ways. The default is to show you all records in the infobase. This allows you to view the search hits in context. You may also view only those records that have hits or an entire partition that has hits. Or, using the <u>HitList</u> pane, you may view the most relevant hits (if a ranked query is performed).

To view records or partitions with hits:

1. Perform a query. See Searching the Infobase, Searching a Subset of the Infobase, or Performing a Relevancy Ranked Search for more information.
2. Choose **Records With Hits** or **Partitions With Hits** from the **View** menu. All of the records which contain search hits are gathered into a single view (extraneous records disappear from the view).
3. Choose **All Records** from the **View** menu again to restore the view.

To use the HitList:

1. Perform a ranked query. See Performing a Relevancy Ranked Search or Simple Ranked Query for more information.

2.   Click the **All** tab at the bottom of the infobase view to display the HitList. The most relevant hits are displayed first in the HitList.
3.   Double-click an item in the HitList to go directly to it in the infobase. Click a column header in the HitList to change how the items are sorted (ascending or descending alphanumeric order).

Table 1.3   Advanced Query Options

Operator or Scope	Example
And	assets liabilities
	assets & liabilities
	assets and liabilities
Or	debit | credit
	debit or credit
Not	^deferred
	not deferred
	recorded^deferred
Exclusive or (Xor)	earned ~ advanced
	earned xor advanced
Phrase	"negative goodwill"
	"realiz* and recog*"
Single character wildcard	uncollect?ble
	defer???
Multiple character wildcard	leas*
	qualif*n*
Ordered proximity	"securities and exchange"/10
Unordered proximity	"securities and exchange" @7
Record proximity	"exempt small"#5
Sentence proximity	"search query"/s
	"search operators"@s
Paragraph proximity	"create build infobase"/p
	"index stop words"@p
Stem (word form)	recognize%
	realize%
Thesaurus (synonym)	liability$
	adjustment$
Contents	[Contents EITF Abstracts] offset*
Partition	[Partition Title] account*
Rank	[Rank 10] recognize income
Fields	[Field issue date: '12/73']
Range	[Field issue date: >'12/73']
Highlighters	[Highlighter lease: classification | capital]
Pop-ups and notes	[Note accounting principle] or [Popup glossary]
Groups	[Group qa] asset liability
Headings	[Heading <level name>,<heading path>: query]
	[Heading Chapter: import files]
	[Heading Chapter, Open: import files]
Levels	[Level <level name>: <query>]
	[Level Document Type: account title]

Food for Thought, Including the GAAP Hierarchy

Mastery of research in documentary databases, such as FARS, is challenging. Considerable past research efforts in semantic analysis of accounting standards and information—more recently applying data mining, statistical, and digital techniques as well as mark-up languages focused on eXtensible Business Reporting Language (XBRL—see http://www.xbrl.org/)—are directed to facilitating understanding, retrieval, and analysis. A challenge arises because language is used more generally in everyday vernacular (such as having an "interest" in a subject matter), as well as in specialized settings (such as the "interest" charged by a financial institution). One approach to distinguishing these meanings is to expand the search, using phrases such as "interest rate." Recall that quotes require exact phrasing for a match, which means that some documents that refer to interest charged but choose different phraseology will not be identified by such a search.

Computers are extremely efficient at matching, comparing, and locating words and phrases. However, since language is written by individuals who often use both generic and professional meanings of words within a single document (let alone within a database), human intelligence and reasoning has to be coupled with the computer's power to effectively locate and interpret the results of any search. Since databases change every time an update occurs, often changing meanings of existing terms and adding new definitions or terms, as well as superseding past guidance, the results of any particular search word or phrase will change as well.

The step of identifying search terms or phrases will reflect the degree of learning and experience of the researcher. Research skill and knowledge work hand-in-hand. In full-text document-retrieval systems such as FARS, a search engine supports Boolean, wildcard, structured, and natural language searching via Folio Views, which is a generic interface. Tradeoffs arise in gaining completeness without having a user buried by irrelevant word uses. For example if a user types warrant* as a wildcard, intended to include warrants, the search will expand to encompassing warranty and warranting, which have distinct use within accounting apart from the intended subject matter.

Since users lose time and patience with excessively expanded searches, too often the approach is to focus on only the top 10 or 20 searches, rather than coupling scanning capabilities of the searcher with the expansive word use identification by the computer. This has led to some researchers' suggestion that a list of terms be provided to novice users to both build vocabulary and reduce frustration (Garnsey et al., 2005). Yet, search strategies are expected to differ among individuals based on their verbal and technical skills, as well as personal style. Just as multiple learning styles exist, approaches to the use of technology, cognitive processes, and research acumen will vary.

A core consideration in selecting from among available passages providing guidance is to respect what is known as the GAAP Hierarchy (do a *query* on the Amended FARS information base using the phrase "GAAP Hierarchy"). If the accounting treatment of a transaction or event is not specified by a pronouncement covered by category (a), which is the highest authority, consider whether the accounting treatment is specified by another source of established accounting principles. If an established accounting principle from one or more sources in category (b), (c), or (d), which are lower levels of authority within the hierarchy, is relevant to the circumstances, any conclusion that another treatment is generally accepted would have to be justified. Whenever a conflict arises between accounting principles relevant to the circumstances from one or more sources in category (b), (c), or (d), the treatment specified by the source in the higher category is to be followed—for example, follow category (b) treatment over category (c). If this is not done, then the conclusion that a treatment specified by a source in the lower category better presents the substance of the transaction in the circumstances would have to be justified.

The goal is to build one's unique ability to search efficiently, given particular database capabilities. For example, FARS permits different approaches to searches and displays of results that can enhance research strategies in certain settings. Rather than be disheartened by an "off the mark" search result, the researcher can build expertise as to the broader use of language in the professional literature and hone his or her skills to avoid or adapt to such distractions in future searches. As the saying goes: "Every job is a self-portrait of the person who did it. Autograph your work with excellence."

Winston Churchill advised: "Never, Never, Never Quit" and Ralph Waldo Emerson observed: "Our chief want in life is somebody who will make us do what we can." The novice can build skills that will make FARS an indispensable resource.

> *Unless you try to do something beyond what you have already mastered, you will never grow.*
> *—Ronald E. Osborn*

References

Garnsey, Margaret R., John O'Neill and Leonard Strokes. "Increasing Student Accuracy in FARS Database Searching" Working Paper, Siena College, 2005.

Hannon, Neal J., and Robert J. Gold. "XBRL Revisited". *Journal of Accountancy* 199(2):64–65, 2005.

National Association of Black Accountants, Inc. *"Commitment to Excellence."* 1986 National Convention, Dallas, TX. pp. C1, C34, C40, C12.

Naumann, Jeffrey W. "Tap Into XBRL's Power the Easy Way." *Journal of Accountancy* 197(5):33–39, 2004.

Self-Review and Cross-Checks

1. If you enter a search and are told there are zero hits, what is likely to be the problem?

   You probably have not opened the infobase. In other words, there is nothing to search. (Remember, once you open the infobase and conduct a search, click on the HitList pane tab to view the hits and the Document pane tab to view the textual information located. The Contents pane tab will provide the count of the types of guidance identified in the hits (such as how many hits relate to APB opinions or FASB statements). The Contents/Document pane tab permits you to view both at the same time.)

2. What if you enter a search and get far fewer hits than you expected?

   You are probably searching only the menu or some smaller subset of information than intended. Check to confirm which infobases are open by clicking Window on the menu bar. Proceed to open the infobase or multiple infobases you wish to search.

3. You specify a search and identify zero hits; you check Window on the menu bar and confirm that the appropriate infobase is open. How should you proceed?

   If the search involves more than a single word, access Search on the menu bar and then select Advanced Query. This will allow you to check the word count of any item within your search phrasing and to see how the structure of your search may have limited your matches in an unintended fashion.

4. You perform a search and notice that most of the document you have accessed is shaded. What is meant by the shading, and how should you proceed?

The shading indicates superseded materials in FARS. There should be a red diamond at the beginning of the shaded material. Click that diamond to read what materials apply in place of the superseded section. Within the AMENDED infobase, clicking on the diamond will explain amendments.

5. In the Document pane, a number of footnotes appear. How do you access the footnotes?

Click the footnote number, the cursor will take the form of a pointing hand, and a pop-up screen will appear. This will contain the text of the footnote.

6. You specify a word search in quotes that generates zero hits, even though you are certain that the phrase should be in the material. How might you proceed to explore the search phrasing?

The same phrasing might be attempted without the quotes. If that generates too many hits, then you might try Advanced Query with quotes but with a proximity delimiter such as /3. Another idea is to try a synonym command outside of quotes to see if a match can be achieved. As an example, if there are zero hits when you search "recording a deferred debit" but 50 hits if you remove the quotes, you might consider using such delimiters. If neither of those options produces the desired result, you might try using deferred debit$. The synonym command enlarges coverage to consider such phrases as deferred-charge account as one example of an additional hit identified.

7. You have performed a search using the FASB-OP infobase and prepared a related report on your findings. Upon reviewing the write-up, an associate points out that you have no references to the work of the Emerging Issues Task Force (EITF) and wonders whether there might be some relevant EITF guidance. How should you proceed?

Your associate has pointed out that FARS only searches the infobases you indicate. Once you have completed a search on FASB-OP, you should check other infobases for relevant information regarding the issue being researched. In this case, you should access File on the menu bar, select Open from the pull-down menu, then apply that command to the folder Nfo, and click on EITF. You can then proceed to search that infobase in the usual manner. Alternatively, you could have concurrently opened the FASB-OP and the EITF databases and accessed Search from the menu bar, selected Advanced Query, typed in the search phrasing, and then clicked Apply to All to trigger a search of all open infobases. Keep in mind that in order to view the HitList for each infobase, you need to access Window and switch among the infobases to which the search was applied. Alternatively, pressing Ctrl+Tab will cycle through the views. You might also consider searching other infobases. FASB-Q&A can be particularly helpful on some issues. The AMENDED infobase would have concurrently integrated EITFs, as would the Topical Index.

8. You perform an advanced query search of the FASB-Q&A and the FASB-OP infobases. Yet, when you view the results generated by the Advanced Query command to apply to all, your hits have no references to FASB-Q&A. Does that mean there are no hits within that infobase?

No, you have to move to the infobase FASB-Q&A to see the hits located, since they would not appear in the HitList for the FASB-OP infobase. In other words, you can use an <u>Advanced Query</u> to search multiple infobases, but you must switch to the respective infobase to view the results of that search for that particular resource. One alternative approach is to open the AMENDED infobase that incorporates such guidance. Another is to use the query template, once the AMENDED resource is accessed, and <u>Search within a single OP document type</u> and choose <u>implementation guides q a</u> before specifying the search phrase.

9. You understand that links are connections between one point in an infobase and another. Distinguish the types of links within an infobase one from the other.

    The links that arise include query links that connect menu items, document references, and topical index references to the related information in the appropriate infobase. Another type of link is the pop-up link that connects footnote references to the text of the footnote. In addition, in FASB-OP, links connect superseded or amended material in one document with the superseding or amending language in another document. Finally, both FASB-OP and FASB-CT link glossary terms with their definitions. Within the AMENDED infobase, a status page is retained for those pronouncements that are omitted because they have been completely superseded and to identify which pronouncement (and paragraph within it) created the amendment(s) reflected.

10. You export tagged records and import them into your word-processing software, but discover the listing is far longer than you expected. What might be the problem?

    If you were searching more than one issue and forgot to clear the tags from the initial research, any records you had previously tagged would be exported, along with the last few that you really intended to bring into your software. Care must be taken to understand that a continuous session within FARS will keep all tagged records until you choose to clear them. Your tags remain until you clear them or exit the FARS system. This facilitates you performing multiple queries and tagging any and all records of use in your research, which is helpful when you want such a collection of cites.

11. You are performing an advanced query and your system crashes, triggering a general protection fault. What may be the cause of this crash?

    If you open too many infobases at one time, such crashes are common, particularly if a system has less than 12 megabytes of RAM. Since FASB-OP and FASB-CT have essentially the same material, they would rarely need to be opened at the same time. The AMENDED infobase automatically incorporates EITFs and other guidance. Reconsider which infobases you really need to have opened and try again. Remember, you can always do a search on one infobase at a time and then combine such searches. Often it is easier to organize your results with such an approach. You merely need to keep track of which infobases you have searched and what your specific search phrasing was, so you can be consistent across the infobases. Remember that by using the AMENDED infobase, you access multiple documents at the same time.

12. Does it matter whether you query "Internal Revenue Service" or "internal revenue service"?

    No, because queries are not case sensitive.

13. If you have more than a single infobase open and use the <u>Search</u> and <u>Select a Query</u> template, will it apply to all the opened infobases?

    No, because query templates cannot be applied to multiple infobases. The <u>Advanced Query</u> dialog box is needed to consider multiple infobases with a single search.

14. How do you clear a query when you are analyzing multiple infobases through use of the advanced query capability?

    You cannot use the <u>Clear Query</u> button, since it does not apply to multiple infobases. To clear a multiple infobase query, it is necessary to clear the query in each of the open infobases individually.

15. What is the logic of ordering of hits on the HitList?

    The default is an ordering by relevance, with the first hit being deemed the most relevant to the search.

16. You wish to identify guidance related to corporate reorganization. What is the difference in the following approaches: "corporate reorganization"; "corporate reorganization"/3; "corporate reorganization"@4; corporate reorganization~bankruptcy; corporate reorganiz*^ bankrupt%; corporate reorganization$; corporate reorgan*? Clearly describe the distinctions and identify the approximate number of hits that result from a search of the FASB-OP (amended) infobase.

    The quoted search phrase matches every character of the terms and results in two hits. The use of /3 means that the words must be within three records of one another and is only operative in the <u>Advanced Query</u> mode; it likewise results in two hits. Within the <u>Advanced Query</u> mode, the use of @4 permits the order of the terms to be reversed and increases the number of hits to 11. The removal of the quotes and the use of ~bankruptcy means that it can be either but not both terms in a record. The result is a total of nine hits. The use of the asterisk on reorganiz* means that different endings to the word would be matched, such as reorganizing *and* reorganization. *The ^ means not bankrupt% and the % permits consideration of words that are forms of the root word* bankrupt, *such as* bankruptcy. *The use of the dollar sign calls for synonyms. The last three searches all result in 12 hits. Note the usefulness of the <u>Advanced Query</u> capability in understanding the structure of the various search commands.*

17. You type "sales"/5 in a search process and notice that the HitList shows the sales term blocked in blue and the number 5, such as paragraph 5 highlighted in blue. What is the problem?

    You intended to do a proximity search but instead of using the required <u>Advanced Query</u> mode, you used <u>Query</u> mode. As a result, your command simply works as a search on both the word sales *and the number* 5.

18. Explain how you can use FARS to distinguish between revenue recognition that is based on the earnings process and that relating to realized or realizable criteria. Concurrently, explain how

FARS can address the nature of revenue for not-for-profit entities. Describe all approaches you could use to explore these questions within FARS.

The *first* approach could be to access FARS, click on the <u>Topical Index</u>, and then click on the "<u>T</u>" and scroll down to <u>Terminology</u> in the Topical Index and see whether terms associated with the question at hand are listed. You will find: Earned CON5, Par. 83; Earnings CON5, Par. 33; Realization CON6, Par. 143; Realized, Realizable CON5, Par. 83 and CON6, Par. 143; Recognition CON5, Par. 6, CON6, Par. 143, and CON7, Par. 12; and Revenue CON6, Par. 78. Each of these can be clicked and viewed on the Document Pane to address the question at hand. Be certain to read the footnotes in each of the linked definitional cites in order to completely consider the core discussion within FARS. This first step clearly bears out that when a researcher is addressing conceptual matters, the concept statements (CON) are likely to be the source of information of primary focus within FARS. The terminology section of the Topical Index does have a listing for Not-for-Profit Organizations, citing FAS116, Par. 209, B51.409, FAS117, Par. 168, C67.407, FAS141, Par. F1, G40.406, FAS142, Par. F1, No5.405. The references with letters and numbers are within the FASB-CT infobase.

The **second** approach extends beyond a vocabulary focus to the subject matter of these same terms, again using the <u>Topical Index</u>. Of relevance under "E", is the Earnings caption, and under "R", the Realization, Recognition, "Recognition and Measurement in Financial Statements," "Revenue Recognition," and Revenues captions. The "Revenue Recognition" caption goes far beyond the Concept statements, bearing out applicable ARBs, APBs, FASs, FTBs, and EITFs. A number of FASB-CT cites are also highlighted. Under "N", you will find Nonprofit Enterprises, which instructs you to "See Not-for-Profit Organizations", since the hyphenated nomenclature is used within GAAP. Under the "Not-for-Profit Organizations" heading are a number of cites, including a highlighting of "See Contributions" which is an alert to the nature of certain inflows in such settings being separate from an earnings process.

The **third** approach that can be powerful when pursuing a theoretical concept such as revenue recognition or a similar "theme" is to access the "<u>Current Text</u>" option on the FARS menu. Click on "<u>General Standards</u>" and you will find an alphabetized table of contents. Scroll down to "R75 Revenue Recognition." Click on the red diamond to the left, and the linkage identifies sources used: ARB 43, Chapter 1A; APB Opinion 10; FASB Statement 48; FASB Statement 111; FASB Technical Bulletin 90-1. You will also find reference to lists of (a) Issues discussed by the Emerging Issues Task Force (EITF; presented in paragraph .1000) and (b) AICPA Accounting Standards Executive Committee (AcSEC) pronouncements (paragraph .2000), both of which provide supplemental guidance for this section. The Summary Communicates the concept of earning and the concept of collection. However, the sources cited do not highlight the Concept statements, and the clarification of terminology—realized relative to earned—is not clearly inferred. The Summary is followed by a number of subheads with text and cross-references, such as: Installment Method of Accounting; Other Guidance on Revenue Recognition; Revenue Recognition When Right of Return Exists (Applicability and Scope); and Criteria for Recognizing Revenue When Right of Return Exists. Supplemental Guidance is cited, associated with Accounting for Separately Priced Extended Warranty and Product Maintenance Contracts, as well as Emerging Issues Task Force (EITF) Issues. The EITFs are grouped by subject matter and related by topic to the guidance in this section, such as "Consideration Given by/Received from a Vendor" or "Long-Term Power Contracts." No Nonprofit entry appears under General Standards, but this brings us to the fourth step to consider related to industry.

A *fourth* approach remains in the FASB-CT infobase but accesses <u>Industry Standards</u> in order to consider how context might affect accounting. The alphabetical list permits consideration of revenue issues focused on different settings that address peculiarities arising from the nature of the enterprise. As an example, presume that revenue recognition in the nonprofit sector has raised the question of when a pledge is considered to be revenue. Click on Industry Standards and then the diamond beside "No5 Not-For-Profit Organizations". Scrolling down will highlight subheads directed to "Reporting of Contributions Received" (.143–.145) and "Recognition of Expiration of Donor-imposed Restrictions" (.146–.147), among others. The Glossary expands on related terms, including an "Unconditional promise to give".

Note that FASB-CT has two other links of potential interest to a researcher. "Current Text Sections That Are Superseded by Pronouncements with Delayed Effective Dates (Appendix E)" should be perused to consider how results in the FASB-OP, AMENDED, and FASB-CT might be affected by these pronouncements. "Schedule of AICPA Practice Bulletins, Audit and Accounting Guides, and Statements of Position (Appendix A)" provides a guide to other potential sources of information on topics of interest. In checking completeness of research in the accounting area, it is prudent to scan this listing and note that these sources are not retrievable from FARS.

The *fifth* approach uses Boolean logic and search phrases. FARS permits word searches and phrase definitions that can be extremely useful in locating citations of direct interest to the question being asked. This approach uses the Toolbar (recall Figure 1.6), which is a collection of buttons for quick access to the most frequently used menu commands. An explanatory box appears with all the Toolbar icons when you place the mouse cursor over the icon. First you access the FARS MENU. Then you access the directory to be searched, such as the Original Pronouncements, as amended. Next, go to the Toolbar and click on Search. Then Click on <u>Query</u>. Type in the phrase for searching: revenue recogni* earn* realiz* realize$. The use of the wildcard * facilitates the search for all variations of a word: for example, recogni* would match to recognize, recognizes, recognizing, recognition . . . ; earn* would match to earns, earning, earned . . . ; realiz* would match to realize, realizes, realized, realizing, realization . . . . The $ adds any synonyms to the term realize. The results in the Document pane go right to the CON5 Highlights. The simpler search phrase earn and realize and recognize has the same first result. The search phrase revenues$ and not-for-profit organizations in the query mode produces a hit at FAS 116, Par. 105 specifically addressing recognition of unconditional promises to give.

The **sixth** approach moves from the query to the <u>Advanced Query</u>. The latter permits transparency as to how frequently each term appears in the infobase being searched and how their intersection influences the results. In particular, if a query has no matches, you can explore the possible reasons why that is the case by checking the advanced query. Moreover, it is easy to identify synonyms through the advanced query approach. Another option within Advanced Query is to use proximity searches and Boolean operators. First, to clear the previous query, click the Clear Query button. Then click on the Advanced Query button or press F2. An advantage of using the same search phrase with the advanced capability within FASB-OP (amended) is it provides the count of matches per term in the search phrase and also reports the number of records the combined search terms identify: in this case, nine. Moreover, synonyms to realize are identified, and these can help in setting a scope for future searches—understand, comprehend, accomplish, complete, perfect, effect, perform, receive, gain, profit, obtain, and acquire. FAS 19, Par. 135 is the first hit reported. There are also cites to FAS 97, FAS 124, FTB86-2, CON 5 (two hits), CON 7 (two hits), and the Table of Contents. An advantage to applying this search to FASB-OP is that original pronouncements bear the shading of superseded guidance, helping *to gain historical perspective. Such a search identifies 16 hits. The first hit cites APB 7, Par. 12 and relates to superseded material describing manufacturing revenue. Conditions cited for the reporting of income include: "(a) credit risks are reasonably predictable, (b) the lessor does not retain sizeable risks of ownership . . . and (c) there are no important uncertainties surrounding the amount of costs yet to be incurred or revenues yet to be earned under the lease." This historical perspective is very much on point in providing an illustration of how concepts have been applied to practice settings. As you evaluate accounting issues, keep in mind:* There is nothing permanent except change. —Heraclitus (540–475? B.C.) *Any historical issue has to be evaluated relative to the GAAP that existed at that point in time.*

The **seventh** *approach uses the query template accessible from the Search menu. This can tailor the search to particular types of documents as well as date ranges.*

The use of the query phrase within the advanced query capability revenues$ and not-for-profit organizations results in 36 hits, identifying FAS 93, 116, 117, and 131, and CON 6 as the relevant literature base. To show the sensitivity of such searches to phrasing, simple adjustment to revenue$ and not-for-profit organizations leads to 155 hits, identifying the synonyms of earnings, income, proceeds, receipts, profit, gain, interest, dividends, capital, wealth, funds, finances, income, means, resources, stocks, credit annuity. Yet, a conspicuous omission in this list is contribution. To explore which terms might have identified this inflow, use contribution$ within advanced query. The results identify contributions, gift, donation, present, offering, grant, addition, improvement, increase, supplement, subsidy, and assistance. The query template Search within a single OP document title *can focus the search phrase just on FAS 116, as an example.*

19. Discuss the pros and cons of each of the available approaches to researching FARS.

   Pros and cons of topical index. *The pros of using a topical index are (a) it is as familiar as any index in the back of a book reference and (b) the nature of subject orientation rather than word orientation tends to help in obtaining an idea of the scope of related subject matter. The cons of using a topical index are (a) the many cross-references to other subheads that would need to be searched for completeness and (b) the nature of the subject orientation rather than the word orientation potentially generates many cites of marginal interest. Note, however, that the "Terminology" option within the Topical Index does offer a word focus.*

   Pros and cons of current text. *The pros of using current text are (a) it provides a short summary of the concept or theme, (b) key dimensions of the concept or theme are highlighted as subheads, helping to scope the question, and (c) cross-references lead to related documentation. The cons of using current text are (a) that the summary may not focus on detailed terminology or critical distinctions due to its intended succinctness and (b) other dimensions of interest may not be included, as is the case of the CONCEPT statements. Unlike a Statement of Financial Accounting Standards, a Statement of Financial Accounting Concepts does not establish generally accepted accounting principles (see CON1 Highlights). In 2007 and thereafter, the Conceptual Framework Project underway jointly by the FASB and IASB plans to consider the entire framework as to purpose and status in the GAAP Hierarchy.*

   Pros and cons of Boolean logic and search phrases. *The pros of Boolean logic and search phrases are (a) the ability to narrow the hits to a combination of ideas and (b) the capability of identifying synonyms for further research into the area of interest. The cons of Boolean logic and search phrases are (a) that they are fraught with the shortcomings of linguistics that use similar terms for very different phenomena and (b) the 50-hit default requires a good deal of scanning* *through materials that may be of limited relevance. Key things to remember in the search process are: (1) you search that directory which is opened, (2) searches produce a hit list in order of relevancy and will return the top 50 hits, (3) if too many databases and too many searches are performed, the system can become unstable and prudence suggests the wisdom of closing FARS and beginning again, (4) if you have no hits, check to ensure you have opened the database to be searched, (5) when a hit list has less information than one wishes to see, you can proceed to the FARS MENU, access the Original Pronouncements, or the amended infobase, choose the type of guidance of interest, scroll down, and access the full pronouncement (this permits reading a match in context and is easily accessed in FARS), and (6) you can copy and paste, export, and blend output from FARS with other software with relative ease.*

20. In the course of your search in FARS, you notice some AICPA publications of relevance, including Statements of Position (SOPs) and Accounting Guides. In addition, mention is made of Securities and Exchange Commission (SEC) literature of potential importance. Are these accessible in FARS as full text documents available for search?

No. The AICPA is the source for both SOPs and Accounting Guides. Some summary information can be accessed at http://www.aicpa.org. The http://www.sec.gov site provides access to the Securities and Exchange Commission guidance. Text files can be downloaded from the SEC site and then searched within your word-processing package or other software with which you have familiarity. Both the AICPA and SEC sites often include information on current developments, exposure drafts, and speeches that can be useful resources when researching issues.

Remember that by clicking Current Text on the FARS menu, a screen will appear that includes a red diamond link labeled Schedule of AICPA Practice Bulletins, Audit and Accounting Guides, and Statements of Position (Appendix A). In addition, certain sections of the General Guidance describe other authoritative guidance, including attention to the SEC. As an example, see E11.171 related to Earnings Per Share, listing SEC guidance on that topic. A Query search of SEC within the FASB-CT infobase generates 38 hits that reference both General Standards and Industry Standards. An Advanced Query using SEC generates 150 hits within the FASB-OP (amended) infobase. The phrase "Securities and Exchange Commission" results in 50 hits. The acronym SOP results in 223 hits. The phrase "Statement of Position" results in 90 hits. The point is that FARS can assist in pointing the accounting researcher in the right direction of other literature of interest.

Other proprietary software products incorporating FARS content with other databases are accessible at a cost. Examples include Comperio (go to http://www.pwc.com and search Comperio for its home page) and Accounting Research (http://www.accountingresearchmanager.com/). Content includes accounting, SEC, and auditing resources. The user interface facilitates easy access to such areas of interest as the regulatory setting, permitting the researcher to drill down into the accounting and auditing enforcement releases. Organization of topics, similar to that found in the Current Text approach of the FARS product is apparent, including business combinations, financial instruments, leases, revenue recognition, and related parties. As with other products, online help capabilities are made available to online subscribers.

CHAPTER 2 – RESOURCES BEYOND THE FINANCIAL ACCOUNTING RESEARCH SYSTEM (FARS)

2

Researching Accounting and Business Issues

Overview of Resources

Before turning to the case assignment in Chapter 2, consider the spectrum of resources available to research accounting and business issues. This overview will prepare you to solve the case exercises at the end of this chapter.

AICPA's Annual *Accounting Trends & Techniques*

Accounting Trends & Techniques is published annually by the American Institute of Certified Public Accountants (AICPA)—the sixtieth edition was published in 2006. This resource tracks 600 companies' common practices relative to each of the financial statements and associated disclosure practices. For information see http://www.aicpa.org. Each edition follows a similar approach, whereby tables are provided summarizing the industry classifications and general nature of the sample. Numerous tables with frequency statistics (counts) describe reporting and disclosure approaches, organized by components of each financial statement, notes to the financial statements, and the auditors' report forms. Examples of actual reporting excerpts are included. This is a useful resource for profiling common accounting choices, identifying patterns over time, and seeing how others describe their accounting choices. Check your library!

Journals

A literature search, directed to accounting, finance, and business journals may identify research coverage of the company and its industry. Examples of journals of likely interest follow, with an asterisk beside those you should check first due to their practice-oriented focus:

ABACUS
Accounting and Business Research
Accounting Horizons*
Accounting, Organizations and Society
The Accounting Review
Advances in Accounting
Auditing: A Journal of Practice and Theory
Behavioral Research in Accounting
Business Horizons
California Management Review (Berkeley)
(Canadian) Accounting Perspectives
Contemporary Accounting Research
The CPA Journal*
Critical Perspectives on Accounting
European Management Journal
Financial Accountability and Management
Government Financial Management*

Harvard Business Review
Issues in Accounting Education
Journal of Accountancy*
Journal of Accounting and Economics
Journal of Accounting and Public Policy
Journal of Accounting, Auditing, and Finance
Journal of Accounting Literature
Journal of Accounting Research
Journal of Finance
Journal of Finance and Economics
Journal of International Accounting, Auditing and Taxation
Journal of the American Taxation Association
Research in Accounting Regulation
Research in Governmental and Nonprofit Accounting

Restatements

A resource of particular interest to accounting researchers is the analysis of financial restatements that has been performed by the United States Government Accountability Office (GAO). In 2002, the GAO released a report concerning changes from January 1997 to June 2002 in the relative number of restatement announcements: *Report on Restatements* (GAO-03-138). *Financial Statement Restatement Database* (GAO-03-395R) facilitated related research by the broader research community. In July 2006, the GAO released a second study focusing on 2002 through September 2005 entitled *Financial Restatements—Update of Public Company Trends, Market Impacts, and Regulatory Enforcement Activities*. All three reports can be accessed at www.gao.gov/cgi-bin/getrpt?GAO-06-678

by simply substituting the desired GAO report number at the end of the link. Downloadable .PDF files are available.

Interactive Databases

A number of interactive databases are available in the library at your university, and increasingly on the Web page for the library. Such information gateways have numerous resources including quick database links, digital collections, full-text journal collections, and instruction on searching and evaluating the Web through various search engines. Research tools are detailed, alongside resources.

Universities frequently have available: Factiva (Dow Jones & Reuters); ArticleFirst, Econ-Lit, Consumers Index, and Worldscope Global (FirstSearch); Business and Company Resource Center containing company profiles, brand information, rankings, investment reports, company histories, and periodicals, including Expanded Academic Index/ASAP and Business & Economics Business Index ASAP (InfoTrac–Thomson Gale); LexisNexis Academic Universe; NewsBank; Findex (CSA); JSTOR (Journal Storage Project); SpringerLink (Springer journals); netLibrary; ScienceDirect (Elsevier); and Periodicals Index Online (Chadwyck-Healey). To provide some idea of scope: Factiva.com has a collection of content from 118 countries in 22 languages including more than 9,000 global publications, 10,000 key Web sites, thousands of company profiles, and pictures from Reuters. It uses Factiva Intelligent Indexing, which permits more focused searches. Other commonly available resources include: World News Connection (Dialog), CQ Weekly (CQ Press), AccuNet/AO Multimedia Archive, *New York Times*, 1851–2003+ (Proquest), Social Sciences Citation Index (ISI), Web of Science (ISI), STAT-USA (Statistical Abstract of the U.S., U.S. Census Bureau), and industry-focused resources such as METADEX (CSA) concerning metals and alloys and Computer Database focusing on periodicals in the computer, telecommunications and electronic industries. International business company profiles are available at Mergent Online, while the General Business File (Thomson Gale) has nearly 200,000 public and private companies. Over 208 economics, financial, and environmental World Development Indicators for the 1960–2004+ time frame are in a database available through the World Bank; other global information can be located in International Financial Statistics (IMF). The Leadership Library is a directory containing information on over 400,000 individuals; the Gale Biography Resource Center contains more than 200,000 individuals' biographies. Numerous publishers have Web sites tied to business, accounting, auditing, and tax areas such as John Wiley & Sons, Inc. (http://www.wiley.com) and Wolters Kluwer (e.g., CCH at www.tax.cchgroup.com). Public libraries frequently provide online database access from your home or other location to similar resources, as well as offering NetLibrary which has books in electronic format.

Internet Search Engines

The Internet has a number of search engines available through which you can perform keyword searches and identify resources. They include the following sites:

http://www.google.com

http://www.altavista.com

http://www.lycos.com

http://www.yahoo.com

http://www.msn.com

http://www.excite.com

http://www.sevenmetasearch.com

http://www.go2net.com

http://www.webcrawler.com

http://www.infoseek.com

http://www.hotbot.com   http://www.finderseeker.com
http://www.ask.com   http://www.looksmart.com
http://usinfo.state.gov   http://www.business.com
http://www.directorieslistings.com   http://www.firstgov.gov

http://www.Top5SearchEngines.com [searches Google Yahoo! MSN AOL and ASK]

http://www.virtualfreesites.com/search.government.html [has Government Search Engines including IRS, Patent Office, Supreme Court, Library of Congress, Government Printing Office, and National Transportation Library]

You can perform a word search and thereby identify Internet resources related to that topic. However, each engine will likely identify different resources due to its respective approach to searching the Web sites, classifying material, and presenting matches. Moreover, given estimates that less than one-third of available Web resources are captured by such search engines (*Wall Street Journal*, April 10, 1998, p. 1), it is particularly prudent to access more than one such resource.

Site-Specific Searches

Beyond general search engines, many Web sites have their own search mechanisms that help to identify information of interest on that site. These search assistants are often more tailored to context, such as requesting that the user read a site map, select a department, and then search content within that category. The box is frequently labeled Search This Site with a box provided in which to type your search, alongside a Go button. Note that Web addresses are called URLs, or uniform resource locators. The standard formats of most sites are translated using hypertext transfer protocol, which is why the lead-in of http:// is needed. The second part of the address usually begins with www. to represent World Wide Web. Beyond the .com for companies, .gov is used for government, .org for organizations, .edu for universities, and a number of international indicators are in use, such as .uk for United Kingdom. Sites are frequently redesigned, updated, and redirected to other URLs.

Tagosphere

Increasingly popular are Web sites intended to expedite others' searches as well as to obtain feedback on one's own search results—the "tagosphere" are places to go to save, share, and search Web pages. Examples include wink.com, which permits users to search those links other users have found to be important, and reddit.com, where users can post a Web link and others can vote on that link's level of interest. Shadows.com permits users to save their favorite Web pages, permitting all to search such favorites. This same site permits users to join online groups to discuss and share pages that are directed to core themes such as politics. In a similar vein, furl.net permits you to save and retrieve Web pages and access recommendations on other related Web pages of potential interest. Users can sign up and receive a daily email of pages that friends have "furled." Kaboodle.com is a shopping site where Web pages can be saved regarding products and others can view and rank—a means by which friends and relations can easily provide comments on their experiences or advice as to acquisitions. Further discussion of this topic is available in an article authored by Jessica E. Vascellaro, "The Next Big Thing in Searching: Yahoo and Others Embrace 'Tagging' as a Better Way to Find and Store Information," *Wall Street Journal* (January 24, 2006), pp. D1, D3.

As tagging is increasingly integrated in search protocols, some issues arise. For example, if search engines focus on those search results that the user has found useful in the past within the filter applied on a subsequent search, then identical search results on the same search engine are no longer replicable by a third party. Moreover, the search effectiveness may be either enhanced or crippled depending on the skill of the previous searcher. This could be problematic for accounts used by multiple parties of differing interests and abilities. The tension between relevance and reliability pervades the information age.

Be Wary When Using Online Interactive Internet Sources—Wikipedia and Blogs

An online interactive encyclopedia, launched in 2001, was reported by 2006 to have hit a million articles and become the tenth most popular site on the Internet (Stacy Schiff, "Annals of Information: Know It All—Can Wikipedia Conquer Expertise?" *New Yorker* (July 31, 2006), pp. 36–43). The idea of the site at http://www.wikipedia.org is for articles to reflect a neutral point of view (N.P.O.V.), with content that would prove both verifiable and previously published. Since anyone can write collaboratively and edit the site using the simple software tool known as "wiki," debate continues as to whether Wikipedia is accurate and how it compares with traditional hard-copy encyclopedias. Unfortunately, individuals may intentionally post information that is inaccurate.

The term *blog* refers to a Web site containing an online personal journal with reflections, comments, and often hyperlinks that are provided by the author. The term's origin dates back to three-masted merchant ships on which captains recorded their voyage details in logs (as recounted by Merriam-Webster's *365 New Words Calendar*). An analogy emerged to the ocean of the Internet, and the term *Web log* was born. Its first meaning was a file recording requests made to a Web server, but then it evolved to refer to online journals and was shortened to "blog." The open nature of the Internet means that such sources may include inaccurate and outdated materials. As a result, be wary in distinguishing such resources from database resources.

You will see a number of articles describing the use of blogs in journals such as *BusinessWeek*. Commentators often cite specialty blogs, since they reflect opinions on current issues. The Analyst's Accounting Observer (AAO) Weblog is an example of a periodic blog by Jack Ciesielski (http://www.accountingobserver.com/blog) dealing with accounting news topics.

Internet Resources

Any Web site, whether interactive with users or not, should be evaluated by the researcher with caution. Check the date at which changes were last made to evaluate the timeliness of postings. Also, remember that Web sites have been co-opted or attacked by hackers, and have threatened the intended quality control practices of Web page sponsors. Evaluate the reputation of sites used.

The Annual Reports Library includes reports from corporations, foundations, and public institutions from around the world at zpub.com/sf/arl/. The site includes a link to the Securities Class Action Clearinghouse at Stanford University. Access to current economic and social data in the United States is offered through Economic and Social Statistics briefing rooms that offer summary statistics and links to agencies responsible for the statistics, thereby permitting access to more detailed data. These sites, available within the White House Web site, include whitehouse.gov/fsbr/esbr.html, as well as whitehouse.gov/fsbr/ssbr.html.

Another useful Web site for locating U.S. government information is fedworld.gov. As an aside, you can design your own version of the U.S. budget, by your personal standards, and then analyze and graph the results, by accessing the following Web site on the Internet: budgetsim.org/NBS.

Government Statistics

U.S. Government Statistics are accessible at http://www.stat-usa.gov. The Council of Economic Advisers provides data useful to the determination of growth rates and payout ratios (see http://origin.www.gpoaccess.gov/eop/). The Federal Reserve Bank of Philadelphia provides quarterly forecasts of long-term inflation; at phil.frb.org/econ/spf/index.html. The Federal Deposit Insurance Corporation (FDIC) site is fdic.gov. The U.S. Library of Congress can be accessed at lcweb.loc.gov. Census information is available at census.gov. Public debt information and details on treasury securities are described at both publicdebt.treas.gov and treasurydirect.gov.

Industry Codes

Industry codes are at census.gov/epcd/www/naics.html and census.gov/epcd/www/sic.html. By accessing custom computer programming services, you will identify that US NAICS 541511 is equivalent to SIC 7371. Other sources for industry information include doc.gov and cnnfn.com which are sites for the Department of Commerce and CNN Money.com (the Internet home of *Fortune* and *Money*), respectively.

Directing attention to industry-focused resources, ISIS is a database of detailed reports on about 7,000 public and private insurance companies in over 100 countries. Until November 2002, this was provided by Thomson Financial Insurance Solutions; at that time it was taken over by Fitch Ratings. In 2005, it became accessible from Wharton Research Data Services—a demo is available at wrds.wharton.upenn.edu. ExecuComp permits industry comparison of compensation, providing salaries and stock options for S&P 1000 firms since 1992—accessible in the Wharton Research Data Services. BANKSCOPE information is accessible through Fitch Ratings and Wharton Research Data Services. Morningstar, which rates mutual funds, is an information source on the industry, categorizing funds into large growth, mid-cap, small value, and similar groups that reflect the nature of the fund and tracking year-to-date returns, expense ratio, total assets, manager tenure, and its own star rating system (morningstar.com).

Business Sites

A number of sites provide information about companies. The Yahoo! Finance site is an example. To access, use this address: http://biz.yahoo.com. Be certain to check out tabs (such as investing) with pull-down menus that lead to a market overview and options that include quotes, charts, news & info, SEC filings, analyst coverage, ownership, and financials. If you access historical prices, you can elicit information for a specified time frame, including daily, weekly, monthly, and dividends information. Options are also available to explore insider trading information.

Company information can be located at http://www. followed by hoovers.com, msn.com, intuit.com, cnn.com, marketcenter.com, bloomberg.com, stockmaster.com, and datamonitor.com. Investorguide.com has menus for stock researh and markets including, charts, news, profile, analysis, and offers. Forbes.com provides links to business stories and a quotes and search function to access company information by typing in the ticker symbol. Most sites have a lookup feature, for finding the company's symbol.

On the MSN.com site, click Money on the menu, then Investing for stock research capabilities including quotes, charts, news, stock ratings, advisor FYI, research wizard, stock screener, and expert picks. In addition, information on IPOs (initial public offerings), up/downgrades, and mutual funds is provided. Charts and historical price information, along with financial highlights, some ratios, and selected news stories can be particularly useful.

For the marketcenter.com site, click on Stocks. The menu provides access to quotes, charts, news, and market overview. These are accessible by simply entering a company's symbol on the stock exchange. The Bloomberg.com site tracks information on news, market data, and investment tools. Stocks, rates, and bond information, alongside currency rates and commodity information are accessible. (**Caution:** Whenever downloading data, make note of how missing information is handled. If a resource uses a zero when no information is accessible, such values can be problematic when you attempt to analyze the information. If spreadsheet downloads are inaccessible, you can copy and paste into a spreadsheet. If that does not align well, you can copy and paste into a word-processing software program, then save as a text file and import into Excel using either the delimited option or the fixed width option. For the latter, you can adjust the lines to create the desired demarcations between columns.)

Business-related sources of potential interest include the links that follow. **Note:** http://www. precedes each parenthetical listing.

The International Chamber of Commerce (iccwbo.org)

Federal Trade Commission (ftc.gov)

The Business Roundtable (businessroundtable.org)

Business Week Online (businessweek.com)

The Council of Institutional Investors (cii.org)

Investor Responsibility Research Center (irrc.org) [to be acquired by Institutional Shareholder Services]

The National Investor Relations Institute (niri.org)

EconPapers (econpapers.repec.org)

New York Stock Exchange (nyse.com)

American Stock Exchange (amex.com)

Chicago Berkeley Options Exchange (cboe.com)

International Organization of Securities (iosco.org)

The Better Business Bureau (bbb.org)

The Confederation of British Industry (cbi.org.uk)

World Development Indicator (devdata.worldbank.org)

The Open Compliance and Ethics Group (oceg.org)

The Bank for International Settlements (BIS) (bis.org)

The National Association of Corporate Directors (nacdonline.org)

S&P Bond Rating Criteria (standardpoor.com) [click on ratings]

Environmental Management Accounting International Website (emawebsite.org)

U.S. Environmental Protection Agency Accounting Project (epa.gov/opptintr/library/pubs/archive/acct-archive)

A number of valuation-related Websites are accessible to businesses and individuals. For example, when exploring the worth of vehicles, one can access kbb.com or autopricing.com. The "value-at-risk" approach to measuring the risk of financial instruments developed by J. P. Morgan is described at jpmorgan.com, which includes information on a number of indices for the United States and a number of other countries. Periodic updates on accounting developments and valuation issues are likewise provided by entities such as Goldman Sachs, Bear Stearns & Co., Credit Suisse, and UBS. The Federal Reserve Web site has such information as interest rates for treasury bills and bonds, foreign exchange rates, and statistics on consumer credit. It can be accessed at federalreserve.gov.

Proprietary services likewise provide information on companies. Returning to Factiva, you can select the option of Company Information, which will connect you to more information based on either the name of the company or its ticker symbol. Resources often available include Standard & Poor's Stock Reports and Net Advantage, Holt Stock Reports, Moody's Investor Service List, and Baseline equity research, among others. Standard & Poor's Corporation Records' Full Reports provide information on exchanges where companies trade, industry classifications in which they operate, business descriptions, recent financials, stock data, news digest, directors, history, subsidiaries and affiliates, and officers.

Global Insight provides economic and financial data, forecasting, consulting, and analytical software (as described at dri-wefa.com). Other types of global database resources are described at worldbank.org. Morningstar is a provider of mutual fund analysis and tracks performance of variable annuities and variable life insurance products (insure.com). Standard & Poor's Insurer Profile is available at data.insure.com/ratings/reports.

Information on salaries is accessible free at www.payscale.com. Standard reports include average salary ranges by company size, degree, experience, gender, and location. Personal finance information is accessible at www.360financialliteracy.org.

The eXtensible Business Reporting Language XBRL is a free XML-based specification that facilitates exchange of financial statements across all software and technologies, including the Internet. Related information can be found at xbrl.org.

Company Sites

When interested in company-specific matters, you can use a search engine to locate that company's Web page. However, the address is often rather easy to deduce. Specifically, companies' Web sites tend to take the form of http://www.companyname.com.

Web sites containing various resources are maintained by a number of firms and associations–often separating free access from a pay-for-service proprietary set of resources. The Big 4 (deloitte.com, ey.com, kpmg.com, pwc.com) provide a number of resources, such as the PricewaterhouseCoopers' daily news feeds and business analyses at cfodirect.com. BDO Seidman, LLP (bdo.com), Grant Thornton International (gti.org), McGladrey & Pullen, LLP (mcgladrey.com), Cherry, Bekaert & Holland, LLP (cbh.com), Holtz Rubinstein Reminick (hrrllp.com), BKD, LLP (bkd.com), and Altschuler, Melvoin and Glasser LLP (AM&G) (amgnet.com) offer articles, case studies, calculators, newsletters, tax tips, and Web links.

Software Tools

A number of software tools are downloadable from the Internet. In the area of statistical sampling, the free program RAT-STATS is available from the Web site oig.hhs.gov/organization/OAS/ratstat.html. Also available is the RAT-STATS User Guide at: oig.hhs.gov/organization/OAS/ratstats/ratstat.pdf.

Calculators for business valuation, leasing, currency, bonds, and stock options' valuation are available at cfo.com/tools. Currency, mortgage, lease/buy, and other calculators can be accessed at bloomberg.com/invest/calculators. Calculators associated with mortgages and loans, as well as leases are at bankrate.com. Stock option valuation tools are at hoadley.net/options/binomialtree.asp?tree. A number of free calculators are accessible at calculator.com, such as one that translates computer data size.

Free resources are available at numerous proprietary sites, such as Practitioners Publishing Company (PPC) (ppc.thomson.com). They include E-practice aids and online demos.

Security issues for banks on the Internet are made available periodically through the FDIC consumer protection and regulation and examinations resources online at fdic.gov. Special alerts are posted periodically.

A number of subscription-based online tools are accessible for accounting research. Of use in exploring resources is the Resourcelinks Business Directory at resourcelinks.net. The AICPA Audit Committee Toolkit is available free from aicpa.org/audcommctr.

Popular Accounting Sites

To identify current information and addresses to accounting resources, check such URLs as Rutgers Accounting Web (RAW) International Accounting Network (http://accounting.rutgers.edu/) with links to numerous professional organizations, including the AAA, AAH, AGA, FASB, GASB, NABA, IIA, IAFEI, and IMA. Click on Accounting Resources which includes the sites for various state societies of CPAs and professional accounting firms.

   Direct Internet addresses for the Web sites of various standard-setters, professional, and government organizations can also be helpful; remember that http://www precedes each parenthetical in the following list:

Financial Accounting Standards Board (FASB) (fasb.org)

Federal Accounting Standards Advisory Board (fasab.gov)

Governmental Accounting Standards Board (gasb.org)

International Accounting Standards Board (iasb.org)

International Accounting Standards Committee (iasb.org) [Also see iasplus.com]

Public Companies Accounting Oversight Board (pcaobus.org)

International Federation of Accountants (ifac.org)

Securities and Exchange Commission (sec.gov)

Government Accountability Office (gao.gov)

Internal Revenue Service (irs.ustreas.gov)

National Association of State Boards of Accountancy (nasba.org)

The Committee of Sponsoring Organizations of the Treadway Commission (coso.org)

American Institute of Certified Public Accountants (aicpa.org)

Institute of Management Accountants (imanet.org)

The Institute of Internal Auditors (theiia.org)

The American Accounting Association (aaahq.org)

Financial Executives International (fei.org)

CFA Institute (cfainstitute.org)

Canadian Institute of Chartered Accountants (cica.ca)

Association of Government Accountants (agacgfm.org)

The Association of Certified Fraud Examiners (acfe.org)

Information Systems Audit and Control Association (isaca.org)

National Center for Nonprofit Boards (ncnb.org)

The Accounting Standards Board in the United Kingdom (frc.org.uk/asb)

Other resources include a Tax and Accounting Sites Directory at taxsites.com that has state boards of accountancy and accounting firm directories. Inspector General Offices have a searchable site at Ignet.gov. Accounting research and career information can be found at accountingnet.com. Auditing information is posted at auditnet.org. AccountingWeb has news and resources for accountants and accounting professionals (accountingweb.com). SmartPros Accounting has details on accounting, ethics and compliance, financial planning, and international laws at accountingnet.com. Resources on the Cost Accounting Standards Board (CASB), which is particularly relevant to government contracting, are accessible at three sites:

   http://www.whitehouse.gov/omb/procurement/casb.html
   http://farsite.hill.af.mil/archive/Far/1997/FARAPB1.HTM
   http://fast.faa.gov/archive/v1198/pguide/98–30C14.htm

EDGAR: http://www.sec.gov

Rather than use the company's site to link to the SEC filings, you can go directly to EDGAR, which stands for Electronic Data Gathering Analysis and Retrieval Service, a free Web site that permits you to search by company and type of filing and read and/or download copies of such filings. The nature of the filings is described at the SEC site. A "Description of SEC Forms" is a menu item under "Filings and Forms," as is a "Quick EDGAR Tutorial," both of which can help to identify the information of relevance in a setting—such as disclosure questions associated with proxy statements, which would be Form DEF 14A. The home page has a menu on the left called Filings & Forms (EDGAR), which should be clicked. On the next screen, select Search for Company Filings. Enter the company name of interest, then click on the filing of interest. When saving a text file and trying to view in your word-processing package, you will likely find the columns align better if you use the eight-point courier font in boldface. A beta test version facilitates a full text word search of two years of SEC filings—particularly useful in identifying specific examples of accounting treatments and events.

Beyond individual companies' information, EDGAR has details on regulators' proposals, including requests for comments and the comment letters received in electronic form. Staff Accounting Bulletins (SABs) are accessible, as are details on the SEC's regulatory activities. The SEC's Report to the President and Congress is among the materials accessible. Downloadable resources provide investor information, news and public statements, speeches, and litigation materials. A menu is provided to link information directed to accountants, broker dealers, EDGAR filers, funds and advisers, municipal markets, and small business. In addition, links are accessible from the home page to the SEC divisions of Corporation Finance, Enforcement, Investment Management, and Market Regulation.

Public Companies Accounting Oversight Board (PCAOB): http://www.pcaobus.org

The Sarbanes-Oxley Act led to the creation of an independent organization known as the Public Company Accounting Oversight Board or PCAOB. That body initially monitored and evaluated the Auditing Standards Board and the activities of the SEC's Practice Section of the American Institute of Certified Public Accountants (AICPA) Division for CPA Firms. However, instead of merely monitoring such activities, the PCAOB decided to set auditing standards itself and to establish an inspection process. The SEC's Web site under Regulatory Actions has a menu item "PCAOB Rulemaking." The PCAOB is not a government agency but instead is a not-for-profit entity. In December 2003, the PCAOB issued its first auditing standard calling for a change in future audit reports whereby rather than stating "conducted in accordance with generally accepted auditing standards" the report would read "conducted in accordance with standards established by the Public Company Accounting Oversight Board." Accounting representations are frequently subject to audit. When reports are issued by entities that are not public, they follow generally accepted auditing standards (GAAS), issued by the AICPA's Auditing Standards Board.

Special-Purpose Databases

Alternative sources of information include a number of special-purpose databases that may be available to you on CD-ROM resources or through various network interfaces. The subject matter of such databases varies widely. In this exercise, you will retrieve information regarding legal cases, financial statements, reporting practices, and the stock market.

For example, interest in legal cases can be explored in Lexis/Nexis. Financial databases would include COMPUSTAT-PC, which permits ease of downloading of a number of financial line items and ratios—not merely for particular companies but for sets of companies that meet selection criteria of interest, such as size or industry type. Stock price information is accessible through CRSP (Center for Research on Security Prices), a database accessible from the University of Chicago, which was initially a mainframe tape-based system but is increasingly being made accessible in various forms, including Intranet-site licensing interfaces. If one wishes to explore stock price movements relative to the market averages of particular companies or sets of companies, long-term trends can be analyzed. These can be evaluated, with corrections for stock splits and stock dividends. Details on generally accepted accounting practices (GAAP) can be accessed through the Financial Accounting Research System (FARS). It permits word searches using Boolean logic to explore accounting questions specific to industry settings and both practice and theory. "Boolean" is named after George Boole, who was an English mathematician in the mid-1800s who developed a logical combinatorial system that symbolically represents relationships between entities that can be various sets or propositions with diverse elements; logical operators would include AND, OR, and NOT (*Webster's Ninth New Collegiate Dictionary*. Springfield, MA: Merriam-Webster, 1985, p. 168).

Lexis/Nexis

Lexis/Nexis is a full-text computer research database, with Lexis representing the law libraries and Nexis representing the business libraries. It maintains well over half a billion documents online, with almost two million added weekly. The coverage includes such publications as the *New York Times*, the *Financial Times*, *BusinessWeek*, and the *Journal of Taxation*.

The legal libraries include M&A (Mergers and Acquisitions library), UCC (Uniform Commercial Code library), BKRTCY (Federal Bankruptcy library), BANKNG (Federal Banking library), TRADE (Federal Trade Regulation library and International Trade library), REALTY (Real Estate library), GENFED (Federal Government Library), and STATES (States library).

The Nexis libraries include NEWS (General News and Business library), LEXPAT (the U.S. Patent and Trademark Office library), MARKET (the Marketing library, which covers advertising, marketing, market research, public relations, product announcements, and similar marketing-related items), PEOPLE (the People library), CMPCOM (the Computers and Communications library), ACCTG (the Accounting library), and COMPNY (the Company library).

Once you access a library, you will be asked to narrow the search by specifying the names of additional file choices. For example, within the NEWS library, you can specify BUS, and all business-related stories from newspapers, magazines, wire services, and transcripts will be accessed. If within NEWS you select PERSON, biographical information can be accessed. Within ACCTG, examples of useful files would include AAER (the Accounting and Auditing Enforcement Releases from the SEC), TAXCFR (Tax Rules), PROSP (Prospectuses), EDGARP(EDGAR Plus), ACCES (Access Disclosure), and PROXY (SEC Proxy Statements).

Within the EDGARP file, you can search for documents like the 10-K and proxy, then within the full text view of the documents, a table of contents is made available that permits you to pull only certain sections of the documents, such as the financial statements.

Examples of useful titles under the COMPNY library are DISCLO (disclosure), ALLMA (M&A reports), SPCORP (company profiles for both public and private firms), USPRIV (U.S. private companies), USPUB (U.S. public companies), and STKRPT (stock reports). Under either GENFED or STATES library, one can obtain cases under the COURTS file.

The search phrasing you can use within Lexis and Nexis includes *Or*, *And*, *W/n* (where *n* refers to the number of words within which you expect to find the words—*stock w/3 dividend* would mean that the cite would include any place these two words were within three words of one another), and *W/p* where articles with the two topics in the same paragraph are identified.

When the results are reported back, a toolbar permits you to select among the Full View, the Kwic View (providing an abstract, including the sentence before and after that term specified), or a Cite View (bibliographical information).

When working on CD-ROM versions of Lexis/Nexis you typically cannot print your sessions or download your work to a disk in the usual fashion. Instead, to record your search on disk, you must first click on File. Then choose Record Session and hit Start. This will record your entire search from choosing the libraries to article searches. If you do not want everything to be recorded, you can hit Pause and later Start, and there will be no recording of the interim actions. When you are finished with the session and log off, you can bring up your documents in Wordpad and then re-save the search as a Word file, aligning the margins to seven inches when in Word to achieve realignment. Note that Wordpad can be found under your accessories section of your computer. The reason for using Wordpad rather than Word is that the latter will sometimes scramble your fonts.

If you are unable to identify the library/file to use for your search, you can conduct a search in the Lexis/Nexis online guide. If you would like to find a library/file on AAERs, you would type .gu AAER and the online service would then tell you that the library is ACCTNG and the file name is AAER. The Lexis/Nexis free help desk is available at 1-800-346-9759. Rather than the CD-ROM version, increasingly, universities are offering Lexis/Nexis Academic Universe on their intranets, with site license access by students and faculty.

Legal Information Institute is an Internet resource of related interest: law.cornell.edu has searchable federal law materials. Also see findlaw.com and refdesk.com. In addition, criminal justice links and other legal resource materials are accessible at criminology.fsu.edu/cjlinks/default.htm. The Government Accountability Office (GAO) is a rich resource, including its publication "Investigator's Guide to Sources of Information," which can be found at gao.gov.

COMPUSTAT and Worldscope

Standard & Poor's PC Plus for Windows and the COMPUSTAT database are built into one system on CD-ROM, which provides financial and market data of U.S. and Canadian corporations, banks, savings and loans, business segments, geographic regions, industry information, indexes, and inactive companies. The system contains a collection of financial data from company annual and quarterly shareholders' reports and SEC 10-K and 10-Q reports. Although the details of any database change over time, the following instructions should be helpful in characterizing the types of commands that can be used to access information and generate analyses.

When accessing the screen showing COMPUSTAT moving horizontally across the screen, view the PC Plus desktop by pressing Enter and you will see some of your options represented by icons on the left border of the screen. These include abilities to find specific companies, create a single report or multiple reports for one or more companies, screen for particular companies, construct a set of companies, business segments, geographic areas, or issues, view a chart of COMPUSTAT data, and view a library of information about companies. To find a specific company, click on Company, click on Look Up. The $C CS Active category should be highlighted, and the available companies will then be listed in the Name List box.

You can access business descriptions by clicking Library, entering the company's ticker symbol (which can be found by clicking the Look Up button if unknown), then clicking on OK.

To screen companies that meet your criteria, click on <u>Screen</u> and on <u>New</u>. The PC will show you a screen template with $C in the base set column and will highlight the Formula column. Type *sic* and hit <u>Enter</u>. The PC inserts what you have just typed into the formula bar and then into the Formula column. It highlights the Min column. The item shows a company's primary SIC code. Note that SIC stands for Standard Industrial Classification code. Until recently, it was the most commonly used code in the United States. In 1997, this framework was replaced by the North American Industrial Classification System (NAICS), which is intended to integrate Canada, Mexico, and the United States as part of the North American Free Trade Agreement (NAFTA). Systems will gradually transfer from SIC to NAICS. If SIC is in use, you could type 7371 for Services-Computer Programming Services and hit <u>Enter</u>. (You can also press the right arrow key to move to the Max column.) Type 7371 and hit <u>Enter</u>. The PC inserts what you have just typed into the Min and Max columns. For, example entering codes 7000 and 7399 tells the PC that you are screening for companies that list any four-digit SIC that begins with 70, 71, 72, and 73 as their primary SIC. Click on Formula column row 2, then click on the <u>Look Up</u> tool, a box with a pair of glasses. The PC shows the <u>Look Up</u> dialog box. Click on the <u>Item</u> button and click on <u>Company</u> in the <u>Category List</u> box. Type Return on Assets; ROA should be displayed on the screen. The ROA concept calculates a ratio. You can click on the <u>Definition</u> button. Click on <u>Paste</u> to insert the item into the formula bar. Click on the check mark to insert the item into the Formula column. The PC highlights the Min column. Type 1 and hit Enter. The Maximum column remains blank. This value tells the PC that you are screening for companies that have a return on assets value of at least 1 percent. Click on the <u>Run</u> button in the toolbar to evaluate the screen criteria. Note that you can screen from any field information in the COMPUSTAT system, including membership in an S&P Index, sales volume, number of employees, or other attributes of interest.

COMPUSTAT Research Insight's main menu has a <u>Research Assistant</u> icon that can be clicked; when the ticker symbol is placed in the field entitled <u>Companies</u>, you can select from among the other options. For example, to generate a list of companies with the same SIC, click on <u>Find Similar Companies</u>, then click <u>Company Specifics</u>, and choose an industry SIC designation. To customize a peer group for comparison, open <u>Research Assistant</u>, and click on <u>Customize</u>. To create a report, click the <u>Open Report</u> icon, select what you wish, and click <u>Finish</u>. From the <u>Run Assistant</u> screen, choose the desired company and click <u>OK</u>. You can customize your report within <u>Report Assistant</u>, including generating historical reports. The <u>Chart Assistant</u> icon can be useful in selecting a chart. To predefine charts, click on <u>Open Chart</u>, highlight the desired chart, click <u>Finish</u>, and when Run Assistant appears, select the desired company and click <u>OK</u>. Clicking on <u>Open Set</u> brings up four folders (Charts, Reports, Screens, and Sets) and uses predetermined sets of information, charts, estimates, comparisons, and similar information for analysis of a company.

Thomson's Worldscope database, which tracks information from 1980, contains more than 22,000 active companies in developing and emerging markets, representing approximately 97 percent of global market capitalization in 53 countries—all countries in the World Bank's IFC Investables Index. Other products include Global Access, Datastream, and I/B/E/S (which includes forecasts, revisions, consensus, and analyst-by-analyst earnings estimates of both U.S. and international companies). See Online Computer Library Center oclc.org for a description of Worldscope and Worldscope Global, as well as access information.

CRSP

CRSP has traditionally been accessed through FORTRAN programming on mainframe systems. However, the tape-based data are increasingly being transferred onto intranet sites, with friendly interfaces. Explore whether your university has CRSP and whether students have access. Find out whether user manuals or other tutorials are available. Since the interface can vary widely, no further details on use are included herein.

Daily stock market quotes are accessible at numerous Web sites, including:

http://stockmaster.com
http://www.pcquote.com
http://finance.yahoo.com
http://www.msn.com
http://www.bloomberg.com

The StockMaster Web site provides current information and summarizes stock-price performance of a company for the last year, providing a graph charting this information relative to the S&P 500. Links are provided at that site to other information associated with the company, including a link to EDGAR. Indices are accessible at spglobal.com, and the site explains the composition of indices (e.g., the weight placed on different sectors of the economy, the sizes of entities included, and the weights on various countries within global indices). Excel worksheets can be downloaded. Similarly, russell.com has a number of indices available, and it explains the approach to forming its indices.

FARS and FASB: http://www.fasb.org

When you access FARS, whether it is on a CD-ROM, through your library, through the network, or on the Internet, the basic system you will find has been well described in Chapter 1 of this book. Review the introductory material under Quick-Start and thereafter, before proceeding. Test your understanding of the FARS materials by working through the Self-Review and Cross-Checks at the end of Chapter 1.

Financial Accounting Research System (FARS)

FARS was designed to be flexible and easy to use. The accounting literature within the infobases can be accessed in three different ways—through the Contents view tab, through the Topical Index references that link to the appropriate text in the infobases, and, finally, through predefined *query templates* and user-defined *queries*.

The graphical interface of FARS for Windows has a look that will be familiar to MS-Word users. Flexible printing functions, simple text *exporting*, a true WYSIWYG text display, and easy-to-follow navigational tools combine to make FARS for Windows an indispensable system for GAAP research. Competency in FARS is one aspect of the CPA Exam. (See http://www.cpa-exam.org where you can access the AICPA Tutorial and related information.)

Whenever performing research on FARS, make a practice of visiting the FASB home page to check for recent developments, including recently issued pronouncements and exposure drafts. The site offers downloadable .PDF files for both. For example, if you accessed that site at the end of October 2006, you would see: "Statement No. 158 News Release New—FASB Standard Provides Enhanced Guidance for Measuring Fair Value—Board Establishes Measurement Framework and Expands Disclosures Associated with Fair Value Measurements (Posted: 09/15/06)," "Tentative Guidance—Statement 133 Implementation Issues New—Issue No. G26 (Posted: 10/10/06) (Comment Deadline: November 14, 2006)," "Proposed

FASB Staff Positions (FSPs) New—Proposed FSP EITF 03-6-a (Posted: 10/20/06) (Comment Deadline: December 19, 2006)," and "Final FASB Staff Positions (FSPs) New—FSP FAS 123(R)-6 (Posted: 10/20/06) FSP FAS 123(R)-5 (Posted: 10/10/06)." Beyond recent additions, a click on Pronouncements & EITF Abstracts will provide directions and conditions for downloading. Any postings subsequent to the cutoff date of your FARS resource will need to be considered when performing an analysis. Unfortunately, .PDF files do not offer the power of the FARS database that facilitates integration of resources, search, and export capabilities. However, the timeliness of Internet access provides an indispensable tool to ensure up-to-date reflection of GAAP.

Another important resource can be accessed by clicking on the FASAC link at the Financial Accounting Standards Board (FASB) home page. Discussion Materials and FASAC Meeting Handouts are posted for past and upcoming meetings and provide insights as to points of contention, theoretical alternatives, and open questions. Moreover, the FASAC meeting minutes reflect FASAC members' commentaries, as do results of annual FASAC surveys. Comment Letters on proposals are posted at fasb.org.

Introduction to Case

Assume it is 2005 and you are in college. Semester break this year is the planned timing for a family reunion. Your uncle has been in Europe for the past year on a start-up venture with a large international corporation and is returning home. You view the event with mixed emotions. On the one hand, you look forward to seeing your uncle. On the other hand, you know your uncle well enough to expect that sometime in the course of the reunion, he will focus on you and inquire about your college education. In particular, he will likely ask: "Show us the return on our investment! What have you learned, and are you getting ahead?" As a business professional, he always uses business jargon and is especially keen on new technology and how well today's college students are mastering this information age.

You decide that this time, you'll be ready. As a result, you have been reading both business and technology news with enthusiasm, looking for an idea for research that will show you are both up-to-date and lucid on technology's application to business. Since your uncle is particularly interested in accounting-associated matters and enforcement proceedings, those are the subject areas about which you are especially curious. You access the *SEC News Digest* (Issue 2005-244, December 21, 2005) and notice the headline under Enforcement Proceedings says: "Commission Voluntarily Dismisses all Claims against Former Officers of TenFold Corporation." Reference is made to a U.S. district court for the District of Utah entering an order on December 19, 2005.

The story seems perfect, as it has business, accounting, and regulatory dimensions, while involving new technology (computer programming services). The question is where to look for details in order to prepare by semester break for the questions that will likely come from introducing such a current event topic. For example, someone might ask what were the original allegations? Someone else might inquire as to why the SEC would wait until the eve of the trial to make a motion for dismissal. Moreover, you have a very real opportunity to describe your mastery of technology by not only preparing your answers to such questions, but also being ready to explain precisely how you found the answers. You have little doubt that broader business questions will follow, such as how investors reacted to the news and what type of events preceded the announcement. Since compensation is one affect asserted of improved financial position, your uncle will pursue detailed follow-up questions, such as whether you happen to know anything about how well the company's managers are compensated or what the aftermath was of the bad press of the allegations, then the good news of the dismissal, including how TenFold Corporation has performed relative to the industry and the overall market.

In short, your uncle is not going to meekly accept your pronouncement of knowledge. If you want to mount a credible defense against his inquisition, you are going to need more ammunition. It is time for a literature search.

Perform Literature Searches

You decide to start by exploring what the press has said about TenFold Corporation. First you focus in the same time frame, and then you move backward and forward in time, to gain a sense of the media coverage in the aftermath of the story of interest. You decide to have *Accounting Trends & Techniques* ready to compare practices reported for TenFold Corporation to those of other companies.

Examples of Search Approaches

Because your first interest is in a business news event, you explore the *Wall Street Journal*, which you know is published by Dow Jones. This leads you to decide to begin with Factiva, the Dow Jones interactive database. You choose the Publications library and perform a search by using the term *TenFold Corporation*, or *TenFold Corp* (databases and media often use the abbreviation "Corp"), and you isolate the search of Dow Jones Selected Publications to the time frame from December 1 through December 22, 2005 (by clicking on Enter Date Frame, then typing the dates), then you click on Run Search.

Another alternative is to access Lexis/Nexis Academic Universe and to select the News Option, then the General News Option, which will then present a screen that calls for keyword searches and also provides tips. You input the keywords "TenFold Corp" and select the narrow search with the additional term of "SEC." You select the source as Major Newspapers and click on the date From/To, inputting 12/1/2005 to 12/22/2005 as the dates of interest. Click the Search button. This permits you to review the media coverage around the time of interest in the *Wall Street Journal*.

A third alternative is InfoTrac, which has an option of "General Business File ASAP." When the keyword search is requested, you input "TenFold Corp" and indicate that you want to look at articles by date after 12/1/2005 (i.e., you click on After and then scroll to select day 1, month December, and year 2005), then click on the Search button). The result will be any articles to date that correspond to the TenFold Corporation and have appeared since December 1, 2005.

Literature search bases are similar in their use. They access categories of subject matter, request a search by you, and return a list of citations, which can then be clicked on to read the underlying article or abstract, depending on the nature of the database. The keyword search formats vary, as described herein. Sometimes fields are required, and in other circumstances you can choose to use the field or to ignore that specification. For example, InfoTrac allows the search to be limited to articles with text, to refereed publications, or to particular journals, but this is optional. Pro-Quest Direct is a useful resource, providing full text access to articles. "Business News" within Lexis/Nexis includes articles from newspapers, magazines, journals, wires, and transcripts. "Industry and Market News" includes coverage of over 25 industries. "Accounting Literature Tips" are provided to users of Lexis/Nexis. The resources accessible relate to menu choices that, among other options, include: Accountant's Liability; Accounting and Auditing Enforcement Release; Accounting Series Releases; Accounting Technology; *Accounting Today*; AICPA Accounting and Auditing

Publications—including the full text of all the articles from *Tax Adviser*; *CPA Letter*; *Journal of Accountancy*, and authoritative and semiauthoritative professional accounting material; OMB (Office of Management and Budget) literature; *Practical Accountant*; and Staff Accounting Bulletins (SABs).

Note that press releases and analyst information can be accessed on the Internet at http://www.infobeat.com. Some articles can be located through http://www.findarticles.com—many can be accessed for free. When interested in accounting topics, you will want to visit the site: http://www.cpaj.com. It has a searchable archive of the *CPA Journal*, allowing content clicks on Accounting & Auditing. As another example of the use of specific sites, search http://www.nytimes.com with the phrase *TenFold Corporation Accounting Litigation SEC*, and you will identify an article of interest.

For practice in building your literature search skills, locate the following *Journal of Accountancy* articles directed to practitioners: Jeffrey W. Naumann, "Tap Into XBRL's Power the Easy Way" (May 2004), pp. 33–39; Neal J. Hannon and Robert J. Gold, "XBRL Revisited" (February 2005), pp. 64–65; and Robert Tie, "XBRL: It's Unstoppable" (August 2005), pp. 32–35.

Consider Restatements Literature: http://www.gao.gov

The information in the GAO reports (cited earlier) has spawned a number of related research articles. As examples, the author has conducted research that addresses the relationship of such restatements to auditor changes, corporate governance, and the market (see "Auditor Changes and Restatements: An Analysis of Recent History," *CPA Journal* LXXV (3): 30–33, 2005; "To What Extent Are Restatements Associated with Changes in Boards?" *NACD-Directors Monthly*, Research Note, Audit and Finance Department, National Association of Corporate Directors (NACD) 19, June 2004; and "Adding Value through Accounting Signals," *California Management Review* 46(4): pp. 120–137, Summer 2004). Locate the three GAO reports on restatements and these three related articles to hone your literature search skills. Restatement literature provides an opportunity to learn from past experiences, including assessing those areas of practice in which errors have been alleged or reported.

•Exercise A

1. Locate any media coverage concerning TenFold Corporation and, in particular, the enforcement proceedings to which the December 2005 announcement relates. Based on your reading of the articles, explain the nature of the allegations that TenFold Corporation and its officers faced.
2. Perform a literature search to identify related articles on TenFold Corporation surrounding the events described, as well as related to performance by the company in the aftermath of this media coverage. Provide citations for what you deem to be particularly useful articles for your research effort. Was a restatement considered or recorded by TenFold Corporation? How does the setting compare or contrast with the various restatements reflected in the GAO reports? Explain why you believe the events unfolded in the manner you recount, particularly the dismissal of the case on the eve of trial.
3. Access Wikipedia and look up an item that would appear to have relevance to the issues involved in the TenFold Corporation research effort. Then look up a subject about which you feel personally well versed. Drawing upon these two results, share your assessment as to the usefulness of this interactive resource and why caution is advised.

Compare Search Engines

Next, you decide to apply several search engines to explore the Internet's resources concerning Ten-Fold Corporation. You give priority to Google, MSN, and Yahoo!, as well as the Top5SearchEngines sites provided earlier in this chapter.

•Exercise B

1. Access three different search engines and perform a word search on TenFold Corporation. Indicate how many hits are identified. Peruse the identified links and discuss the extent to which the first 10 sites identified prove to be relevant. Give a Web address for one source identified via the search engine that you find of relevance to your research. Understand that search engines can change over time, as can the names of Web sites; links may be added to resources and databases may change hands through acquisitions and mergers. Browsers from search engines can facilitate locating an updated site that varies in the format of the Internet address, as such change occurs.
2. Use the search engines to see if they can assist you in finding Litigation Release No. 17852 (Nov. 20, 2002). [SEC v. TenFold Corp., et al., (D. Utah 2:03-CV-00442 TC)] (LR-19504).
3. Identify whether other search engine sites are accessible that provide relevant information.
4. Do you believe "tagosphere" will enhance the quality of Internet research? Explain.

Use Internet Resources

The Internet is undergoing constant change; however, a number of sources can be counted on as providing both useful and relevant information when researching accounting and business issues. This exercise will assist you in gaining the ability to find your way on the information highway.

When interested in company-specific matters, a company's Web page address is rather easy to deduce. Specifically, companies' Web sites often have the following form: http://www. companyname.com. If you substitute TenFold for company name, you will find yourself at the Web page of TenFold Corporation. Topics highlighted at the site include: Read Me First!; Industry Awards; Quick Links; and In the News. Many company sites embed easy linkages to other Web sites that contain information concerning the entity, such as stock charts, historical prices, statistical supplements, SEC filings, fundamentals, and information on Wall Street analysts. You will notice as you move around a site that the Web address will have words added behind the .com access you used. Such suffixes describe the file location within that site's server.

As you access the varied business sites to explore TenFold Corporation, you will find it helpful to use the company's symbol—TENF or TENF.OB. The SIC for the company is 7371.

•Exercise C

1. Access the company site for TenFold Corporation and go to In the News. Determine if there are any relevant press releases for your research. Then proceed to use the other investor and financial information links to assess how TenFold Corporation appears to be doing during and in the aftermath of this media event. Consider the level of executives' compensation as well as the types of compensation arrangements used by TenFold Corporation. Such data can be accessed at investor.reuters.com, clicking on Officers & Directors, then Basic Compensation and Option Compensation.

2. Identify the competitors of TenFold Corporation. Give the names of the first five in the alphabetized list accessed on Yahoo! How are competitors defined? What is an effective way of defining competitors? Justify your position. (Check the Industry Center http://biz.yahoo/ic, Sector Technology, for companies matching the Industry: Business Software & Services.)

3. Access the Yahoo! site and generate a stock price chart that includes price information before and after the November 20, 2002, and the December 19–21, 2005, events. (Also check earnings per share (EPS) information, including estimates and recommendations.) Does the stock market appear to have reacted in any manner to the media coverage?

4. Have blogs addressed any of the events affecting TenFold Corporation? Be specific. Explain the limitations of blogs as a source of information. Why is caution advisable? Which business sites, beyond Yahoo!, are of use in identifying key competitors? How consistent are the sets of competitors identified by the different resources you access?

Access EDGAR and PCAOB Sites

Go directly to the free SEC Web site known as EDGAR (Electronic Data Gathering Analysis and Retrieval Service) and search by company and type of filing. Access the beta test version and try a text word search to identify SEC filings that include accounting treatments and events similar to those at issue in the TenFold Corporation setting.

•Exercise D

1. Access the SEC EDGAR site and identify all filings that are contained therein for TenFold Corporation. Indicate the types of filings you find, the number, and the last filing listed on the date you check the filings—including the type of the last filing and the date it was made available on the Web.

2. Using the EDGAR site, explain what types of SEC filings exist and when they must be filed.

3. Using the Search capability within EDGAR, type *executive compensation*, and follow the links to explore where this topic is addressed by SEC filings. Identify the SEC publication you find most instructional. Access the DEF 14A materials for TenFold Corporation to specifically address the compensation practices of the company relative to both its management and board.

4. Access the PCAOB Web site and describe how its guidance relates to TenFold Corporation. Consider issues including the relative size of TenFold Corporation, its events from the initial public offering (IPO) to date, and the applicability of Sarbanes-Oxley related provisions.

Use Special-Purpose Databases

Within COMPUSTAT, look for TenFold Corporation by typing *TenFold Corp* in the Name box in the upper right of the dialog box. Click on Paste and then the Close button. Click on View Data and then OK. You can choose what data you want to see by clicking on Look Up and then Item (the button on the left, second down). For example, if you wanted to find the price/earnings (PE) ratio for TenFold Corporation, click on Name List and type in *price/ear*. The name list highlights the PE item. Now double-click on Price/Earnings-Monthly and click on Close. Click on View Data and on the up and down arrows to see the years you want. Click on New Item and repeat the process.

Predefine charts by clicking on Open Chart, highlighting the desired chart, and clicking Finish. When Run Assistant appears, select TenFold and click OK. Clicking on Open Set brings up four folders (Charts, Reports, Screens, and Sets). Analyze TenFold by clicking on the various charts to explore the resource.

You have a curiosity about two basic issues at this point that were among allegations made by the SEC in its Accounting and Auditing Enforcement Release dated November 20, 2002. The first relates to revenue recognition. The second involves the disclosure of risks.

•Exercise E (depending on which databases are accessible)

1. Access the Lexis/Nexis Academic Universe or CD-ROM version, if it is available. Consider the litigation you have seen cited both in the media and among the disclosures in SEC filings. Perform a search of the Lexis portion of Lexis/Nexis to identify the cases and their general nature.

   To do so using Lexis/Nexis Academic Universe, access Legal Research and a descriptive screen on Basic Legal Research will show subheads of Secondary Literature, Case Law, Codes & Regulations, Patent Research, and Career Information. If you select Get a Case, the first bullet under Case Law, then a screen will appear offering the option to retrieve a case by citation or by party name. From the materials you have accessed, you should be able to locate the case caption(s). Note that Lexis/Nexis Academic Universe asks for input of the parties permitting you to type, for example, TenFold Corporation or the SEC as a party to litigation. In other words, you need not have the legal citation requested. Hit the Search button and under the document list will be the citations, any of which you can choose to review. If Lexis/Nexis is unavailable, check Internet resources such as those described herein and http://courtsonline.org. Since you have an interest in a particular case, you could also seek information in hard-copy form from a law library. Moreover, SEC filings will contain descriptions of litigation. When it is the SEC filing the case, sec.gov posts litigation and enforcement releases.

   Compare the description you access from SEC filings to that found in the Lexis/Nexis or similar data source. If you were responsible for drafting the disclosure found in the SEC filing, what adjustments to its content would you recommend?

2. Using the COMPUSTAT database, download a report on the information available for Ten-Fold, as well as a similar report for the key competitors within their industry. If COMPUSTAT is unavailable, check to see what resources with company financial information are available at your library. Compare the ease of use, quality of information, and relative advantages and disadvantages of these resources, relative to the Internet sources described herein.

3. Using CRSP, download all information available for TenFold (i.e., all stock prices since its IPO). Also download a market index accessible through CRSP. If CRSP is unavailable, check to see what resources with companies' stock price data are available at your library and how they compare to the information accessible on the Internet. You should be able to locate both a time-series database of the stock prices of TenFold since its IPO and a market index for the same time frame on the Internet.

4. Access FARS.

(a) Open the Financial Accounting Research System (FARS) main menu. Click on the Topical Index. After refreshing yourself by reading the Chapter 1 coverage of searches and use of the topical index, click on R and explore the issue of revenue recognition. Explain your findings on guidance relevant to your curiosity regarding revenue recognition, particularly as it relates to TenFold Corporation.

(b) Alternatively, use the search capabilities. Specifically, click on Open, FARS, Open, Nfo, Open, FASB-OP (amended), and click Search at the top of the toolbar. Select Query and then type *computer programming services revenue recognition timing* and click on OK. Select the Document view (using the tabs toward the bottom of the screen). Identify the relevant guidance, as cited in the top bar of the view, and describe what must be the criteria met for revenue recognition. Compare and contrast with SAB 101, downloadable from sec.gov.

(c) Describe how you would suggest finding accounting guidance within FARS relative to the disclosures associated with risks that are described in the SEC's litigation release. Be specific as to the search you perform and what you locate in terms of guidance.

• Exercise F: Identify the Acronym—Internet Puzzle

Acronyms dominate the literature and are important to master. Work the following crossword puzzle backwards. In other words, list out the numbers Down and Across, and then write out what the acronym stands for and describe its nature. Some will be apparent from the steps you complete in Chapter 2, as well as materials in Chapter 1. Others will require that you search the Internet and locate the translation of the acronym into something relevant to business, government, not-for-profit, or accounting.

CHAPTER 3 – BUILDING YOUR BUSINESS VOCABULARY

Defining Terms and Solving Problems through the Financial Accounting Research System (FARS)

Going Straight to the Source

Have you wondered if parenthood comes with a manual of required phrases? For example, do your parents ask "Do you live in a barn?" whenever you leave a door partly open and do they use phrases intended to break your bad habits of saying "well," "you know," or "like"—such as "a well is a hole in the ground," "no, we don't know," or "like what?" Moreover, there is the popular rhetorical question many parents use: "If all your friends jumped off a bridge, would you?" And then there is this exchange: "Dad, what does affinity mean?" "There's the dictionary. Look it up!" Pause. "But Dad, why can't you just tell me?" With a grin, Dad might say, "Go straight to the source; why take my word for it?". . . "Awesome."

In a similar vein, in building your mastery of the language of business, you can go to the source: the Financial Accounting Research System (FARS). Every source outside of the pronouncements has less authoritative weight. An opportunity is at hand to gain familiarity with the standards that describe the language of business. In addition to building your vocabulary, you can compare this authoritative definition to other explanations of the term or concept that have been offered in conversation and in your readings. Are the differences important? As you use FARS, you will gain familiarity with how to perform searches on information databases that are becoming increasingly important tools for all professionals to master. These skills will serve you well in your career. This chapter includes separate FARS-directed problems (Tables 3.1–3.40) for each of the main subject areas in an introduction to the language of business.

Using FARS to Master Business Terminology

This chapter consists of three types of assignments organized by subject matter. The first pertains to key vocabulary, identified as basic, intermediate, or advanced in nature. All of these terms can be located in the FARS database under the Terminology Topical Index. Specifically, the terms listed have definitions within FARS that can be found by clicking on <u>T</u> and scrolling down to the Terminology heading. By clicking on the columnar items, you can go to the key passages and review those definitions. This is an important self-study tool for the subject matter in each table. The self-study process builds experience with the official literature and hones one's ability to comprehend the type of guidance essential to career endeavors.

By using those links within the Topical Index, the definitions of the terms can be identified in the professional literature. You are to keep track of the literature citations found and read through the definitions. To demonstrate your understanding of each term, draft a sentence using the new vocabulary, in line with the FARS definitions you have reviewed. Create your own dictionary for review and future reference. Refer to Chapter 1 for assistance with various approaches you may take to assembling your own document. Moreover, the definitions from the Topical Index will help you solve the problems that follow the tables and address similar subject matter. You can tag these definitions, export the cited passages, and create your own document for self-review of key terms, based on FARS. Should you plan to eventually take the Certified Public Accountant (CPA) exam, the ability to find and retrieve such passages is currently a facet of that exam process. (See http://www.cpa-exam.org where you can access the AICPA Tutorial and related information.) You may wish your dictionary to include both quotations directly from FARS and interpretive points that you have observed in your study of the materials at each link. In particular, you may note that the links relate to different pronouncements and display a variety of meanings for the same terminology, depending on the context. Explore the synonym capability within FARS to both build your vocabulary and gain an appreciation of whether a word is unique or versatile in its use.

After the vocabulary assignment, the second type of assignment for each topic has a table for you to complete. The information you uncover as you complete these tables, alongside your mastery of the self-study vocabulary will help you solve the third type of assignment which includes short-answer problems and questions for discussion. Some self-study questions and answers (Self-Study Q&A, identified as **Q:** and *A.*) are included within the problem sets. Replicate the steps described in the Q&A to master the search process and facilitate related discussion of your findings.

For each of the topics in the complete-the-table assignments, first use the recommended search and try to identify that source in the professional literature most helpful to understanding the meaning of the term. You are asked to apply these instructions to FARS, complete each table, and respond to the related questions per topic.

The citation expected should include a reference to the document type, number, and para-graph. As an example, assume that you access FARS, click on <u>File</u>, <u>Open</u>, select <u>Nfo</u>, <u>Open</u>, select <u>FASB-OP</u>, click <u>Open</u>, and click <u>Search</u>. Then you type in the query *vocabulary*. If you view the <u>Document</u> pane, it will have a clear reference at the top of the screen that reads ATB-1, Par. 1. This is what you need to complete the next to last column of each table (i.e., the column labeled "Citation for Definition: Provide Full Reference"). The actual content shown in the window has the phrase:

> "1. The committee on terminology was constituted in 1920 and assigned the task of compiling a vocabulary of words and expressions used peculiarly in accounting and of gradually preparing definitions thereof."

Reading the content for the prioritized search will not only prepare you to define each term but will also provide the background for solving the problems associated with each table. Keep in mind that the citations you provide may well reference more than a single paragraph, as you deem best describes the concept or term of interest.

FARS does not always give a specific definition for each term. However, the meanings of the terms usually can be inferred from the context in which they are used. Analyze the surrounding words or sentences to deduce a term's meaning. You are also asked to suggest other searches of relevance for each of the terms in the table. Your suggestions will likely involve exploring alternative Boolean operators, proximity adjustments with advanced search, and synonyms for the concepts or terms cited. Be creative in exploring and suggesting other searches. Chapter 1 will be of use in completing the tables and associated questions.

You may find additional searches of FARS to be useful in responding to the questions, beyond those cites you have included in your dictionary or those required for completion of the table. In responding to the problems, highlight the specific citation you believe ties in to your solution. You are encouraged to experiment and gain improved skill at finding the answers to various questions likely to arise in practice and theory.

As additional guidance to completing assignments, consider the following example.

Example of Assignment and Solution

ASSIGNMENT:

Your professor has made an assignment from the Accounting Standards topical area in Chapter 3. Specifically, you have been asked to create a dictionary of the Intermediate terms (i.e., the middle column of the Vocabulary table). To demonstrate your understanding of each term, you are expected to draft a sentence using the new vocabulary, in line with the FARS definitions you have reviewed. In addition, you are asked to complete the first three entries from Table 3.1Table 3.1, as well as Problem #5.

SOLUTION:

The *first step* to creating a dictionary of terms in the Vocabulary table is to proceed to the FARS Menu, click on the Topical Index, click on the letter T, scroll down to Terminology, and find each of the three terms and the citations indicated. The results can be placed in a tabular arrangement as follows:

Vocabulary: Citations for each term from FARS, located in the Terminology section of the Topical Index. These should be a part of the dictionary entries.

Intermediate

Consolidated Statements	ARB51, 1	C51.401
Income Taxes	FAS109, 289	I27.410
Statutory Accounting Practices	FAS60, 66	In6.431

The *next step* is to prepare the dictionary. This will require clicking on each of the entries and copying and pasting the results into your response. You can use the Go Back button to return to the Terminology listing. (Alternatively, you can tag and export passages.) All items under Terminology are in alphabetical order and all of the Vocabulary tables are likewise in alphabetical order within each column of terms. This permits you to efficiently assemble a dictionary. The first draft of your response follows:

Consolidated Statements

"PURPOSE OF CONSOLIDATED STATEMENTS
ARB51, Par. 1

1. The purpose of consolidated statements is to present, primarily for the benefit of the shareholders and creditors of the parent company, the results of operations and the financial position of a parent company and its subsidiaries essentially as if the group were a single company with one or more branches or divisions. There is a presumption that consolidated statements are more meaningful than separate statements and that they are usually necessary for a fair presentation when one of the companies in the group directly or indirectly has a controlling financial interest in the other companies."   -

"Glossary
C51.401

.401 Consolidated statements. Consolidated statements present, primarily for the benefit of the shareholders and creditors of the parent company, the results of operations and the financial position of a parent company and its subsidiaries essentially as if the group were a single enterprise with one or more branches or divisions. [ARB51, ¶1]"

Income Taxes

"FAS109, Par. 289

Income taxes

Domestic and foreign federal (national), state, and local (including franchise) taxes based on income."

I27.410 ".410 Income taxes. Domestic and foreign federal (national), state, and local (including franchise) taxes based on income. [FAS109, ¶289]"

Statutory Accounting Practices

"FAS60, Par. 66

Statutory accounting practices

Accounting principles required by statute, regulation, or rule, or permitted by specific approval, that an insurance enterprise is required to follow when submitting its financial statements to state insurance departments."

"In6.431

.431 Statutory accounting practices. Accounting principles required by statute, regulation, or rule, or permitted by specific approval, that an insurance enterprise is required to follow when submitting its financial statements to state insurance departments. [FAS60, ¶66]"

The first thing you will notice is that these direct quotes, when copied and pasted, are often duplicative of one another. This is because the current text citations are drawn from the pronouncements. In addition, for some terms there are multiple references in the database and, sometimes more than one meaning is ascribed to a term depending on the context. Since the table you have prepared for the response has all citations from the Terminology section of FARS, you can select one of the overlapping quotes for use in your dictionary. Save your document for study.

> *To complete the assignment associated with the Vocabulary table*, you must draft sentences that demonstrate your understanding of each of these Intermediate terms. Possible responses follow.
>
> In order to gain an overall understanding of Coca-Cola's operations, I studied the consolidated financial statements which combine operations of majority-owned companies.
>
> Income taxes are payments to some type of governmental entity, based on income that is measured in accordance with tax requirements of that entity.
>
> An insurance company not only prepares and files financial statements in accordance with generally accepted accounting principles, but also is required to file reports to insurance regulators that are in accordance with statutory accounting principles.

Proceeding to the first three terms in Table 3.1, the results of the search recommended are noted, and suggestions are offered for additional searches. The latter can vary widely.

As the table footnote marked with a single asterisk indicates at the bottom of Table 3.1, "Access FARS, click on File, Open, Nfo, Open, and select FASB-OP (amended), click Search, enter query."

Type in the search recommended and you will identify the citations listed. Note that the order of the results will vary depending on the version of FARS in use, since the pronouncements change over time. You will want to scan the HitList to determine those discussions you find most useful in gaining an understanding of the meaning of the term. Feel free to consider other resources beyond FARS that might help to inform your research, such as checking the Financial Accounting Standards Board (FASB), AICPA, or Securities and Exchange Commission (SEC) Web sites for definitions and developing guidance. However, concentrate on alternative query approaches within FARS. For example, could the Advanced Search capabilities of FARS simplify the process, or could a Query applied to the Topical Index help to consider the context in which a particular term has been used? For this assignment, by opening Topical Index, using the query of Financial Reporting, you will have a number of items on the Hit List. By scrolling through the results, you will find that Financial Reporting is a distinct entry in the Topical Index, although its definition is not listed under the "T" for Terminology and "definition" is not a subhead under the entry. Yet, of particular relevance to the assignment is the subhead found, entitled Relation to Financial Statements CON1, ¶5-8. It is wise to make a practice of performing a search of the Topical Index, since it concurrently considers all Infobases' tables of contents and is powerful in reminding you of the various dimensions of a single term or phrase that are reflected in the professional literature. The completed Table 3.1 for the three terms assigned follows:

Table 3.1   Accounting Standards COMPLETE THIS TABLE –**Example of Solution**

Terms	**Search Recommended* (Semicolons are not part of the search but are used as separators.)**	**Citation for Definition: Provide Full Reference**	**Other Searches You Would Suggest**
Financial reporting	Financial reporting defin*	CON 1, Par. 5, 17, 29, 33	Financial information Query identifies FAS 35 Summary
Financial statements	Financial statements of business	CON 5, Par. 5, CON 6, Par. 1, 3, 20	Financial statements FAS24, Par. 5, superseded by FAS 131 Appendix C, Par. 128—FAS 95, Par. 152 is linked with glossary
Generally accepted accounting principles (GAAP)	GAAP hierarchy for financial statements	FAS 111, Par. 25	Open the Topical Index and enter the query *GAAP*. This will identify a heading for GAAP with a Subhead of Conflict Between Principles, citing FAS111, ¶7 and A06.112.
			Other resources: Statement of Auditing Standards (SAS) 69 with Summary of GAAP Hierarchy in GAAS. Also see http://fasb.org for a related discussion, as well as http://www.aicpa.org.

Next, complete Problem #5: "Describe the GAAP hierarchy". A response follows.

5. The GAAP hierarchy is explained in the word search results from generally accepted accounting principles (GAAP): FAS111, Par. 25. This passage follows, along with the footnotes that can be clicked, copied, and pasted, for completeness.

"Summary of GAAP Hierarchy under SAS 69

FAS111, Par. 25

25. The chart below summarizes the GAAP hierarchy for financial statements of nongovernmental entities [4] under SAS 69.

Established Accounting Principles

> Category (a)—FASB Statements and Interpretations, APB Opinions, and AICPA Accounting Research Bulletins
> Category (b)—FASB Technical Bulletins, cleared [5] AICPA Industry Audit and Accounting Guides, and cleared AICPA Statements of Position
> Category (c)—Consensus positions of the FASB Emerging Issues Task Force and cleared AICPA AcSEC Practice Bulletins
> Category (d)—AICPA Accounting Interpretations, FASB Implementation Guides (Q&As), and widely recognized and prevalent industry practices

Other Accounting Literature

Other accounting literature, including FASB concepts Statements; APB Statements; AICPA Issues Papers; International Accounting Standards Committee Statements; GASB Statements, Interpretations, and Technical Bulletins; pronouncements of other professional associations or regulatory agencies; AICPA Technical Practice Aids; and accounting textbooks, handbooks, and articles."

"FAS111 Footnote 4—"Rules and interpretive releases of the Securities and Exchange Commission (SEC) have an authority similar to category (a) pronouncements for SEC registrants. In addition, the SEC staff issues Staff Accounting Bulletins that represent practices followed by the staff in administering SEC disclosure requirements. Also, the Introduction to the FASB's EITF Abstracts states that the Securities and Exchange Commission's Chief Accountant has said that the SEC staff would challenge any accounting that differs from a consensus of the FASB Emerging Issues Task Force, because the consensus position represents the best thinking on areas for which there are no specific standards" (quoted from footnote 3 of SAS 69)."

"FAS111, Appendix, Footnote 5—As used in SAS 69, cleared means that the FASB has indicated that it does not object to the issuance of the proposed pronouncement. Footnote 4 of SAS 69 states that it should be assumed that such pronouncements have been cleared by the FASB unless the pronouncement indicates otherwise."

This paragraph is elaborated upon in FAS 111, paragraphs 17, 18, and 19, which outline the SAS 69 information.

Although not assigned, it is strongly recommended that you read over all Self-Study Q&A within this chapter as a means of building your FARS search competencies. Hence, when considering the subject of Accounting Standards, you would *proceed to self-study by reading through and replicating the steps in Problems #6, #7, and #8.*

■ **ACCOUNTING STANDARDS**

> *Vocabulary: Create your dictionary of the following terms from FARS.*
>
> | Basic | Intermediate | Advanced |
> |---|---|---|
> | Accounting Policies | Consolidated Statements | Articulation |
> | Accounting Principle | Income Taxes | Attribute |
> | Accounting Pronouncement | Statutory Accounting Practices | |
> | Complete Set of Financial Statements | | |
> | Elements of Financial Statements | | |
> | Financial Position | | |
> | Full Set of Financial Statements | | |
> | Tax | | |
>
> CHECK THE TERMINOLOGY SECTION OF THE TOPICAL INDEX AND READ LINKS TO BUILD COMPRE-
> HENSION. RECORD THE CITATIONS TO THE LITERATURE FOR FUTURE REFERENCE. USE EACH TERM
> IN A SENTENCE.

Table 3.1   Accounting Standards COMPLETE THIS TABLE

Terms	Search Recommended* (Semicolons are not part of the search but are used as separators.)	Citation for Definition: Provide Full Reference	Other Searches You Would Suggest
Financial reporting	Financial reporting defin*		
Financial statements	Financial statements of business		
Generally accepted accounting principles (GAAP)	GAAP hierarchy for financial statements		
Emerging Issues Task Force (EITF)	**		
Financial Accounting Standards Board (FASB)	Financial Accounting Standards Board Mission		
Interpretations***	Interpretation and mission and accounting		
Technical bulletins****	Purpose of Technical Bulletins		
International Accounting Standards	International Accounting Standards		

Table 3.1 Accounting Standards   Page **3-9**

Terms	Search Recommended* (Semicolons are not part of the search but are used as separators.)	Citation for Definition: Provide Full Reference	Other Searches You Would Suggest
Tax policy	"tax policy"; "tax-planning strategy"; tax$ strategy$		
Statements of Financial Accounting Concepts*****	Statements of Financial Accounting Concepts are intended		
Governmental Accounting Standards Board (GASB)	Government Accounting Standards Board		

*Access FARS, click on <u>File</u>, <u>Open</u>, <u>Nfo</u>, <u>Open</u>, and select <u>FASB-OP (amended)</u>, click <u>Search</u>, enter query.

**After selecting FASB-OP, on the menu presented, click on <u>EITF Abstracts</u> and then <u>Introduction</u>.

***After selecting FASB-OP, on the menu presented, click on <u>AICPA Accounting Interpretations (AIN)</u> and peruse the topics; then return to the FASB-OP menu and click on <u>Interpretations (FIN)</u> and peruse the topics.

****After selecting FASB-OP, on the menu presented, click on <u>Technical Bulletins (FTB)</u> and peruse the topics.

*****Also, select <u>Statements of Financial Accounting Concepts (CON)</u> from menu and read topics covered.

Table 3.1 Accounting Standards

1. In what sense does the FASB influence trend analysis (i.e., the ability to compare and analyze information over time)?

2. Why do generally accepted accounting principles diverge among companies at an international level?

3. How might tax policy influence decision making in Germany and Japan, compared to the same dynamic in the United States?

4. What is the difference between financial statements and financial reporting? What are the objectives of financial reporting?

5. Describe the GAAP hierarchy.

6. SELF-STUDY Q&A. **Q:** Where does FARS describe the measurement scale used in financial reporting?
    A. *Access the Topical Index, go to M and locate MEASUREMENT. The subhead Description* links to CON1, Par. 2 and CON5, Par. 65-72. Read through this material. You will find that CON5, Par. 71 is entitled Monetary Unit or Measurement Scale.

7. SELF-STUDY Q&A. **Q:** How many standard setters were involved in the promulgation of Accounting Principles Board Opinions? How many standard setters are involved in the promulgation of Financial Accounting Standards? How many individuals are involved in reaching a consensus in the EITF process?
    A. *Access the opening FARS menu and click on* Original Pronouncements. *Then click on* Accounting Principles Board Opinions (APB). *If you click on APB 1 and scroll through the shaded*

area, you will find at the end "Accounting Principles Board (1962–1963)" with a listing of names numbering 20. If you go back and click on APB 31, the last item on the list, and again scroll through the shaded area, you will find at the end "Accounting Principles Board (1973)" with a listing of names numbering 17. This indicates that the number of standard setters varied by opinion.

Follow a similar process to quantify the size of the FASB since its origin. On the Original Pronouncements *screen, click* Statements of Financial Accounting Standards (FAS); *on the next menu, click on FAS 1. As you scroll down the shaded area, right before the Appendix, you will find the words: "This Statement was adopted by the unanimous vote of the seven members of the Financial Accounting Standards Board" followed by a list of the board members. Proceed to the last FAS listed and click. Watch for the heading "Members of the Financial Accounting Standards Board:" and you will again find a listing of seven names. This heading is usually located right after the dissent section of the guidance (assuming a board member has dissented).*

Finally, click on EITF Abstracts *on the opening FARS menu. The next screen allows you to click on* List of Task Force Members (Appendix A). *Listed are the Chairman and current members that number 14 and current observers that number 3. Note their affiliations.*

8. SELF-STUDY Q&A. **Q:** The format of the Statements of Financial Accounting Standards (FAS) has changed over time. Compare an early standard that was issued to the most recent FAS. Describe the typical format and the changes therein that you observe.

A. *Access the opening FARS menu and click on* Original Pronouncements. *On the* Original Pronouncements *screen, click* Statements of Financial Accounting Standards (FAS); *on the next menu, click on FAS 2. Become familiar with that format and then compare it with later pronouncements, including the most recent statement included in the FARS resource you are accessing.*

The typical format of an FAS is an issuance date and an effective date, an itemization of what other standards are affected, amended, or superseded, as well as cites to interpretations and related issues. Then a summary of the statement is provided, articulating reasons for issuing the statement, differences from prior guidance, how changes improve financial reporting, relationships between conclusions and the conceptual framework, and the effective date of the statement. The core of the pronouncement will include an introduction, scope, provisions, financial statement presentation dimensions, and disclosure, as applicable. The effective date and mode of transitioning to the new standard will be detailed. At the end of the core statement, before detailing the voting results is a highlighted message: "The provisions of this Statement need not be applied to immaterial items." The results of the vote of the Board are detailed, including dissents and their reasoning. After the statements, implementation guidance may be provided, sometimes in the form of an appendix. Then background information and the basis for conclusions in the statement are articulated. Such a basis will frequently cite comment letters analyzed and the reason for changes from exposure draft provisions. Disclosure illustrations are frequently provided, as are details on amendments to existing pronouncements. Related excerpts from concept statements, a glossary, and endnotes with citations are common.

You will notice that the focus on objectives, benefits, and the relationship to concepts is evidenced in more recent standards such as FAS 142 Goodwill and Other Intangible Assets, *issued in June 2001, but this elaboration will not be found in most of the earlier guidance.* FAS 156 Accounting for Servicing of Financial Assets an amendment of FASB Statement No. 140, *issued in March 2006, includes a Summary with sections addressing Reasons for Issuing This Statement, How This Statement Improves Financial Reporting, and Effective Date and Transition. Then FAS 156 proceeds to Objective, Scope, and Key Terms, thereafter setting forth its Amendments to FAS 140, using a redlining approach. This example bears out that the content of the pronouncement and whether it is an amendment of earlier statements affects its format.*

Table 3.2 Concepts   Page **3-11**

■ CONCEPTS

Vocabulary: Create your dictionary of the following terms from FARS.

Basic	Intermediate	Advanced
Conservatism	Conversion	Enterprise
Earned	Current Exchange Rate	Foreign Entity
Earnings	Economic Interest in an Entity	Fresh-Start Measurement
Entity	Foreign Currency	Nonpublic Enterprise
Entity-Specific	Foreign Currency Financial Statements	Public Business Enterprise
Feedback Value	Foreign Currency Transactions	Public Enterprise
Historical Cost	Foreign Currency Translation	Publicly Traded Enterprise
Materiality	Functional Currency	Publicly Traded Entity
Nonpublic Entity	Industry Segment	Reporting Enterprise
Predictive Value	Intercompany Profit	Transaction Date
Public Entity	Local Currency	Transaction Gain (Loss)
Recognition	Monetary Assets	Translation
Reporting Date	Monetary Liabilities	Translation Adjustment
Representational Faithfulness	Reporting Currency	
Revenue	Reporting Unit	
Timeliness	Spot Rate	

CHECK THE TERMINOLOGY SECTION OF THE TOPICAL INDEX AND READ LINKS TO BUILD COMPRE-HENSION. RECORD THE CITATIONS TO THE LITERATURE FOR FUTURE REFERENCE. USE EACH TERM IN A SENTENCE.

Table 3.2   Concepts COMPLETE THIS TABLE

Concepts	Are these assumptions (A), principles (P), or constraints (C)? Classify each concept.	Search Recommended*	Citation for Definition: Provide Full Reference	Other Searches You Would Suggest
Cost benefit		"cost benefit constraints"		
Monetary unit		Monetary unit		
Going concern		Going concern		
Industry practice		Specialized industry practice		
Matching		Matching		
Full disclosure		Objective of full disclosure		

Concepts	Are these assumptions (A), principles (P), or constraints (C)? Classify each concept.	Search Recommended*	Citation for Definition: Provide Full Reference	Other Searches You Would Suggest
Economic entity		Economic entity		
Periodicity		Period*		
		Reporting period		
Revenue recognition		Recogniz* revenue*		

*Access FARS, click on <u>File</u>, <u>Open</u>, <u>Nfo</u>, <u>Open</u>, and select <u>FASB-OP (amended)</u>, click <u>Search</u>, enter query.

Problems

1. An individual who is also a partner in a CPA firm is expected to maintain his or her personal checking account separate from the business checking account based on what fundamental concept? Explain.

2. A business, Diehl Incorporated, has operated for 10 years. In its first year of operations, it acquired a tract of land for $30,000. Since that date, the market value has fluctuated significantly. By the fifth year of operation, the value had reached $100,000, and by the tenth year, market value for the tract of land was $200,000. How should this land be recorded on the balance sheet of Diehl Incorporated in the (a) first year of operations? (b) fifth year of operations? (c) tenth year of operations? How are recognition and measurement related?

3. A company purchased an electric pencil sharpener that is estimated to have a useful life of five years. Nonetheless, the company is considering expensing the pencil sharpener rather than recording it as an asset. What concept must justify such an action?

4. Does industry practice define GAAP? Explain. (*Hint:* Revisit the GAAP hierarchy.)

5. If full disclosure is a goal, why not merely publish all books and records of a public company? (*Hint:* Consider cost benefit.)

6. SELF-STUDY Q&A. **Q:** Go to FARS, open the FASB-OP (amended) infobase, use Advanced Query and identify the synonyms listed for *conservatism* and then for *conservative*. Are any of these synonyms helpful in understanding the meaning of the term *conservatism* within the accounting literature?

    A. *The search phrase conservatism$ does not add any synonyms within FARS. In contrast, the search phrase conservative$ identifies traditional, unchanging, conventional, inflexible, stable, and moderate. These words are not helpful to discerning the meaning of conservatism. They merely bear out the diversity of use of the word* conservative *within the English language. Moreover, this exercise bears out the importance of using that form of a word usually applied in technical language that is assigned a unique meaning, rather than searching on a variant of that word, having multiple uses in more general conversational settings.*

7. SELF-STUDY Q&A. **Q:** FARS not only defines materiality, it likewise describes materiality. Where is such a description available?

    A. *Access the Topical Index, go to M and locate materiality. One of the subheads is "Description" with a link to CON2, Par. 123-132. Read through the description.*

Table 3.3 The Accounting Information System   Page **3-13**

■ THE ACCOUNTING INFORMATION SYSTEM

Vocabulary: Create your dictionary of the following terms from FARS.

Basic	**Intermediate**	**Advanced**
Accrual	Financial Flexibility	Estimated Cash Flow
Collections	Income Available to Common Stockholders	Expected Cash Flow
Transaction	Net Carrying Amount	

CHECK THE TERMINOLOGY SECTION OF THE TOPICAL INDEX AND READ LINKS TO BUILD COMPRE-HENSION. RECORD THE CITATIONS TO THE LITERATURE FOR FUTURE REFERENCE. USE EACH TERM IN A SENTENCE.

Table 3.3   The Accounting Information System COMPLETE THIS TABLE

Terms	Search Recommended* (Semicolons are not part of the search but are used as separators.)	Citation for Definition: Provide Full Reference	Other Searches You Would Suggest
Double entry accounting	Double entry accounting		
Cash basis accounting	"cash basis accounting"		
Net cash flow	"net cash flow is" defin*; computation of net cash flow		
Net income	Net income defin*		
Balance sheet equation	Double entry accounting balance sheet		
Balancing the books	Balancing the books trial balance		
Miscellaneous account	Caption line item immaterial miscellaneous; "miscellaneous income"		

*Access FARS, click on File, Open, Nfo, Open, and select FASB-OP (amended), click Search, enter query.

Problems

1. What are the advantages of double-entry accounting?
2. Lancione Incorporated purchased $30,000 of goods for cash and an additional $20,000 on credit. It made cash sales of $40,000 and credit sales of $70,000. The cost of the goods sold was $45,000. The company paid off $12,000 of the balance owed to suppliers. What would be the net cash

flow using cash basis accounting? What would be the net income if accrual accounting were used? Read the cites listed in the topical index under "A" Accrual Basis of Accounting, as well as Accrual Accounting and Related Concepts.

3. When asked to explain the economic transaction that led to the journal entry below, a new accounting student responded: "Cash was debited $30 and Accounts Receivable was credited $30." Has the student responded correctly? Explain your answer.

Cash   30
   Accounts Receivable 30

4. During a review of a new client who was considering issuing securities, an accountant ran across a "miscellaneous account" on the books. It seemed particularly unusual because every month it was charged, sometimes with a debit and sometimes with a credit. Moreover, the magnitude of the adjustment ranged from pennies to thousands of dollars. Bewildered, the accountant asked the client's bookkeeper what had been recorded in the account. The bookkeeper responded that every time the trial balance was run, whatever amount was needed to make it balance had been charged to the "miscellaneous account." The accountant called his partner and said "We've got a problem here." Explain what he meant. What is the scope of the problem?

5. If you were a lender, would you prefer to receive cash basis financial statements or accrual basis? Explain.

6. SELF-STUDY Q&A. **Q:** Go to FARS, open the FASB-OP (amended) infobase, use Advanced Query, and input the search phrase "balance* books$"/20. How does such a phrase work? What is the message of the search result identified?

   A. *This phrase uses a wildcard, a synonym, and a proximity capability. The message is that deferred taxes balances reflect differences in books maintained on a tax basis and those kept on a financial accounting basis. The citation identified is FAS 141, Par. B223.*

7. SELF-STUDY Q&A. **Q:** Go to FARS, open the Topical Index, access the heading articulation, identify the cites described for the definition. Then find the specific description that ties to double entry accounting.

   A. *Under "A" you will find articulation, which includes the subhead "Definition CON6, 20-21." By reading these cites you will find "CON6, Footnote 14—The two relations described in this paragraph are commonly expressed as (a) balance at beginning of period + changes during period = balance at end of period and (b) assets = liabilities + equity. "Double entry," the mechanism by which accrual accounting formally includes particular items that qualify under the elements definitions in articulated financial statements, incorporates those relations."*

8. SELF-STUDY Q&A. **Q:** Find where within FARS the users of financial information are identified.

   A. *Under "U" in the Topical Index you will find the entry USERS OF FINANCIAL INFORMATION with the subhead Description, linked to CON1, Par. 24–27.*

Table 3.4 Income Statements   Page **3-15**

■ INCOME STATEMENTS

Vocabulary: Create your dictionary of the following terms from FARS.

<u>Basic</u>	<u>Intermediate</u>	<u>Advanced</u>
Expenses	Allocation	Incremental Costs of Incidental Operations
Extraordinary Items	Allocation Period	Incremental Direct Acquisition Costs
Gains	Functional Classification	Incremental Direct Costs
Income from Continuing Operations	Gains and Losses Included in Comprehensive Income but Excluded from Net Income	Incremental Revenue from Incidental Operations
Income Taxes	Incidental Operations	Incurred but Not Reported Claims
Losses	Income Tax Expense (Benefit)	Incurred Claims Cost (by Age)
Operating Cycle	Incurred Cost	Interest Methods of Allocation
Ordinary Income or Loss	Loss	
Pretax Accounting Income	Proceeds	
Profit		

CHECK THE TERMINOLOGY SECTION OF THE TOPICAL INDEX AND READ LINKS TO BUILD COMPRE-
HENSION. RECORD THE CITATIONS TO THE LITERATURE FOR FUTURE REFERENCE. USE EACH TERM
IN A SENTENCE.

Table 3.4   Income Statements COMPLETE THIS TABLE

Terms	Search Recommended* (Semicolons are not part of the search but are used as separators.)	Citation for Definition: Provide Full Reference	Other Searches You Would Suggest
Income statement	"income statement is"		
Natural business year	Operating cycle natural business year		
Unusual items	Unusual items defin*		
Discontinued operations	Discontinued operations defin*		
Divestiture	"divestiture of assets"		
Loss from operations	Defin* loss from operations		

Terms	Search Recommended* (Semicolons are not part of the search but are used as separators.)	Citation for Definition: Provide Full Reference	Other Searches You Would Suggest
Allocation of overhead	Allocation of overhead		
Proceeds from sale of operations	Proceeds from sale of operations; proceeds from sale of property		

*Access FARS, click on <u>File</u>, <u>Open</u>, <u>Nfo</u>, <u>Open</u>, and select <u>FASB-OP (amended)</u>, click <u>Search</u>, enter query.

Problems

1. What is meant by a natural business year?

2. How do unusual items differ from extraordinary items?

3. Why is income from continuing operations typically reported as a subtotal on the income statement?

4. A segment of business is being disposed of (i.e., discontinued), with divestiture expected. While an interim loss from operations is incurred, the disposal of the line of business will result in a gain. Explain how the measurement date influences income statement presentation. What types of costs and expenses are permitted to be associated with the determination of the gain or loss on disposal? How much time can elapse between the measurement date and the disposal date, in order for the presentation in accordance with the discontinued operations of a segment of business to apply? Explain how groups of assets are handled relative to previously reported segments of operations.

5. What is meant by the term *operating income*? Is it an accounting-based term or is it an analyst's term? Explain.

6. The *Wall Street Journal* article on October 1, 2001 (pp. C1–C2) in the "Heard on the Street" column, authored by Steve Liesman, described how "Accountants, in a Reversal, Say Costs from the Attack Aren't 'Extraordinary'." The technical issue is entitled "Accounting for the Impact of the Terrorist Attacks of September 11, 2001," EITF Issue No. 01-10, reflecting discussions on both September 20 and 28, 2001 in the EITF Meeting Minutes. Read through the EITF material and explain in your own words why this event was not permitted to be treated as an extraordinary item. (*Hint:* Access the *Wall Street Journal* article and similar media coverage as background for your response.)

7. SELF-STUDY Q&A. **Q:** Find the definition of "allocation of costs" in the Topical Index.
   A. *The Topical Index identifies: "Definition CON6, 142."*

Table 3.5 Balance Sheets   Page **3-17**

■ BALANCE SHEETS

> *Vocabulary: Create your dictionary of the following terms from FARS.*
>
> | **Basic** | **Intermediate** | **Advanced** |
> |---|---|---|
> | Assets | Internal Rate of Return | Capital Maintenance |
> | Capitalize | Prematurity Period | Development Stage Enterprises |
> | Earned | Relative Fair Value Before Construction | Indirect Project Costs |
> | Entity | Subscriber Related Costs | Project Costs |
> | Revenue | | |
>
> CHECK THE TERMINOLOGY SECTION OF THE TOPICAL INDEX AND READ LINKS TO BUILD COMPRE-
> HENSION. RECORD THE CITATIONS TO THE LITERATURE FOR FUTURE REFERENCE. USE EACH TERM
> IN A SENTENCE.

Table 3.5   Balance Sheets COMPLETE THIS TABLE

Terms	Search Recommended* (Semicolons are not part of the search but are used as separators.)	Citation for Definition: Provide Full Reference	Other Searches You Would Suggest
Balance Sheet	"statement of financial position"		
Entity principle	Economic entity		
Line items	Specif* line items statement of financial position		
Order of line items	Order of presentation statement of financial position line items		
Prepaid advertising	Prepaid advertising		
Earned subscriber revenue	Earned subscriber revenue		
In construction	In construction		
Partially in service	Partially in service		
Organization costs	Start up organization costs		
Capitalization	"capitalization of costs"		

*Access FARS, click on File, Open, Nfo, Open, and select FASB-OP (amended), click Search, enter query.

Problems

1. Two students of financial accounting are reviewing their understanding of assets. John asserts, "Football teams record players' contracts as assets." Cynthia asks, "How can they? Most assuredly, people can't be owned, and how can they possibly be quantified in dollar terms?" Explain to the two students why the contracts of professional athletes, in fact, can be recorded as assets.

2. A businesswoman, Christina Lancione, who sells a line of cosmetics part-time has a Cadillac, which she uses for business purposes as well as for personal errands. How should the automobile be recorded on the books maintained for the cosmetics business, and why?

3. What determines the order in which line items are arranged on a balance sheet?

4. When asked to explain the economic transaction that led to the journal entry below, a new accounting student responded, "Prepaid advertising has been used up." Has the student responded correctly? Why or why not?

Prepaid Advertising	800	
Cash		800

5. Cable television companies experience what is termed a *prematurity period* which is expected not to exceed two years and may be shorter. During this period, the cable television system is partially under construction and partially in service. Its beginning will be with the first earned subscriber revenue and its end will be determined according to plans for completion of the first major construction period. During this period, a number of costs are likely to be incurred related to the costs of cable television plant, materials, direct labor, and construction overhead. In addition, subscriber-related costs will be incurred, as will general and administrative expenses. Subscriber-related costs include costs to obtain and retain subscribers, costs of billing and collection, bad debts and mailings, repairs and maintenance of taps and connections, franchise fees related to revenues, or number of subscribers, and programming costs as well as direct selling costs. Another type of cost is that related to initial subscriber installation costs, for which initial hookup revenue is generated. Do you believe such costs should be accumulated and reported in the financial statements? If so, why? Respond to each of the types of costs described.

6. SELF-STUDY Q&A. **Q:** Find the essential three characteristics of assets.
    A. *Click on the definition under "Assets" in the Topical Index, access the link, and read to find "characteristics of assets CON6, Par. 26."*

7. SELF-STUDY Q&A. **Q:** Using FARS, provide an example of an unclassified balance sheet.
    A. *Click on STOCKBROKERAGE INDUSTRY in the Topical Index and you will see the subhead of Unclassified Balance Sheet, with links to FAS6, Par. 7 and B05.102.*

Table 3.6 Cash Flows   Page **3-19**

■ CASH FLOWS

Vocabulary: Create your dictionary of the following terms from FARS.

<u>Basic</u>	<u>Intermediate</u>	<u>Advanced</u>
Liquidity	Economic Resources	Financial Capital Maintenance Concept
Working Capital	Reacquisition Price of Debt	Project Financing Arrangements

CHECK THE TERMINOLOGY SECTION OF THE TOPICAL INDEX AND READ LINKS TO BUILD COMPRE-HENSION. RECORD THE CITATIONS TO THE LITERATURE FOR FUTURE REFERENCE. USE EACH TERM IN A SENTENCE.

Table 3.6   Cash Flows COMPLETE THIS TABLE

Terms	Search Recommended* (Semicolons are not part of the search but are used as separators.)	Citation for Definition: Provide Full Reference	Other Searches You Would Suggest
Statement of Cash Flows	"statement of cash flows is"		
Operating activities	Operating activities		
Investing activities	Investing activities defin*; "investing activities include"		
Financing activities	"financing activities include"		
Cash outflows for income tax paid	Cash outflows for income tax paid		
Income statement classifications	Income statement classifications		
Noncash investing and financing activities	Noncash investing and financing activities		
Direct method	Direct method cash flow defin*		
Indirect method	Indirect method operating cash flow		

*Access FARS, click on <u>File</u>, <u>Open</u>, <u>Nfo</u>, <u>Open</u>, and select <u>FASB-OP (amended)</u>, click <u>Search</u>, enter query.

Problems

1. What is the purpose of a statement of cash flows?

2. What classifications are used for the statement of cash flows, and how do they compare to classifications used on the face of the income statement?

3. Describe the type of noncash investing and financing activities that are required to be disclosed with statements of cash flows.

4. The FASB mentions that cash outflows for income taxes paid cannot be allocated to operating, investing, and financing activities. Do you agree? Why or why not?

5. State the principal advantage of (a) the direct method of reporting net cash flow from operating activities and (b) the indirect method.

6. How is interest classified on the Statement of Cash Flows, and why? If you were a standard-setter and chose to revisit guidance in this area, would you continue classifying interest in this manner? Why or why not?

7. SELF-STUDY Q&A. **Q:** Go to FARS, open the FASB-OP (amended) infobase, use Advanced Query, and use the search phrase *statement of cash flows format*. How many cites are identified? Now, change the search phrase to *statement of cash flows formats*. Are the same number of citations identified? How do they compare to the first set of search results?

   A. *The six citations from the first search phrase include FAS 95, Par. 2, Par. 67, and Par. 129; FAS 102, Par. 21; FAS 130, Par. 9; FAS 133, Summary. The four citations from the second search phrase include FAS 7, Par. 10 and Par. 11; FAS 95, Par. 130; FAS 117, Par. 82. The searches do not overlap whatsoever and cover different aspects of the nature of how statements of cash flow are formatted. In particular, the first search identifies the reasoning for a change from working capital and funds language toward cash, as well as pointing out certain unique considerations involving investment companies. The second search references illustrations of cash flow statements and focuses on unique considerations for development stage enterprises. The point of this self-study question is to bear out the difference that can result from merely including or choosing to exclude a single letter from a search phrase.*

Table 3.7 Time Value of Money   Page **3-21**

■ TIME VALUE OF MONEY

Vocabulary: Create your dictionary of the following terms from FARS.

<u>Basic</u>	<u>Intermediate</u>	<u>Advanced</u>
Best Estimate	Benchmark Interest Rate	Return on Plan Assets
Bias	Components of Economic Value	Systematic Risk
Discount Rate	Future Economic Benefits	Time Value of an Option
Expected Present Value	Risk Premium	Variable Annuity Contract
Interest Rate	Traditional Approach	
Present Value		

CHECK THE TERMINOLOGY SECTION OF THE TOPICAL INDEX AND READ LINKS TO BUILD COMPRE-
HENSION. RECORD THE CITATIONS TO THE LITERATURE FOR FUTURE REFERENCE. USE EACH TERM
IN A SENTENCE.

Table 3.7   Time Value of Money COMPLETE THIS TABLE

Terms	Search Recommended* (Semicolons are not part of the search but are used as separators.)	Citation for Definition: Provide Full Reference	Other Searches You Would Suggest
Time value of money	Time value of money		
Future value	"future value"		
Compounding	Compounding; Compounding of interest		
Risk-adjusted discount rate	"Risk-adjusted discount rate"		
Return on investment	Return on investment		
Discounting the note	Discounting the note; Interest on receivables		
Negative loan amortization	Negative loan amortization**		

*Access FARS, click on <u>F</u>ile, <u>O</u>pen, <u>N</u>fo, <u>O</u>pen, and select FASB-OP (amended), click <u>S</u>earch, enter query.
**Access FARS, click on <u>F</u>ile, <u>O</u>pen, <u>N</u>fo, <u>O</u>pen, and select <u>EITF</u>, <u>S</u>earch, enter query, and then click on link to access EITF.

Problems

1. Real estate sales in the 1980s frequently involved graduated payment and insured mortgages, with negative loan amortization, meaning that principal could actually increase over the life of the obligation (because the cash payment was insufficient to cover interest). How did these attributes influence revenue recognition?

2. The federal consumer Truth-in-Lending law requires that interest rates on consumer loans be stated in annual percentage terms. Why do you think this provision is required?

3. Assume that CLeeVan Company makes a 120-day 9 percent $20,000 note on January 3, 20x1. All interest is payable at maturity. On February 1, 20x1, the note was discounted at a 10 percent rate. Record the discounting of the note. How would the discounting be recorded if the note was not discounted until March 1, 20x1?

4. You are offered a chance in one of three lotteries, which have the following related prizes: (1) an annuity of $1,000 a year for 20 years; (2) an annuity of $1,500 a year for 15 years, beginning after 5 years have elapsed; (3) a lump sum of $50,000 at the end of 18 years. Rank these three lottery prizes by value from highest to lowest. Quantify the basis for your ranking, assuming you demand a 10 percent return on your investments. [*Hint*: You can use spreadsheet software to compute present value (PV); for example, Excel has a PV command available to compute a present value of an annuity, using the command = PV(rate,nper,pmt,fv,type) in which nper is the number of periods that an equal amount is paid and type is 0 if payment is at the end of the period and 1 if the payment is at the beginning of the period, with 0 as a default. Note that the command can be entered with only the first three terms specified.]

5. On the Public Broadcasting System, December 27, 1987, Adam Smith's "Money World" reported that had the Native Americans invested the $28 received for Manhattan, at a 12 percent rate of return, the 1987 value would be far more than the value of New York City. In fact, the amount to which the $28 would have grown would exceed the total 1987 gross national product. To demonstrate how quickly compounding can earn a return, assume that you decide to save $100 a quarter for seven years, earning 12 percent a year. What amount would you have saved by the end of the seven-year period?

6. Your younger brother wants to attend a university in Paris to major in art. He asks you to lend him $100 a month for the next two years. In return, he promises to repay $3,500 at the end of the second year. He is certain by that date he will be selling his paintings. (a) If you demand a 30 percent return on risky investments, should you agree to lend the money? (b) What rate of return would you earn on the lending arrangement? (c) Would your return increase or decrease if instead you commit to lend $200 every two months for two years? Why?

7. SELF-STUDY Q&A. **Q:** Identify an example of a computation within FARS that involves the time value of money.
   A. Go to FARS, open the FASB-OP (amended) infobase, use Advanced Query, with the search phrase illustrate comput* present value. *The guidance identified includes FAS 90, Par. 5 (citing Par. 20 and 23, as well as an illustration in its Appendix A) and FTB87-2, Par. 38. Also see the Topical Index, under P, entry PRESENT VALUE TECHNIQUE.*

8. SELF-STUDY Q&A. **Q:** Find a glossary within FARS that describes terminology used in lending activities.
   A. Go to FARS, access the Topical Index under L and you will find LENDING ACTIVITIES. The links identified include a Glossary at FAS91, Par. 80 and L20.401-404.

Table 3.8 Cash   Page **3-23**

■ **CASH**

Vocabulary: Create your dictionary of the following terms from FARS.

<u>Basic</u>	<u>Intermediate</u>	<u>Advanced</u>
Cash Equivalents	Restriction	Daylight Overdraft or Other Intraday Credit

CHECK THE TERMINOLOGY SECTION OF THE TOPICAL INDEX AND READ LINKS TO BUILD COMPRE-
HENSION. RECORD THE CITATIONS TO THE LITERATURE FOR FUTURE REFERENCE. USE EACH TERM
IN A SENTENCE.

Table 3.8   Cash COMPLETE THIS TABLE

Terms	Search Recommended* (Semicolons are not part of the search but are used as separators.)	Citation for Definition: Provide Full Reference	Other Searches You Would Suggest
Cash	"cash includes"; cash currency bank accounts		
Bank overdrafts	Bank overdrafts		
Compensating balance	Compensating balance		
Restricted cash	Restricted cash xor donations		

*Access FARS, click on <u>File</u>, <u>Open</u>, <u>Nfo</u>, <u>Open</u>, and select <u>FASB-OP (amended)</u>, click <u>Search</u>, enter query.

Problems

1. What is included in the definition of cash? Distinguish between cash and cash equivalents.

2. Can two companies, Gladden Corporation and Fuson Company, with identical assets differ in their presentation of cash and cash equivalents? Explain.

3. What is the purpose of a compensating balance?

4. Give an example of a restricted cash balance. How should such a balance be presented in the financial statements?

5. What does a negative cash balance signify? How should it be classified?

6. SELF-STUDY Q&A. **Q:** Go to the Assets heading in the topical index, link to the cite identified as a definition, and find that particular passage discussing the value of money.
   A. CON6, Par. 29 and footnote 20.

■ SHORT-TERM INVESTMENTS

Vocabulary: Create your dictionary of the following terms from FARS.

Basic	Intermediate	Advanced
Current Market Value	Financial Asset	Current Cost/Constant Purchasing Power
Derivative Financial Instrument	Firm Commitment	Embedded Call
Derivative Instrument	Forecasted Transaction	Freestanding Call
Fair Value	Interest-Only Strip	Guaranteed Interest Contract
Financial Instrument	LIBOR Swap Rate	Guaranteed Investment Contract
Investments by Owners	Master Netting Arrangement	Guaranteed Mortgage Securitization
Mortgage-Backed Securities	Purchasing Power Gain or Loss	Market-Related Value of Plan Assets
Notional Amount	Right of Setoff	Undivided Interest
Relevance	Securitization	Unilateral Ability
Reliability	Setoff	
Underlying	Standby Commitment	
Verifiability		

CHECK THE TERMINOLOGY SECTION OF THE TOPICAL INDEX AND READ LINKS TO BUILD COMPRE-HENSION. RECORD THE CITATIONS TO THE LITERATURE FOR FUTURE REFERENCE. USE EACH TERM IN A SENTENCE.

Table 3.9   Short-Term Investments COMPLETE THIS TABLE

Terms	Search Recommended* (Semicolons are not part of the search but are used as separators.)	Citation for Definition: Provide Full Reference	Other Searches You Would Suggest
Short-term investments	"short-term investments"; "classification fair value financial instrument"		
Marketable securities	Marketable securities line item; "equity securities"		
Investment in Equity and Debt Securities	Accounting guidance investment* in equity and debt securities		
Impairment of securities	Impairment of securities; Impair* and sec*		

Table 3.9 Short-Term Investments   Page **3-25**

Terms	Search Recommended* (Semicolons are not part of the search but are used as separators.)	Citation for Definition: Provide Full Reference	Other Searches You Would Suggest
Market value accounting	Market value accounting for short-term investments		
Portfolio basis	Portfolio basis; "Portfolio basis" and "financial instrument"		

*Access FARS, click on File, Open, Nfo, Open, and select FASB-OP (amended), click Search, enter query.

Problems

1. How are impairments in short-term investments reported?

2. What are the categories into which debt and equity securities are to be classified? Can financial instruments have both debt and equity characteristics? Give an example.

3. In examining international accounting standards, through the 1980s, the United Kingdom, France, Germany, the Netherlands, Sweden, Switzerland, and Japan all reported short-term marketable securities at the lower of cost or market value. This was a time when much diversity existed internationally. Why do you believe these countries were reasonably homogeneous in their choice of accounting for short-term marketable securities?

4. On November 15, 1991, the U.S. Securities and Exchange Commission (SEC) sponsored a market value conference titled "Relevance in Financial Reporting: Moving toward Market Value Accounting." In announcing the conference, the brochure explained that the discussion would focus on whether market-based measures would be a useful and relevant alternative to historical cost information for decision makers, including investors, analysts, regulators, creditors, and management. Opponents of the market value accounting frequently cited lack of reliability, excessive cost, and an expected increase in reported volatility as insurmountable obstacles to market value accounting. Explain what discussion points you would expect to have raised regarding (a) relevancy, (b) reliability, (c) cost, and (d) volatility? [*Hint*: Search FARS using the phrase *dissent management intent* and consider implications of the associated discussion identified.] Also see FAS 157.

5. Can an identical derivative instrument held by two different companies be accounted for in a different manner by each company? Why or why not?

6. Assume that you went to a Las Vegas casino with 10 dollars and won $2,000 on the first day of your vacation. On the second day, you lost the entire $2,010. Would you say that you lost $10 or $2,010? Does this scenario imply anything about how marketable securities are recorded? Why or why not?

7. SELF-STUDY Q&A. **Q**: Go to FARS, open the FASB-OP (amended) infobase, use Advanced Query to search the phrase *accounting for marketable securities investments on financial*

statements. Read the citations identified and, in particular, explain what is meant by "look through" an investment.

A. *CON 5, Par. 50, Table of Contents titles of FASB statements and FINs, and FASB Staff Position 115-1/124-1 are the cites, with the first and last being particularly informative regarding the subject matter being searched. The term "look through" appears in the FSP, Par. 4a.(2): "Investors shall not "look through" the form of their investment to the nature of the securities held by an investee. For example, an investment in shares of a mutual fund that invests primarily in debt securities would be assessed for impairment as an equity security under this FSP."*

8. SELF-STUDY Q&A. **Q:** Provide an example of a derivative that is an investment.

   A. *Go to FARS, open the FASB-OP (amended) infobase, use Query, with the search phrase* derivatives as an investment. *The results tie to FAS 138, Par. 40 and explicitly cite variable annuity products as investment contracts.*

9. SELF-STUDY Q&A. **Q:** Identify a setting in which investment in derivatives might be prohibited.

   A. *Go to FARS, open the FASB-OP (amended) infobase, use Advanced Query, with the search phrase* derivatives investment prohibited. *The results tie to FAS 132(R), Par. 5 (2). That cite identifies the narrative description of investment policies and strategies as potentially identifying permitted and prohibited investments including the use of derivatives. The context involves disclosures about pensions and other postretirement benefit plans.*

10. SELF-STUDY Q&A. **Q:** Explore the use of synonyms within FARS by opening the FASB-OP (amended) infobase, using Advanced Query, and *typing value$ investment$.* Peruse the results and describe the scope of valuation and investments identified in FARS.

    A. *The results first characterize valuation as encompassing assessments, appraisals, substance, estimation, evaluation, ratings, and judgment. Then the investment aspect of the search recognizes money, certificates of deposit, share, and property among the synonyms.*

11. SELF-STUDY Q&A. **Q:** Identify the discussion in FARS that addresses the debate concerning reporting of realized and unrealized gains and losses on investments by not-for-profit organizations.

    A. *Within FARS open the FASB-OP (amended) infobase, using Advanced Query, and type* not-for-profit realized and unrealized invest$ gains and losses report. *The results will highlight FAS 124, Par. 38, FAS 135, Par. 20, and FASB Staff Position FAS115-1/124-1. Only the first of these cites directs attention specifically to not-for-profit organizations. This can be seen quickly by clicking on* HitList *and scrolling down the page, looking for the highlighted phrase* not-for-profit.

Table 3.10 Receivables   Page **3-27**

■ RECEIVABLES

Vocabulary: Create your dictionary of the following terms from FARS.

<u>Basic</u>	<u>Intermediate</u>	<u>Advanced</u>
Credit Card Fees	Nonrecourse Financing	Expected Residual Returns
Net Realizable Value	Primary Beneficiary	Fronting Arrangements
Recorded Investment in	Purchaser's Incremental	Reinsurance Receivables
the Receivable	Borrowing Rate	
Recoverable Amount	Recourse	
Reserve for Bad Debts	Variable Interest Entity	
Valuation Allowance	Variable Interests	

CHECK THE TERMINOLOGY SECTION OF THE TOPICAL INDEX AND READ LINKS TO BUILD COMPRE-HENSION. RECORD THE CITATIONS TO THE LITERATURE FOR FUTURE REFERENCE. USE EACH TERM IN A SENTENCE.

Table 3.10   Receivables COMPLETE THIS TABLE

Terms	Search Recommended* (Semicolons are not part of the search but are used as separators.)	Citation for Definition: Provide Full Reference	Other Searches You Would Suggest
Trade receivables	Trade accounts and notes receivable*; "trade receivables are"; Receivables from customers separate		
Nontrade receivables	Receivable* xor trade; "receivables from"		
Factoring with recourse	Factoring with recourse; Transfers of receivables with recourse		
Factoring without recourse	Factoring without recourse		
Notes receivable	"notes receivable"; secured and unsecured notes		
Installment receivable	Installment receivable from installment sale		

*Access FARS, click on <u>File</u>, <u>Open</u>, <u>Nfo</u>, <u>Open</u>, and select <u>FASB-OP (amended)</u>, click <u>Search</u>, enter query.

Problems

1. How do you compute the net realizable value of receivables?

2. What is the difference between trade and nontrade receivables, and how should they be presented on a balance sheet?

3. Would you expect the charge for factoring with recourse to be higher or lower than the charge of factoring without recourse? Why?

4. Define an installment receivable.

5. If a customer does not pay on a timely basis and is charged an interest rate for late payment, how does this affect the reporting of the related receivable?

6. What is the relationship of variable interest entities (VIEs) to receivables? Do such entities relate in any manner to the Enron debacle? Explain.

7. SELF-STUDY Q&A. **Q:** Identify the discussion in FARS that addresses the estimation of uncollectible receivables.

   A. *Within FARS open the FASB-OP (amended) infobase, using Advanced Query, and type* uncollect?ble receivables estimate. *The results will highlight FAS 5, Par. 23; FAS 113, Par. 120; FAS 154, Par. 2; FIN 39, Par. 17; and CON6, Par. 34. The first citation is particularly helpful.*

Table 3.11 Inventories   Page **3-29**

■ INVENTORIES

Vocabulary: Create your dictionary of the following terms from FARS.

Basic	**Intermediate**	**Advanced**
Inventory	Take-or-Pay Contract	Product Financing Arrangements
Direct Selling Costs	Throughput Contract	

CHECK THE TERMINOLOGY SECTION OF THE TOPICAL INDEX AND READ LINKS TO BUILD COMPRE-HENSION. RECORD THE CITATIONS TO THE LITERATURE FOR FUTURE REFERENCE. USE EACH TERM IN A SENTENCE.

Table 3.11   Inventories COMPLETE THIS TABLE

Terms	Search Recommended* (Semicolons are not part of the search but are used as separators.)	Citation for Definition: Provide Full Reference	Other Searches You Would Suggest
Periodic inventory	Periodic inventory relative to perpetual inventory		
Perpetual inventory	"perpetual inventory"		
Pilferage expense	Pilferage expense		
Cost flow assumptions	Cost flow assumptions inventory		
Physical flow of goods	Physical flow of goods		
Inventory method	Choice of inventory method; "first-in-first-out"; inventory is accounted for first-in-first-out		
Matching	Matching; cost of goods sold determination		
Retail method	Retail method of estimating inventory		

*Access FARS, click on File, Open, Nfo, Open, and select FASB-OP (amended), click Search, enter query.

Problems

1. Which system provides the more accurate estimate of pilferage expense: periodic or perpetual? Why?

2. How does a cost-flow assumption relate to the physical flow of goods?

3. In what sense is last in, first out (LIFO) said to produce better matching? What do you suspect was the reason claimed by the media for a number of companies changing to LIFO in the late 1970s and early 1980s?

4. Do generally accepted accounting principles (GAAP) permit selling expenses be made a part of inventory costs?

5. Do generally accepted accounting principles (GAAP) permit interest to be capitalized into the cost of inventory? Explain.

6. If a production plant experiences problems that create abnormally large unfavorable cost variances, do generally accepted accounting principles (GAAP) permit such variances to be capitalized into inventory cost?

7. SELF-STUDY Q&A. **Q:** Identify the discussion in FARS that addresses inventory problems.

   A. *Within FARS open the FASB-OP (amended) infobase, using Advanced Query, and type* inventor* problem*. *The results will highlight an APB 17, Par. 21 cite that is shaded; APB 29, Par. 16; FAS 34, Par. 44; FAS 52 Dissent, Par. 64, and Par. 153; FAS 89, Par. 124; FAS 101, Par. 47; FAS 133, Par. 377; and Q&A. 131,#8. A perusal of these cites bears out the problem areas of cost deferral, nonmonetary asset issues of fair valuation and swapping of inventory, qualifying assets for interest capitalization, foreign currency implications for locally sourced inventory and internationally priced inventory items, current cost considerations, regulated industry issues, and aggregation issues associated with segmental reporting. Open the EITF Infobase and perform the same search.*

8. SELF-STUDY Q&A. **Q:** Are handling costs a part of inventory costs?

   A. *No. Within FARS open the FASB-OP (amended) infobase, using Query and enter the phrase* handling cost. *The first item on the HitList will be FAS 151 Summary. That cite clarifies "the accounting for abnormal amounts of idle facility expense, freight, handling costs, and wasted material (spoilage)... be recognized as current-period charges regardless of whether they meet the criterion of "so abnormal".*

Table 3.12 Inventory Valuation   Page **3-31**

■ INVENTORY VALUATION

Vocabulary: Create your dictionary of the following terms from FARS.

Basic	**Intermediate**	**Advanced**
Cost	Cost Accrual	Cost Accumulation
Lower of Cost or Market (Rule)	Holding Gain or Loss	Historical Cost/Constant Purchasing Power
Net Realizable Value	Observable Market Price	

CHECK THE TERMINOLOGY SECTION OF THE TOPICAL INDEX AND READ LINKS TO BUILD COMPRE-HENSION. RECORD THE CITATIONS TO THE LITERATURE FOR FUTURE REFERENCE. USE EACH TERM IN A SENTENCE.

Table 3.12   Inventory Valuation COMPLETE THIS TABLE

Terms	Search Recommended* (Semicolons are not part of the search but are used as separators.)	Citation for Definition: Provide Full Reference	Other Searches You Would Suggest
Fair market value	Fair market value of inventory		
Cost principles	Cost principles inventory valuation		
Writedowns	Writedowns inventory		
Price recovery	"price recovery"		
Trade discounts	"trade discount"		
Inflation	Inflation		

*Access FARS, click on File, Open, Nfo, Open, and select FASB-OP (amended), click Search, enter query.

Problems

1. Declines in the fair market value of inventory below cost principle at the date of interim financial statements require writedowns of assets to lower of cost or market when near-term price recovery is uncertain. Does this appear to be consistent or at odds with the historical cost or periodicity concept?

2. What are trade discounts?

3. In a period of inflation, how would we expect inventory values to compare if the same company makes calculations using FIFO, LIFO, and weighted-average cost-flow assumptions?

4. When using the lower of cost or market method, how is market defined?

5. How do markups affect inventory valuation if the retail method is applied?

6. SELF-STUDY Q&A. **Q:** Changing prices have been accounted for in financial statements in a variety of ways over the past years. Identify this phenomenon in FARS relevant cites.

    A. *Within FARS, open the Topical Index and proceed to C, where you will find the entry CHANG-ING PRICES: REPORTING THEIR EFFECTS IN FINANCIAL REPORTS. Of particular use in displaying the variety of approaches is the Glossary included in FAS89, Par. 44 and C28.401-419. By going into the FASB-OP infobase and perusing the titles of original pronouncements, you will see the superseded standards addressing price changes.*

7. SELF-STUDY Q&A. **Q:** How many standards were issued after 12/73 that addressed inflation or changing prices in the title of the pronouncement?

    A. *Access FARS, open FASB-OP (amended), click Advanced Query and enter [Field issue date: >'12/73']. Then scan the 234 titles for an indication of the topic. You will identify FAS 33 issued September 1979, FAS 39 issued October 1980, FAS 40 issued November 1980, FAS 41 issued November 1980, FAS 46 issued March 1981, FAS 54 issued January 1982, FAS 70 issued December 1982, FAS 82 issued November 1984, and FAS 89 issued December 1986. It is not a coincidence that all but one of these pronouncements were issued in the 1979 to 1984 time frame. To understand this flurry of standard-setting activity, access the* www.federalreserve.gov *Web site and review the historical trend of interest rates and inflationary measures.*

Table 3.13 Property Plant and Equipment   Page **3-33**

■ PROPERTY PLANT AND EQUIPMENT

Vocabulary: Create your dictionary of the following terms from FARS.

Basic	**Intermediate**	**Advanced**
Barter	Maintenance Costs	Exchange Contract
Equity	Nonmonetary Assets	Exchange Price
Exchange (Exchange Transactions)	Nonmonetary Liabilities	Income-Producing Real Estate
Nonreciprocal Transfer	Nonmonetary Transactions	Physical Capital Maintenance Concept
Productive Assets	Similar Productive Assets	Value-in-Use

CHECK THE TERMINOLOGY SECTION OF THE TOPICAL INDEX AND READ LINKS TO BUILD COMPRE-HENSION. RECORD THE CITATIONS TO THE LITERATURE FOR FUTURE REFERENCE. USE EACH TERM IN A SENTENCE.

Table 3.13   Property Plant and Equipment COMPLETE THIS TABLE

Terms	Search Recommended* (Semicolons are not part of the search but are used as separators.)	Citation for Definition: Provide Full Reference	Other Searches You Would Suggest
Property plant and equipment	Property plant and equipment classif* statement of financial position		
Land	"land"		
Investment in land	"investment in land"		
Equipment	"equipment"		
Capitalized interest	"capitalization of interest"; accounting treatment of interest capitalization on fixed assets		
Interest expense	"interest expense include"; recording of interest incurred when purchasing fixed assets		
Pledged asset	"pledged asset"		

Terms	Search Recommended* (Semicolons are not part of the search but are used as separators.)	Citation for Definition: Provide Full Reference	Other Searches You Would Suggest
Self-constructed asset	Self-constructed asset under construction; Self-constructed asset under construction interest incurred capitalization		
Cost of equity capital	"cost of equity capital"		
Book value	"book value"		

*Access FARS, click on File, Open, Nfo, Open, and select FASB-OP (amended), click Search, enter query.

Problems

1. What is the distinction between land as a noncurrent asset and land held by a real estate company?

2. If a company purchases equipment on credit, is the interest capitalized? Why or why not?

3. Do pledged assets differ in value from assets that are not pledged?

4. When the amount of interest to capitalize on self-constructed assets is determined, how is the cost of equity capital reflected?

5. If two assets are exchanged without any cash changing hands, will the new asset be recorded at the book value of the asset given up? Explain your answer.

6. Three of the seven members of the Financial Accounting Standards Board dissented to the final FASB Statement No. 34. What do you think their reasons were for dissenting?

7. SELF-STUDY Q&A. **Q:** Identify where FARS discusses the accounting by an entity for its development of computer software for its own use.

   A. See the Topical Index entry Computer Software, subhead of "Definitions" for Software Product. The citation is to FAS86, Par. 2 and Co2.101, as well as Q&A.86 #1 and Co2.802. Direct particular attention to Co2.101's footnote 1.

Table 3.14 Depreciation   Page **3-35**

■ DEPRECIATION

Vocabulary: Create your dictionary of the following terms from FARS.

Basic	**Intermediate**	**Advanced**
Depreciation Accounting	Idiosyncratic Risk	Salvage
Useful Life	Risk	Service Potential

CHECK THE TERMINOLOGY SECTION OF THE TOPICAL INDEX AND READ LINKS TO BUILD COMPREHENSION. RECORD THE CITATIONS TO THE LITERATURE FOR FUTURE REFERENCE. USE EACH TERM IN A SENTENCE.

Table 3.14   Depreciation COMPLETE THIS TABLE

Terms	Search Recommended* (Semicolons are not part of the search but are used as separators.)	Citation for Definition: Provide Full Reference	Other Searches You Would Suggest
Units of production	Units of production		
Straight line	"straight line depreciation"		
Depreciable basis	"depreciable basis"; depreciable basis is computed as		
Sum of the years' digits	"Sum of the years digits method"		
Double declining balance	"declining balance depreciation"		
Accelerated depreciation	Accelerated depreciation		
Group depreciation	"group depreciation"		
Risk of computation with software	Risk of depreciation computation with software		

*Access FARS, click on File, Open, Nfo, Open, and select FASB-OP (amended), click Search, enter query.

Problems

1. Will the units-of-production method result in a write-off patttern similar to the pattern produced by the straight-line method?

2. How does the depreciable basis calculation apply to the straight-line, sum-of-the-years'-digits, and double-declining-balance methods?

3. What is meant by the term *accelerated depreciation*?

4. What is the most distinctive aspect of group depreciation?

5. What types of risks arise from the use of software to compute depreciation?

6. Under GAAP, is it permissible for two companies in the same industry and operating the same asset to depreciate that asset using a different method of depreciation? Is it acceptable for the two companies to assign different salvage values? Is it acceptable for the two companies to assign different useful lives?

7. SELF-STUDY Q&A. **Q:** Identify where FARS provides guidance on accounting for changes in method of depreciation, amortization, and depletion.
   A. *Access the FASB-OP (amended) infobase and use Query to search the phrase* change in method of accounting for depreciation amortization depletion. *The result is FAS 154, Par. B24.*

Table 3.15 Depletion   Page **3-37**

■ **DEPLETION**

Vocabulary: Create your dictionary of the following terms from FARS.

Basic	**Intermediate**	**Advanced**
Exploratory Well	Probable Mineral Reserves in Extractive Industries Other Than Oil and Gas	Development Well
Field	Proved Area	Reservoir
Mineral Resource Assets	Proved Mineral Reserves in Extractive Industries Other Than Oil and Gas	Service Well
Oil and Gas Producing Activities	Proved Reserves	Stratigraphic Test Well

CHECK THE TERMINOLOGY SECTION OF THE TOPICAL INDEX AND READ LINKS TO BUILD COMPRE-HENSION. RECORD THE CITATIONS TO THE LITERATURE FOR FUTURE REFERENCE. USE EACH TERM IN A SENTENCE.

Table 3.15   Depletion COMPLETE THIS TABLE

Terms	Search Recommended* (Semicolons are not part of the search but are used as separators.)	Citation for Definition: Provide Full Reference	Other Searches You Would Suggest
Depletion	Depletion of property		
Successful efforts	Successful efforts accounting framework		
Full cost accounting	Full cost accounting framework		
Natural resources	Natural resources		
Extraction	"extraction"		
Legal life of intangibles	Legal life of intangibles		

*Access FARS, click on File, Open, Nfo, Open, and select FASB-OP (amended), click Search, enter query.

Problems

1. Distinguish between successful efforts and full cost accounting.
2. If an oil well costing $60,000 is expected to produce 500,000 barrels and 100,000 barrels have been extracted, what is the depletion expense?

3. The debate over successful efforts and full cost accounting has been both heated and affected by political intervention. Use FARS to describe the evolution of current accounting practices as they relate to oil and gas.

4. One of the underlying concepts associated with oil and gas accounting is that of a cost center. Describe what is meant by a cost center and how it is distinct from a single discrete asset basis of accounting.

5. SELF-STUDY Q&A. **Q:** How do disclosures regarding reserves relate to oil and gas accounting? **A.** *Within FARS open the FASB-OP (amended) infobase, using Advanced Query enter the search phrase* reserve oil gas disclosure require. *The HitList references three items: FAS 19, Par. 244; FAS 69, Par. 43 and 113. FAS 69, Par. 43 explains: "The SEC initiated the development of that new accounting method (which it referred to as reserve recognition accounting [RRA]) by requiring supplemental disclosures on that basis." It likewise notes that "The SEC took those actions because it believed that neither the full cost nor the successful efforts method provided sufficient information on the financial position and operating results of oil and gas producing enterprises." Paragraph 113 is of interest due to its attention to whether disclosures are warranted for enterprises that are not publicly traded.*

Table 3.16 Impairments   Page **3-39**

■ IMPAIRMENTS

> ***Vocabulary: Create your dictionary of the following terms from FARS.***
>
> | **Basic** | **Intermediate** | **Advanced** |
> |---|---|---|
> | Captive Insurer | Allocated Contract | Cost-Sharing (Provisions of the Plan) |
> | Insurance Contract | Gross Premium | Credited Service Period |
> | Insurance Risk | Group Insurance | |
>
> CHECK THE TERMINOLOGY SECTION OF THE TOPICAL INDEX AND READ LINKS TO BUILD COMPRE-
> HENSION. RECORD THE CITATIONS TO THE LITERATURE FOR FUTURE REFERENCE. USE EACH TERM
> IN A SENTENCE.

Table 3.16   Impairments COMPLETE THIS TABLE

Terms	Search Recommended* (Semicolons are not part of the search but are used as separators.)	Citation for Definition: Provide Full Reference	Other Searches You Would Suggest
Impairment	Impairment defin*		
Idle property	"idle facility"		
Permanent improvement	"term property improvements"; "property improvements"		
Asset write-offs	Asset writeoffs		
Write-downs of assets	Writedowns of assets		
Involuntary conversion	Involuntary conversion		
Uninsured	"uninsured"; self-insured loss		
Insured	Recording insured losses; Insurance proceeds for loss; Measuring and recording insured loss on property; Loss on fire		

*Access FARS, click on File, Open, Nfo, Open, and select FASB-OP (amended), click Search, enter query.

Problems

1. If property is idle, should depreciation be recorded? Should permanent impairment be recorded? Are write-downs of assets appropriate in such a setting?

2. What is a common source of asset write-offs?

3. How does the recording of an insured involuntary conversion differ from that of an uninsured involuntary conversion?

4. Write-downs have been criticized in the literature. What is the nature of such criticism?

5. SELF-STUDY Q&A. **Q:** Explain the consequence of an impaired intangible asset.

   A. *Use the FASB-OP (amended) infobase, access Advanced Query, and type the search phrase* if an intangible asset impaired determin*. *The three hits that result are FAS 142, Par. 12 and 46 and CON 7, Par. 119. The first citation explains: "An intangible asset shall not be written down or off in the period of acquisition unless it becomes impaired during that period" and references footnote 11: "FAS142, Footnote 11—However, both Statement 2 and Interpretation 4 require amounts assigned to acquired intangible assets that are to be used in a particular research and development project and that have no alternative future use to be charged to expense at the acquisition date." The second citation explains the disclosure requirements for an impairment loss involving an intangible asset. The third citation includes a reference to FAS 121.*

6. SELF-STUDY Q&A. **Q:** FAS 121 includes the provision, in its summary, that: "Restatement of previously issued financial statements is not permitted." Use FARS to provide other examples in the official literature that specifically do not permit application retroactively.

   A. *Use the FASB-OP (amended) infobase, access Advanced Query, and type the search "not permit*" and "retroactive*". Among the HitList items are FAS 92, Par. 72 and FAS 133, Par. 48.*

Table 3.17 Intangible Assets   Page **3-41**

■ INTANGIBLE ASSETS

Vocabulary: Create your dictionary of the following terms from FARS.

Basic	Intermediate	Advanced
Amortization	Customer Relationship	Detail Program Design
Capitalize	Development	Product Design
Goodwill	Research	Product Enhancement
Intangible Asset Class	Testing	Product Maintenance Contracts
Intangible Assets	Working Model	Product Masters
Negative Goodwill		

CHECK THE TERMINOLOGY SECTION OF THE TOPICAL INDEX AND READ LINKS TO BUILD COMPRE-
HENSION. RECORD THE CITATIONS TO THE LITERATURE FOR FUTURE REFERENCE. USE EACH TERM
IN A SENTENCE.

Table 3.17   Intangible Assets COMPLETE THIS TABLE

Terms	Search Recommended* (Semicolons are not part of the search but are used as separators.)	Citation for Definition: Provide Full Reference	Other Searches You Would Suggest
Tangible assets	"tangible assets"		
Patents	Patents received or applied for; Patents are intangible		
Research and development	Research and development		
Pledged asset	"pledged asset"		
Defense cost of patent	Patent litigation; Cost of successfully defending a patent infringement		
Amortization of intangibles	Amortization of intangible assets		
Period of amortization	Period of amortization for intangible assets		
Capitalization	Capitalization intangible assets; Purchased intangibles capitalizable		
Patent dispute	Patent dispute		

*Access FARS, click on File, Open, Nfo, Open, and select FASB-OP (amended), click Search, enter query.

Problems

1. How do tangible assets differ from intangible assets?

2. Provide examples of intangible assets.

3. Since research and development costs are intended to result in a new product on which a patent will be granted, they are capitalized as an asset in the patent account. Is this statement true or false? Explain.

4. Do pledged assets differ in value from assets that are not pledged?

5. If patent rights are disputed, how are the costs of defending the patent handled in the accounting records?

6. Define the terms *goodwill* and *negative goodwill.*

7. Over what period should intangibles be amortized?

8. SELF-STUDY Q&A. **Q:** Is there a maximum life that applies to intangible assets?

   A. *Use the FASB-OP (amended) infobase, access Query, and type the search phrase* intangible maximum life. *The first hit is FAS 142, Par. B53 which specifically states: "The Board therefore concluded that a recognized intangible asset should be amortized over its useful life to the reporting entity and that there should be no limit, presumed or maximum, on that amortization period."*

Table 3.18 Current Liabilities   Page **3-43**

■ CURRENT LIABILITIES

Vocabulary: Create your dictionary of the following terms from FARS.

<u>Basic</u>	<u>Intermediate</u>	<u>Advanced</u>
Carrying Amount of the Payable	Annual Effective Tax Rate	Liability for Claim Adjustment Expenses
Compensated Absences	Constructive Obligations	Liability for Future Policy Benefits
Current Liabilities	Income Taxes Currently Payable (Refundable)	Liability for Unpaid Claims
Debt	Obligations	Pay-Related Plan
Deferral	Short-Term Obligations	Tax Consequences
Liabilities	Tax	Tax-Planning Strategy

CHECK THE TERMINOLOGY SECTION OF THE TOPICAL INDEX AND READ LINKS TO BUILD COMPRE-HENSION. RECORD THE CITATIONS TO THE LITERATURE FOR FUTURE REFERENCE. USE EACH TERM IN A SENTENCE.

Table 3.18   Current Liabilities COMPLETE THIS TABLE

Terms	**Search Recommended* (Semicolons are not part of the search but are used as separators.)**	**Citation for Definition: Provide Full Reference**	**Other Searches You Would Suggest**
Accounts payable	Accounts payable defin*		
Notes payable	"notes payable";		
	distinction in notes and accounts payable		
Utility bills	Utility bills;		
	Electricity used to light;		
	Obligations for electricity used		
Payroll	Payroll expense and obligations defin*		
Property taxes	Property taxes		
Interim financial statements	Interim financial statements defin*;		
	Interim financial reporting;		
	Integral interim statements		

*Access FARS, click on <u>File</u>, <u>Open</u>, <u>Nfo</u>, <u>Open</u>, and select <u>FASB-OP (amended)</u>, click <u>Search</u>, enter query.

Problems

1. How do accounts payable differ from notes payable?

2. Utility bills are typically recorded by a company upon payment, as is payroll. If the fiscal year-end precedes a monthly utility bill's payment by one week and payday by two days, how are such obligations commonly recorded?

3. In January, Kiernan Company paid $24,000 of property taxes. The company prepares interim financial statements. What should be reflected as property tax expense for the first quarter?

4. Describe the circumstance that results in a current liability for deferred taxes.

5. SELF-STUDY Q&A. **Q:** Identify the discussion in FARS that addresses the classification of short-term and long-term liabilities, as well as receivables.

   A. *Within FARS open the FASB-OP (amended) infobase, then use Advanced Query, and type short-term and long-term classification receivables and liabilities. The results will highlight ARB43Ch. 3A,Par. 7; CON7, Par. 119; and Table of Contents FASB Statements. Read through the first citation, including its footnotes to gain a clear understanding of the distinction between current and noncurrent.*

6. SELF-STUDY Q&A. **Q:** Identify the discussion in FARS that addresses the treatment in interim financial statements of changes in accounting principle.

   A. *Within FARS, access the Topical Index, go to I and then Interim Financial Reporting. One of the subheadings is Definition which also has a subhead of "Ordinary Income or Loss" that cites FAS144, Par. C19 and I73.402, as well as FAS154, Par. C18 and FIN18, Par. 5. FAS154, Par. C18 directly addresses the question.*

Table 3.19 Contingencies   Page **3-45**

■ CONTINGENCIES

Vocabulary: Create your dictionary of the following terms from FARS.

Basic	**Intermediate**	**Advanced**
Contingencies	Contingency Consideration	Conditional Contract
Probable	General Reserve	Extended Warranty Contracts
Reasonably Possible	Obligations	Retroactive Benefits
Remote	Preacquisition Contingencies	Retroactive Reinsurance
Uncertainty		

CHECK THE TERMINOLOGY SECTION OF THE TOPICAL INDEX AND READ LINKS TO BUILD COMPRE-
HENSION. RECORD THE CITATIONS TO THE LITERATURE FOR FUTURE REFERENCE. USE EACH TERM
IN A SENTENCE.

Table 3.19   Contingencies COMPLETE THIS TABLE

Terms	Search Recommended* (Semicolons are not part of the search but are used as separators.)	Citation for Definition: Provide Full Reference	Other Searches You Would Suggest
Warranty obligations	Warranty obligations		
Retroactive adjustment	Retroactive adjustment reversal of revenue or billings		
Range	Range of estimated contingency		
Litigation	Litigation		

*Access FARS, click on <u>File</u>, <u>Open</u>, Nfo, <u>Open</u>, and select <u>FASB-OP (amended)</u>, click <u>Search</u>, enter query.

Problems

1. Under what conditions must liabilities be accrued on the books of a company for contingencies?

2. Joe Dillon Company has estimated its long-term warranty obligations to range from $600,000 to $700,000 on product A. Its new product B also has a warranty, but the company has no basis for quantifying the amount of customers' potential claims. How would these long-term warranty obligations be reported in the financial statements, and why? [Also check the <u>sec.gov site</u>].

3. The health care industry has been affected by the existence of predefined procedures and related cost-reimbursement formulas for physicians' services. Insurers regularly audit the billings received for their compliance with guidelines on appropriate procedures, as well as for the reasonableness of the time charges. Medicare diagnostic related group (DRG) payment rates for wages often result in retroactive adjustment. An example of a retroactive adjustment would be where a billing by a physician was considered to be too high for the procedure performed, or the procedure was deemed unnecessary for the circumstances at hand. How should this affect

accounting (i.e., how would you expect the anticipation of retroactive adjustments to be captured by the information system)?

4. A suit for breach of contract seeking damages of $1,000,000 was filed against a company on July 1, 20x1. The company's legal counsel believes that an unfavorable outcome is probable. A reasonable estimate of the court's award to the plaintiff is in the range of $100,000 to $500,000. No amount within this range is a better estimate of potential damages than any other amount. What should be recorded in the financial statements?

5. SELF-STUDY Q&A. **Q:** The accounting treatment of guarantees has been described as distinct from the usual approach to contingencies. Find the passage in FARS that recognizes such a debate.

A. *Within FARS open the FASB-OP (amended) infobase, using Query, type the search phrase* guarantee* not contingent liabilit*. *The first item on the HitList is FIN 45, Par. A39 that states:* "If, at the inception of the guarantee, no liability is recognized under Statement 5 for the contingent loss related to the guarantee, the liability to be initially recognized for the guarantor's obligations under the guarantee should be the fair value of the guarantee. In the unusual circumstance that, at the inception of the guarantee, a liability is recognized under Statement 5 for the related contingent loss, the liability to be initially recognized for the guarantor's obligation under the guarantee should be the greater of (a) the amount that satisfies the fair value objective as discussed in paragraph 9 or (b) the contingent liability amount required to be recognized at inception of the guarantee by Statement 5." *This passage explains the distinction that arises but does not bear out the debate. In order to find the citation for the debate, use the search phrase* respond* guarantee* not contingency 5 *and the first hit is FIN 45, Par. A36 which states:* "Respondents also commonly argued that the requirement to record a liability for the guarantor's obligation is not a legitimate interpretation of Statement 5 but rather a change in GAAP. Similar to the arguments concerning Concepts Statement 6, respondents stated that the requirement to recognize a liability for an event that is unlikely to occur (performance under the guarantee) is a significant change in accounting from that required by Statement 5. Respondents argued that a liability should be recognized only when the loss under the guarantee is both probable and reasonably estimable, in accordance with Statement 5. Other respondents stated that an Interpretation could not address recognizing a liability for a noncontingent obligation to stand ready and still be an interpretation of Statement 5 because Statement 5 addresses only loss contingencies. They argued that any requirement for recognition of a liability amounted to a change in GAAP and could come only through the issuance of a Statement of Financial Accounting Standards."

Table 3.20 Long-Term Liabilities   Page **3-47**

■ LONG-TERM LIABILITIES

Vocabulary: Create your dictionary of the following terms from FARS.

<u>Basic</u>	<u>Intermediate</u>	<u>Advanced</u>
Amortization	Callable Obligations	Attached Call
Collateral	Effective Settlement	Call Option
Debt Security	Expected Losses	Derecognize
Discount Rate	Financial Liability	Equitable Obligations
Effective Interest Rate	Indirect Guarantee of Indebtedness of Others	Federal Home Loan Mortgage Corporation (FHLMC)
Implicit Rate	Interest Rate Implicit in the Lease	Federal National Mortgage Association (FNMA)
Interest Rate	Minimum Guarantee	Gap Commitment
Long-Term Obligations	Put Option	Government National Mortgage Association (GNMA)
Market	Reacquisition Price of Debt	Internal Reserve Method
Security	Subjective Acceleration Clause	Servicing Asset
Security Interest	Subordinated Financial Support	Servicing Liability

CHECK THE TERMINOLOGY SECTION OF THE TOPICAL INDEX AND READ LINKS TO BUILD COMPREHENSION. RECORD THE CITATIONS TO THE LITERATURE FOR FUTURE REFERENCE. USE EACH TERM IN A SENTENCE.

Table 3.20   Long-Term Liabilities COMPLETE THIS TABLE

Terms	Search Recommended* (Semicolons are not part of the search but are used as separators.)	Citation for Definition: Provide Full Reference	Other Searches You Would Suggest
Face value	Face value of liability is defined as glossary		
Coupon rate	"coupon rate"		
Real rate	Real versus nominal rate of interest		
Nominal rate	"nominal rate"		
Stated rates	"stated rate"		
Rates incurred	Interest rate incurred		
Rate paid	Interest rate paid on liability		
Market rates	"market rates"		

Terms	Search Recommended* (Semicolons are not part of the search but are used as separators.)	Citation for Definition: Provide Full Reference	Other Searches You Would Suggest
Unsecured debt	Unsecured debt; Collateral		
Subordinated debt	Subordinated debt defin* glossary		
Callable convertible debt	Callable convertible debt defin* glossary		
Term bond	Fixed term of existence for bonds; Example bond liabilities financial instrument		
Serial bond	"serial bonds"		
Debt swaps	Debt swap* transaction* defin*		
Defeasance	Defeasance defin* glossary; Accounting treatment for defeasance		
Straight-line amortization	"straight-line amortization"		
Premium	"bond premium"		
Discount	Bond discount defin*		
Imputed rate	Imputation of interest defin* How to imput* interest		

*Access FARS, click on <u>File</u>, <u>Open</u>, <u>Nfo</u>, <u>Open</u>, and select <u>FASB-OP (amended)</u>, click <u>Search</u>, enter query.

Problems

1. Practitioners have posed the following question to those who set the standards: Should long-term debt be classified as a current liability if the long-term debt agreement contains a subjective acceleration clause that may accelerate the due date? How do you believe the standard-setters responded? Why? (*Hint*: Examine the FASB Technical Bulletins.)

2. If a 10 percent, $100,000 bond is issued in each of the following markets, would the proceeds be greater than, equal to, or less than the face value of (a) 15 percent market? (b) 8 percent market? (c) 10 percent market?

3. Interest rates are referred to as coupon rates, real rates, effective rates, nominal rates, stated rates, rates incurred, rates paid, and market rates. Which of these terms are synonymous and which differ from each other?

Table 3.20 Long-Term Liabilities   Page **3-49**

4. Define the following terms: (a) unsecured debt, (b) subordinated debt, (c) callable convertible debt, (d) term bond, (e) serial bond, (f) debt swaps, (g) defeasance.

5. Peterson Incorporated issued a $500,000, 10 percent, 20-year bond at 97. Record the issuance of the bond and amortization for the first year using the straight-line method. Is the straight-line method of amortizing a bond issued at a discount acceptable under generally accepted accounting principles (GAAP)? Why or why not?

6. You want to furnish your dormitory room. A local furniture store advertises that you can buy any desk in the store on September 1, 20x1, and not pay the bill for two years (i.e., not until September 1, 20x3). No interest will be charged. You buy a desk for $300. (a) What is the stated interest on this transaction? Is this the interest you incurred? Why or why not? (b) Assume you determine that the value of the desk is $270. What was the implicit interest rate? (c) Assume that you cannot determine the value of either the desk or the note, but you have an imputed borrowing rate of 10 percent. What should the recorded value of the desk be?

7. SELF-STUDY Q&A. **Q:** Use FARS to support the assertion that a Premium on Bonds Payable is not a liability in its own right.

A. Go to V in the Topical Index and you will find the entry VALUATION ALLOWANCES with the subhead of Definition, linked to CON6, Par. 34, V18.401, and CON6, Par. 43. The last cite specifically supports the assertion, explaining that such "valuation accounts" as premiums or discounts on bonds payable "are part of the related liability and are neither liabilities in their own right nor assets."

■ STOCKHOLDERS' EQUITY

Vocabulary: Create your dictionary of the following terms from FARS.

Basic	Intermediate	Advanced
Common Stock	Comprehensive Income	Cumulative Accounting Adjustments
Convertible Debt	Conversion of Debt	Equity Restructuring
Cost Method	Conversion Rate	Restricted Share
Equity	Convertible Security	Restricted Stock
Equity Method Investments	Junior Stock	Reverse Treasury Stock Method
Equity Security	Other Comprehensive Income	Time of Restructuring
Market	Participant	Treasury-Stock Method
Preferred Stock	Participation Right	Troubled Debt Restructuring

CHECK THE TERMINOLOGY SECTION OF THE TOPICAL INDEX AND READ LINKS TO BUILD COMPRE-HENSION. RECORD THE CITATIONS TO THE LITERATURE FOR FUTURE REFERENCE. USE EACH TERM IN A SENTENCE.

Table 3.21   Stockholders' Equity COMPLETE THIS TABLE

Terms	Search Recommended* (Semicolons are not part of the search but are used as separators.)	Citation for Definition: Provide Full Reference	Other Searches You Would Suggest
Stockholders' equity	"balance-sheet presentation of stockholders' equity"		
Par value	"par value"		
Market value	"market value"		
Owners' equity	Owners' equity defin*		
Proprietorship	"proprietorship"		
Partnership	"partner"		
Voting rights	"voting rights"		
Cumulative	"cumulative preferred stock"		
Preemptive	"preemptive"		
Participating	"participating preferred stock"		
Convertible	"convertible"		
Treasury stock	Treasury stock defin*		

*Access FARS, click on File, Open, Nfo, Open, and select FASB-OP (amended), click Search, enter query.

Table 3.21 Stockholders' Equity   Page **3-51**

Problems

1. Are *par value* and *market value* synonymous? What purpose do they serve?

2. How do owners' equity accounts for a proprietorship differ from those of a partnership?

3. A company issues straight debt (bonds) with a 5 percent stated rate, convertible debt A with a 4.5 percent stated rate, and convertible debt B with a 2 percent stated rate. Common stock yields approximately an 8 percent return. Describe the promises granted by convertible debt and their relative value to the bondholder and explain how, if at all, they influence the accounting treatment.

4. Outline the principal types of transactions that can influence stockholders' equity.

5. What rights are typically granted to common stockholders? Briefly describe the nature of each right. Describe the typical differences between preferred stock and common stock.

6. Indicate whether the following attributes commonly apply to common stock (C) or preferred stock (P): (a) voting rights; (b) participative; (c) cumulative; (d) preemptive; (e) convertible.

7. JKenny Incorporated issued 500,000 shares of stock for $20 a share. The par value of the stock was $10 a share. It concurrently reissued 1,000 shares of treasury stock, previously purchased for $15,000, at the same $20-per-share market price. The corporation uses the cost method of accounting for treasury stock. Record the necessary journal entries.

8. SELF-STUDY Q&A. **Q**: Find the FARS location where a Statement of Investments by and Distributions to Owners is described.

   A. *The Topical Index, under S, has the entry STATEMENT OF INVESTMENTS BY AND DIS-TRIBUTIONS TO OWNERS with a subhead labeled "Description, Nature, and Recognition Considerations" with a link to CON5, Par. 55-57. Read through this material.*

■ **CONTRIBUTED CAPITAL**

Vocabulary: Create your dictionary of the following terms from FARS.

Basic	Intermediate	Advanced
Contribution	General Reserve	Contributory Plan

CHECK THE TERMINOLOGY SECTION OF THE TOPICAL INDEX AND READ LINKS TO BUILD COMPRE-
HENSION. RECORD THE CITATIONS TO THE LITERATURE FOR FUTURE REFERENCE. USE EACH TERM
IN A SENTENCE.

Table 3.22   Contributed Capital COMPLETE THIS TABLE

Terms	Search Recommended* (Semicolons are not part of the search but are used as separators.)	Citation for Definition: Provide Full Reference	Other Searches You Would Suggest
Contributed capital	Invested and earned contributed capital;		
	The contributed portion of capital		
Gifts	Gifts by owners to corporations;		
	Recording of gifts to not-for-profit organizations		
Paid-in capital in excess of par	Stated capital paid-in capital in excess of par		

*Access FARS, click on File, Open, Nfo, Open, and select FASB-OP (amended), click Search, enter query.

Problems

1. A gift of land worth $50,000 was granted to a corporation by a municipality. How would this be recorded?

2. SELF-STUDY Q&A. **Q:** Identify the Characteristics of Equity of Business Enterprises, using FARS.
   A. *Within FARS, open the FASB-OP (amended) infobase, using Query type "characteristics of equity of business enterprises" and you will receive the hit CON6, Par. 212. Alternatively, access the Topical Index, go to C, click on* capital, Description, *and that precise paragraph will likewise be identified. In particular, the discussion describes capital contributions.*

Table 3.23 Retained Earnings   Page **3-53**

■ RETAINED EARNINGS

Vocabulary: Create your dictionary of the following terms from FARS.

Basic	**Intermediate**	**Advanced**
Dividends	Distributions to Owners	Dividends to Policyholders
Stock Dividend	Stock Split	General Reserve

CHECK THE TERMINOLOGY SECTION OF THE TOPICAL INDEX AND READ LINKS TO BUILD COMPRE-HENSION. RECORD THE CITATIONS TO THE LITERATURE FOR FUTURE REFERENCE. USE EACH TERM IN A SENTENCE.

Table 3.23   Retained Earnings COMPLETE THIS TABLE

Terms	Search Recommended* (Semicolons are not part of the search but are used as separators.)	Citation for Definition: Provide Full Reference	Other Searches You Would Suggest
Retained earnings	Presentation of retained earnings		
Cumulative preferred stock	Cumulative preferred stock		
Date of declaration	Date of declaration		
Plant expansion	Appropriat* of retained earnings for plant expansion		
Appropriations	Appropriations		

*Access FARS, click on File, Open, Nfo, Open, and select FASB-OP (amended), click Search, enter query.

Problems

1. Is a dividend analogous to interest expense? Explain your response.

2. Bill Jones Incorporated has not declared dividends on its $100 par-value 6 percent preferred stock for two years. This year there are 40,000 shares outstanding, and dividends are declared for $2 million. If the preferred stock is cumulative, what journal entry will be recorded as of the date of declaration?

3. One thousand shares of an $18 par value stock of Drew Sheehan Corporation was subjected to a three-for-one stock split. Prior to the stock split, the market value of the shares was $54. Describe the effects of the stock split in specific terms.

4. Andrea Tecce Corporation with $90,000 retained earnings wishes to earmark $10,000 for an intended purchase of land for plant expansion. Record the necessary journal entry. How does this entry affect total earnings?

5. SELF-STUDY Q&A. **Q:** Can treasury stock transactions affect retained earnings? Support your response with a citation from FARS.

A. Yes. By accessing FASB-OP (amended) and using Advanced Query in FARS, you can enter the search phrase treasury stock retained earnings *to identify ARB 43, Ch. 1B, Par. 7, which describes the effect on retained earnings.*

6. SELF-STUDY Q&A. **Q:** Can stock retirements affect retained earnings? Support your response with a citation from FARS.

A. Yes. By accessing FASB-OP (amended) and using Advanced Query in FARS, you can enter the search phrase stock retirement retained earnings *to identify ARB 43, Ch. 1B, Par. 7, which describes the effect on retained earnings.*

7. SELF-STUDY Q&A. **Q:** Can restatements affect retained earnings? Support your response with a citation from FARS.

A. Yes. By accessing FASB-OP (amended) and using Advanced Query in FARS, you can enter the search phrase restatement retained earnings to identify APB 9, Par. 26, which observes: "When financial statements for a single period only are presented, this disclosure should indicate the effects of such restatement on the balance of retained earnings at the beginning of the period and on the net income of the immediately preceding period." Also retrieved will be FAS 154, Par. 25, which is particularly on point.

Table 3.24 Dilutive Securities   Page **3-55**

■ DILUTIVE SECURITIES

Vocabulary: Create your dictionary of the following terms from FARS.

<u>Basic</u>	<u>Intermediate</u>	<u>Advanced</u>
Economic Interest in an Entity	Blackout Period	Broker-Assisted Cashless Exercise
Employee	Combination Award	Calculated Value
Employee Share Ownership Plan	Combination Plan	Closed-Form Model
Exercise Price	Derived Service Period	Cross-Volatility
Freestanding Financial Instrument	Dilution (Dilutive)	Excess Tax Benefit
Grant Date	Explicit Service Period	Lattice Model
Issuance of an Equity Instrument	Fixed Award	Market Condition
Issued, Issuance, or Issuing of an Equity Instrument	Implicit Service Period	Modification
Principal Stockholder	Intrinsic Value	Performance Condition or Performance Award
Reload Option and Option Granted with a Reload Feature	Minimum Value	Replacement Award
Settle, Settled, or Settlement of an Award	Nonvested Shares	Requisite Service Period (and Requisite Service)
Share Option	Nonvested Stock	Restriction
Share-Based Payment (or Compensation) Arrangement	Service Inception Date	Service Condition
Share-Based Payment (or Compensation) Transaction	Service Period	Share Unit
Stock Appreciation Rights	Tandem Award	Short-Term Inducement
Stock Option	Tandem Plan	Variable Stock Option, Purchase and Award Plans
Stock-Based Compensation Plan	Warrant	Vest, Vesting, or Vested
Terms of a Share-Based Payment Award		Volatility

CHECK THE TERMINOLOGY SECTION OF THE TOPICAL INDEX AND READ LINKS TO BUILD COMPRE-HENSION. RECORD THE CITATIONS TO THE LITERATURE FOR FUTURE REFERENCE. USE EACH TERM IN A SENTENCE.

Table 3.24   Dilutive Securities COMPLETE THIS TABLE

Terms	Search Recommended* (Semicolons are not part of the search but are used as separators.)	Citation for Definition: Provide Full Reference	Other Searches You Would Suggest
Look-back share options	"look-back"		
Graded vesting	"graded vesting"		

*Access FARS, click on <u>File</u>, <u>Open</u>, <u>Nfo</u>, <u>Open</u>, and select <u>FASB-OP (amended)</u>, click <u>Search</u>, enter query.

Problems

1. What is the key advantage of stock appreciation rights over stock options from the perspective of the holder?

2. What is a warrant?

3. In 2006, a series of articles in the *Wall Street Journal* appeared on the topic of "backdating" investigations involving stock options. As an example, the July 1, 2006 front-page story indicated "Authorities Signal Hard Line as Backdating Investigations Extend to Over 80 Companies." Does FARS address this issue? Explain. [*Hint*: Check the <u>sec.gov site.</u>]

4. SELF-STUDY Q&A. **Q:** Identify that cite in FARS clarifying the effect of dilutive securities on earnings per share.
   A. *By accessing FASB-OP (amended) and using Query in FARS, you can enter the search phrase "dilutive securities" to identify FAS 135, Par. 4.*

5. SELF-STUDY Q&A. **Q:** International Rectifier's 8-K filed May 11, 2006 reported that "After reviewing its accounting for share-based payment awards pursuant to Statement of Financial Accounting Standards No. 123R, 'Share-Based Payments,' the Company determined, as described below, that it should correct the classification in its consolidated cash flow statements for the excess tax benefits generated from the exercise of stock options. In the first and second quarters of fiscal 2006 the Company had presented these excess tax benefits as operating cash flows, while SFAS 123R requires their presentation as financing cash flows." Identify the specific FARS cite that sets forth the requirement erroneously applied to the first two quarters of 2006. Why might such an error have arisen?
   A. *Access FARS, open FASB-OP (amended), and use Query to enter the search phrase* excess tax benefits statement of cash flows classif* financing. *The result will be FAS 123(R) Par. A96, which explicitly sets forth the requirement. The second item on the HitList is Par. B223, which provides some insight as to why such an error may have arisen. FAS 123(R) includes an exception to the general approach in FAS 95. This problem bears out the importance of timely attention to the recent developments in standard setting because such exceptions often arise as context varies.*

Table 3.25 Earnings Per Share   Page **3-57**

■ EARNINGS PER SHARE

Vocabulary: Create your dictionary of the following terms from FARS.

Basic	Intermediate	Advanced
Antidilution	Dilution (Dilutive)	Call Option
Basic Earnings per Share	Exercise Price	Contingent Issuance
Diluted Earnings per Share	If-Converted Method	Contingent Stock Agreement
Earnings per Share	Option	Contingently Issuable Shares
Income Available to Common Stockholders	Potential Common Stock	Purchased Call Option
Weighted Average Number of Shares	Rights Issue	Reverse Treasury Stock Method

CHECK THE TERMINOLOGY SECTION OF THE TOPICAL INDEX AND READ LINKS TO BUILD COMPRE-HENSION. RECORD THE CITATIONS TO THE LITERATURE FOR FUTURE REFERENCE. USE EACH TERM IN A SENTENCE.

Table 3.25   Earnings Per Share COMPLETE THIS TABLE

Terms	Search Recommended* (Semicolons are not part of the search but are used as separators.)	Citation for Definition: Provide Full Reference	Other Searches You Would Suggest
Per share computations	Required disclosure of per share information;		
	Cash flow per share earnings per share;		
	"computing basic eps"		
Fully diluted earnings per share	Simplify compute fully diluted EPS		

*Access FARS, click on <u>F</u>ile, <u>O</u>pen, <u>N</u>fo, <u>O</u>pen, and select <u>FASB-OP (amended)</u>, click <u>Search</u>, enter query.

Problems

1. What is typically reported in per-share terms on the statement of earnings?
2. What is the difference between earnings per share and fully diluted earnings per share?
3. SELF-STUDY Q&A. **Q**: Find the FARS location where a Statement of Earnings and Comprehensive Income is described. How has earnings per share disclosure reflected the concept of "all inclusive income"?
   A. *The Topical Index, under S, contains the entry STATEMENT OF EARNINGS AND COMPRE-HENSIVE INCOME with the subhead "Description, Nature, and Recognition Considerations,"*

linked to CON5, Par. 30-41. Specific mention of "all inclusive income" within Par. 35 elaborates on this concept and Par. 34 depicts the separate line items that may appear on a statement of income. The presentation of earnings per share from continuing operations, as distinct from earnings per share associated with extraordinary items is an example of the reflection of all-inclusive income on the face of the income statement.

4. SELF-STUDY Q&A. **Q**: Does FARS indicate that restatement of earnings per share is proscribed?

   A. *No. If you use the Advanced Query capability on the FASB-OP (amended) infobase and apply the search phrase* earnings per share proscribe, *only one cite is identified, which is FAS 16, Par. 21, and it specifically advises: "This Statement is also not intended to proscribe restatements of earnings per share that are required by APB Opinions No. 15, 'Earnings Per Share,' and 16 or by other APB Opinions and FASB Statements."*

   However, admonitions also appear in the FARS database regarding earning per share disclosures more generally. By using the Query capability with the same search phrase, the first cite remains the same, but a later item in the HitList cites FAS 95, Par. 123, containing the admonition: "To report other data on a per share basis invites the danger that investors, creditors, and others may confuse those measures with the conventional accounting measure of earnings per share."

Table 3.26 Investments   Page **3-59**

■ INVESTMENTS

Vocabulary: Create your dictionary of the following terms from FARS.

Basic	**Intermediate**	**Advanced**
Business Combination	Corporate Joint Ventures	Beneficial Interests
Consolidated Statements	Cost Method	Consolidated Affiliate of the Transferror
Control	Earnings or Losses of an Investee	Contingency Consideration
Investee	Equity Method Investments	Transfer
Investments by Owners	Pooling-of-Interests Method	Transferee
Investor	Purchase Method	Transferor
Subsidiary		

CHECK THE TERMINOLOGY SECTION OF THE TOPICAL INDEX AND READ LINKS TO BUILD COMPRE-
HENSION. RECORD THE CITATIONS TO THE LITERATURE FOR FUTURE REFERENCE. USE EACH TERM
IN A SENTENCE.

Table 3.26   Investments COMPLETE THIS TABLE

Terms	Search Recommended* (Semicolons are not part of the search but are used as separators.)	Citation for Definition: Provide Full Reference	Other Searches You Would Suggest
Investment	Accounting for investments in stock$ other companies		
Marketable securities	"equity securities"		

*Access FARS, click on <u>F</u>ile, <u>O</u>pen, <u>N</u>fo, <u>O</u>pen, and select <u>FASB-OP (amended)</u>, click <u>S</u>earch, enter query.

Problems

1. Distinguish between pooling of interests and purchase-based consolidations. Which is proscribed by generally accepted accounting principles (GAAP)?

2. If an investor holds 15 percent of a stock or 25 percent of a stock, does that difference in holdings have an effect on the accounting treatment of the investor? Be specific. What if that same investor held 60 percent of a company's stock?

3. SELF-STUDY Q&A. **Q:** Where is the topic "common control" discussed by FARS?

    A. The Topical Index, under C, the entry contains "Common Control" and refers to the definition of this term in Relation to Statement 141 which is EITF 02-5. Specific mention is made that the Task Force did not reach a consensus on the issue of how to determine whether common control of separate entities exists. It likewise provides an example of SEC guidance being highlighted in an unresolved EITF setting.

■ REVENUE RECOGNITION

Vocabulary: Create your dictionary of the following terms from FARS.

Basic	Intermediate	Advanced
Realization	Advance Royalty	Contingent Rentals
Realized, Realizable	Repurchase Agreement (Repo)	Customer Support
Recognition	Reverse Repurchase Agreement (Reverse Repo)	Maintenance
Substantive Terms Unrealized	Royalties	Service Providing Efforts

CHECK THE TERMINOLOGY SECTION OF THE TOPICAL INDEX AND READ LINKS TO BUILD COMPREHENSION. RECORD THE CITATIONS TO THE LITERATURE FOR FUTURE REFERENCE. USE EACH TERM IN A SENTENCE.

Table 3.27   Revenue Recognition COMPLETE THIS TABLE

Terms	Search Recommended* (Semicolons are not part of the search but are used as separators.)	Citation for Definition: Provide Full Reference	Other Searches You Would Suggest
Line items	Line items def*; Sequence of line items assets liquidity		
Advances from customers	"advances from customers"		
Unearned revenue	"unearned revenue"		
Completed-contract method	"completed contract method"		
Percentage of completion method	"Percentage of completion method"		
Cash basis accounting	"cash basis accounting"		
Installment sales	"installment sales"; "installment method"; revenue recognition installment sales method retail land sales		
Substance versus form	Substance versus form		

*Access FARS, click on File, Open, Nfo, Open, and select FASB-OP (amended), click Search, enter query.

Table 3.27 Revenue Recognition   Page **3-61**

Problems

1. What type of line item is "advances from customers"? Is this type of line item the same as "unearned revenue"? Why?

2. Distinguish between revenue realization and recognition.

3. How does the completed-contract method differ from the percentage-of-completion approach to income recognition for a long-term construction contractor?

4. Give an example of when a type of cash-basis accounting is prescribed by GAAP and why this is the case.

5. How does the idea of substance over form relate to revenue recognition?

6. SELF-STUDY Q&A. **Q**: Use the Search capability within the tool bar of FARS, with the FASB-OP (amended) infobase open, to narrow the HitList to FSP documents that direct attention to revenue recognition. What are the hits identified?

   A. *On the tool bar, click* <u>Search</u> *and then click* <u>Search FSP documents only</u>. *Enter the query* revenue recogn* *and eight items are identified. Specifically, the hits refer to FSP FASB 97-1, superseded FSP FASB 106-1, FSP FASB 106-2, FSP FASB 143-1, FSP FASB 150-4, FSP FIN 45-3, FSP EITF 85-24-2, FSP SOP 94-6-1. However, the FSP FASB 150-4 demonstrates the inexact nature of word searches, since it highlights the term "Revenue" within the context of the "Internal Revenue Code" and later refers to recognition of expense. The number of FSPs identified suggests the pervasive attention to revenue recognition within authoritative literature.*

■ ACCOUNTING FOR INCOME TAXES

Vocabulary: Create your dictionary of the following terms from FARS.

Basic	Intermediate	Advanced
Discount Rate	Carrybacks	Deductible Temporary Difference
Event	Carryforwards	Deferred Tax Asset
Income Taxes	Current Tax Expense or Benefit	Deferred Tax Expense or Benefit
Tax	Deferral	Deferred Tax Liability
Tax Consequences	Income Taxes Currently Payable (Refundable)	Taxable Temporary Difference
Taxable Income	Tax-Planning Strategy	Temporary Difference

CHECK THE TERMINOLOGY SECTION OF THE TOPICAL INDEX AND READ LINKS TO BUILD COMPRE-HENSION. RECORD THE CITATIONS TO THE LITERATURE FOR FUTURE REFERENCE. USE EACH TERM IN A SENTENCE.

Table 3.28   Accounting For Income Taxes COMPLETE THIS TABLE

Terms	Search Recommended* (Semicolons are not part of the search but are used as separators.)	Citation for Definition: Provide Full Reference	Other Searches You Would Suggest
Accelerated Cost Recovery System (ACRS)	"acrs guidelines"; acrs rollover effect		
Rollover effect	Tax strategy of rolling over equipment before reversal of timing effects; Rollover effect		
Payroll withholding taxes	"payroll withholding"; payroll withholding tax		
Taxation of partnerships	Taxation of partnerships		
Timing differences	"timing differences"		
Permanent differences	"permanent differences"		
Liability method	"liability method"		

Table 3.28 Accounting For Income Taxes   Page **3-63**

Terms	Search Recommended* (Semicolons are not part of the search but are used as separators.)	Citation for Definition: Provide Full Reference	Other Searches You Would Suggest
Deferred method	"deferred method"; fas 109 accounting for income tax		
Expected tax rate	Expected tax rate		
More likely than not	"more likely than not"; more likely than not		
Discounting	Discount* of tax liabilit*		

*Access FARS, click on <u>File</u>, <u>Open</u>, <u>Nfo</u>, <u>Open</u>, and select <u>FASB-OP (amended)</u>, click <u>Search</u>, enter query.

Problems

1. A common line item in financial statements was "deferred charges," as was "deferred taxes." Does the accounting framework provide clear direction as to whether such balances are likely to be debits or credits? Why or why not? Do you believe this somehow detracts from the elegance of double-entry accounting? Why or why not?

2. Is the Accelerated Cost Recovery System (ACRS) method for tax purposes more analogous to the straight-line or accelerated method of depreciation? Explain your response.

3. What is a sign that Steve Turley Corporation, or any other company, is effectively using the rollover effect to its advantage?

4. How do payroll withholding taxes affect a company's recorded income?

5. How are partnerships taxed?

6. On April 8, 1985, the FASB presented its tentative conclusion that the effects of tax timing differences are assets and liabilities (liability method), rather than deferred debits and credits (deferred method). While the deferred method does not adjust balances to reflect a subsequent change in taxes, the proposed liability method uses expected tax rates and adjusts balances for future changes. (a) Under the new tax rates applied in 1988, what would be the expected change in deferred tax balances under the liability method when compared with those of 1987? Would there be a predictable income effect? (b) If discounting is applied to deferred taxes, what are the expected effects on reported liabilities? [*Hint*: An excellent resource regarding tax rates at different points in time is "Instructional Resource: Using Tax History to Teach the Concepts of Tax Planning," by William D. Samson, *Issues in Accounting Education* 13(3):655-92, especially Table 1, pp. 679-81, August 1998.]

7. In letters responding to the FASB's discussion memorandum entitled "An Analysis of the Issues Related to Accounting for Income Taxes," approximately 88 percent opposed discounting of deferred taxes. (a) What do you believe are the reasons for this opposition? (b) Do you personally favor or oppose the discounting of deferred taxes? Why?

8. SELF-STUDY Q&A. **Q**: Is the phrase "deferred tax" used within the FASB Technical Bulletins? Where and how many times?

   A. *Use the Search capability within the toolbar of FARS, with the FASB-OP (amended) infobase open, then narrow the HitList by selecting <u>Search Within a Single OP Document Type.</u> Click on FASB Technical Bulletins twice and it will appear in the Document type box. Then click your cursor in the query for: box and type "deferred tax." Three hits are identified. All are located in FTB87-2. In order to view the higlighted term for the first cite, you must access the popup screen for the second footnote paragraph 3. The second cite is Par. 38. The third cite shows the inexactness of word searches, because it highlights words in two distinct headings in columnar format: Deferred Charge and Tax Expense.*

9. SELF-STUDY Q&A. **Q**: Use FARS to locate in the professional literature guidance an example of how to account for a change in tax rates.

   A. *Open the FASB-OP (amended) infobase and the Advanced Search capability, entering the phrase* change in "tax rates"/10 accounting treatment. *The citation identified is FSP FAS 109-2. Note paragraph 4 in particular and click on the diamond icon.*

Table 3.29 Accounting For Pensions   Page **3-65**

■ ACCOUNTING FOR PENSIONS

Vocabulary: Create your dictionary of the following terms from FARS.

Basic	Intermediate	Advanced
Actuarial Present Value	Assumptions	Accumulated Benefit Obligation
Benefit	Attribution	Accumulated Plan Benefits
Benefits	Benefit Formula	Actual Return on Plan Assets Component (of Net Periodic Pension Cost)
Defined Benefit Pension Plan	Benefit Information	Actuarial Present Value of Accumulated Plan Benefits
Defined Contribution Pension Plan	Benefit Information Date	Benefit/Years-of-Service Approach
ERISA	Benefit Security	Career-Average-Pay Formula (Career-Average-Pay Plan)
Fund	Benefits of Servicing	Expected Long-Term Rate of Return on Plan Assets
Gain or Loss	Contributory Plan	Expected Return on Plan Assets
Measurement Date	Curtailment	Explicit (Approach to) Assumptions
Net Periodic Pension Cost	Funding Agency	Final-Pay Formula (Final-Pay Plan)
Pension Benefits	Funding Policy	Flat-Benefit Formula (Flat-Benefit Plan)
Pension Plans	Mortality Rate	Gain or Loss Component (of Net Periodic Pension Cost)
Plan Administrator	Multiemployer Plan	Interest Cost Component (of Net Periodic Pension Cost)
Plan Amendment	Multiple-Employer Plan	Market-Related Value of Plan Assets
Plan Assets	Plan's Benefit Formula	Nonparticipating Annuity Contracts
Plan Curtailment	Return on Plan Assets	Participating Annuity Contract
Prepaid Pension Cost	Service	PBGC (Pension Benefit Guaranty Corporation)
Prior Service Cost	Settlements	Pension Benefit Formula (Plan's Benefit Formula or Benefit Formula)
Projected Benefit Obligation	Single-Employer Plan	Plan Assets Available for Benefits
Retroactive Benefits	Suspension	Plan Termination/Reestablishment
Supplemental Actuarial Value	Turnover	Service Cost Component (of Net Periodic Pension Cost)
Vested Benefit Obligation		Unfunded Accrued Pension Cost

Basic	**Intermediate**	**Advanced**
Vested Benefits		Unfunded Accumulated Benefit Obligation
		Unrecognized Net Gain or Loss
		Unrecognized Prior Service Cost

CHECK THE TERMINOLOGY SECTION OF THE TOPICAL INDEX AND READ LINKS TO BUILD COMPRE-HENSION. RECORD THE CITATIONS TO THE LITERATURE FOR FUTURE REFERENCE. USE EACH TERM IN A SENTENCE.

Table 3.29   Accounting For Pensions COMPLETE THIS TABLE

Terms	**Search Recommended* (Semicolons are not part of the search but are used as separators.)**	**Citation for Definition: Provide Full Reference**	**Other Searches You Would Suggest**
Assumed rate of return	"assumed rate of return"		
Actuary	"actuary"		

*Access FARS, click on File, Open, Nfo, Open, and select FASB-OP (amended), click Search, enter query.

Problems

1. Define the following pension-related terms: (a) service cost, (b) prior service costs, (c) vesting.

2. Pension funds use an assumed rate of return in computing the actuarial present value of pension plan benefits. What is the nature of an assumed rate of return and what would happen to the pension liability as the percentage moves up, for example by 4 percent?

3. Distinguish between a defined benefit and a defined contribution plan.

4. *BusinessWeek* in a Special Report entitled "Sinkhole" by Nanette Byrnes (June 13, 2005, pp. 68–76) reported that studies had estimated that over 14 million nonfederal government workers and 6 million retirees were owed $2.37 trillion by in excess of 2,000 agencies, cities, or states (p. 71). The article observes that the public sector lacks the equivalent of the Pension Benefit Guaranty Corporation (PBGC), although state constitutions guarantee pension promises in most states. Has the accounting literature accessible in FARS addressed such issues? Who determines the accounting treatment for the type of obligation described? What is the PBGC? Discuss the implications of the obligations for the citizenry.

5. SELF-STUDY Q&A. **Q**: Identify the FARS passage that describes the accounting for an acquired company's pension plan that is underfunded.

    A. *Access the FASB-OP (amended) infobase and using Advanced Query type* acquired pension underfund* *which will link to Implementation Guides—Q&A 87, Questions and Answers 81-100, with #88 highlighted. Both underfunding and overfunding are addressed. See FAS 158.*

Table 3.30 Postretirement Benefits   Page **3-67**

■ POSTRETIREMENT BENEFITS

Vocabulary: Create your dictionary of the following terms from FARS.

Basic	Intermediate	Advanced
Active Plan Participant	Attribution Period	Accumulated Postretirement Benefit Obligation
Dependency Status	Full Eligibility Date	Actual Return on Plan Assets Component (of Net Periodic Postretirement Benefit Cost)
Employee	Pay-Related Plan	Assumed Per Capita Claims Cost (by Age)
Full Eligibility (for Benefits)	Plan	Curtailment (of a Postretirement Benefit Plan)
Fully Eligible Plan Participants	Plan Amendment	Defined Benefit Postretirement Plan
Gross Eligible Charges	Plan Demographics	Defined Contribution Postretirement Plan
Health Care Cost Trend Rates	Plan Participant	Expected Postretirement Benefit Obligation
Inactive Employees	Plan Termination	Gain or Loss Component (of Net Periodic Postretirement Benefit Cost)
Medicare Reimbursement Rates	Substantive Plan	Interest Cost Component (of Net Periodic Postretirement Benefit Cost)
Net Incurred Claims Cost (by Age)		Net Periodic Postretirement Benefit Cost
Per Capita Claims Cost by Age		Nonparticipating Insurance Contract
Postemployment Benefits		Participating Insurance Contract
Postretirement Benefit Plan		Postretirement Benefits Other Than Pensions
Postretirement Benefits		Postretirement Health Care Benefits
Prior Service Cost		Service Cost Component (of Net Periodic Postretirement Benefit Cost)
Retirees		Settlement (of a Postretirement Benefit Plan)
Termination Benefits		Unfunded Accumulated Postretirement Benefit Obligation
Transition Asset		Unrecognized Transition Asset
Transition Obligation		Unrecognized Transition Obligation

CHECK THE TERMINOLOGY SECTION OF THE TOPICAL INDEX AND READ LINKS TO BUILD COMPRE-HENSION. RECORD THE CITATIONS TO THE LITERATURE FOR FUTURE REFERENCE. USE EACH TERM IN A SENTENCE.

Table 3.30 Postretirement Benefits COMPLETE THIS TABLE

Terms	Search Recommended* (Semicolons are not part of the search but are used as separators.)	Citation for Definition: Provide Full Reference	Other Searches You Would Suggest
Funded postretirement benefit plan	"funded postretirement benefit plan"		
Fully funded for tax	"fully funded for tax"		
Obligations related to employees	"obligations related to employees"		

*Access FARS, click on File, Open, Nfo, Open, and select FASB-OP (amended), click Search, enter query.

Problems

1. When the FASB passed the pronouncement on postretirement benefits (FAS 106), there was a "Gray Panthers" protest. Why do you believe this was a controversial proposal? [Also see FAS 158.]

2. SELF-STUDY Q&A. **Q**: Identify where FARS describes the journal entries related to health care changes in premiums associated with pension-related obligations.

   A. Access the FASB-OP (amended) infobase and using Query, type the search phrase chang* premium* healthcare* journal entry. *This links Implementation Guides—Q&A 87, Questions and Answers 1-20, with #4 highlighted. The passage requires an analogy to be drawn between the role of premiums and the consequences of recording actions by a regulator. Further guidance is available in FAS 87, Par. 261, depicting journal entries given certain funding status. Alternatively, type in the search phrase* match$ postretirement *and FSP FASB 106–2 will be identified. This discussion concerns the accounting related to Medicare Prescription Drugs, reflecting attention to the employer's share of cost and the subsidy provided.*

Table 3.31 Leases   Page **3-69**

■ LEASES

Vocabulary: Create your dictionary of the following terms from FARS.

Basic	Intermediate	Advanced
Bargain Purchase	Bargain Purchase Option	Direct Financing Leases
Capital Leases	Bargain Renewal Option	Estimated Economic Life of Leased Property
Executory Costs	Implicit Rate	Estimated Residual Value of Leased Property
Fair Value of the Leased Property	Inception of the Lease	Leveraged Lease
Lease	Initial Direct Costs	Money-Over-Money Lease Transactions
Lease Term	Interest Rate Implicit in the Lease	Sale-Leaseback Accounting
Lessee's Incremental Borrowing Rate	Penalty in Lease Arrangement	Sales Recognition
Minimum Lease Payments	Renewal or Extension of a Lease	Sales-Type Lease
Operating Lease	Unguaranteed Residual Value	Wrap Lease Transactions
Residual Value	Unrelated Parties	

CHECK THE TERMINOLOGY SECTION OF THE TOPICAL INDEX AND READ LINKS TO BUILD COMPRE-HENSION. RECORD THE CITATIONS TO THE LITERATURE FOR FUTURE REFERENCE. USE EACH TERM IN A SENTENCE.

Table 3.31   Leases COMPLETE THIS TABLE

Terms	Search Recommended* (Semicolons are not part of the search but are used as separators.)	Citation for Definition: Provide Full Reference	Other Searches You Would Suggest
Guaranteed residual value	"guaranteed residual value is"		
Penalty for failure to renew	"penalty for failure to renew"; penalty for failure to renew defin*		
Lease commitments	"lease commitments are"		
Blindpool syndication	Blindpool syndication def*		

Terms	Search Recommended* (Semicolons are not part of the search but are used as separators.)	Citation for Definition: Provide Full Reference	Other Searches You Would Suggest
Lease note disclosures	Disclosure in notes of lease agreements		
Economic life test	Economic life test		
Transfer of ownership	"transfer of ownership"		
Leaseholds	"leasehold improvements"		

*Access FARS, click on File, Open, Nfo, Open, and select FASB-OP (amended), click Search, enter query.

Problems

1. Real-estate developers sold an office building to a public real-estate blindpool syndication. Then, a sale and leaseback arrangement was reached. How should this be recorded?

2. Why do leaseholds sometimes appear as long-term assets?

3. What is the typical content of notes to financial statements that relate to lease commitments?

4. What are the criteria used to distinguish a capital lease from an operating lease?

5. SELF-STUDY Q&A. **Q**: Identify where FARS describes the claimed effect of capitalization on the leasing industry, relative to the notion of off-balance sheet financing.
   A. *Access the FASB-OP (amended) infobase and using Query, type the search phrase* capitaliz* leases off balance sheet financing. *CON 2, Par. 101 is identified.*

6. SELF-STUDY Q&A. **Q**: How many FASB Interpretations (FINs) contain some reference to leasing?
   A. *Access the FARS toolbar, click on* Search, *select Search Within a Single OP Document Type, double click on* FASB Interpretations *and it will appear in the Document Type: box. Then enter in the query for: box the term* leas*. *You will notice that* least *is among the words highlighted but use of* lease* *removes the relevant term of* leasing. *Refine the search by entering* leas* ^least. *The HitList identifies FIN 6, 9, 18, 19, 21, 23, 24, 26, 27, 39, 43, 44, 45, 46, and 46(R). These results bear out how pervasive the topic of leasing is within the authoritative literature.*

7. SELF-STUDY Q&A. **Q**: Use Advanced Query's Check Branches capability to identify how many of the table of contents for varied professional pronouncements use some form of the word *lease*.
   A. *Access FARS, open the FASB-OP (amended) infobase, click on the* Contents *lower tab and click on* Table of Contents. *Then click on* Advanced Search, *click on* Checked Branches, *then type in the* search lease%. *The result is seven of the table of contents. The same incidence is found using the search phrase* leas*. *The listings on the HitList bear out the details by type of table of contents: APB 5, 7, 27, and 31; AIN-APB 7; FAS 13, 17, 23, 28, and 98; FIN 21, 23, and 24; FTB 79-10, 85-3; Staff Implementation Guide Q&A 91; and FSP FIN 46(R)-4.*

Table 3.32 Accounting Changes   Page **3-71**

■ ACCOUNTING CHANGES

Vocabulary: Create your dictionary of the following terms from FARS.

Basic	Intermediate	Advanced
Accounting Changes	Change in Accounting Estimate	Change in Accounting Estimate Effected by a Change in Accounting Principle
Accounting Principle	Change in Accounting Principle	Cumulative Accounting Adjustments
Accounting Pronouncement	Change in the Reporting Entity	Direct Effects of a Change in Accounting Principle
Consistency	Retrospective Application	Indirect Effects of a Change in Accounting Principle

CHECK THE TERMINOLOGY SECTION OF THE TOPICAL INDEX AND READ LINKS TO BUILD COMPRE-
HENSION. RECORD THE CITATIONS TO THE LITERATURE FOR FUTURE REFERENCE. USE EACH TERM
IN A SENTENCE.

Table 3.32   Accounting Changes COMPLETE THIS TABLE

Terms	Search Recommended* (Semicolons are not part of the search but are used as separators.)	Citation for Definition: Provide Full Reference	Other Searches You Would Suggest
Prospective	change* accounting prospective*		
Cumulative effect of an accounting change	cumulative effect type change		

*Access FARS, click on <u>File</u>, <u>Open</u>, <u>Nfo</u>, <u>Open</u>, and select <u>FASB-OP (amended)</u>, click <u>Search</u>, enter query.

Problems

1. Do differences exist in the depreciation accounting for (a) changes in estimates and (b) changes in accounting method? Explain your response in detail.

2. Kip Makuc's High Tech purchased 100 personal computers on January 2, 20x1, estimating 5-year useful lives and a salvage value of $1,000 per computer. Straight-line depreciation was applied to the $500,000 purchase price. However, by 20x3, it was determined that technology had advanced to such a degree, the terminals would need to be replaced by the end of 20x4. Moreover, due to tax law changes that made it attractive to decrease reported net income, per books, the corporation switched to the sum-of-the-years'-digits in 20x3. The tax law change determined the alternative minimum tax on reported net income, creating an influence by tax

law on financial statement presentation. Make all necessary journal entries to reflect the personal computers in the company's books over their useful life.

3. SELF-STUDY Q&A. **Q:** Identify in FARS a disclosure for a change in inventory method.

   A. Access the FASB-OP (amended) infobase and using Advanced Query type, the search phrase change in accounting for inventory. *This will be identified in FAS 154, Par. A7.*

Table 3.33 Error Analysis   Page **3-73**

■ ERROR ANALYSIS

Vocabulary: Create your dictionary of the following terms from FARS.

Basic	**Intermediate**	**Advanced**
Accounting Changes	Error in Previously Issued Financial Statements	Restatement

CHECK THE TERMINOLOGY SECTION OF THE TOPICAL INDEX AND READ LINKS TO BUILD COMPRE-HENSION. RECORD THE CITATIONS TO THE LITERATURE FOR FUTURE REFERENCE. USE EACH TERM IN A SENTENCE.

Table 3.33   Error Analysis COMPLETE THIS TABLE

Terms	Search Recommended* (Semicolons are not part of the search but are used as separators.)	Citation for Definition: Provide Full Reference	Other Searches You Would Suggest
Irregularity	"irregularity"; misstatement		
Correction	"correction of error"		

*Access FARS, click on File, Open, Nfo, Open, and select FASB-OP (amended), click Search, enter query.

Problems

1. An insurance premium of $1,600 was prepaid in 20x1 covering the years 20x1, 20x2, 20x3, and 20x4. The entire amount was recorded as an expense in 20x1. No other errors occurred during 20x1 and no corrections were made for the error. Ignoring any tax considerations: (a) What was the effect on net income in 20x1? (b) What was the effect on net income in 20x2? (c) What was the effect on retained earnings as of the end of 20x1? (d) What was the effect on assets as of the end of 20x1? (e) What was the effect on retained earnings as of the end of 20x2? (f) As of what date will retained earnings be accurately reported?

2. A customer called and complained that an order for 15,000 parts, serial number A278, had been filled with 15,000 parts, serial number B278. The customer noted that although a check had been mailed three days before, a stop-payment was being issued. The parts would be returned within the week. The customer requested that the actual order be filled immediately and that your company incur the costs of express transit to ensure delivery by the next day. Following the phone call, you wish to investigate the accuracy of the complaint. Moreover, you need to decide how to proceed, including what actions to take and what journal entries to record. Explain what steps are appropriate and why.

3. SELF-STUDY Q&A. **Q:** Does FARS address irregularities?
   A. No. Advanced Query of FASB-OP (amended) has one hit with a distinct meaning.

■ STATEMENT OF CASH FLOWS REVISITED

Vocabulary: Create your dictionary of the following terms from FARS.

Basic	Intermediate	Advanced
Adequate Compensation	Affiliated Enterprise	Financially Interrelated Organizations
Agent	Affiliates	Full Set of Financial Statements
Cash Equivalents	Immediate Family	Mutual Enterprise
Investor	Permanent Investor	Sponsor
Related Parties	Principal Owners	Trustee
Seller	Small Business Issuer	Variance Power

CHECK THE TERMINOLOGY SECTION OF THE TOPICAL INDEX AND READ LINKS TO BUILD COMPRE-HENSION. RECORD THE CITATIONS TO THE LITERATURE FOR FUTURE REFERENCE. USE EACH TERM IN A SENTENCE.

Table 3.34   Statement of Cash Flows Revisited COMPLETE THIS TABLE

Terms	Search Recommended* (Semicolons are not part of the search but are used as separators.)	Citation for Definition: Provide Full Reference	Other Searches You Would Suggest
Statement of cash flows	"statement of cash flows"; defin* statement of cash flows; "a statement of cash flows as part of a full set of financial statements"		
Cash management	"cash management"; objective of enterprises' cash management programs		
Family loans	loans to family members		
Concessions to creditors	concessions to creditors		
Small business	"small business"		
Charge-offs of loans	write-offs and charge-offs of loans		
Investing activities	"investing activities"		
Net cash flows	net cash flows within the statement of cash flows defin*		

Table 3.34 Statement of Cash Flows Revisited   Page **3-75**

Terms	**Search Recommended* (Semicolons are not part of the search but are used as separators.)**	**Citation for Definition: Provide Full Reference**	**Other Searches You Would Suggest**
Gross cash flows	gross cash flows in statement of cash flows defin*		
Indirect method	"indirect method"		
Reconciliation to net income	"reconciliation to net income";		
	adjusting net income to net cash flow remove		
Write-offs of receivables	"write-offs of receivables"		
Internal control	"internal control"		

*Access FARS, click on <u>File</u>, <u>Open</u>, <u>Nfo</u>, <u>Open</u>, and select <u>FASB-OP (amended)</u>, click <u>Search</u>, enter query.

Problems

1. It has been asserted that one of the most inexpensive ways for companies to finance themselves is to take control of the cash they already have. Many claim that U.S. corporations are "quite primitive" in their cash management. What do you believe are the problems? How would you quantify the related costs? What steps might be taken to make cash management more effective?

2. In the 1980s, it was observed that the 14 million small businesses in the United States provided about half of all private sector jobs and generated almost 40 percent of the gross national product; the role of small business in the economy has been growing. Yet, money for such businesses has been represented to be a nightmarish experience. About three-quarters of new businesses are reported to get at least part of their financing from friends and relatives. What types of concessions can small businesses grant to providers of capital to obtain the cash resources they need? Be specific.

3. A very real control problem relates to write-offs of accounts receivable and charge-offs of loans. Numerous cases are available in which officers and employees systematically diverted written-off accounts or charged-off loan recoveries to their own use. Clearly, controls must be established over such recoveries. Accounts written off or loans charged off are potential assets. In fact, member banks of the Federal Reserve Bank are able to recover over a quarter of their charged-off loans. As it turns out, they were not entirely uncollectible. How would you establish control over accounts written off and loans charged off? Why do you think these types of transactions are difficult to control?

4. If items meet the definition of cash equivalents that are part of a larger pool of investments, they are properly considered investing activities. The FASB allows these items not to be segregated and treated as cash equivalents. What desirable attribute of accounting information seems to be lacking as a result of this decision? How is this problem addressed by the FASB?

5. What is the general requirement for reporting of cash receipts and payment—gross or net? Why? Provide an example of an exception to such a requirement.

6. The indirect method of presenting a statement of cash flows requires that net income be reconciled to net cash flow from operating activities. To do so, what must be removed from net income?

7. An article entitled "Capital Pains: Big Cash Hoards" by Ian McDonald appeared in the *Wall Street Journal* on July 21, 2006 (p. C1) and reported that research by Standard & Poor's (S&P) had quantified as of the first quarter, the 174 companies in the S&P Industrials Index, which excludes financial firms and utilities, held over $295 billion in cash. If this was combined with the treasury-shareholdings, it would represent nearly 20 percent of their total stock market value. Why do you think the researchers couple treasury shares with cash in their analysis of "cash hoards"?

8. The *Wall Street Journal* reported on July 27, 2006, "Firms Ponder What Constitutes Cash" (p. C3, by Steven D. Jones). Specifically, the FASB was being contacted by companies to respond to what they represented to be a case of the "Big Four" accounting firms usurping the FASB as to what constituted a cash equivalent. Reportedly, some cases of auditing firms assembling a "not cash list" had evolved, leading even to restatements of prior years, on the premise that "highly liquid" was being interpreted by such auditors in a different manner than intended by standard setters. Since some companies were allowed to treat even 30-year maturity auction-rate securities and variable-rate demand notes as cash equivalents based on the contention that frequent auctions maintained deep markets and sufficient liquidity, an appeal was being made to the FASB to provide due process and gain consistency in treatment. What do you think of the disagreement reflected among companies and their auditors? Is it appropriate for different auditing firms to reach different judgments as to which instruments qualify as cash equivalents for a given company? Why or why not?

9. SELF-STUDY Q&A. **Q:** Locate in FARS a discussion of the complementary nature of financial statements.

   A. The Topical Index, under R, contains the entry RECOGNITION AND MEASUREMENT IN FINANCIAL STATEMENTS. A subhead under Definition has "Financial Flexibility" linked to CON5, Par. 24 which explicitly states: "Financial statements complement each other." Examples of how each type of financial report complements the other are provided.

Table 3.35 Full Disclosure   Page **3-77**

■ FULL DISCLOSURE

Vocabulary: Create your dictionary of the following terms from FARS.

Basic	**Intermediate**	**Advanced**
Changes in Financial Position	Complete Set of Financial Statements	Right of Setoff
Materiality	Completeness	Setoff
Understandability	Full Set of Financial Statements	

CHECK THE TERMINOLOGY SECTION OF THE TOPICAL INDEX AND READ LINKS TO BUILD COMPRE-HENSION. RECORD THE CITATIONS TO THE LITERATURE FOR FUTURE REFERENCE. USE EACH TERM IN A SENTENCE.

Table 3.35   Full Disclosure COMPLETE THIS TABLE

Terms	Search Recommended* (Semicolons are not part of the search but are used as separators.)	Citation for Definition: Provide Full Reference	Other Searches You Would Suggest
Full disclosure	"full disclosure"; transparency		
MD&A	MD&A		
General purpose financial statements	"general purpose financial statements"		
Notes to the financial statements	required notes to the financial statements		
Offsets	offset* defin* permitted; general principle that offsetting is improper statement of financial position		
Concentration	"concentration"		
Off-balance sheet financing	"off-balance sheet financing"		

*Access FARS, click on <u>File</u>, <u>Open</u>, <u>Nfo</u>, <u>Open</u>, and select <u>FASB-OP (amended)</u>, click <u>Search</u>, enter query.

Problems

1. The SEC requires disclosures in SEC filings only for material items (SEC SX 210.4-02). What are the pros and cons of such a policy?

2. What is the general purpose financial statement beyond the income statement, balance sheet, and statement of retained earnings?

3. How can notes to the financial statements be of use?

4. In reviewing a company's detailed journals and subsidiary ledgers, you note that a single company is both a supplier and a customer. It seems to you rather strange that this entity's balance represents 20 percent of outstanding receivables and likewise represents about 15 percent of outstanding payables. Is it appropriate for such a situation to arise? Can the receivables and payables be offset? Why or why not? Would the net amount be important information? Why or why not? Is there any disclosure you would recommend to such a company?

5. Give an example of a possible source of off-balance-sheet financing.

6. SELF-STUDY Q&A. **Q**: Locate in FARS a discussion of de-recognition and how it relates to the topic of offsets.
   A. *The Topical Index, under R, has the entry RIGHT OF SETOFF, with the subhead "Definition" and links to FIN39, Par. 5 and B10.101A. In particular, see FIN39, Par. 5, footnote 3.*

7. SELF-STUDY Q&A. **Q**: While reading a public filing, you notice a reference to a spinoff. Find in FARS where such transactions are described. Are other terms used to describe such events?
   A. *The Topical Index, under S, contains the entry SPINOFF, with a subhead of "Description", linked to APB29, Par. 5 and N35.102. Such passages do indicate that other terms are used to describe "plans of reorganization that involve disposing of all or a significant segment of the business (the plans are variously referred to as spin-offs, split-ups, and split-offs)."*

Table 3.36 Not-For-Profit Considerations   Page **3-79**

■ **NOT-FOR-PROFIT CONSIDERATIONS**

> *Vocabulary: Create your dictionary of the following terms from FARS.*
>
> | **Basic** | **Intermediate** | **Advanced** |
> |---|---|---|
> | Collections | Donor-imposed Condition | Change in Permanently Restricted Net Assets |
> | Conditional Promise to Give | Donor-imposed Restriction | Change in Temporarily Restricted Net Assets |
> | Contribution | Donor-restricted Endowment Fund | Change in Unrestricted Net Assets |
> | Endowment Fund | Permanent Restriction | Maintenance of Net Assets |
> | Functional Classification | Permanently Restricted Net Assets | Net Asset Information |
> | Funds or Fund Balances | Restricted Support | Net Assets |
> | Not-for-Profit Organizations | Temporarily Restricted Net Assets | Net Assets Available for Benefits |
> | Promise to Give | Temporary Restriction | Unrestricted Net Assets |
> | Unconditional Promise to Give | Unrestricted Support | Voluntary Health and Welfare Organizations |
>
> CHECK THE TERMINOLOGY SECTION OF THE TOPICAL INDEX AND READ LINKS TO BUILD COMPRE-
> HENSION. RECORD THE CITATIONS TO THE LITERATURE FOR FUTURE REFERENCE. USE EACH TERM
> IN A SENTENCE.

Table 3.36   Not-For-Profit Considerations COMPLETE THIS TABLE

Terms	Search Recommended* (Semicolons are not part of the search but are used as separators.)	Citation for Definition: Provide Full Reference	Other Searches You Would Suggest
Investment objective of not-for-profit organizations	investment objective of not-for-profit organizations		
Pledges	"pledges"		

*Access FARS, click on File, Open, Nfo, Open, and select FASB-OP (amended), click Search, enter query.

Problems

1. What are the investment objectives of a not-for-profit organization?

2. How should an endowment fund be presented in financial statements? When a restriction by donor applies, how is it accounted for in the not-for-profit setting?

3. When a not-for-profit organization receives a pledge of support, how is this accounted for relative to contributions?

4. How are investments held by not-for-profit organizations to be recorded?

5. SELF-STUDY Q&A. **Q:** Identify the types of collections that may be of relevance in the not-for-profit sector, as described by FARS.

   A. *The Topical Index, under C, contains the entry COLLECTIONS—WORKS OF ART, HISTORICAL TREASURES, AND SIMILAR ASSETS. Of particular use is footnote 6 of C67.111.*

Table 3.37 Financial Statement Analysis   Page **3-81**

■ FINANCIAL STATEMENT ANALYSIS

Vocabulary: Create your dictionary of the following terms from FARS.

Basic	Intermediate	Advanced
Comparability	Debt Security	Annual Effective Tax Rate
Current Assets	Distributions to Owners	Dividends to Policyholders
Debt	Equity Security	Estimated Cash Flow
Dividends	Industry Segment	Financial Position of an Investee
Equity	Stock Dividend	Foreign Entity
Inventory	Stock Split	Foreign Geographic Area
Working Capital	Treasury-Stock Method	

CHECK THE TERMINOLOGY SECTION OF THE TOPICAL INDEX AND READ LINKS TO BUILD COMPRE-
HENSION. RECORD THE CITATIONS TO THE LITERATURE FOR FUTURE REFERENCE. USE EACH TERM
IN A SENTENCE.

Table 3.37   Financial Statement Analysis COMPLETE THIS TABLE

Terms	Search Recommended* (Semicolons are not part of the search but are used as separators.)	Citation for Definition: Provide Full Reference	Other Searches You Would Suggest
Financial statement analysis	"financial statement analysis"		
Line items	selection of line items relationship to financial analysis and comparability		
Classes of current assets	"current assets"; "classes of current assets are"		
FIFO	FIFO financial statement analysis		
Inflation	"inflation"		
Dividends	"dividends"; dividends financial statement analysis		
Declaration of a dividend	"declaration of a dividend"		
Payment of a dividend	payment of a dividend		
100 percent payout	paying out all earnings in the form of dividends		

Terms	Search Recommended* (Semicolons are not part of the search but are used as separators.)	Citation for Definition: Provide Full Reference	Other Searches You Would Suggest
Cash flow per share	"cash flow per share"		
Ratio analysis	analysis with ratios		
Treasury stock	treasury stock is def*		
Debt to equity ratio	"debt to equity ratio"		
Interim financial statements	"interim financial statements"; "interim financial reporting"		
Discrete view	"discrete approach"		
Integral view	integral approach interim reporting		
Segment disclosures	"segment disclosures"; "operating segment disclosures"; segment$ disclosure*$		
Back orders	sales orders unfulfilled; "unfulfilled commitments"		

*Access FARS, click on File, Open, Nfo, Open, and select FASB-OP (amended), click Search, enter query.

Problems

1. Although a number of line items may appear in the current section of a balance sheet, what are the four general classes of current assets into which these items can be categorized?

2. Jeri & Glen Enterprises has used the FIFO method of inventory over a period of rapid inflation. The corporation has a policy of 100 percent payout of net income in the form of dividends. Recently, the company has noticed a steep decline in net income and in volume of sales. Back orders have climbed. What is the most likely problem?

3. Of the following transactions, does each increase (I), decrease (D), or have no effect (N) on the ratio of debt to equity (i.e., total liabilities divided by the sum of total liabilities and total stockholders' equity)? (a) a two-for-one stock split; (b) the declaration and payment of a cash dividend; (c) the declaration of a 5 percent stock dividend; (d) issuance of stock; (e) purchased treasury stock.

4. Why doesn't the FASB permit cash flow per share to be reported? Note that some respondents to the exposure draft for the statement of cash flows asked if the board intended to preclude the reporting of per-unit amounts of cash flow that were distributable under the terms of a partnership

Table 3.37 Financial Statement Analysis   Page **3-83**

agreement or other agreement between an enterprise and its owner. How do you believe the FASB responded to this question? Explain.

5. Many respondents to the statement of cash flow exposure draft commented negatively as to the usefulness of working capital as a concept of funds. They questioned its relevance, since positive working capital was not necessarily an indication of liquidity and negative working capital was not necessarily an indication of illiquidity. Do you agree with this overwhelming majority view of responses? Why or why not?

6. What are the major classes of ratios and what is the information content of each class?

7. Distinguish between the discrete and the integral method to interim reporting. Which is the approach embraced by GAAP? Do you agree with GAAP?

8. Describe the reporting requirements for segment operations and how they might be used by an investor.

9. SELF-STUDY Q&A. **Q:** Ratio analysis is affected by account classification, particularly by current asset and current liability demarcations. Identify in FARS those citations that discuss the nature of these balance sheet classifications.

   A. The Topical Index, under B, contains the topic BALANCE SHEET CLASSIFICATION: CURRENT ASSETS AND LIABILITIES. By accessing the link under definition, subhead "Current Assets", you will be directed to ARB43, Ch.3A, Par. 4 and B05.401 and then subhead "Current Liabilities" will lead to ARB43, Ch.3A, Par. 7 and B05.402. Be certain to read through the footnotes referenced. Also of relevance are the subheads "Short-Term Obligations" (FAS6, Par. 2 and B05.405) and "Subjective Acceleration Clause" (FAS78, Par. 10 and B05.405A).

■ INTERNAL CONTROL DESIGN AND EVALUATION

Vocabulary: Create your dictionary of the following terms from FARS.

Basic	Intermediate	Advanced
Control	Events	Circumstances (Affecting an Entity)
Management	Internal Events	Intermediary
Small Business Issuer	Internal Transactions	Loss Averse
Specific Risk		

CHECK THE TERMINOLOGY SECTION OF THE TOPICAL INDEX AND READ LINKS TO BUILD COMPRE-
HENSION. RECORD THE CITATIONS TO THE LITERATURE FOR FUTURE REFERENCE. USE EACH TERM
IN A SENTENCE.

Table 3.38   Internal Control Design and Evaluation COMPLETE THIS TABLE

Terms	Search Recommended* (Semicolons are not part of the search but are used as separators.)	Citation for Definition: Provide Full Reference	Other Searches You Would Suggest
Internal control	"internal control"		
Sequence checks	completeness; counting documents sequence		
Receiving reports	receiving goods		
Small business	"small business"		
Vacation	"vacation"		
Bank checks	"checks"		
Paid invoices	paid invoices		
Control risk	control risk		
Board of directors	board of directors		
Situation pressures	situation pressures legal; economic or legal pressure		
Fraud	fraud$		

*Access FARS, click on File, Open, Nfo, Open, and select FASB-OP (amended), click Search, enter query.

Table 3.38 Internal Control Design and Evaluation   Page **3-85**

Problems

1. A manager was asked whether periodic sequence checks were made of receiving reports. The manager responded, "No, but the receiving reports are prenumbered." Evaluate the control implications of this verbal exchange.

2. A friend of yours has a small business. Her CPA asked her the following questions: (a) What is done when employees are on vacation? (b) What is done when one employee goes to lunch? She asks you why the CPA made these inquiries. How would you respond? What are desirable responses to these questions from a control standpoint?

3. In your review of a company's internal controls, the following practices were observed. (a) Whenever one of the two normal check signers plans to be out of the office for a day, he will sign a set of 20 blank checks to ensure that his absence won't hinder business operations. (b) When payments are made, original invoices from suppliers are filed; no notation is made on these invoices to indicate that they have been paid. Comment on the risks posed by these practices.

4. The concept of corporate governance has long been debated, particularly in terms of who should serve on the board of directors. Some contend that representatives of labor, owners, suppliers, customers, the community, and management should be a part of the board. What do you think is a desirable composition of a board of directors, and why? What are the implications for internal control of your recommendations for membership?

5. What types of situational pressures do you believe might motivate individuals to commit fraud against a company?

6. On June 7, 2006, an article entitled "IRS Reviews Denied Extensions after Admitting It Made Errors" by Tom Herman appeared in the *Wall Street Journal* (p. D2). The IRS explained that the error stemmed from its incorrect date stamping on paper extension requests submitted to the Fresno, California IRS office. What internal control practice might have avoided such an error?

7. SELF-STUDY Q&A. **Q:** A good deal of attention has been directed to the Sarbanes-Oxley law and, in particular, to the costs of compliance. For example, the U.S. House of Representatives government reform subcommittee observed that the Business Roundtable (representing chief executive officers of large companies) in 2006 reported that 40 percent of its members will pay more than $10 million each this year to comply with the 2002 Sarbanes-Oxley law. A study by AMR Research, a Boston-based research firm, estimated a total of $6 billion would be spent in 2006 by U.S. companies in order to comply. The Section 404 provisions associated with internal control were the subject of an SEC advisory panel's recommendation in December 2005 that only the largest 20 percent of public companies be required to have outside accountants certify their systems of protecting assets, reporting financial information, and complying with regulations. However, the SEC decided not to grant such an exemption. Do the accounting pronouncements in FARS accord any attention to internal control, Sarbanes-Oxley, or Section 404 in particular? Do accounting standard-setters ever grant the sort of exemption from accounting pronouncements that the SEC Advisory Panel recommended with respect to Section 404? Explain the basis for your response, describing the searches you perform and their results.

A. Access FARS, open the FASB-OP (amended) infobase, and use Advanced Query to check for the incidence of the words associated with the matters of interest. A search of internal controls *results in no hits, but the deletion of the "s" to internal control identifies seven cites. However, when these are scanned, one sees the shortcomings of a word search, since* internal *is in reference to the Internal Revenue Code or internal events, and* control *is directed to a controlling interest sort of* *meaning. This effort would not have been needed had the search phrase "internal control*" been used initially, which would have generated no hits whatsoever.*

Clear the previous queries and enter in Advanced Query the phrase Sarbanes-Oxley *and FAS 123(R), par B7 will be indicated, with a popup screen for footnote 139. The context addresses criticism that voluminous accounting guidance existed for share-based arrangements that constituents said was disjointed, rule-based, and form-driven: "That guidance was identified by the United States Securities and Exchange Commission (SEC) as an example of rules-based accounting standards. (SEC, Study Pursuant to Section 108(d) of the Sarbanes-Oxley Act of 2002 on the Adoption by the United States Financial Reporting System of a Principles-Based Accounting System, March 25, 2003 [www.sec.gov/news/studies/principlesbasedstand.htm])." The second item identified within FARS is also found in FARS 123(R), in Par. B246, tied to footnote 168 which gives the formal source for the Sarbanes-Oxley Act referenced: "Public Law 107-204—July 30, 2002, Section 180(b)(1)(A)(v)." Of interest is that this second cite relates to the question posed as to exemption. The discussion acknowledges: "Many respondents said that more time would be needed to adopt this Statement, often citing the ongoing implementation with the Sarbanes-Oxley Act[168] as a constraint on available resources. Moreover, the effective date proposed in the Exposure Draft was predicated on a targeted issuance date for this Statement of no later than November 15, 2004. In light of those comments and the fact that this Statement is being issued later than projected, the Board concluded that the effective date of this Statement should be deferred beyond the date proposed in the Exposure Draft." In other words, exemption is not granted but a deferral is provided, in recognition of cost and time constraints.*

"Section 404" in Advanced Query results in no hits within FARS. In other words, the accounting standards have not accorded any attention to internal control, Sarbanes-Oxley, or Section 404 except in a cross-referencing manner that acknowledges criticisms leveled and competing demand for resources by the FASB's constituents. Note that those desiring details on Section 404 as well as Sarbanes-Oxley can find a wealth of information on the Internet, particularly at the Public Company Accounting Oversight Board (PCAOB) Web site at www.pcaobus.org*.*

To explore the last question as to whether exemptions are granted by accounting standard-setters, access Advanced Query and input exempt**. In a quick scan, you will notice that tax-exempt appears in the citations, suggesting a more effective search would be* exempt* ˆ tax-exempt*. The search shows 118 matches. A quick scan unveils that a number of exemptions have been granted over time, as have grandfather clauses that accomplish a similar objective. However, often when asked to make exemptions, the accounting standard-setters have chosen not to do so, for example, FAS 16, Par. 56 observes: "The Board concluded that there was no equitable basis for exempting certain preexisting contingencies and not others." The Dissent to FAS 25 has an interesting discussion relative to the SEC and registered companies.*

Table 3.39 Regulated Industry   Page **3-87**

■ REGULATED INDUSTRY

Vocabulary: Create your dictionary of the following terms from FARS.

Basic	Intermediate	Advanced
Allowable Costs	Cost Recovery Method	Endowment Contract
Regulatory Lag	Deposit Method	

CHECK THE TERMINOLOGY SECTION OF THE TOPICAL INDEX AND READ LINKS TO BUILD COMPRE-
HENSION. RECORD THE CITATIONS TO THE LITERATURE FOR FUTURE REFERENCE. USE EACH TERM
IN A SENTENCE.

Table 3.39   Regulated Industry COMPLETE THIS TABLE

Terms	Search Recommended* (Semicolons are not part of the search but are used as separators.)	Citation for Definition: Provide Full Reference	Other Searches You Would Suggest
Regulated operations	"regulated operations"		
Rate-making process	"rate-making process"		

*Access FARS, click on File, Open, Nfo, Open, and select FASB-OP (amended), click Search, enter query.

Problems

1. How are profits on sales to regulated affiliates to be recorded?

2. Do accounting requirements set forth by regulators have to comply with generally accepted accounting principles (GAAP)?

3. SELF-STUDY Q&A. **Q:** Identify the relevant FARS guidance for an industry that is deregulated.
   A. Using FARS, access FASB-OP (amended) infobase and type in the Query: deregulation of
certain industries accounting treatment. *The result is FAS 101, Par. 1.*

■ SPECIALIZED INDUSTRY CONSIDERATIONS

Vocabulary: Create your dictionary of the following terms from FARS.

Basic	Intermediate	Advanced
Amenities	Callable Obligations	Area Franchise
Annuity Contract	Capacity Contract	Assessment Enterprise
Broadcaster	Ceding Enterprise	Assuming Enterprise
Cable Television Plant	Claim Adjustment Expenses	Book Entry Securities
Claims	Cleanup Call	Continuing Franchise Fee
Coding	Credit Life Insurance	Contractually Specified Servicing Fees
Commitment Fees	Daypart	Costs Incurred to Rent Real Estate Projects
Common Costs	Initial Services	Costs Incurred to Sell Real Estate Projects
Credit Card Fees	Net Premium	Franchise Agreement
Life Insurance Enterprises	Origination Fees	Franchisee
Morbidity	Parity Adjustment	Franchisor
Mortality	Phase	Fraternal Benefit Society
Mortgage Banking Enterprise	Phase-in Plan	Initial Franchise Fee
Motion Picture Films	Preacquisition Costs	License Agreement for Program Material
Property and Liability Insurance Enterprise	Restate-Translate	License Agreements
Record Master	Settlement Period	Mortgage Guaranty Insurance Enterprise
Reinsurance	Subrogation	Network Affiliation Agreement
Reinsurer	Termination	Nonforfeiture Benefits
Risk of Adverse Deviation	Termination Rate	Normal Servicing Fee Rate
Separately Priced Contracts	Title Plant	Participating Life Insurance Contract
Term Life Insurance	Translate-Restate	Prospective Reinsurance
Title Insurance Enterprise	Whole-Life Contract	Reciprocal or Interinsurance Exchange

CHECK THE TERMINOLOGY SECTION OF THE TOPICAL INDEX AND READ LINKS TO BUILD COMPRE-
HENSION. RECORD THE CITATIONS TO THE LITERATURE FOR FUTURE REFERENCE. USE EACH TERM
IN A SENTENCE.

Table 3.40 Specialized Industry Considerations   Page **3-89**

Table 3.40   Specialized Industry Considerations COMPLETE THIS TABLE

Terms	Search Recommended* (Semicolons are not part of the search but are used as separators.)	Citation for Definition: Provide Full Reference	Other Searches You Would Suggest
Specialized industry	Specialized industr*		
Industry-specific guidance	Industry-specific guidance		

*Access FARS, click on File, Open, Nfo, Open, and select FASB-OP (amended), click Search, enter query.

Problems

1. Where are many of the definitions associated with particular industries located within FARS? Be specific. How can you efficiently access such resources to explore an industry?

2. Using the Topical Index, see how many entries you can identify that direct you to cites that focus on a specialized industry. List the industries identified for future reference.

3. SELF-STUDY Q&A. **Q:** Specialized industries often have tailored disclosure expectations. Use FARS to identify Oil and Gas Producers' complete set of financial statements.
   A. *The Topical Index, under O, contains the topic OIL AND GAS PRODUCING ACTIVITIES with subheads of Definition and Complete Set of Financial Statements. Links include FAS69, Par. 1, Oi5.400, and FAS95, Par. 152.*

4. SELF-STUDY Q&A. **Q:** The *Wall Street Journal* reported in an article entitled "Tracking the Numbers: Outside Audit H&R Block Leans More on Loan-Servicing Fees—A Change in Assumptions on Mortgage-Related Assets May Give Pause to Investors" by Steven D. Jones on March 7, 2006 (p. C3) that changes in its valuation generated more noncash income than reported as the total income for the mortgage unit in the second quarter of the fiscal 2006. The valuation of mortgage servicing rights (MSRs) which is that business of processing mortgage paperwork and collecting monthly payments for a fee is based on the present value of future streams of loan-servicing income. Identify the cite in FARS that sets forth such an accounting treatment. Why might such a valuation change regularly and represent a large proportion of an income statement for such an entity?
   A. *Access FARS, open FASB-OP (amended), use Query, and enter the search phrase* mortgage servicing rights present value. *The result is FAS 140, Par. 276. Illustrative guidance regarding the determination of fair value is in Par. 343. FAS 140, Par. 359 describes the various estimates and choices underlying valuation. They suggest multiple reasons for regular changes in valuation and, if such assets are a large part of an entity's operations, one would expect such changes to have a potentially large effect. Also see FAS 156, an amendment of FAS 140.*

CHAPTER 4 – BRAIN TEASERS:

Using the Financial Accounting Research System (FARS) to Untangle the Mystery

Introduction to Brain Teasers

The "Brain Teasers" in this chapter use an active dialogue approach of individuals discussing a conceptual or practice problem that needs to be analyzed. The search phrases you will use must be designed to identify resources that can shed light on the issue at hand. In addition, you are asked to explore a number of resources beyond FARS. A Bonus Question appears for each Brain Teaser which tends to be a straightforward, directed question, that facilitates enhancement of FARS search skills. Depending on the topic within the Brain Teaser, you will find additional questions in varied subject matter from across the accounting curriculum, including Accounting Theory, Auditing, Tax, Not-for-Profit, Advanced Accounting, and International.

As you proceed to solve the Brain Teasers, keep in mind the following ten points:

1. Searches of the *Topical Index* are helpful in identifying sources from all Infobases.
2. Open the Infobase before you attempt to search.
3. Historical questions may require that you access *FASB-OP* rather than *FASB-OP (amended)*.
4. If a question is focused upon *EITFs*, then open EITF Abstracts from the main menu.
5. If a question is focused upon *FSPs*, use the toolbar in FARS to click Search and then select from the pull down menu Search FSP documents only.
6. If a question is focused upon a particular type of pronouncement, use the toolbar in FARS to click Search and then select from the pull down menu Search within a single OP document type.
7. If a question is focused on a particular standard, use the toolbar in FARS to click Search and then select from the pull down menu Search within a single OP document title.
8. Query can be a powerful tool for broad searches and then narrowed with Boolean operators.
9. Advanced Query can add proximity capabilities to your search and inform you of the relative frequency of particular words within an Infobase.
10. The process of research often requires several steps, involving more than a single search approach, and potentially moving from a broad search to focused consideration of a document type or title.

EXAMPLE OF BRAIN TEASER WITH SOLUTION: What Has Changed in the Conceptual Framework?

Isn't The Objective of Financial Reporting Much the Same?

Mark: I just read the Preliminary Views (PV) document on the current Conceptual Framework project that I downloaded from fasb.org. It was issued July 6, 2006 and the deadline for comments is November 3, 2006. I've been asked to give an update at our staff meeting on the new PV, but I'm stymied. I had this déjà vu feeling when I read the document. It seems to me that the single overarching objective of general purpose external financial reporting for business entities is much the same. Moreover, the four major factors they describe as important qualities of decision-useful financial information are relevance, faithful representation, comparability (including consistency), and understandability.

Johanna: Those do sound familiar. I do have one suggestion; I just read an interview with the FASB Board collaborator on that project; it was in *The FASB Report*, downloadable from fasb.org, dated August 31, 2006. Let me look up my download—it's the first two pages of the *Financial Accounting Series* No. 263. Anyway, it's bound to help sort out what is new.

Mark: Good idea.

Johanna: Moreover, why not access FARS and compare what the current framework has to say, in explicit terms? Even if the same words are used, often both meanings and priorities change over time with the standard-setters.

Required:

Use FARS to determine how the four major factors Mark has identified in the recent PV document are defined and used in the current conceptual framework. Access the other sources cited to prepare a brief update for the staff meeting.

BONUS QUESTION:

Does the conceptual framework suggest stewardship as an objective of financial reporting?

SOLUTION:

An approach to exploring how FARS reflects the qualitative characteristics of information is to go to the FARS site and open the Topical Index to perform a Query. This is powerful since it concurrently searches all tables of contents of the FARS infobases when you type *qualitative characteristics of information*. A key result displays that the Topical Index has a heading of "Qualitative Characteristics" which also highlights the glossary and suggests various subtopics, citing where they are elaborated upon within FARS. The dominant source is clearly CON2, although some links are to other parts of the Conceptual Framework in FARS.

You can download the Preliminary Views document and *The FASB Report* from fasb.org, as well as considering FARS and other resources within fasb.org. (For example, see FASAC meeting materials, including: Joint Conceptual Framework Project, Financial Accounting Standards Advisory Council June 2005 Attachment F, June 13, 2005.) With this information you prepare the following handout (see box) that you will distribute to update the professional staff. It has four sections. The first is your description of Statements of Financial Accounting Concepts (SFAC or CON) and a summary from CON2 of the current hierarchical approach to accounting qualities. The second addresses the Conceptual Framework Improvements Project. The third focuses on the Preliminary Views (PV) document. The fourth describes things to come, based on historical literature addressing both the conceptual framework and international harmonization.

Added historical perspective explaining "Why Does the FASB Have a Conceptual Framework?" can be found in the Financial Accounting Standards Board publication *Understanding the Issues* (FASB, August 2001). Authors John M. (Neel) Foster, then an FASB member, and L. Todd Johnson, then Senior Project Manager explain: "Concepts Statements do not affect practice directly. They do not require changes in generally accepted accounting principles, amend, modify or interpret existing accounting or disclosure standards or require changes in accounting procedures or require disclosure of practices that might be in conflict with the concepts.... The framework affects practice only by means of its influence in the development of new accounting standards" (p. 1). Similarly, historical perspective on the role of constraints is provided within FARS: see APB Statement No. 4, *Basic Concepts and Accounting Principles Underlying Financial Statements or Business Enterprises* (October 1970), par. 24. An example of a FARS cross-citation to the conceptual framework is in the dissent to SFAS 69, *Disclosures about Oil and Gas Producing Activities,* an amendment of FASB Statements 19, 25, 33, and 39 issued November 1982, which states: "Elsewhere, the Board has stated that relevance and reliability are the two primary qualities that make accounting useful for decision making and has adopted the position that if either of those qualities is completely missing, the information will not be useful (FASB Concepts Statement No. 2, Qualitative Characteristics of Accounting Information)."

UPDATE ON PRELIMINARY VIEWS (PV) CONCEPTUAL FRAMEWORK
FARS Framework: Statements of Financial Accounting Concepts (SFAC or CON) have a purpose of setting "forth fundamentals on which financial accounting and reporting standards will be based." (CON1, Objectives of Financial Reporting by Business Enterprises, issued November 1978, highlights.) They "are intended to establish the objectives and concepts that the Financial Accounting Standards Board will use in developing standards of financial accounting and reporting." Their format is similar to SFASs, including the possibility of dissents, frequent inclusion of a glossary, and extensive background and appendices.
CON2: Hierarchy of Accounting Qualities
Consider User-Specific Qualities
Consider Pervasive Constraint that Benefits Must Exceed Costs
PRIMARY DECISION-SPECIFIC QUALITIES OF <u>RELEVANCE</u> AND RELIABILITY MUST EACH BE PRESENT TO SOME DEGREE
Dimensions of Relevance could be predictive value or feedback value. Timeliness is a consideration.
Dimensions of Reliability include verifiability and <u>representational faithfulness</u>.
CON2 Qualitative Characteristics of Accounting Information issued May 1980, Summary explains: "The hierarchy separates user-specific qualities, for example, <u>understandability</u>, from qualities inherent in information. Information cannot be useful to decision makers who cannot understand it, even though it may otherwise be relevant to a decision and be reliable."
SECONDARY AND INTERACTIVE QUALITIES INCLUDE Neutrality
Seek <u>Comparability including Consistency</u> but consider interaction with PRIMARY QUALITIES in the hierarchy. Hence, if a choice has to be made among alternative accounting recording and disclosure approaches and one approach provides more of a primary qualitative characteristic, the conceptual framework would describe such an approach as preferable.
MATERIALITY determines threshold for recognition and disclosure. (See CON2, par. 33.)
Background of the Conceptual Framework Improvements Project:
The Financial Accounting Standards Board (FASB) has admitted to contradictions among its individual Statements of Financial Accounting Standards (SFASs) and the Statements of Financial Accounting Concepts. As a result, the board has announced a conceptual framework improvements project that will try to align the conceptual framework and existing standards. The joint project between the FASB and IASB face the added challenge that the conceptual framework each developed do not always agree with one another. The Board added the Conceptual Framework project to its agenda on October 20, 2004 explaining it was a "joint project with the IASB to develop a common conceptual framework that is based on and builds on the existing frameworks" (Financial Accounting Series No. 264 January 31, 2005, *The FASB Report*, Technical Plan Beginning January 1, 2005, p. 1). Financial Accounting Series No. 267-A (April 18, 2005), *The FASB Report* Technical Plan — April 1, 2005 through September 30, 2005, p. 4 explains that a joint project is being undertaken with the IASB with the "goal of developing standards that are

more principles-based, internally consistent, internationally converged, and that lead to financial reporting that provides the information needed for investment, credit, and similar decisions" (p. 4).

PRELIMINARY VIEWS (PV) CONCEPTUAL FRAMEWORK DOCUMENT
Overview: This PV is a step in the FASB and IASB joint project to update existing conceptual frameworks and only concerns the objective of financial reporting and the qualitative characteristics of decision-useful financial information.
1. In an interview with board member Michael Crooch, *The FASB Report* observes that "the basic objective of financial reporting is much the same" and explains its focus on a wide group of primary users "to provide information that is useful to present and potential investors and creditors and others in making investment, credit, and similar resource allocation decisions."
2. Both accrual accounting and cash flow information is emphasized, alongside management explanations and other information. The amounts, timing, and uncertainty surrounding an entity's cash flow prospects are focal points.
3. Important qualities of good information include relevance, faithful representation (REPLACING reliability in the current framework, but intended to mean complete, verifiable, and neutral with none of the three being subordinated subqualities), comparability (including consistency), and understandability.
4. Neither complexity nor difficulty for users' understanding are reasons to exclude relevant financial information.

Examples of Things to Come
The Exposure Draft Proposed Statement of Financial Accounting Standards: The Hierarchy of Generally Accepted Accounting Principles (Financial Accounting Series No. 1300-001, April 28, 2005) expects to consider the role of Concepts Statements in its conceptual framework project and specifically notes that the IASB accords a higher standing to its conceptual guidance than does the FASB. Whether and how to converge the hierarchy is expected to consider the SEC's recommendation that the FASB's conceptual framework be designated as authoritative literature once improvements to the framework are completed (pp. i and ii).
Preliminary Views documents on later phases are expected in 2006 or later.   Based on a brief literature review, an example of one issue to be tackled concerns the reconciliation of Comprehensive Income in the U.S. relative to the UK's split of overall financial performance into two broad components termed "trading" and "capital." (Source: Financial Accounting Series No. 181-A, January 1998 Special Report—*Reporting Financial Performance: Current Developments and Future Directions*)

Solution to the BONUS QUESTION merely requires that attention be accorded to a word search of stewardship within FARS.

Go to FARS, open the Topical Index, and type the Query *stewardship*. Two citations are returned in the results:

Stewardship	CON1, ¶50-53
... Not-for-Profit Organizations	CON4, ¶40-42
Management Stewardship	CON4, ¶40-42

Par. 50 of CON1 specifically states: "Financial reporting should provide information about how management of an enterprise has discharged its stewardship responsibility to owners (stockholders) for the use of enterprise resources entrusted to it." Similarly, par. 40 of CON4 states: "Financial reporting should provide information that is useful to present and potential resource providers and other users in assessing how managers of a nonbusiness organization have discharged their stewardship responsibilities and about other aspects of their performance."

These passages suggest that information usefulness includes information on stewardship, with particular attention to both business and nonbusiness use. However, if you go to Advanced Query and type in the phrase *objective financial reporting stewardship*, zero hits are returned.

Moving from the Topical Index infobase that focuses on tables of contents to the FASB-OP (amended) infobase, again type in the Advanced Query the phrase *objective financial reporting stewardship*. Three hits are returned in the HitList: the FAS 35 Dissent, FAS 124, par. 35, and CON4, par. 67. By clicking the <u>Documents Tab</u>, you can read through these results. The second cite states: "Fair value information assists users in assessing management's stewardship and performance—thus helping to meet the third objective of financial reporting discussed in Concepts Statement 4." The table found in CON4, par. 67 explicitly compares par. 40 of CON4 to par. 50 of CON1 as they describe objectives. You will want to offer this evidence from FARS in support of your affirmative answer to the bonus question.

This example of a Brain Teaser with Solution bears out the usefulness of FARS in understanding the current framework of guidance from standard setters. It also demonstrates the importance of checking the <u>fasb.org</u> site for subsequent developments, following the date at which your FARS resource cuts off. Since the standard-setting process can take years to move projects from its Agenda through Preliminary Views, and eventually to pronouncements, the <u>fasb.org</u> site is a key complement. Once a document such as a PV is issued, you can access comment letters that permit you to consider others' points of view. Moreover, you can read publications that contain updates and perspectives from board members and their professional staff. In line with resources introduced in Chapter 2, numerous other modes of research can be applied, including literature searches, databases, and Internet sites.

As you proceed to solve various Brain Teasers, depending on the topic, you will find additional questions in varied subject matter from across the accounting curriculum, including Accounting Theory, Auditing, Tax, Not-for-Profit, Advanced Accounting, and International. Refer to these when practicing your skills in research throughout your study of accounting.

Brain Teaser 1: How Many Standards Have Been Issued by FASB?

Isn't It The Last Numbered Pronouncement?

Ed: I just read that the Financial Accounting Standards Board has issued a pronouncement that is numbered 155!

Eve: That's only half of the story. Remember that we had the Accounting Principles Board (APB) before the Financial Accounting Standards Board (FASB), and some of the APB opinions are still effective.

Ed: Oh, you're right. We even have some Accounting Research Bulletins (ARBs) that are still effective.

Eve: Moreover, the FASB has issued *more* than 155 pronouncements.

Ed: What do you mean?

Required:

Use FARS to explain what Eve means.

BONUS QUESTION:

How many ARBs are still effective?

Auditing Issue:

You are involved in an engagement that includes auditing prior years' financial statements. What is the easiest way to determine which accounting standards were effective during a particular time period?

Tax Issue:

How many standards have been issued in which the title itself recognizes a tax dimension?

Brain Teaser 2: Dissents Portending Future?

Always Read the Dissent

Maureen: I remember my undergraduate professor's suggestion that whenever we read a financial accounting standard, we should carefully read through the dissents, if any are reported.

Jeannie: It would seem with the reasonably small size of the FASB that the members could reach total consensus. Given that the Statements of Financial Accounting Standards set generally accepted accounting principles (GAAP) for the entire country, why not require that at least all the board members be convinced before moving forward?

Maureen: Well, as a matter of fact, my understanding is that it was proposed to change the voting rules, not to total consensus, but to a different mix of required votes for approval, and it caused a real political debate. It seems many thought that the shift toward more approving votes being required was perceived to be a strategy that was intended to cause a stalemate, which would slow down the standard-setting process.

Jeannie: Oh, how could it get any slower? The stock options project began in the early 1980s and took well over a decade before the SFAS No. 123 was issued. Then SFAS No. 123 was revised after that, not to mention SFAS No. 148. I believe the pension projects spanned over a decade as well and now are under revision again!

Maureen: You do have a point. Perhaps that is why timeliness is one of the virtues of accounting that could not withstand a total consensus requirement by the Board.

Jeannie: Well, I can tell you that sometimes the dissents seem more logical, or at least they accurately portend what will need additional attention in the future.

Maureen: Do you have something particular in mind?

Jeannie: As a matter of fact, I do. I vaguely remember hearing about a dissent that specifically warned that the way the statement had been written implied that a new materiality standard was being set. Well, that warning was ignored, and sure enough, a later statement had to be issued by the FASB to address that very point.... I am pretty sure it was associated with materiality.

Maureen: I, for one, would like to see that. Could you find the dissent, as well as the superseding SFAS, so we could look it over?

Jeannie: Thank goodness for technology! With the Boolean logic in FARS, I'm sure this should not be too difficult. . . . Let's go to the program and try.

Required:

Use FARS to find the dissent to which Jeannie is referring, as well as the subsequent Statement of Financial Accounting Standards (SFAS) issued to correct the problem highlighted in the original pronouncement's dissent. If you had been a member of the original board, do you believe you would have joined the majority position or the dissent? Why or why not?

BONUS QUESTION:

How many of the Statements of Financial Accounting Standards (SFASs) were adopted by the unanimous vote of the seven members of the FASB?

Accounting Theory Issue:

Has the FASB ever explicitly noted that the materiality box that is rather standard on each Statement, stating "The provisions of this Statement need not be applied to immaterial items" does not apply to a particular aspect of a professional pronouncement?

Auditing Issue:

It has been asserted that the dissents to SFASs are of particular use to an auditor in evaluating whether Rule 203 should be invoked in the expression of an auditor's report. Do you agree with this assertion? Why? Cooperative steps have been taken between the American Institute of Certified Public Accountants (AICPA) and FASB to set aside the Rule 203 exception. Explore the AICPA and FASB Web sites regarding these steps and consider whether you view this as a step forward or a step back and why. Is there any analogy to the United States' Rule 203 in the international literature?

Tax Issue:

Using FARS, identify those dissents to SFASs that involve some dimension of taxes.

Brain Teaser 3: Hybrid Historical Cost and Market Value—Why the Mix?

What's a Hybrid?

Ken: I keep seeing in the financial press references to *hybrid* accounting. What's a hybrid?

Pat: The term I've seen just as often is *multiattribute* accounting. The point of the articles I've read seems to be that we accountants have not decided whether historical cost or market value is the "right" valuation basis, so now we have a hybrid throughout the balance sheet.

Ken: If the issue is between historical cost and market value, why is the term *multiattribute* popular? Doesn't the term *multi* mean more than just two choices?

Pat: Actually, far more than two values do appear on the balance sheet. Think about the lower of cost or market concept applied to inventory—that's neither an historical cost nor a market value, but a bit of a blend of the two. Then we have some estimates, such as net realizable receivables, that likewise blend historical cost transactions with a concurrent estimate of which of those amounts may prove to be uncollectible.

Ken: Now that you mention it, I don't even think that our historical cost and market value definitions are all of similar ilk. For example, we write down an historical cost of a fixed asset through depreciation and report book value thereafter. It would seem that book value is neither historical cost nor market value.

Pat: I have concern that when we say market value, many think of the New York Stock Exchange as the source of value, whereas many entities hold securities that are not traded on well-developed markets. The question becomes "what is the essence of market value that we do report in such cases?"

Ken: I think the problem of hybrids is worsening. The concept of impairment accounting moves away from either a clear market value or an historical cost concept. It seems to often rely on an estimated cash flow projection based on tailored intended use of the asset in question. Without an arm's-length transaction and potentially no secondary market to speak of for specialized assets, it would seem that the basis of accounts in the balance sheet would have a plethora of definitions.

Pat: Multiattributes indeed! You know, I've been asked to speak on the topic of account valuation to a group of analysts. I think a great "take-away" would be examples of the basis of accounting presently in GAAP, especially how market value is defined in relation to various pronouncements.

Ken: I wonder if it would be possible to analyze the pros and cons of historical cost, market value, or some selected alternative basis of accounting.

Pat: That's a great idea! I certainly hope the standards would imply why the diversity of definitions has evolved. If not, just posing the question of "why the difference" would be food for thought.

Ken: I'll give you a hand. Let's access FARS. You know, one angle to consider is that historical cost and market value equal one another at the date of acquisition. You could point that fact out and then pose the question, "So why and how do they differ?"

Required:

Use FARS and prepare a table on all definitions you are able to identify as to the specific basis of accounting used in valuation. As you prepare the table, keep track of how you went about finding each definition and be prepared to brainstorm with colleagues about other effective means of identifying definitions of this type. In the table itself, be certain to include full citations and the succinct definitions found. Read the materials surrounding the excerpts to see if they can help you develop an explanation as to why the particular definition was included in the guidance. In other words, what are its comparative advantages relative to alternatives? In addition to preparing a table of citations and definitions as to basis of valuation, prepare a list of the pros and cons of historical cost relative to market value. Keep in mind that the table and the list are intended to be self-contained handouts for distribution to a group of professionals involved in financial statement analysis. By focusing on a particular audience, you may find it easier to develop a handout that effectively communicates.

BONUS QUESTION:

Does Statement of Financial Accounting Standards No. 155 "Accounting for Certain Hybrid Financial Instruments" eliminate the use of different measurement attributes for financial instruments?

Accounting Theory Issue:

If fair value is an arm's-length market price, then the assumptions as to how the asset can be used are embedded in the market rather than being an entity-specific belief by the current owner. Moreover, it focuses on price and does not make allowance for transactions cost. Do these two observations receive attention in the professional literature? Do you agree with the standard-setters' perspective on each of these dimensions of fair value?

Auditing Issue:

You are auditing the reported value of a financial instrument that was purchased by the auditee from a related party. Assume the financial instrument is convertible preferred stock issued by a private company. How would you proceed to evaluate the reasonableness of the financial statement representation? What particular auditing challenges are faced in such a setting?

Brain Teaser 4: Cash Basis or Accrual Basis?

Is Accrual Accounting Superior to Cash Basis?

Alicia: In the finance literature, there seems to be an emphasis on cash. Stock prices are discussed as the present value of future cash flows. Most of the capital budgeting applications in which investment decisions are made appear to focus on the cash required at acquisition and the cash flows expected during the life of that investment. If cash is so important, why is accrual accounting the focus in GAAP?

John: A problem with just following the cash is that you can collect cash or pay cash and really have little economic activity underlying those cash exchanges. Indeed, I can structure terms of payment almost any way I choose in a contract, including so-called balloon payments, where almost all the cash changes hands at the end of a contract. If all accounting statements did was track the cash, little information would be provided as to how the cash had actually been generated, invested, or lost.

Alicia: Last night on the news, there was a story about a college student who had managed to run up almost $20,000 in credit card debt, while still an undergraduate. On a cash basis, if someone thought he had received that $20,000 for some actual economic service, that would clearly be way off the mark. I mean, cash acquired through debt has to be different from cash that one receives because he or she has performed some service or sold some asset. In fact, receiving cash from selling something is not at all the same as receiving cash as an employee for providing services. After all, you can only sell an asset once, whereas services can continue to be provided, generating recurring cash flows.

John: I remember someone once asserting that cash flow was all that was important, and accountants just "mess things up" by imposing the accrual accounting framework on the analysis of cash flows. It made no sense when I heard it, and the more I learn about economic activity, the less sense that assertion makes. Besides, we accountants, after all, do prepare statements of cash flow as well. However, we respect the differences in operating, financing, and investing activities.

Alicia: Of course, I've never quite understood why we call interest an "operating item" and not a "financing item." Nonetheless, I agree that the Statement of Cash Flows alone or the publication of an entity's bank statement would in no way reflect performance effectively. Yet, it is obvious that many investors are at least confused as to the nature of accrual accounting and its importance relative to cash flow analysis.

John: I wonder whether GAAP explain the importance of accrual accounting relative to a cash basis.

Alicia: Let's find out.

Required:

Use FARS to identify what standard-setters have said as to the superiority of accrual accounting relative to a cash basis. Do you agree with the justification offered for accrual accounting? Explain.

BONUS QUESTION:

Identify which accounting pronouncement specifically observes: "This Statement relies on a basic premise of generally accepted accounting principles that accrual accounting provides more relevant and useful information than does cash basis accounting."

Accounting Theory Issue:

When is a "cash-basis method" used within the accounting literature? Do you view such a method as complementary or preferable to accrual accounting in the settings you have identified?

Auditing Issue:

Would a cash basis be easier or harder to audit than an accrual basis? Why?

Tax Issue:

Does FARS suggest the existence of guidance that sponsors the idea that certain earnings may be accounted for on an accrual basis while the related income taxes are accounted for on a cash basis?

Not-for-Profit Issue:

When did most not-for-profit organizations change from a cash or "modified cash" basis to accrual accounting?

Brain Teaser 5: Where Are Charitable Donations on Corporate Income Statements?

Why Is There No Line Item for Charitable Donations?

Christine: I believe in giving to charities, and I know that corporate America does as well. Yet, every time that I read a financial statement, even those from my socially responsible mutual fund companies, I notice that the income statement has no separate line item reporting charitable donations. My question is, why?

Christina: That's a good question. I would think companies would want credit for their charitable gifts.

Charlie: You no doubt have noticed, though, that very few line items appear on the income statement. I mean, it's not easy to discern what was spent on employees' salaries, or even whether research and development expenses were incurred, in some cases.

Christine: You're right about the simplicity of the usual income statement. I mean, a handful of line items are typical. The press releases tend to have even fewer line items. Yet, I know the Securities and Exchange Commission (SEC) is a proponent of full disclosure.

Christina: Sometimes I've been able to find additional detail in the notes to the financial statements, even though it's not provided as a line item. Yet, I don't recall seeing details on charitable donations in the notes, so your question remains unanswered.

Charlie: Well, given GAAP are supposed to provide guidance on reporting, there must be some explanation for the line items we see reported and those that appear to be missing.

Christine: You're right, let's see if we can solve the puzzle.

Sophia: Can I help?

Required:

Use FARS to find an explanation for why certain line items dominate the income statements of public companies. Does the absence of a line item mean that expense was not incurred? Specifically, is the apparent absence of charitable donations as a line item indicative of corporate companies not making contributions? Explain. Choose a major company in which you have an interest and access its Web page. See if that company's home page references community activities and charitable donations. Note the scope and types of disclosures provided. Do your findings correspond to the income statement presentations by that company? Are your findings reconcilable to the guidance you located in FARS? Explain.

BONUS QUESTION:

Apply the search phrase *line item charit** to the FASB-OP (amended) infobase. Does the passage identified bear any relationship to the question of where information on charitable donations might be located? Explain.

Accounting Theory Issue:

The FASB Report (Financial Accounting Series, No. 279 April 26, 2006) reports that the Financial Statement Presentation joint FASB/IASB project was undertaken "to establish a common, high-quality standard for presentation of information in the financial statements, including the classification and display of line items and the aggregation of line items into subtotals and totals." A Preliminary Views and Discussion paper is expected in the first quarter of 2007. Access the FASB and IASB Web sites to explore developments. Do any of the materials imply that the incidence of charitable contributions as a line item on corporate financial statements will be more likely in the future? Would you judge this project to be principles-based or rules-based in nature?

Auditing Issue:

You are auditing a grocery store chain that has adopted the practice of having each cashier ask every customer if he or she "would like to round up to the nearest dollar" and contribute the difference to charity. How would such a practice influence the audit process? Identify the associated risks and any particular complications for the auditor in evaluating the fairness of the financial statements' representations associated with such charity projects.

Tax Issue:

Does FARS contain information on the tax effects of charitable contributions? Be specific.

Not-for-Profit Issue:

You are the chief executive of a not-for-profit hospital and just read an article entitled "Cleveland Clinic Defends Gift from a Vendor" by David Armstrong in the *Wall Street Journal* (August 8, 2006, pp. B1, B4). The article reports that a company providing radiation therapy to the hospital's cancer patients had donated a $500,000 gift for a research chair. What is the nature of the problem and can accounting practices be of help in addressing the matter?

Advanced Accounting Issue:

Does FARS provide direction on the consolidation of foundations?

Brain Teaser 6: Deferred Debits and Deferred Credits

What Is the Nature of a Deferred Debit and How Does It Differ from a Deferred Credit?

Cynthia: I thought that accounts within information systems were supposed to be clearly labeled to communicate with financial statement users. Yet, I have seen references to deferred debits and to deferred credits, and I find those titles unclear. I mean, what is a deferred debit? Is it a balance sheet item? How should it be classified and why? How is it different from a deferred credit? What is the effect on cash flows of such items?

John Jr.: You always have 50 questions. The basic question to which you really want an answer is from where do they come: what generates a deferred debit or a deferred credit?

Cynthia: You're right. That is the basic question, and I suppose if we understand the answer of how they originate, we could deduce the answer to some of my other questions.

John Jr.: I remember a professor recounting how deferred taxes were being referred to as "UGOs" or "Unidentified Growing Objects" because their size relative to total assets was anything but trivial.

Cynthia: I also recall some discussion of *dangling debits* when the standard-setting community was debating the issue of how derivatives and hedges should be recorded. I don't remember any details, but I do think more than taxes are involved in the area of these deferred debits and credits.

John Jr.: There's one way to find out. Let's search FARS and see if we can find some explanations for when deferred debits and credits arise.

Required:

Use FARS to answer each of the questions posed by both Cynthia and John Jr.

BONUS QUESTION:

Does FARS contain a specific proscription that some item not be classified as a deferred credit?

Accounting Theory Issue:

Does FARS contain any conceptual discussion of deferred credits? Elaborate.

Auditing Issue:

Your auditee's balance sheet contains the caption "deferred charges." You use inquiry procedures and discover that this includes: (a) the discount resulting from the determination of present value in cash or non-cash transactions involving a note receivable; (b) issue costs associated with a note payable; and (c) the tax effect of an estimated provision for warranties. Are each of these appropriately classified within the nomenclature of the caption? Why or why not? What additional aspects of the items need to be explored in order to complete the audit of the reporting presentation?

Tax Issue:

Has the Emerging Issues Task Force in its EITFs directed attention to deferred tax debits?

Not-for-Profit Issue:

Rosemary and Wiley who are directors for a not-for-profit organization have listened to the dialogue between Cynthia and John Jr. They ask whether deferred debits and credits have any relevance to them and why that might be the case. What should be the response?

Brain Teaser 7: Time Value of Money: Gone Today but Here Tomorrow?

Why the Inconsistent Attention to Time Value of Money in Evaluating Impairments?

Nancy: I'm more than a little perplexed.

Dave: What about?

Nancy: I've been reading the guidance on fixed assets and the treatment of impairments.

Dave: Did you have insomnia last night, or what?

Nancy: Seriously, I have a client with a large book value for fixed assets, and I have to determine whether our team needs to accord attention to the area of impairment. And the problem I have is that it seems to me that present value is not used at all in considering whether current book values exceed future cash flows. However, if the future cash flows in nominal, undiscounted dollars are expected to fall below the recorded book value, then it's a whole new ballgame.

Dave: I see your point. We had an impairment situation with a client last year, and you are right that when an impairment trigger occurs, the impairment guidance requires that future cash flows be discounted to evaluate the amount that should be recorded as the basis.

Nancy: I find it more than a little curious that time value of money is used for cash flows when you value impaired assets, while they are not used to determine impairment. Why is this the case?

Dave: Well, it would certainly make a difference if the trigger involved discounting, wouldn't it? Now you have me perplexed. I'm still reeling from the asset retirement obligation guidance: sorting out how the liability is discounted and accretion expense is recognized using the credit-adjusted risk-free interest rate in effect when the liability was initially recognized for asset retirement obligations.

Nancy: One step at a time. Let's take a careful look at the present value literature and the impairment guidance and see if we can figure out the reason for the inconsistency.

Kathryn: Can I help?

Required:

Use FARS to determine the logic of time value of money concepts being used in a manner that appears to be inconsistent. Explain how you believe fixed assets would be affected if the present value of money was consistently used both in assessing triggers for impairment analysis and in valuing assets deemed to be impaired. Provide a numeric example to illustrate the effects described. Be certain to clearly state your assumptions and show the related calculations to demonstrate your perspective and related conclusions.

BONUS QUESTION:

Are discount rates intended to capture both the time value of money and risk exposure? Why or why not? A company uses an assumption of a discount rate for pension benefits of 6.75% in the current year, whereas the rate used in the prior year was 7.25%. The weighted average interest rate on outstanding commercial paper in the current year is 1.71%, while the weighted average rate on senior notes is 6.48%. Do these observations have any bearing on your evaluation as to the propriety of the interest rate used in impairment measurement for assets? Why or why not?

Accounting Theory Issue:

If a creditor measures impairment of a loan based on the present value of expected future cash flows, should the change in present value attributable to the passage of time be reported as a reduction of bad-debt expense or as interest income?

Auditing Issue:

The *Wall Street Journal* reported "IBM Ruling Paves Way for Changes to Pensions: Appeals Court's Reversal of Discrimination Finding to Aid Cash-Balance Plans" (by Ellen E. Schultz and Theo Francis, August 8, 2006, p. A3). Moreover, Congressional pension reform has been reported to encourage cash-balance plans. The nature of a cash-balance plan is that benefit pay is based on an employee's pay in each year, rather than being tied to an average salary amount, and a single rate is applied to determine that annual amount. The formula then applies a hypothetical interest rate. The nature of the IBM ruling was a finding that since all ages receive the same percentage of the pay, it is age neutral.

You are aware that one of your auditees had delayed a transition from an existing defined benefit plan due to the earlier IBM court decision. Even though a chance exists that the case will be appealed yet again and be reversed, the auditee is contemplating proceeding to a cash-balance plan. In a meeting with the audit committee, one of the directors poses the question to you as to why the older employees of IBM contend that the result of IBM's change to a cash-balance plan had harmed them, reducing their total pension by an estimated 20 to 50 percent.

Can you provide an answer by applying your knowledge of the time value of money? If the auditee requested you to consult regarding alternative pension plans, should you provide such assistance?

Brain Teaser 8: What Do We Record When Interest Rates Diverge?

Stated, Implicit, Imputed, and Effective Interest Rates: What If They Diverge?

Bill: We have to record some interest for the financing element of the transaction.

Alex: The question is, what amount? There is no stated rate on the instrument itself.

Bill: Even if there were a stated rate, since the instrument's transaction value was different from the face of the instrument, an effective interest would have to be recorded, and that would differ from whatever stated rate was reported. Of course, that does not even apply here.

Alex: One approach would be to determine an implicit rate, whereby we back into the rate by looking at the cash flows.

Bill: That means we have to know the cash flows on both sides of the transaction, right? Do we have that detail?

Alex: I'm not sure if we do or not.

Bill: The other alternative is an imputed rate. That entails looking at the borrowing rate on other instruments. I think we need to do some research before we make a decision.

Alex: I read you. I'll access FARS and prepare a table of definitions of stated, effective, implicit, and imputed rates. Alongside the definitions, I'll see if the standards provide a clear example of where each approach is to be used.

Bill: If it's not clear which definition and context fits our transaction, what should we do if the approaches diverge? While you're doing the research, be on the lookout for whether these are mutually exclusive definitions, or whether there is some basis for choosing from among varying approaches.

Alex: I'll see what I can do.

Required:

Use FARS to prepare the table described. In your judgment, are the definitions and examples you have identified mutually exclusive, or is there an overlap that requires judgment? If you were to apply these definitions to a single transaction and found there to be a divergence, how would you proceed? Why might the approaches generate different interest rates for a single transaction? Could a single company apply different definitions to multiple transactions? Choose a company and access its 10-K filing from http://www.sec.gov. Read through the financial statements and accompanying notes, and list every interest rate identified, alongside the type of transaction to which it relates. Why might a single company record disparate interest rates on different transactions?

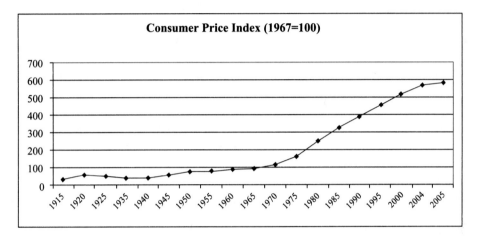

Figure 4.8-1 Given economic indicators vary over time, is it surprising reported rates of any given company likewise vary? [Sources: Bureau of Labor Statistics, U.S. Department of Labor. *The World Almanac and Book of Facts 2006*, Shoreview, MN: Pearson Education, p. 79. In 2006, a proposal that the CPI be reported to three decimals was made, suggesting that would better inform those evaluating the economy with respect to inflation (see the *Wall Street Journal*).]

BONUS QUESTION:

Do accounting standards sometimes prescribe current rates and at other times historical rates? Explain.

Auditing Issue:

An auditee purchased a $300,000 asset on credit and was told it was "interest free" and need not be paid off for four years. The auditee has assumed an imputed rate parallel to the 1.71% currently incurred on outstanding commercial paper in order to record the transaction. Explain how you would proceed to audit the appropriateness of this accounting treatment.

Brain Teaser 9: Inventoriable Costs?

What's All the Fuss about *Dot-Coms?*

Erin: It seems as though I can't pick up a newspaper or business journal without seeing some commentary on the accounting practices of *dot-coms*.

Patrick: I don't see what the fuss is about.

Erin: Well, I read an article that reminded me of an old case I had when I was in cost accounting called "The Clever President," ... only in reverse.

Patrick: Oh, I think we had that case, too. I'm foggy on recollection, but wasn't it about some CEO who negotiated to be compensated on reported income when he took the helm at a troubled company, proceeded to report big profits, and then resigned, leaving with a huge bonus?

Erin: Yes, and the so-called cleverness had to do with shoveling costs into inventory, building a stockpile of two years' worth of sales, and thereby enhancing gross profit and, in turn, net income.

Patrick: Remind me of why that worked.

Erin: Well, the idea has to do with fixed cost allocation. Since fixed costs don't change as production increases, by stockpiling inventory through doubling or even tripling production, the fixed costs were spread over two to three times as many units, cutting the per-unit allocation to only a half or a third of its previous level.

Patrick: In other words, the inventoriable costs in total grew as inventory grew, but the per-unit cost shrunk because of the per-unit fixed cost assignment. Now I remember.

Erin: As I understand the *dot.com* debates, a good deal has to do with whether things should have been inventoried rather than treated as period costs. You might look at the problem as the reverse of "The Clever President" case.

Patrick: I'm confused. If "The Clever President" case is supposed to illustrate an abuse of accounting, then how is it that the opposite is also an abuse?

Erin: Well, two wrongs never make a right.

Patrick: I hear you, but I still don't agree.

Erin: Okay, here's an example of the problem. The *dot.coms* have a line item they call "fulfillment costs." These costs are described as including costs attributable to receiving, inspecting, and warehousing inventories, as well as picking, packaging, and preparing customers' orders for shipment. The line item of fulfillment costs is being included in marketing expenses as a period cost. In other words, they are not being treated as a product cost at all. The question raised is whether they should be inventoriable costs.

Patrick: What's the harm if everything hits net income anyway? It sounds conservative to me.

Erin: Remember, conservatism for its own sake is not laudable. Accounting is intended to be neutral. Moreover, *where* something hits the income statement matters. By taking inventoriable costs and placing them as a period expense, the gross profit looks a great deal better than it ought to look to investors and others supplying capital. I've seen estimates that argue this maneuver can effectively quadruple the gross profit on sales.

Patrick: Why have the *dot.coms* presumed they have the choice of not placing at least some of these fulfillment costs into cost of goods sold? Isn't GAAP clear on this matter?

Erin: Well, income statements are not required to include a gross profit caption. Some companies use a presentation by nature of expense, rather than by function. You do have a good question as to what GAAP require. We certainly have to figure the situation out, because we have a new client that is a *dot.com*, and I'm certain we'll be asked for our view on the classification of costs. Let's see what we can find in the authoritative literature.

Required:

Use FARS to provide a basis from which Patrick and Erin can formulate a position as to the appropriate classification of the fulfillment cost components described in this case. Provide citations and key excerpts, and prioritize the guidance identified, based on the GAAP hierarchy. Given your research, what is your view regarding the appropriate accounting practice?

BONUS QUESTION:

Is profit-sharing an inventoriable cost?

Accounting Theory Issue:

Using FARS, describe the nature of hedges of inventory transactions and related debate as to how cash flows from such hedges ought to be classified. Could you envision an argument being made that costs related to such hedging activities be inventoriable? Identify within the EITF Abstracts an example of journal entries that involve both inventory and derivative activity.

Auditing Issue:

As an auditor, you independently evaluate which of the accounts in the auditee's income statements correspond to inventoriable costs. Describe any assumptions necessary for you to classify each of the following captions (*a.* through *bb.*). Either indicate *yes they are inventoriable* or *no they are not*, clarifying how your judgments rely on your assumptions.

a. Costs of services	*h.* Foreign currency adjustments when included by the company	*o.* Salaries and benefits	*v.* Depreciation and amortization
b. Delivery and branch expenses	*i.* Freight-out expense	*p.* Warehouse operations	*w.* Financing costs
c. Bad debt expense	*j.* Product cost of revenue	*q.* Engineering, research and development expenses	*x.* Restructuring and other severance charges
d. Commissions	*k.* Products and integration services	*r.* Store operating, general and administrative expenses	*y.* Cost of equipment sold
e. Fixed asset impairment charges	*l.* Income tax expense	*s.* Advertising expense	*z.* Directors' fees and remuneration
f. Indirect costs	*m.* Lease expense	*t.* Unfavorable overhead variance	*aa.* Rebates
g. Material, labor, and other production costs	*n.* Reimbursable expenses	*u.* Sales and marketing	*bb.* Cost of hardware resale revenue

Advanced Accounting Issue:

What is one of the key adjustments required for either equity method accounting or consolidations that relates to inventory accounting practices?

International Accounting Issue:

Search FARS to identify what changes in the inventory accounting area were prompted by a desire for international comparability.

Brain Teaser 10: Valuation of Inventory and Purchase Commitments

How Many Ways Are There to Value Inventory? What About Purchase Commitments?

Wayne: I read somewhere that an enormous number of choices are available for valuing inventory. I thought the main approach was historical cost. In other words, what you pay for it is the value of the inventory.

Quentin: What about retailers? I know there's a retail method of accounting, and there's an approach that records mark-ups and mark-downs.

Wayne: I wonder at how the retail method can work, given profits are not supposed to be recorded until sales are made.

Quentin: Oh, I think it's similar to removing transfer pricing profits from the financial statements for third parties. In other words, the profit embedded in the retail valuation is adjusted out of the numbers to ensure against premature profit recognition.

Wayne: What about purchase commitments? These days, sole-source suppliers are popular. If a purchase commitment is made to that supplier, is that purchase commitment valued in the financial statements? If no valuation appears in the balance sheet, is there disclosure required in the notes?

Quentin: That's an interesting question. We know that executory contracts such as compensation packages are commitments to purchase services of an employee, and yet I don't believe we record those commitments.

Wayne: I wonder what the reasoning is regarding whether purchase commitments are recorded and, as you say, whether they are recorded for goods but not for services.

Quentin: We can find out the answer. Let's explore the FARS database and see if it can help sort this out.

Required:

Use FARS to provide a listing of all of the approaches cited regarding the valuation of inventory. Likewise, describe the accounting treatment prescribed for purchase commitments. Be specific as to whether valuations appear on the financial statements and/or in the notes to the financial statements. Determine if there is a different treatment for executory contracts, such as executives' compensation, relative to purchase commitments. What do you believe is the reasoning for the accounting treatments you identify? Specifically, why is there such a variety of inventory valuations permitted? Why is the treatment distinctive for inventory relative to purchase commitments? Explain the approach prescribed for executory contracts.

BONUS QUESTION:

If a decline of inventory value is due to seasonal price fluctuations, must inventory at the interim date be written down to lower of cost or market?

Accounting Theory Issue:

The accounting literature frequently describes what respondents to earlier exposure drafts have contended. One example is where respondents are described as having recommended that retailers who use the retail method of accounting be permitted recognition of sales returns when merchandise actually is returned for refund or credit. Locate within FARS what the respondents' rationale was for this recommendation. Do you believe their points have merit?

Auditing Issue:

You audit a company that has long-term purchase commitments. The auditee has represented that the valuation account for estimated loss on purchase commitments is zero. How would you proceed to evaluate the propriety of this representation?

Tax Issue:

What was the *Insilco* Tax Court Decision and how and why did it affect financial accounting? The *Wall Street Journal* reported "Big Oil's Accounting Methods Fuel Criticism: LIFO Leaves the Likes of Exxon with Big Balance-Sheet Reserves as Gas-Pump Prices Slam Drivers" (by David Reilly, May 8, 2006, pp. C1, C3). The assertion is made that the use of LIFO had raised the company's cost, lowered net profit, and thereby trimmed the tax bill. Mention is made of potential tax reform that would repeal LIFO. In particular, attention is directed to the 2005 Exxon disclosure of initial cost relative to replacement cost resulting in a cumulative difference or "LIFO Reserve" over $15 billion. What do you think of such media coverage tying inventory accounting practice to pricing and suggesting a focus on tax consequences?

Advanced Accounting:

Is there a circumstance when intercompany profits should not be eliminated in consolidated financial statements if the transfer price is reasonable?

Brain Teaser 11: Are Capital Expenditure Numbers Comparable?

Why Might Capital Expenditures of One Company Differ from Those of Another?

Shareena: I have been asked to analyze the relative capital expenditures by a set of competitors in three industries. I'm to include a comparison of property, plant, and equipment investments by each entity. I have set up a prototype spreadsheet for collecting information from the financial statements, and I am wondering what other details I should record. It will be much easier if I can identify what I need so that I don't have to "go to the well" twice.

Alan: Describe what you have so far.

Shareena: I thought I would track the last 10 years. I'll record the beginning and ending balances of property, plant, and equipment—including the accumulated depreciation numbers. In addition, from the cash flow statement I'll collect all purchases and sales, as well as retirements of fixed assets. I thought I should record whatever details there are on useful life and salvage values. What do you think?

Alan: You're on the right track. However, what about self-constructed assets? What are the industries you are analyzing? Is it likely that self-constructed assets would be a prominent part of their operations?

Shareena: I hadn't even thought about that dimension. Indeed, one of the industries in particular is likely to self-construct assets.

Alan: That means you will want to consider the element of capitalized interest. Consider the hypothetical that two of the companies you are analyzing both self-construct assets, but one has high leverage, while the second one has virtually no leverage.

Shareena: I'm not that acquainted with interest capitalization. Where should I look to gain a background on that issue, so I can decide what information I ought to track?

Alan: I suggest you begin with FARS. Why not prepare an executive summary as to how interest capitalization can influence the companies you are analyzing as to their investment in property, plant, and equipment? Be specific as to what attributes of the company can influence what actually is recorded on the balance sheet, as well as both the cash flow statement and the income statement. Then integrate the implications from your summary into your data collection spreadsheet. I'll be happy to review your next draft.

Shareena: Thanks. As usual, your assistance is invaluable.

Alan: Two other considerations also deserve attention. Remember that environmental expo-
              sures can affect the capitalized cost base of companies, as can their legal obligations
              associated with the retirement of assets. Comparability is tricky.

Required:

Use FARS to draft the executive summary and to propose a worksheet format for data collection. Be
specific as to the information fields you need to collect and why. Be certain in the executive summary
to include specific cites to the key determinants of self-constructed asset valuations according to
GAAP. Your executive summary should completely address Alan's hypothetical. From a managerial
accounting perspective, would you suggest that other information be considered beyond the GAAP
framework? Why or why not? Could the capitalized interest issue be affected by the environmental
exposures as well as obligations associated with retirement of assets?

BONUS QUESTION:

Do standard-setters specifically proscribe certain types of assets from having capitalized interest
assigned in the process of construction?

Accounting Theory Issue:

Can the comparability of capital expenditures be affected by the treatment of pre-production design
and development costs?

Auditing Issue:

An auditee has always been an all equity firm. However, because the company is breaking ground
on a new office building, it has likewise issued debt with the intent of capitalizing interest during
the construction period. As an auditor, how would you evaluate the risks associated with such an
action? Will such action have implications for analytical procedures applied in the current audit?
Explain.

Brain Teaser 12: Why the Proposed Staff Accounting Bulletin (SAB)?

What GAAP Does Not Require

Brian: I make a point to browse the EDGAR site of the SEC periodically, just to review current proposals and to determine which ones have been finalized and what they have to say.

Elizabeth: So do I. That Web site is such a resource, and so easy to access!

Brian: I noticed a proposal that relates to estimates of useful life and salvage value of property, plant, and equipment. The interesting aspect of the proposed Staff Accounting Bulletin (SAB) was its recognition that GAAP do not require certain disclosures.

Elizabeth: I've been thinking about the proposal in light of industry practices. I was preparing a presentation on diversity within industries and noted that some companies disclose useful lives for buildings of 3 to 25 years, with others in the same industry reporting 20 to 50 years. Ranges are reported by some entities, while other companies give a single figure, like 30 years or 40 years.

Brian: It's not just in regard to buildings. I noted that machinery and equipment disclosures often have ranges, such as 4 years to 20 years.

Elizabeth: I recall the proposed SAB's interest in disclosure requirements pertaining to adjustments in useful life and salvage value.

Brian: There is an irony historically. I remember when I was an undergraduate student, the 10-K SEC filings had some detailed exhibits for property, plant, and equipment that provided some added insights regarding accumulated depreciation, but those were eliminated from the requirements. I think it was part of a simplification movement.

Elizabeth: What goes around comes around. I wonder if any changes in GAAP have occurred in the interim that might explain why the SAB was proposed in 2000.

Brian: Why don't we prepare a joint analysis? It might be a basis for writing a commentary to the SEC proposal and could also lead to an article comparing industry practices.

Elizabeth: Good idea. Let's begin with a catalogue of current GAAP, including the citations, date of requirement, and specific guidance in the areas of useful life, salvage value, and changes therein.

Brian: Then we can expand to an actual practices analysis, using Lexis/Nexis.

Required:

Use FARS to prepare the catalogue of current GAAP associated with useful life, salvage value, and changes in either of these estimates. Focus on disclosure requirements associated with any of these three dimensions. Based on your work, explain why you believe the SEC might have decided to propose additional disclosures in this area. Would you support such increased disclosures? Why or why not? Select three companies in the same industry and collect information as to what they disclose regarding the three dimensions of interest—useful life, salvage value, and changes in either. Explain why you believe these estimates are sufficiently informative or ought to be revised. If the latter, what specific changes would you propose?

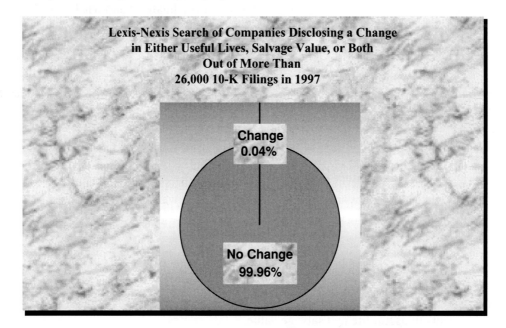

Figure 4.12-1   An example of the relative rarity of disclosure of changes in useful life and salvage value.

BONUS QUESTION:

A simplification movement is referenced as an explanation for the SEC's elimination of the detailed property, plant, and equipment schedule. *The FASB Report* (Financial Accounting Series No. 278-B, March 31, 2006) describes "Efforts to Reduce Complexity." Does FARS suggest that such efforts have been a consideration by standard-setters historically? In your opinion, is this a laudable objective? Why or why not?

Accounting Theory Issue:

With what frequency do accounting standards permit a range of disclosure in lieu of a point estimate? Theoretically, do you find such guidance to be sound?

Auditing Issue:

The company you are auditing performs heavy construction and has a number of varied-size and type of tractors that have useful lives ranging from 5 years to 20 years. One type of tractor, which corresponds to half of this class of asset, has been changed from 8-year lives to 10-year lives for the purpose of computing depreciation expense. In your judgment, is the disclosure practice of 5- to 20-year lives for this class of assets sufficient for reporting purposes? What additional information is needed, if any, and what assumptions are implicit in your evaluation?

Tax Issue:

Have accounting standard-setters been challenged by constituents as inappropriately providing a "roadmap" for taxing authorities through their disclosure requirements?

Brain Teaser 13: Is Goodwill Indefinite or Indeterminate?

If Indeterminate Duration, Why Capitalize Goodwill but Not Research and Development?

Reneé: The politics and theory of accounting sometimes are hard to separate. I was reading that in order to gain support for the elimination of pooling of interests accounting, the FASB had decided not to require amortization of goodwill. What is it that justifies a presumed indefinite life for goodwill?

Raj: You don't find compromise to be sufficient justification?

Reneé: Not at all. For the standards to guide professionals in reaching judgments, I think we need to retain the elegance of theoretical justification.

Raj: I suppose the theoretical explanation for no amortization is that the asset will have to be evaluated for impairment.

Reneé: Well, that may be true, but consider the fact that impairment tests are now called for with plant and equipment, but depreciation is still recorded. It would seem that in parallel fashion, we could do impairment tests on goodwill and nonetheless amortize the balance.

Raj: It must be some sort of analogy between land and goodwill, contending that both are indefinite in life, since land is not depreciated.

Reneé: I can buy the idea that as long as land is not being depleted, it should hold its value, but I have difficulty seeing the analogy between tangible land and intangible goodwill.

Raj: What about works of art? They have intangible value: Picasso is certainly not valued based on the cost of the canvas and oils.

Reneé: It's not the valuation of the intangible initially that is the issue, it's the concept that the value persists indefinitely. After all, the premium paid on a company that is merged into another would not seem to rival a Picasso or Monet in durability of intrinsic value.

Raj: I seem to remember that many years back, a common approach was to capitalize goodwill and then not to amortize it at all. A debate ensued regarding how one should compare companies with goodwill on their balance sheets to other entities that never made acquisitions and hence had no such goodwill on their balance sheets.

Reneé: Some analysts reportedly set goodwill aside in their evaluations, which in itself raises questions as to its perceived value, let alone its indefinite value status!

Raj: I have to admit that I find it ironic that an ill-specified asset category such as goodwill is capitalized and potentially unamortized, while research and development expenses—by and large—are expensed.

Reneé: The benefits are deemed indeterminate for R&D since so many projects are initiated in order to achieve the single commercially successful product or process. Of course, many a failed merger fills the history of business. One thing for certain, the argument of no amortization of goodwill because the life is indeterminate would seem to argue more for expensing than indefinite capitalization.

Raj: Isn't it somewhat incredulous that goodwill is deemed indeterminate or indefinite in life when 10-K filings have repeatedly presented estimated amortization periods, often ranging from 5 to 40 years?

Reneé: I'm enough of a history buff that I'm very curious about the historical development, as well as the contrasts drawn among intangibles such as goodwill relative to R&D.

Raj: I have a minor in history, and I firmly believe that those who do not have an understanding of the past are destined to repeat its mistakes.

Required:

Use FARS to provide an historical account, with appropriate citations as to how goodwill has been accounted for at various points in time, as well as research and development (R&D). Check the FASB Web site http://www.fasb.org for related details and proposals that may not yet be reflected in FARS. Can you find an elegant theoretical framework to explain the accounting treatment of each, as well as the practice of recording no amortization of goodwill—remembering the presumption that impairment analysis is required? Prepare a brief presentation of your framework or an explanation of why you believe the treatments are irreconcilable without reference to the political context of standard-setting activities.

BONUS QUESTION:

How often have standard-setters used the term "arbitrary" in their guidance and what is meant by this term?

Auditing Issue:

In the last quarter of the fiscal year, a subsidiary of your auditee received an unfavorable arbitration ruling that affected its ability to recover disputed amounts for past and future performance under a contract with a major customer. This subsidiary had a related goodwill balance of $33 million prior to this ruling. Subsequent to the ruling, using a discounted cash flow analysis of the reporting unit, the company recorded a goodwill impairment charge of $13 million, leaving a $20 million balance in goodwill. How would you proceed to audit the propriety of both the recorded impairment loss and the remaining intangible asset balance?

Brain Teaser 14: Why Must Triggers Arise for Impairment of Assets Whereas Goodwill Is Tested Annually?

Is Goodwill More Prone to Impairment?

Dasaratha: Why do standard-setters require that goodwill be tested every year for impairment?

Takeshi: That's a good question. In fact, in some circumstances the testing has to be even more frequent! Yet, we are not required to do so for property, plant, and equipment, are we?

Dasaratha: No. As I recall, the standard-setters thought that an annual test on all property, plant, and equipment would be cost prohibitive. I wonder why that contention failed to prevail for goodwill?

Takeshi: Let's find out by accessing FARS.

Required:

Use FARS to find out why goodwill must be tested at least every year, while the same requirement does not apply to property, plant, and equipment.

BONUS QUESTION:

How many EITFs relate to how to test goodwill for impairment? What are their topics?

Accounting Theory Issue:

Does the impairment test for goodwill use undiscounted future cash flows or discounted future cash flows? What is the reasoning for such treatment relative to other types of assets?

Auditing Issue:

FAS 142, par. 26 states: "The annual goodwill impairment test may be performed any time during the fiscal year provided the test is performed at the same time every year. Different reporting units may be tested for impairment at different times." What are the audit implications of such timing considerations? Be specific.

Brain Teaser 15: When Is the Stand-Ready Obligation of a Guarantee Deemed Not Probable?

Don't Contingencies Have To Be Probable In Order To Be Recorded?

April: Is a guarantee a contingency?

Trevor: Why do you ask?

April: I wondered whether Financial Accounting Standard No. 5 was the controlling guidance as to whether or not a guarantee is reported.

Trevor: What type of guarantee?

April: The company of interest is a seller-guarantor for a customer's loan. Specifically, the company has issued such a guarantee to facilitate the customer obtaining funds to pay the seller for the assets being purchased. It's improbable that any default will arise on the loan.

Trevor: If it's so improbable, why did the bank demand the guarantee? In any case, remember standard-setters often issue specific guidance that differs in important ways from more general standards. That seems to particularly occur with regard to added disclosure requirements, even if reported numbers on the face of the financial statements are unaltered. I suggest you use FARS and be thorough in researching the current treatment of such guarantees.

Required:

Use FARS to identify the controlling guidance for this type of guarantee. In particular, clarify the role of probability as it relates to the issue of recording and disclosing guarantees. Explain what other guarantees might arise and whether their treatment would be distinct from the case at hand. For example, what is the accounting treatment prescribed for minimum revenue guarantees granted to a business or to its owners?

BONUS QUESTION:

When creditors account for an impairment of a loan, how should changes in observable market prices or the fair value of the collateral be recorded? When evaluating whether a debt security is impaired, can an investor combine separate contracts (a debt security and a guarantee or other credit enhancement)?

Accounting Theory Issue:

Trace the evolution of how loan guarantees have been addressed by the EITF.

Auditing Issue:

The seller-guarantor has been unable to identify any transactions for identical or similar guarantees, deciding that expected present value is the appropriate measurement technique to apply. In the audit process, you note that the company has applied the interest rate of 9 percent to its analysis of contractual cash flows of the transaction, thereby reflecting expectations about future defaults. That same 9 percent rate was used to discount expected cash flows. Is this the appropriate application of the technique? Explain.

Not-for-Profit Issue:

A community foundation has a loan guarantee program to assist not-for-profit organizations in obtaining bank financing at a reasonable cost. Upon the issuance of the guarantee, would the community foundation recognize a liability for the fair value of that guarantee or would it be considered merely a conditional promise to give?

Brain Teaser 16: Expected to Be Refinanced?

Is Anticipating Refinancing Analogous to a Gain Contingency?

Tricia: I don't understand why you are making me reclassify my long-term debt as current. You and I both know that I will be refinancing before the maturity date hits, and then I will rollover the existing debt into a new instrument, and never have a real short-term payout in the current fiscal year.

Ira: I know you are unhappy about the reclassification, but generally accepted accounting principles (GAAP) are very clear on this issue.

Tricia: I thought substance was supposed to dominate form. Your balance sheet portrayal certainly seems to emphasize form and ignore the substance of the way we do business.

Ira: The substance of the situation is that you have not as yet renegotiated or refinanced that debt. If you were to anticipate refinancing, in substance, you would be including a sort of gain contingency attitude in your accounting treatment. We conservative accountants do not anticipate gains.

Tricia: How did gain enter the picture? I'm talking about the balance sheet, not the income statement!

Ira: I know. I was just making an analogy. I mean, you cannot be certain that the refinancing will occur until it happens.

Tricia: Actually, you've made not refinancing more of a possibility. Lenders want healthy current ratios, and thanks to your classification of that debt, the economic picture for my business has really been tarnished.

Ira: You made my point. If a possibility exists that refinancing will not occur, then the last thing you should do is call the debt with maturity nine months from now a long-term commitment. Your credibility with your financial statement users would really "go south."

Tricia: Is there any action I can take to change this short-term liability to a long-term liability?

Required:

Use FARS to provide an answer to Tricia. Be specific as to what GAAP require with respect to the classification of debt to be refinanced. Do you believe that Ira made a good analogy when he mentioned the issue of gain contingency? Explain your point of view and include citations from FARS to support your perspective.

BONUS QUESTION:

What was the dissenter's point of view regarding the statement that guides the classification of debt expected to be financed?

Accounting Theory Issue:

Have standard-setters expressed a point of view as to the advisability of accounting treatments based on plans and intent?

Auditing Issue:

If your auditee represents that refinancing has occurred in time to retain a long-term classification of debt, what audit steps are needed to corroborate that representation?

Tax Issue:

Taxing authorities could issue an assessment and a demand for payment at any time, suggesting that a liability stemming from uncertainty in income taxes is similar to a due-on-demand note. Does this mean that because the timing of payment is uncertain, the liability should be classified as current?

Brain Teaser 17: Extinguishing Debt Was Extraordinary?

How Could This Be, Unless It Was Troubled Debt Forgiven?

Kristin: I was reading over the historical financial statements of a number of public companies for some research I've been doing. I have been paying particular attention to the nature of extraordinary items. I cannot get over the fact that the extinguishment of debt has been reported as an extraordinary item. I mean, what is extraordinary about paying off one's debt?

Ali: Good question. Are you certain it was just paid off in the normal course of business? I mean, could it be that the company had some hard times and negotiated some type of troubled debt arrangement with its creditors? I could see where that might be something out of the ordinary.

Kristin: Interesting that you should mention troubled debt restructuring. Another thing that struck me in reading through this set of financial statements was the incidence of gains from troubled debt by the very companies in trouble. I mean, it just does not make sense to me that one can generate gains from borrowing, let alone from getting into an economic hardship situation.

Ali: It does sound ironic. It seems to me we need to find out the whole story. I mean, what is the definition of an extraordinary item? Has it changed over time? What is the appropriate accounting treatment when debt is extinguished in the normal course of business, and why? When troubled debt restructuring occurs, why might a gain result?

Kristin: And for completeness, how is the gain from troubled debt restructuring to be recorded? Is it an extraordinary item, and if it is not, why is that—given the past treatment of the extinguishment of debt?

Ali: I've read where such troubled debt restructuring might involve off-balance-sheet financing. I'm a bit uncertain as to what is meant by that term and how it could influence the accounting results. For example, could a troubled debt agreement bring something that was off the balance sheet onto that financial statement?

Required:

Use FARS to find out the whole story on the questions posed by Kristin and Ali. In all cases, provide the citations that support your answer.

BONUS QUESTION:

The FASB has explained that the historical approach to classifying the gains and losses associated with extinguishment of debt was "intended to be a temporary measure." How much time elapsed between that temporary measure and attention to the issue by standard-setters?

Accounting Theory Issue:

Identify those activities of the EITF that concern whether gains and losses on debt extinguishment are classified as extraordinary.

Auditing Issue:

Your audit client has extinguished debt early and wishes to report it as an extraordinary item. Is such a classification permitted? What steps would you take as an auditor to ascertain whether the classification is permissible?

Tax Issue:

Identify an EITF associated with the classification of gains and losses on debt extinguishment that attributes its narrow scope to a tax consideration. What is that tax consideration?

Advanced Accounting Issue:

Identify an EITF associated with the classification of gains and losses on debt extinguishment that addresses consolidation-associated matters.

Brain Teaser 18: What Happens When You Barter with Stock?

Does It Matter Whether It's Treasury Stock or Newly Issued Stock?

Jacob: I acquired this land for my business by issuing stock. I did not pay a penny. Since it's my stock, and I decided how much to give up for the land, does that mean I get to determine the value of the land on my balance sheet?

Ruth: You could have issued the stock to somebody else, taken the cash received, and paid for the land, right?

Jacob: I suppose I could have, but I didn't.

Ruth: The fact that you could have does imply there is some value for the stock and that it can be determined by referring to the market for that stock.

Jacob: I also bartered for some equipment. I exchanged some treasury stock for those assets. I suppose you're going to suggest that I could have reissued that treasury stock to somebody else, taken the proceeds, and purchased the equipment instead. While I could have, I didn't.

Ruth: What exactly did you expect the advantage to be of bartering with treasury stock? For that matter, why did you issue stock for the land rather than merely pay cash?

Jacob: Frankly, I thought that would allow me to set the value of both the land and the equipment. I mean, when you pay cash, that is the amount paid—open and shut. Whereas, when you barter with goods, services, or in my case stock, don't I have some discretion then?

Ruth: Do you believe you paid a fair price in stock?

Jacob: Certainly. I mean, I would not have given up the stock unless I thought I received fair value in exchange.

Ruth: You just explained why an "arm's-length exchange" between two parties is expected to arrive at a fair value that is recorded as the historical cost of the assets acquired.

Jacob: Are you telling me that the identical value would be recorded in my barter exchanges as if I had given up cash instead of stock or treasury stock?

Required:

Use FARS to find out whether Jacob has more discretion in the recording of his bartering exchanges than he would have had by paying cash. Provide specific citations to support your conclusion. Is your answer affected by whether the barter arrangement involved newly issued stock or treasury stock?

BONUS QUESTION:

Identify all occurrences of the word *barter* within the accounting literature accessible in FARS.

Accounting Theory Issue:

How does "historical practice" relate, if at all, to how barter transactions are recorded?

Auditing Issue:

What audit challenges are associated with barter exchanges? How would you proceed to audit the amounts entered on the books? Specifically, if your auditee issued treasury stock to acquire land, how would you proceed to audit the related transaction?

Brain Teaser 19: What Is the Substance of an Appropriation of Retained Earnings?

What Does a Dated Retained Earnings Imply?

Norvald: I have been studying retained earnings-related disclosures in financial statements. Appropriations of retained earnings are frequently reported. I recall in the past, hearing about retained earnings as though it represented a surplus, and I also remember the term "reserve for plant expansion" somewhere along the line. Now, what I am trying to recall is the exact distinction between those characterizations and appropriations.

Celeste: I remember that retained earnings are the accumulation of all prior years' net profit, less net loss, and less dividends declared. I remember appropriations being a sort of earmarking of those retained earnings for special purposes.

Norvald: Yes, but when an earmarking occurs, does that also mean cash is set aside for some purpose, or does it merely represent a sort of claim against the retained earnings?

Celeste: My recollection is that retained earnings have nothing to do with cash. In fact, I'm reasonably certain that if you examine the Statement of Cash Flows for one of those companies with an appropriation, you will see nothing related to appropriations as either a cash source or use. I agree with your claim idea, but certainly it's not a liability. I mean, retained earnings are the shareholders' interests, not a creditor's claim.

Norvald: You're right there. I was thinking more in line of a restriction of some sort. In other words, there has to be some purpose for an appropriation, and if it is not cash and does not involve a third-party claim, then it must be something else.

Celeste: You mentioned earlier the notion of reserves and surplus. I'm reasonably certain that the standard-setters discourage use of those terms. Too many people think of reserves as something tangible or put aside, while surplus almost sounds like you don't need it. Neither term would seem to fit retained earnings very well, or for that matter, restrictions on retained earnings.

Norvald: There is something else I've noticed in my research. Every so often, I see that a date appears beside retained earnings.

Celeste: I do remember that there is some type of transaction that leads to a requirement of retained earnings being dated, and not just in one year, but for a time period.

Norvald: We are indeed rusty on some of the details we once knew. I'm going to access FARS and see if I can get some answers.

Required:

Use FARS to find out the precise circumstances under which appropriations of retained earnings arise and what they represent. Confirm the recollections of Norvald and Celeste concerning: (a) the discouragement of the terms *surplus* and *reserve*; (b) the noninclusion of appropriations on the Statement of Cash Flows; and (c) the nature of the restriction that is represented by appropriations. When are dates associated with retained earnings, and for how long must they be disclosed? Describe the type of transactions that lead to such dating of the retained earnings balance and the rationale for requiring that particular type of disclosure.

BONUS QUESTION:

Is it permissible to set up an appropriation of retained earnings for loss contingencies?

Auditing Issue:

Your auditee is a closely held, family-owned business and has a substantial balance in retained earnings. This year, management of the auditee has specified a large appropriation for future plant expansion. What steps will you take to evaluate this action and its financial reporting implications? What are the risks associated with this type of business and transaction?

Tax Issue:

What is a tax reason that a company might choose to appropriate retained earnings?

Not-for-Profit Issue:

How does an appropriation of retained earnings compare to a restriction imposed on a not-for-profit by its managers or directors?

Brain Teaser 20: Stock Option Compensation Dilutes Earnings per Share?

Is Such Dilution Adequately Reflected?

Miguel: I remember many of my MBA colleagues contemplating job offers that were loaded with stock options. The market was hot, and it seemed a far better potential than cash compensation. Of course, that story changed dramatically when the market plummeted.

Flemming: Some of my friends are with companies who have repriced the stock options that are "under water," just to ensure the employees receive some portion of what they were expecting. Yet, I remember that the whole point of options was to create incentives aligned with stockholders. In other words, if the stock price benefits, the employees benefit. Otherwise, no return results. This repricing seems to be a convoluted back door to changing options effectively to cash compensation. In other words, you win whether your price goes up or not, because we choose to lower the price you paid when the bottom drops out of the market.

Miguel: I guess that part of the argument is that the employees are not responsible for the general market decline, and they only accepted the options in lieu of cash because they expected the total compensation would at least compare with other offers.

Flemming: Yet, do you really think the employees were responsible for the hot market run-up? I mean, I haven't heard of employees saying, "No I don't want the benefits that accrued to my stock options, because I wasn't responsible for their increase in value: the market was responsible." It sounds a good deal like "heads I win, tails you lose."

Miguel: Indeed, those who lose do seem to be the stockholders. The repricing and eventual exercise of options creates a dilutive effect on the already issued stock.

Flemming: I would say that as soon as the stock options are issued, a dilutive effect occurs. Consider the analogy that we split the pie of a corporation among 500,000 existing shares of common stock. The board of directors then turns around and issues stock options that can be exercised and become an additional 200,000 shares. It seems to me that the slice of the pie represented by one share has fallen from 1/500,000th to 1/700,000th, and that is a smaller slice, no matter how you cut it. No pun intended.

Miguel: You are assuming that all 200,000 shares become a reality, through exercise of the stock options. I've also read a lot of controversy regarding whether the reduction of net income for compensation expense based on fair value actually creates an inappropriate dual effect on diluted earnings per share; I mean "earnings per share would be hit twice," right?

Flemming: No, I don't agree. Moreover, I believe the 200,000 share figure is more likely than zero shares, particularly with this repricing phenomenon we're observing.

Miguel: That must be part of the reason that some corporate boards proposing changes in their stock option plans have been met with defeat by stockholders' voting power. I believe they understand dilutive effects, especially when the game of repricing has increased in popularity.

Flemming: What I am really curious about is whether the earnings per share that are reported quarterly, and annually for that matter, show this dilutive effect of stock compensation. Does it? I'm also a bit curious as to the tax effects.

Required:

Use FARS to answer Flemming's question. Is there a difference in your response as it regards quarterly and annual earnings per share (EPS)? Elaborate on what information stockholders receive as to the influence of stock compensation on their ownership share. Do you believe it is sufficient disclosure? Explain. What are the tax effects? Given repricing and current accounting treatment, do you believe options motivate employees to perform in line with stockholders' interests? Discuss the basis for your beliefs.

BONUS QUESTION:

Are companies at liberty to report EPS-based figures that are not required by GAAP on the face of an income statement as a separate line item?

Auditing Issue:

Choose a company of personal interest, access the latest 10-K filing at http://www.sec.gov, and read the note disclosure associated with stock options. *Note:* You can "copy" and "paste special" the text file for the SEC 10-K filing into a word-processing program such as Word and use the Find function to locate the stock option note. It is usually deep in the notes to the financial statements, around the note concerning pensions through 2001, with this location augmented in 2002 and thereafter with disclosures in the Summary of Accounting Policies. Use the disclosures found to recompute the reported option value. How would you evaluate the evidential weight of your recomputation? Explain.

For your information, examples of calculator sites you could use for comparison include: http://www.cfo.com/tools and http://www.hoadley.net/options/binomialtree.asp?tree.

Brain Teaser 21: Do Treasury Stock Transactions or Stock Options Have Any Relation to Insider Trading?

What is Spring-Loaded?

Xiao: I just read that the Public Company Accounting Oversight Board (PCAOB) and the Securities and Exchange Commission (SEC) seem to disagree as to whether insider trading is an issue associated with the timing of stock option grants.

Dawn: We also need to add another term to our glossaries: "spring-loading."

Xiao: *The Economist* also refers to "bullet-dodging."

Dawn: Yes, I saw that July 2006 issue as well. Granting options shortly before announcing good news is called "spring-loading," while delaying a grant until after bad news is announced is referred to as "bullet-dodging." A clear distinction is made between either of those events and backdating.

Xiao: The *Wall Street Journal* had an article by David Reilly entitled "Accounting Regulator Urges Closer Look at Options Dating" on July 29–30, 2006, page B5. The discussion suggested that past audits be revisited if an auditor receives credible "information" of potential improper practices involving backdating of employee stock options. Backdating has been described as setting grant dates and exercise prices of options retroactively to precede a run-up in the underlying shares to maximize the options' value.

Dawn: Advisors to the PCAOB met June 13, 2006 and discussed the legal problems that could arise from spring-loading as well as backdating, potentially posing insider trading concerns. Spring-loading suggests that option grants were ahead of market-moving news.

Xiao: Let me pull up the article I was just reading. It's from Bloomberg, an article by Vineeta Anand, dated July 6, 2006, and it's titled "Timing Option Grants Isn't Insider Trading, SEC's Atkins Says." Yet, the PCAOB advisors appear to have a different opinion. Here's an article dated June 13, 2006 from Reuters, by Kevin Drabaugh and Joel Rothstein, "Audit Panel Advisers Voice Backdating Worries." It refers to spring-loading and the potential insider trading issue. Of course, the PCAOB may be anticipating the next move in regulation and merely alerting the audit community to the risk exposure from such claims.

Dawn: If this "spring-loading" options argument holds, why would the same argument not apply to treasury stock transactions? Going a step further, what about the timing of initial public offerings?

Required:

Use FARS to explore whether any attention has been directed to the "spring-loading" question as it might pertain to stock options, treasury stock, or other types of transactions involving a company's own stock. [*Hint*: Also check http://www.sec.gov.]

BONUS QUESTION:

In 1999, Microsoft reported that it was stopping a practice of pricing its stock options for employees at the monthly share-price low in recruiting negotiations. At the time, analysts reportedly asked the company if this would reduce its ability to hire the best brains. In 2003, Microsoft announced its entire abandonment of stock options. The Sarbanes-Oxley Act of 2002 required option grants to be disclosed within 48 hours on Form 4s. Given these historical events, why has a so-called backdating scandal erupted in 2006?

Accounting Theory Issue:

Prior to FAS 123(R), most companies' reporting on stock options appeared in notes to the financial statements rather than on the face of the income statement. Is there any theoretical basis for expecting that the placement on income statements has led to greater scrutiny of the details associated with stock options than that level of attention accorded when information was located in notes to the financial statements?

Auditing Issue:

The PCAOB advisory board member interviewed about the nature of the information that is expected to prompt auditor inquiry, as discussed in the newspaper article cited in the dialogue, suggests that a reported correlation in an academic study does not mean that a restatement will be forced but does mean that an auditor should start asking questions. The PCAOB advisors have called for guidance that an audit inquiry be prompted if information becomes available that something may have been amiss. Do you agree that an academic study would be "information" of potential improper practices involving backdating of employee stock options? Explain.

Tax Issue:

Can transactions among shareholders affect the tax attributes of the company itself?

Brain Teaser 22: Why Do Transfers among Portfolios of Investments Affect Accounting?

Isn't That Doing Business with Itself? Why Is Intent Rather Than Realization Determinative?

Milly: I read that regulators were sanctioning a large financial institution for its accounting treatment of investments.

Jean: What was the nature of the mishandling?

Milly: It seems that management has to express its intent as to whether an investment held is to be in a trading portfolio or is to be held to maturity. That intent determines which portfolio contains an instrument and, in turn, determines the accounting treatment.

Jean: I was under the impression that accounting dealt with what actually happened as opposed to what somebody intended to happen. I know that some areas of practice require estimations, but it would seem that for investments, one could just watch what was done and then record it when it happened.

Milly: Actually, the reality sounded even stranger. What I gathered from the media coverage is that the financial institution first assigned an investment to one portfolio and then later in that same day, due to some dramatic market fluctuations, it switched certain investments from one portfolio to another. The result was a differing accounting treatment that had a substantial difference from what would have occurred had the "original intent" of the management not been altered.

Jean: Now that sounds like the company is doing business with itself. I mean, if it can create different accounting treatments merely from shifting its own assets among its own portfolios, that doesn't sound like any type of arm's-length exchange!

Milly: It does sound a bit like you and I being able to make money by taking our change from the right pocket and placing it in the left pocket.

Jean: I agree. It just doesn't sound logical. Maybe the media left something out that was important to know.

Required:

Use FARS to explain how management intent influences the accounting for investments, if at all. Also describe how transfers among portfolios can affect the accounting result. Consider the dialogue between Milly and Jean relative to what you find out from your study of FARS. Specifically, is this an example of accounting reflecting transactions of a business with itself? Why or why not? Is the absence of a market exchange problematic? Do you concur with the current accounting treatment of investments in marketable securities? Explain.

BONUS QUESTION:

Has the Emerging Issues Task Force (EITF) addressed held-to-maturity investment classification and changes therein? If so, identify the relevant guidance.

Accounting Theory Issue:

To avoid calling into question the entity's intent to hold other debt securities to maturity in the future, must certain financial assets received or retained in a desecuritization likewise be held to maturity?

Auditing Issue:

Assume that your auditee has reclassified certain securities from the held-to-maturity portfolio to the trading portfolio. What steps are needed to audit this transaction and how might the findings from the audit steps influence the financial presentation for the reporting period, as well as the following year? Be specific.

Tax Issue:

Is there a reflection of tax considerations when computing the effect of dividends on preferred stock held by an Employee Stock Ownership Plan (ESOP) on earnings per share?

Not-for-Profit Issue:

Are not-for-profit organizations given the same ability as business enterprises to measure debt securities that will be held to maturity at amortized cost?

Brain Teaser 23: When Does Channel Stuffing Transform Sales into Consignment Sales?

What Role Does Collectibility Play?

Dorn: A company with aggressive selling tactics to independent distributors seems to face many more challenges today. The SEC has that Staff Accounting Bulletin on revenue recognition where the "bottom line" seems to be a warning to take care and not to anticipate revenue.

Greg: Channel stuffing has always been an issue with independent distributorship networks. When a manufacturer's or wholesaler's sales topple, instinctively, the sales force begins to push its customers. The question becomes, just how many additional sales can any single distributor actually bring to fruition?

Dorn: I always wonder what type of side agreements might be necessary to get the distributor to go along. For example, does the sales representative promise to take back any unsold merchandise?

Greg: It seems that any such commitment transforms the sale into a consignment sale, resulting in no real revenue for the manufacturer or wholesaler.

Dorn: Assume that no commitment was made regarding returns, but the salesman is aware of a marginal financial situation of the distributor and its customers. Then it would seem collectibility becomes an issue, particularly in the wake of channel stuffing.

Greg: Then the question becomes, is this actually an installment sale, in which case, the revenue picture changes as well.

Dorn: I wonder what type of bright lines exist in the literature, if any, to help the chief financial officers, as well as the auditors, understand when sales get transformed into consignment sales and when even those might better be regarded as installment sales?

Greg: Let's find out; we can use FARS.

Required:

Use FARS to identify any bright lines that distinguish when sales should be reported as consignment sales. Likewise, explore the guidance associated with determining when the installment sales approach should be applied. Is there special attention in the standards to channel stuffing? In what sense does channel stuffing relate to either the need for consignment sales accounting or installment sales? Explain.

BONUS QUESTION:

Should a company's reported revenue be the gross amount billed to a customer, even if the manner of operations is to retain a commission or fee for that amount and pay the remainder to a supplier? Is it appropriate to reflect reimbursements received for out-of-pocket expenses incurred as revenue?

Accounting Theory Issue:

In a Sale-Leaseback Transaction with Repurchase Option, if the property is fully rented at the time of the sale and the seller agrees to make up any decrease in rentals resulting from lease terminations during a specified period after the sale, would such receipts be reflected as income to the buyer?

Auditing Issue:

Why is revenue recognition considered a special audit risk area? How can recorded revenue be effectively audited? If channel stuffing was suspected, how should the auditor proceed? What are round-trip transactions? [*Note*: Such transactions are reflected in Figure 4.23-1, as are any restatements due to improper revenue accounting. This includes improper recognition, questionable revenues, mistakes, or improprieties that led to misreported revenue. The total number of listed companies was 6,473 in 2005 and the number of companies restating was 439, or 6.8%.]

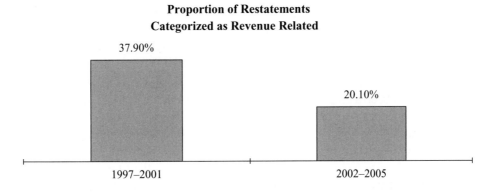

**Proportion of Restatements
Categorized as Revenue Related**

Figure 4.23-1 United States Government Accountability Office Report, Issued July 2006: *Financial Restatements* (GAO-06-678).

Brain Teaser 24: Why Can the Same Company Have Both a Tax Asset and a Tax Liability?

How Do Tax Assets Differ from Recording Contingent Gains?

Peggy: I was looking at a balance sheet of a company that reported both a tax asset and a tax liability for the same year.

Jessica: Why wouldn't you either owe the Internal Revenue Service or have it owe you?

Peggy: That's exactly my quandary.

Jessica: With all the recent changes in tax law and legislation altering rates and deductions over time, how do companies determine their tax obligation or claim? Do they presume that even if something will not occur until several years in the future and could always be rescinded, that once legislation exists in any given year, that is the right rate to estimate the numbers in the financial statements? Is there a role for the probability of altering such legislation in any given four-year period?

Peggy: I remember that this issue received a good deal of attention when the retroactive tax adjustments of the Clinton era occurred. I believe some guidance speaks directly to which rate is used under what circumstances.

Jessica: I have always been a bit puzzled by the idea of a tax asset. Given the nature of tax law over time, I wonder why such numbers are not analogous to the entire area of litigation. My understanding is that gains from awards in litigation cannot be anticipated in any manner. Essentially, the award must be realized in order to reflect the results of that award in the accounting statements. Yet, for taxes, it is as though the future anticipated reward for some tax strategy is permitted to get into the books. We all understand that the entire legal framework on which the gain is based can change at any given point in time. Moreover, can't some of these tax assets be a part of ongoing tax audits and disputes in tax courts? I must be missing something.

Peggy: As a matter of fact, one area that I believe dovetails with your thought process is the entire matter of net operating loss carryforwards. Legislation permits past losses to offset future gains, but after all, such losses are worth nothing if the entity continues to have net losses throughout the period that such an offset is permitted. Does that not seem like a gain contingency if an asset is created in anticipation of claiming that carryforward?

Jessica: I remember discussing the matter of a likelihood aspect to tax assets that is phrased "more likely than not." A bit of a mystery exists in my mind. I recently read through an international standard IAS 37, titled "Provisions, Contingent Liabilities and Contingent Assets." Paragraph 2b of that standard stated, "... it is probable (i.e., more likely than not) that an outflow of resources embodying economic benefits will be required to settle the obligation." This parenthetical seems at total odds with the U.S. literature. I know that there is a sort of 'bright-line distinction' between *probable* and *more likely than not* that is being communicated by the FASB.

Required:

Use FARS to find out how it is possible for a single company to present both a tax asset and a tax liability. Do you believe that a tax asset constitutes a gain contingency? Why or why not? Support your position with appropriate citations. Is the *more likely than not* threshold in the tax asset accounting treatment different from the usual meaning of *probable* within the standards? Justify your position, providing related citations.

BONUS QUESTION:

An enterprise determines a tax position with a $200,000 benefit qualifies for recognition and should be measured but management has limited information about a taxing authority's view of the company's tax position. Management believes that a 60 percent chance exists that when examined, the company would settle for $150,000 of the benefit rather than $200,000. What tax benefit would be recognized in the financial statements?

Auditing Issue:

Recent debates associated with the Sarbanes-Oxley Act of 2002 and activities of the Public Company Accounting Oversight Board (PCAOB) relate to possible threats of tax work to independence. In particular, the PCAOB has intermittently considered the issue of tax shelters and tax consulting to determine whether they create a particular problem. Why do you believe such a concern exists?

Tax Issue:

Access FASB Interpretation No. 48 issued in June 2006 and explain its expected effect on deferred tax assets and deferred tax liabilities. [If the version of FARS does not include this FIN, go to the http://www.fasb.org Web site to access the pronouncement. Note that it is advisable to visit that site frequently to ensure awareness of recent developments subsequent to the time the FARS version to which you have access may have been released.]

Brain Teaser 25: Isn't the Corridor Approach for Pensions and Postretirement Benefits Smoothing?

Do Expected Relative to Actual Returns Matter If a Defined Contribution Plan Replaces a Defined Benefit Plan?

Andy: The corridor approach that is applied to pensions and postretirement benefits is a conundrum. It seems to be merely a smoothing device endorsed by the Financial Accounting Standards Board (FASB). Is smoothing a worthy objective for reporting?

Alice: I believe one of the most common complaints among lobby letters written to the FASB concerns the volatility of earnings. The claim is that a smoother depiction of operations facilitates forecasts and is thereby a desirable outcome.

Andy: I would think that accountants ought to report results no matter how volatile and then let the forecasters do the smoothing of the data set. I mean, macroeconomic statistics can be accessed as seasonally adjusted or in raw form. Why not provide the economic results, however disparate over time, and let the users of those numbers grapple with the question of how they can be used, looking forward?

Alice: Intellectually, I think a "fly in the ointment" is the periodicity principle. Any entity has numerous multiperiod asset and liability balances that inevitably involve long-term estimates. That makes it no simple matter to derive the single figure for reporting purposes as of any given date. I think pensions and postretirement benefits are great examples of long-term obligations that are a challenge to determine in one year. Those related commitments will not actually be met for 20 to 50 years!

Andy: Nonetheless, if you have asset investments to meet that liability 20 years later, you have to admit that you do know what return you actually earned on those assets as of a point in time, right?

Alice: Even then, it would seem you're asking whether market value can be effectively derived at a single point in time, even if some investments are subject to a buy-and-hold strategy that arguably fails to earn the current market return because they are not traded at propitious points in time.

Andy: I suppose that those are the types of concerns, in part, that lead companies to change from defined benefit to defined contribution plans. Then all the company does is contribute a given amount today, and the rest of the picture is the employee's responsibility. If the employee pursues buy-and-hold strategies, or trades actively, that individual accrues the benefits or losses and the company has met the specified obligation of original contribution. I suppose you could also say the shift to a defined contribution plan is itself a smoothing device, since the contributions should be far smoother in quantity than any defined benefit plan accounting effects would be!

Alice: Maybe the corridor approach is a means to encourage companies not to shift to defined contribution plans for such reasons, by providing an alternative means of having relative stability.

Andy: Yes, perhaps, but the substance of a defined benefit plan seems very different to me from the defined contribution plan. For example, presume that I expect a 10 percent return and only earn a 2 percent return on a defined benefit plan's assets. I will have to meet the same commitment regardless of my return, which means in effect that I have to make up an 8 percent shortfall. Whereas, for defined contribution plans, an expected return does not even enter the picture.

Alice: It does from the employees' point of view, most assuredly. They have to decide whether to go to work for a company offering a defined contribution plan or a defined benefit plan. If the former, the employee has investment responsibility, which means expected return can be critical in his or her financial planning.

Andy: You're right, I should not have said that expected return does not even enter the picture. It has to be an ingredient to a company's analysis of what type of pensions and benefits to offer.

Alice: Getting back to the corridor approach, how does that work? Is it symmetrical, and if so, is there not a type of anticipated gain that results? How do we reconcile that with conservatism? Do we make a distinction between the accounting for unexpected and expected gains and losses?

Andy: You bring up an interesting point. I've thought about the issue of discounting as well. It seems that the discounting of pension and postemployment retirement benefits is well accepted, and yet discounting isn't applied to a number of other accounting areas, even though they involve long-term estimates. Why is that the case? Could one say the result is a conservative reflection of the obligation, relative to the undiscounted number?

Alice: I agree about the lack of consistency among standards being an issue, but I would think present value is virtually always a preferred means of reflecting current claims.

Andy: We choose not to discount the short-term obligations for time value of money, yet a year's interest is far from trivial. Besides, it isn't easy to set the appropriate rates for either expected return or discounting. Perhaps it would be a "wash", and the entire accounting approach could be simplified.

Alice: Whenever I hear the phrase "it's a wash," I always have a concern as to what exactly is being *washed out*. You're suggesting that the expected return would offset the effect of discounting, right? I can appreciate the fact that some things need aggregation, and in so doing, certain offsets do become embedded in the assessment. Yet, aren't return and discount distinctive concepts?

Andy: You have a legitimate point.

Alice: I think one of the interesting aspects of pensions involves the requirement that accumulated benefit obligations be compared with the fair value of plan assets as a basis for a minimum liability accrual. I wonder how symmetry fits into the picture, if at all? If the fair value of plan assets impounds unexpected gains and losses, not realized due to a buy-and-hold strategy, is the accounting treatment any different?

Andy: I started with a few questions, and now we have a set of them. I'm going to roll up my sleeves and see whether FARS can help to solve some of our queries.

Required:

Use FARS to formulate a brief position paper regarding the pros and cons of the corridor approach as it relates to smoothing. Also assume that your company is contemplating a change from a defined benefit to a defined contribution plan. Prepare a short information sheet for fellow employees as to the differences between the two types of plans, from the point of view of the individual employee's responsibilities relative to those of the company. Finally, prepare an executive summary for top management as to the anticipated differences in accounting effects of a defined contribution plan relative to the former defined benefit plan. Explain specifically which accounting-associated estimates will no longer have to be made, and provide cites to support your key findings. Comment on the role of discounting and the expected rate of return in the accounting for either pensions or postretirement benefits. Could a "wash" type of approach simplify the picture, or would it merely muddy the picture? Explain your reasoning, using FARS citations in support.

BONUS QUESTION:

Is a Cash Balance Pension Plan a defined benefit or defined contribution plan?

Accounting Theory Issue:

Pensions, their obligations and insured status, alongside their likely future as to design, types of promises made, accounting treatment prescribed, funding requirements and positions, legal and tax status granted, and other dimensions are being actively debated in courtrooms, Congress, union halls, and FASB headquarters. Explain the issues, describing developments as you can assess from media coverage and from the standard-setters' and lawmakers' Web sites.

Auditing Issue:

How would the audit of a defined benefit plan differ from that of a defined contribution plan?

Brain Teaser 26: Lease Accounting—Why Is It Asymmetrical?

A Bargain Purchase from Whose Perspective?

Miklos: A single lease transaction can spawn one type of lease accounting for the lessor and another for the lessee. It always puzzles me that symmetry is not an inherent part of a transaction. Indeed, some of the recent media sensations have involved contracts between two parties in which one side recognizes the revenue but the other side does not book the transaction until a later period in time. I understand that internal decision making affects the recording of transactions, but in a way, a transaction would seem to have two sides of the same coin. I would expect the factual coin would drive both sides of the recording process. Yet, I know that does not result under lease accounting.

Salvatore: Perhaps that is why the FASB has stated that lease accounting is broken and needs attention.

Miklos: A number of groups have recommended that all lease transactions be capitalized, alongside all executory contracts.

Salvatore: You remind me of the interesting irony that the minimum lease payment under current lease accounting guidance is to exclude executory costs. Not that executory costs and executory contracts are synonyms. . . .

Miklos: There are a number of intricacies to current guidance. The volume of related guidance alone is mind boggling.

Salvatore: One concept I have difficulty with in practice is determining when a bargain purchase exists. It seems to me that what one party may deem a bargain may not be similarly viewed by another.

Miklos: I have seen transactions that claimed at the point of initial negotiation that a bargain purchase option existed, yet at the end of the lease, no such purchase occurred. If it had really been a bargain, you would expect that the purchase would be automatic.

Salvatore: I just think a real challenge exists in recording what could be a 99-year lease, anticipating what happens almost a century from today. Talk about forward-looking information!

Miklos: The reason all of this is on my mind is that I'm about to dive into the accounting treatment for a set of proposed lease arrangements. The client wants to understand the accounting consequences if they decide to proceed with the leases as currently written.

Required:

Use FARS to prepare a list of all guidance within the system that deals with the accounting for leases, as a resource for Miklos. In addition, determine whether any requirement of symmetry exists and explain for a given type of lease why the lessor's accounting can differ from that of a lessee's. Since the issue of bargain purchase will need attention by Miklos, define what that term means and its effects on the accounting for leases. The dialogue suggests that part of the decision on whether to move forward with a proposed lease will be the accounting treatment for that lease. Do you believe it is appropriate for the sequence of the events in decision making to include the accounting ramifications of a transaction? Why or why not? If the entity were to adjust the lease transaction to ensure that a particular accounting approach would apply, would that be acceptable? Do you consider it prudence and/or earnings management to consider accounting implications of business transactions during their negotiation? Are such actions normal, advisable, acceptable, and/or objectionable? Explain.

BONUS QUESTION:

Do standard-setters specifically proscribe certain types of assets from being the subject of a lease and thereby ineligible for lease accounting?

Accounting Theory Issue:

The FASB and the International Accounting Standards Board (IASB) are collaborating on a project to reconsider accounting for leases, in light of past criticism and papers such as the SEC's Off-Balance Sheet Report and the G4+1 1996 and 1999 Special Reports. Evaluate these criticisms and developments to date.

Auditing Issue:

If your auditee approached you three times in the course of the year to inquire as to whether the proposed structuring of a single lease qualified for operating lease treatment as distinct from capital lease accounting, would that influence either the way you would proceed with the audit or your auditor's report? Why and how?

Brain Teaser 27: How Are Changes in Warranties to Be Recorded?

What If We Make the Change in the Third Quarter?

Daniel: The company has changed from one warranty arrangement to another. Competition has made that a necessity. I've been asked to analyze the accounting implications of that change.

Mary Anne: I suggest you access FARS and prepare an analysis of which accounts will be affected by the change, in what direction, and then the implications for both reported income and the balance sheet accounts.

Daniel: There's been some discussion about whether our existing customers should be provided with some improved warranty status, particularly if they have recently made purchases. We want to keep rapport with our current customers, rather than merely attracting new customers. If we do increase the benefits of products sold in the past, does that mean we made an error? Or is this merely a change in estimate? Do I record it retroactively, currently, or prospectively?

Mary Anne: FARS will help with those questions as well.

Daniel: We have some choices as to when we make the final decision and the timing of the accounting treatment, right? If we decide in the third quarter instead of the fourth quarter, does that mean the consequence of our accounting will differ for the year?

Mary Anne: Do you think it should? I suggest that you prepare two draft documents. The first should be an analysis of the change and its effects on the accounts. The second should be an outline of the relevant accounting citations, including regarding your interim reporting issue. I'll review those when they are completed.

Daniel: I'll do my best.

Katie: I'll help.

Required:

Use FARS to prepare both reports for Mary Anne's review. Be certain to distinguish between accounting changes and accounting errors and their implications for accounting treatment.

BONUS QUESTION:

Are warranties recorded in the same manner as guarantees?

Accounting Theory Issue:

Are companies estimating warranty liabilities permitted to draw on others' experience or are they to restrict their knowledge base to company-specific experience?

Auditing Issue:

If an auditee initiates a warranty program for the first time in the current year, how is that to be reported and what disclosures are required? Assume that in the second year of the program, it is determined that the number of claimants estimated in the prior year represented an 80 percent understatement. Would this information result in the reporting of an accounting error? Why or why not? If an auditor's report were to be reissued on the prior year's financial statement, would any adjustment to the associated accounting—given the benefit of hindsight—be appropriate? Explain.

Tax Issue:

Locate guidance that illustrates a tax effect of warranties.

Brain Teaser 28: Does the Statement of Cash Flows Give the Full Picture?

What about Noncash Transactions?

Chee: For years, the expression "off-balance-sheet financing" has been in vogue. I think we ought to introduce the phrase "off-cash-flow-statement" transactions.

Shyam: I can understand why a company might want a liability off their balance sheet, but what do you have in mind with the cash flow statement?

Chee: In similar vein, why not avoid showing a large outflow of cash by merely negotiating some sort of noncash transaction? Couldn't that really distort the picture?

Shyam: Now you are arguing substance versus form, assuming the users of cash flow statements care about more than cash.

Chee: Assume a company owes $40 million to a creditor and when it comes due, simply exchanges preferred stock for that debt instead of paying cash. That constitutes a noncash exchange and would not appear on the statement of cash flows.

Shyam: Granted, but it will appear somewhere in a report of noncash transactions.

Chee: That's my point. How is it any different from saying you can go to the notes to the financial statements to learn more about off-balance-sheet items?

Shyam: I agree that you have a point. Then there is the quagmire of how stock options interact with reporting earnings and cash flows, especially tax-related cash flows.

Chee: What about transactions like stock dividends or stock splits?

Shyam: Would the user of a cash flow statement have an interest in appropriations of retained earnings, and if so, should there be some type of linkage as to where they ought to look for such "signs of future outflows?"

Chee: Our financial statement analysis course ought to be extremely clear as to what the differences are among operating, investing, and financing categories in the Statement of Cash Flows, what the problems are that arise in gathering the details, and what might be elsewhere, yet relevant.

Shyam: I agree. We need a roadmap. Barter arrangements were one of the issues that received attention in regulating revenue recognition issues for advertising among dot.coms. We ought to tie that in as an example of the problem at hand.

Required:

Use FARS to prepare the roadmap. Specifically define the difference in operating, investing, and financing cash flows. Explain the nature of noncash transactions and be comprehensive in listing the sorts of transactions that might appear in such a presentation. What latitude does a company have in terms of where to report such disclosures? Use the http://www.sec.gov EDGAR resource to identify a company with noncash transactions reported and indicate the company name, the type of transaction, and where it is reported in the 10-K filing. Explain whether stock dividends, stock splits, and appropriations of retained earnings are relevant, in your judgment, to the evaluation of the cash flow statement. Where can information on any of these transactions be found under GAAP? Provide cites from FARS in support of each aspect of your roadmap and related explanations. In your judgment, does the Statement of Cash Flows give the full picture? Why or why not? Is disclosure of cash flow by segment required? Why or why not? What about segments' noncash items, must they be reported?

BONUS QUESTION:

Should cash outflows for debt issue costs be classified as a financing activity or as an operating activity? How are the proceeds of a borrowing to be classified if the debt is intended as a hedge of an investment?

Accounting Theory Issue:

How should the cash paid upon settlement of an asset retirement obligation be classified in an enterprise's statement of cash flows?

Auditing Issue:

Assume your auditee issued a newly created class of preferred stock in exchange for a set of assets from a company divesting its interests in a related line of business. What audit risks are associated with this structuring of a transaction rather than an outright purchase using cash? Are there particular implications for the content, format, or disclosures associated with the Statement of Cash Flows? Explain.

Tax Issue:

Identify the guidance provided on how to handle tax-associated cash flows in transitioning to FAS 123(R).

Not-for-Profit Issue:

How does the result of negative amortization that represents significant noncash interest income affect a not-for-profit entity's cash flow reporting?

Brain Teaser 29: Why Are Segment Disclosures Non-GAAP?

What Information Is Provided at Interim?

Connor: I've been interested in segment-level disclosures as a means of exploring capital allocation within a company. In other words, in which segments is the corporate office investing and how? My problem is that I wanted to do some time-series comparisons. However, I understand that the entire approach to defining segments changed in the 1990s. Does that mean that I should not include any data earlier than the point of the change in the accounting for segmental disclosures?

Andra: You're right about the definition of segments changing. The focus is now on how managers operate their business. If a certain segmental approach is demonstrated in the internal reporting framework of a business, the managers are thereby contending that this is the relevant approach to analyzing the operations of the business. Hence, it is that management strategy that guides the definition of segments. They have little relationship to the segments disclosed prior to the change by FASB. I remember that when the earlier standards were in place, they were preceded by governmental line-of-business regulations. I attended a conference in which a speaker highlighted the fact that competitors were the first ones that requested to be on the list to receive such line-of-business details. I wonder if competitors have an even greater interest in the new disclosures, or if the earlier approach was of more use?

Benjamin: Another wrinkle in the new approach relates to what is reported. The segment disclosures can be non-GAAP if that happens to be what is used in the internal report. The argument is similar to the initial definition of segments: If management does not find it useful in its internal reports to allocate costs or to use GAAP accounting, then whatever basis is used in the internal report can be the essence of these segment disclosures. Of course, a "plug" is required to show the difference in those numbers and what would have been GAAP, but the plug I believe may be an amalgamation of differences in revenue recognition, cost tracking, allocations, and other things.

Connor: That sounds as though it may be such a hodgepodge as to be uninformative.

Andra: I know that many expressed a concern about the lack of comparability, not merely among companies but even over time for a given company. If management changes its internal reporting framework, the segmental disclosures are expected to likewise fluctuate.

Benjamin: We all know that restructuring is far from a rare event.

Connor: Consider acquisitions, divestitures, spin-offs, downsizing, rightsizing, and the rest of the possibilities.

Andra: Another problem is that if you're interested in any information on interim dates, I'm not certain which segmental disclosures are required in the interim reports. For some aspects, it may be only once a year that you can look inside and investigate the parts or segments of the entity.

Benjamin: I think when you dispose of a segment, some sort of interim disclosure is required. You will need to check on what is to be reported at interim.

Connor: Another aspect of interest to my work is the identification of major customers. Has that changed as well?

Andra: To actually figure out which common costs and what types of disclosures are expected, you ought to access FARS. It should answer those questions, the current requirements associated with major customers, and the extent to which annual and interim reporting apply to anything having to do with segments.

Connor: I need an understanding of this non-GAAP dimension, because it certainly sounds as though I won't even be able to compare revenue figures. What if a single entity uses different revenue recognition for different lines of business? Does that mean the revenues among segments within a single entity even fail the comparability test?

Benjamin: Good questions, and I believe conceptually that could occur. You need to check to see if the FASB considered such a possibility and included any safeguards at all.

Andra: What if management's internal reports choose not to break an operation into segments? Is it not possible for management to state that its strategy is to manage the company as a single holistic unit? Would that mean no details for segments? Or is that a circumstance that FASB precluded?

Connor: I better get to work and find some answers.

Required:

Use FARS to answer the questions raised concerning segment reporting. Be certain to define the criteria used to define segments, any minimum number of segments that must appear, the annual relative to interim requirements, the non-GAAP latitude permitted, and the issue of major customers. In your opinion, are these segmental disclosures preferable to the previous standards on segmental disclosures? Why or why not? Do segmental disclosures inform the classifications depicted in Figure 4.29-1?

Taxonomy or Classification Systems

MANAGEMENT ASSERTIONS:

Existence/Occurrence   Presentation

Valuation/Allocation   Ownership/Incidence/Property

Completeness

QUALITY OF EARNINGS

Transparency   Recurring Nature/Components of Earnings

Origin   Market Reaction to Earnings

Relationship to Cash Flows

ASSET QUALITY

Asset-Specificity   Relative "Hardness" or "Softness" of Asset

Liquidity of the Market

PERSISTENCE OF EARNINGS

Recurring or Nonrecurring   Persistence Relative to Varied Time

                                                 Horizons

Figure 4.29-1 Approaches to Classifying Financial Statement Representations.

BONUS QUESTION:

Does the segmental disclosure guidance apply to nonpublic entities?

Accounting Theory Issue:

Under what circumstances can operating segments that do not meet the quantitative thresholds prescribed in the literature be aggregated?

Auditing Issue:

Your auditee has four lines of business, which in order to be aggregated to a consolidated total must be adjusted by 10 percent for intersegment revenue. Approximately half of this quantity applies to a segment that only earns revenue of half as much from external customers. In auditing segmental disclosures, what level of evidence must be collected regarding each segment's reported revenue, income, and total assets? Is the extent of work affected in any manner by the nature of intersegment revenue? Why or why not?

Not-for-Profit Issue:

Does the segmental disclosure guidance apply to not-for-profit entities?

Brain Teaser 30: When Can Analogies Be Used?

Have Standard-Setters Ever Proscribed an Analogy?

Mohan: When we are unable to find guidance that specifically addresses a particular area of practice, we are permitted to reason by analogy, focusing on the substance of economic transactions being evaluated, right?

Virginia: Given the diversity of economic activity, standards will not exist for every specific context that arises. Practice has to involve reasoning by analogy.

Mohan: Of interest is a 1984 Staff Accounting Bulletin (SAB) 57, "Valuation of Contingent Warrants Issued to a Company's Customers," which contained a footnote in which the staff describes its own use of analogies and advises caution as others use such an approach. The point the SEC makes is that its staff may not always be persuaded that a registrant's analogies result in preferable accounting.

Virginia: I recently accessed the Codification of SABs, and as I recall, there is a question that presumes analogies will be drawn. Let me pull up what I downloaded. Yes, here it is: "How does the staff intend SABs to be applied in circumstances analogous to those addressed in SABs?" It's Topic 6, Section C.

Mohan: The reason I started this discussion was that I saw an exposure draft, "Proposed Statement of Financial Accounting Standards: The Hierarchy of Generally Accepted Accounting Principles." I have it right here; the citation is Financial Accounting Series No. 1300-001, April 28, 2005. It states: "If the accounting treatment for a transaction or event is not specified ... an enterprise shall consider accounting principles for similar transactions or events and other accounting literature." Footnote 3 clarifies: "An enterprise shall not follow the accounting treatment specified in accounting principles for similar transactions or events in cases in which those accounting principles either prohibit the application of the accounting treatment to the particular transaction or event or indicate that the accounting treatment should not be applied by analogy" (p. 2).

Required:

Use FARS to determine whether analogies have been explicitly proscribed and if so, in which circumstances.

BONUS QUESTION:

Provide examples where analogies have been encouraged in the professional literature.

Brain Teaser 31: What Are the 10 Most Important Assumptions?

Are They the Same for All Companies?

Marsha: Last night, I was reading the professional literature on impairments. I noticed that the FASB decided *not* to require disclosures of the assumptions used to estimate expected future cash flows and the discount rate used when fair value is estimated by discounting expected future cash flows.

Kevin: I would have thought those assumptions are important. I mean, probabilities can vary widely, as can discount rates.

Marsha: The FASB explained that without disclosure of the other assumptions used in estimating expected future cash flows, disclosure of the discount rate generally would not be meaningful to financial statement users.

Kevin: Yet, FASB requires disclosure of the assumed weighted-average discount rate in the pension area. That seems rather inconsistent, doesn't it? I suppose I would find it difficult to rank order the 10 most important assumptions that ought to be required for disclosure.

Marsha: Do the standards advise us as to which are the most important assumptions requiring disclosure?

Required:

Use FARS to determine whether the standards indicate which are the most important assumptions requiring disclosure. What reasoning is provided, if any, for the apparent inconsistency in requirements?

BONUS QUESTION:

Explain why a word search using "assumption" may neither be relevant nor complete in analyzing the issues raised in the dialogue.

Accounting Theory Issue:

Identify those subject areas in which assumptions are required by the FASB to be disclosed. Do you believe these include what you would theoretically assess to be the most important accounting assumptions? Why or why not?

Brain Teaser 32: What Makes One GAAP Preferable to Another?

Can Different GAAP Be Deemed Preferable by Companies in the Same Industry?

Wendy: When standard-setters promulgate new standards, they are presumed, definitionally, to be preferred. However, when GAAP has alternatives available for voluntary choice by entities, public companies are required to provide preferability letters from their independent auditors that the voluntary change in accounting principle is to a more preferred accounting principle.

Matthew: One apparent reason for such regulation is to deter voluntary changes that harm the consistency of information across time for the reporting entity. Another is to have an independent check on the voluntary process of changing accounting principles.

Wendy: Ostensibly the reason for permitting choices within GAAP is because context matters in discerning the preferred accounting approach. As a result, preferability letters at any point in time are expected to reflect circumstance-specific evaluation of the past accounting principle used to that being adopted.

Matthew: As I recall, the SEC in its Codification of Staff Accounting Bulletins (SAB 103), posted since May 2003, sets forth Topic 6, which discusses reporting requirements for accounting changes and preferability determinations, in particular.

Wendy: Given the obvious costs of change, why would a company make a voluntary change in accounting? I mean, is it not enough of a burden having to change everything that is required by the standard-setters and regulators?

Matthew: I have seen allegations that voluntary accounting changes are only pursued when income increasing. However, empirical research does not generally support such a proposition.

Wendy: Common sense suggests the preferability letter itself highlights that a public entity has chosen to change one of its past accounting principles, implicitly inviting scrutiny of that decision and its justification.

Matthew: Consider the Fannie Mae experience. Let me show you something I ran across, written by former Chief Accountant of the SEC Walter P. Schuetze (November 29, 2004). It's a letter to members of the FASB, copying Mr. Don Nicolaisen of the SEC, stating: the "labyrinth of detailed rules" disputed with disagreements among Fannie Mae (whose application had been thought in accordance with SFAS 133 by both KPMG and E&Y) and OFHEO (concurred with by D&T), led to a request for arbitration by the SEC Chief Accountant. Given these types of events, how should management and the board deal with settings where the advice from regulators and that of CPA firms diverge?

Required:

Use FARS to describe what makes one GAAP preferable to another. Review the SEC's guidance in the area of preferability letters and provide an example of such a company filing. [*Note*: Since the fourth quarter and year-end filings correspond, the SEC permits the 10-K filing (the annual report, Exhibit 18), rather than 10-Q filing (the quarterly report) of preferability letters. Similarly, 8-Ks (reports on unscheduled material events or corporate changes deemed of importance to shareholders or to the SEC) may include preferability letters, tied to such events as mergers and acquisitions. On occasion, preferability letters are filed with proxy statements (DEF 14-A) and share filings.] How would you respond to Matthew's query?

BONUS QUESTION:

What explanation is provided by standard-setters for permitting more than a single method to be in conformance with GAAP?

Accounting Theory Issue:

Accounting Principles Board Opinion 2 (APB 2), paragraph 13 in the FASB-OP (amended) infobase of FARS, explicitly states: "[It] shall be considered preferable [for] the allowable investment credit [to] be reflected in net income over the productive life of acquired property [(the deferral method). However,] treating the credit as a reduction of federal income taxes of the year in which the credit arises [(the flow-through method)] is also acceptable." Interpret what this phrasing means for practice and, in particular, its theoretical grounding and how it happened to become part of GAAP. Provide a more recent example of a similar standard-setting approach.

Auditing Issue:

Auditors of public companies have posed the question to the SEC: "If one client of an independent accounting firm changes its method of accounting and the accountant submits the required letter stating his view of the preferability of the principle in the circumstances, does this mean that all clients of that firm are constrained from making the converse change in accounting (e.g., if one client changes from FIFO to LIFO, can no other client change from LIFO to FIFO)?" Access the Web site http://www.sec.gov and answer this question.

Tax Issue:

Does the fact that a cost is capitalizable for tax purposes, in itself, indicate that it is preferable, or even appropriate, to capitalize that cost for financial reporting purposes?

Brain Teaser 33: Are Independent Directors Good for Accounting?

Does Independent Mean Uninterested?

Denny: Independent directors are less subject to management control and hence improve the infrastructure of markets. Clearly, that is good for the accounting profession. In particular, audit committees comprised purely of independent directors can better withstand any pressure from management to take actions that might not be in the best interest of stockholders.

James: Warren Buffet seems to argue that having a vested interest in the company is far preferred to an independent status for board membership; at least that's how I understand his position.

Required:

Use FARS to explain what "independent" means. Is any attention accorded to the role of directors, particularly independent directors, within FARS? What is your view as to whether independent directors are good for accounting?

BONUS QUESTION:

Within FARS is the statement: "Without disclosure to the contrary, there is a general presumption that transactions reflected in financial statements have been consummated on an arm's-length basis between independent parties." Find this quote and elaborate on its meaning.

Auditing Issue:

What happens when a public company has a disagreement between its management and its auditors? Explain. What role does the audit committee have in such a setting? What is the required composition of an audit committee? Be specific.

Not-for-Profit Issue:

How does corporate governance for a not-for-profit entity differ from that of a profit-oriented entity?

International Accounting Issue:

The corporate governance literature internationally frequently refers to a dichotomy of insider/outsider, rather than independent/not independent. What is meant by the two dichotomies? Which do you believe is the preferred focus and why?

CHAPTER 5 – CASES TO ACCOMPANY THE FINANCIAL ACCOUNTING RESEARCH SYSTEM (FARS)

5

OUTLINE

Figures and Tables

CASE 1

New Financing: Do Credit Agreements Pose Unique Accounting and Disclosure Challenges? Gunther International

Gunther International has had a rocky road, financially. You joined the company upon graduation and recall having heard about it being significantly restructured in September 1992. It was then that two shareholders assumed control of the corporation and infused additional capital. Your department has been rocked by recent discoveries of accounting issues that have caused a delay in reported numbers. You assisted in crafting the language that appeared in the 8-K filing:

> Item 5. Other Events.
>
> On June 23, 1998, the registrant issued a press release announcing that it does not expect to release its final results for the fourth quarter and the full fiscal year ended March 31, 1998 until later in July 1998. A copy of the press release is attached hereto as an exhibit. During the course of the year-end audit, the Company's auditors, Arthur Andersen LLP, identified errors in the accumulation of contract costs and certain items of expense that were not properly accounted for. The Company, with the assistance of its auditors, is continuing to review the nature and extent of these matters, as well as the effect these matters may have on the Company's financial results. Based on the information that is available at this time, the Company currently expects to report a net loss for the fiscal year ended March 31, 1998 of approximately $2.4 to $3.0 million. The Company also expects

to restate its results for each of the first three quarters of fiscal 1998. Previously issued financial statements for the interim periods of fiscal 1998 should not be relied upon.

The net losses referred to above are expected to result in a violation of certain financial covenants contained in the Company's senior credit facility. The Company has informed representatives of its senior lender about these matters and intends to meet with them to discuss a satisfactory resolution of the situation. If a satisfactory resolution is not reached, the Company may suffer an event of default under its senior credit facility and the Company's ability to continue to borrow thereunder may be impaired.

The Company is moving forward at an aggressive pace to definitively announce its financial results as quickly as possible. The Company continues to maintain a large installed base of customers using its products and believes that its products continue to be well received in the market place. The Company expects to have a record backlog of sales under contract in excess of $5 million as of June 30, 1998.

The Company's expectations are preliminary and are subject to the completion of its year-end audit. The estimated amount of loss, anticipated release of final results and the potential consequences of these matters, including without limitation the resolution of expected violations under the Company's senior credit facility discussed in this report constitute forward-looking statements, and the Company's actual results could differ from those discussed above . . . . *(Source: 8-K filed 6/23/98)*

As the 8-K suggests, a good deal of uncertainty surrounds the financing arrangements of the company going forward. The treasurer's department has been working long hours to explore the options. They requested financial numbers under the existing, though somewhat tenuous financing arrangement. While in preliminary form, assume you have access to something similar to what eventually appeared as the restated financial disclosures in Tables 5.1-1 and 5.1-2.

Table 5.1-1   Summary Financial Data—Income Statement Related*

	Year Ended March 31, 1998	Year Ended March 31, 1997	Year Ended March 31, 1996
Sales:			
Systems	$ 8,630,103	$ 8,716,473	$ 8,458,700
Maintenance	6,454,716	4,911,794	4,022,562
Total Sales	15,084,819	13,628,267	12,481,262
Cost of Sales:			
Systems	7,030,092	5,573,323	5,821,526
Maintenance	4,771,692	4,088,858	2,826,853
Total Cost of Sales	11,801,784	9,662,181	8,648,379
Gross Profit	3,283,035	3,966,086	3,832,883
Operating Expenses:			
Selling and Administrative	5,050,863	4,680,946	4,213,832
Research and Development	618,735	435,404	255,243

	Year Ended March 31, 1998	Year Ended March 31, 1997	Year Ended March 31, 1996
Total Operating Expenses	5,669,598	5,116,350	4,469,075
Operating Loss	(2,386,563)	(1,150,264)	(636,192)
Other Expenses:			
Interest Expense, Net	(245,552)	(184,426)	(243,363)
Net Loss	$(2,632,115)	$(1,334,690)	$(879,555)
Net Loss Per Share	$ (0.61)	$ (0.32)	$ (0.23)

*The summary financial data presented should be read in conjunction with the information set forth in the financial statements and notes thereto. *Source:* January 14, 1999 10-KSB/A filing by Gunther International.

Table 5.1-2   Summary Financial Data—Balance Sheet Related*

	1998 (As Restated)	1997 (As Restated)
Current Assets	$3,118,386	$3,616,493
Total Assets	8,036,929	8,663,040
Current Liabilities	7,981,871	5,661,800
Long-Term Debt, less current maturities	1,884,551	2,213,618
Stockholders' Equity (Deficit)	(1,829,493)	787,622

*The summary financial data presented should be read in conjunction with the information set forth in the financial statements and notes thereto. *Source:* January 14, 1999 10-KSB/A filing by Gunther International.

The reason for the tenuous situation with the creditors is the reported error that resulted in the debt covenant violations on the line of credit held by Bank of Boston. Credit agreements, often the lifeblood of a company, can take a variety of forms, with diverse covenants and commitments. Gunther's solution to this covenant violation has been to find new financing and pay off the line of credit with the Bank of Boston. You have worked with colleagues in both the controller's office and the treasurer's department to craft the following language for inclusion in yet another 8-K filing:

> GUNTHER ANNOUNCES COMPLETION OF COMPREHENSIVE FINANCING TRANSACTION
>
>   NORWICH, CT (October 2, 1998)—Gunther International, Ltd. (NASDAQ: SORT) today announced it has successfully completed a comprehensive $5.7 million financing transaction, the proceeds of which have been utilized to completely restructure and replace the Company's pre-existing senior line of credit, fund a full settlement with the Company's third party service provider, and provide additional working capital to fund the Company's ongoing business operations.
>
>   Under the terms of the transaction, a newly formed limited liability company organized by the Tisch Family Interests and Mr. Robert Spiegel (the "New Lender") loaned an aggregate of $4 million to the Company. At the same time, the Company's senior lender reached an agreement with the guarantor of a portion of the Company's senior line of credit (the "Guarantor") whereby the Guarantor consented to the liquidation of approximately $1.7 million of collateral and the application of the proceeds of such

collateral to satisfy and repay in full a like amount of indebtedness outstanding under the senior credit facility. The balance of the indebtedness outstanding under the senior credit facility, approximating $350,000, was repaid in full from the proceeds of the new financing. The Company executed a new promissory note in favor of the Guarantor evidencing the Company's obligation to repay the amount of the collateral that was liquidated by the senior lender. The Company's obligations to the Guarantor are completely subordinated to the Company's obligations to the New Lender. In addition, approximately $1.4 million of the new financing was utilized to pay the Company's third party service provider all amounts that were due and owing to the service provider for performing maintenance on Company systems.

To induce the New Lender to enter into the financing transaction, the Company, the New Lender, Park Investment Partners, Gerald H. Newman, the estate of Harold S. Geneen (the "Estate"), Four Partners, and Robert Spiegel Entered into a separate voting agreement, pursuant to which they each agreed to vote all shares of Gunther stock held by them in favor of (i) that number of persons nominated by the New Lender constituting a majority of the Board of Directors, (ii) one person nominated by the Estate and (iii) one person nominated by Park Investment Partners. In addition, the Company granted the New Lender a stock purchase warrant entitling the New Lender, any time during the period commencing on January 1, 1999 and ending on the fifth anniversary of the transaction, to purchase up to 35% of the pro forma, fully diluted number of shares of the Common Stock of the Company, determined as of the date of exercise. The exercise price of the warrant is $1.50 per share.

Contemporaneously with the consummation of the transaction, Frederick W. Kolling III and James H. Whitney resigned from the Board of Directors, and Thomas Steinberg and Robert Spiegel were elected to fill the vacancies created by the resignations. Another inside director, Alan W. Morton, resigned from the Board prior to the consummation of the transactions.

The Company is continuing to review the previously announced issues regarding the accumulation of contract costs and the recognition of revenues and expenses relating to the Company's systems business. The Company expects to be in a position to release information concerning the results of the review by the end of October.

Gunther International, Ltd. is a leading manufacturer of intelligent document finishing systems and ink jet printing solutions. *(Source: 8-K, filed 10/7/98)*

Requirement A.1: Disclosure

As soon as the 8-K is released, the company's attention is directed toward the anticipated filing of a 10-K, which will need to provide full disclosure concerning this new financing arrangement in accordance with generally accepted accounting principles (GAAP). You have been asked to outline all associated accounting and disclosure issues that arise as a result of this transaction. The intent is that your outline will become a basis for a joint presentation with the controller to the board of directors.

1. List all relevant FARS references in the order of relevance to the transaction.
2. Clearly set forth permissible alternatives.
3. Draft your recommendation, as to both accounting for and disclosing of the transaction.

Hints Regarding Solution

a. Develop a comprehensive list of search words associated with the transaction.

b. Consider how the former arrangement might have been recorded in comparison to the current transaction, including potential balance sheet, income statement, and cash flow implications.

c. Consider broader disclosure requirements' association with particular transactions.

d. Context matters to accounting and disclosure decisions. Carefully consider the inter-relationship of the two press releases, giving particular attention to the various stakeholders affected by your recommendations.

Requirement A.2: Interdisciplinary Considerations

The board of directors is expected to be very interested in details concerning the transaction, making it imperative that interdisciplinary considerations be discussed as a part of your presentation.

1. Why is corporate governance so interrelated with credit arrangements?
2. Why are warrants frequently integrated into lending contracts?
3. Do contracts in economic settings generally slip into default when problems with past representations in financial statements arise? Be specific.
4. What are the consequences of delaying financial statement information for four months or longer?
5. Describe and justify a management strategy for Gunther International, in light of these past events.

Requirement B: Subsequent Filings

On January 14, 1999, Gunther International filed a 10-KSB/A (accessible at http://www.sec.gov) that contained the following disclosures:

> The undersigned registrant hereby amends its Annual Report on
> Form 10-KSB for the fiscal year ended March 31, 1998 to amend Items 6 and 7 of Part II
> and Item 13 of Part III, as set forth in this amendment.
> ITEM 6. MANAGEMENT'S DISCUSSION AND ANALYSIS OR PLAN OF
> OPERATIONS. SUMMARY OF RECENT EVENTS . . . The Audit Committee's review
> has since been completed and it has been determined that accounts receivable were
> overstated and accounts payable and deferred service revenues were understated at March
> 31, 1997 and costs and estimated earnings in excess of billings on uncompleted contracts
> were overstated at March 31, 1998. As a result, the accompanying financial statements
> and management's discussion and analysis of financial condition and results of operations
> include restated results as of and for the years ended March 31, 1997 and 1998. Also,
> certain amounts were reclassified between selling and administrative expenses, cost of
> sales, and research and development expenses to more appropriately reflect the results of
> operations. The effect of the restatement for the year ended March 31, 1997 was to reduce
> operating results to a net loss of $(1,334,690), or $(0.32) per share, from net income of
> $258,889, or $0.06 per share. The effect of the restatement for the year ended March 31,

1998 was to decrease the net loss to $(2,632,115), or $(0.61) per share, from a net loss of $(2,701,819), or $(0.63) per share.

On October 2, 1998, the Company entered into a $5.7 million comprehensive financing transaction with the Bank of Boston, Connecticut, N.A. (the "Bank"), the Estate of Harold S. Geneen (the "Estate") and Gunther Partners LLC (the "New Lender"), the proceeds of which have been utilized to restructure and replace the Company's pre-existing senior line of credit, fund a full settlement with the Company's third party service provider and provide additional working capital to fund the Company's ongoing business operations. Under the terms of the transaction, the New Lender loaned an aggregate of $4.0 million to the Company. At the same time, the Bank reached an agreement with the Estate, which had guaranteed a portion of the Company's senior line of credit, whereby the Estate consented to the liquidation of approximately $1.7 million of collateral and the application of the proceeds of such collateral to satisfy and repay in full a like amount of indebtedness outstanding under the senior credit facility. The balance of the indebtedness outstanding under the senior credit facility, approximately $350,000, was repaid in full from the proceeds of the new financing. The Company executed a new promissory note in favor of the Estate evidencing the Company's obligation to repay the amount of the collateral that was liquidated by the Bank. The Company's obligations to the Estate are subordinated to the Company's obligations to the New Lender. The principal balance of the $4.0 million debt is to be repaid in monthly installments of $100,000 from November 1, 1998 and continuing to and including September 1, 1999, $400,000 on October 1, 1999 and the balance shall be due on October 1, 2003. Interest shall be paid quarterly, at the rate of 8% per annum, beginning January 1, 1999 and continuing until the principal and interest due is paid in full. The debt is secured by a first priority interest in all tangible and intangible property and a secondary interest in patents and trademarks. . . .

The promissory note in favor of the Estate for approximately $1.7 million is to be repaid at the earlier of one year after the Company's obligations to the New Lender are paid in full or on October 2, 2004. Interest, at 5.44% per annum, shall accrue on principal and unpaid interest, which is added to the outstanding balance and is due at the time of principal payments. The indebtedness is secured by all tangible and intangible personal property of the Company but is subordinated to all rights of the New Lender. (*Source: January 14, 1999, 10-KSB/A filing by Gunther International*)

1. Given these subsequent disclosures, would you propose any adjustments to the accounting or disclosure suggestions you presented prior to the resolution of the restatement? Explain the basis for your response.
2. Would you expect the new lender to make any adjustments to the current contractual arrangement when the credit arrangement is reconsidered at renewal?
3. What would be the accounting or disclosure implications of your expectations? Explain how the following subsequent development might influence your expectations, if you were requested to update your evaluation as of July 1999.

On June 29, 1999, a 10-KSB filing states within the Management's Discussion and Analysis (Item 6, Subhead Liquidity and Capital Resources):

The company did not make its required payments on their respective due dates and certain other information required by the loan agreement was not provided to the New Lender.

The New Lender waived these deficiencies. As of March 31, 1999, all amounts due on the
debt had been paid. . . .

In the event the Company is unable to meet its payment obligations through April 1,
2000, in accordance with the Note Loan and Security Agreement, the new Lender will be
willing to renegotiate the payment terms based upon available cash flow such that the
payment terms would be acceptable to both the Company and the Lender. *(Source:
10-KSB filing 6/29/99)*

Requirement C: The Aftermath

At fiscal year ended March 31, 2001, in its 10-KSB/A fiiling as of July 3, 2001, events associated
with the past financing arrangements are detailed, alongside the following disclosure:

> Through June 30, 1999, the Company had made principal payments to Gunther Partners
> LLC aggregating $800,000, plus interest. In September 1999, the Company experienced a
> deficiency in operating cash flow and Gunther Partners LLC agreed to lend the Company
> an additional $800,000 and to otherwise restructure the payment terms of the note. As
> amended, the outstanding balance due Gunther Partners LLC is due in principal
> installments of $200,000 commencing on October 1, 2001 through April 1, 2002;
> $100,000 on May 1, 2002; and $2,500,000 on October 1, 2003. If, at any time prior to
> October 1, 2001, the accumulated deficit of the Company improves by $1.0 million or
> more compared to the amount at June 30, 1999 of $14.4 million (a "Triggering Event"),
> then the principal payments otherwise due from October 1, 2001 through May 1, 2002
> shall . . . become due in consecutive monthly installments beginning on the first day of the
> second month following the Triggering Event. On April 4, 2000, the Company borrowed
> an additional $500,000 from Gunther Partners LLC.
>
> In June 2001, the Company entered into a recapitalization agreement (the
> "Recapitalization Agreement") with the Estate, Gunther Partners LLC and certain other
> stockholders. The Recapitalization Agreement provides that the Company will effectuate
> a registered public offering ("Rights Offering") of up to 16,000,000 shares of its Common
> Stock (the "Offered Shares") to its existing stockholders by subscription right on a
> pro-rata basis at a subscription price of $0.50 per share. The rights to subscribe to the
> Offered Shares will be granted at a ratio to be determined by the Board of Directors of the
> Company (the "Basic Subscription Right"). In addition, the Company's stockholders will
> be granted the right to "oversubscribe" for additional shares not purchased by other
> stockholders, up to the total amount of the Offered Shares (the "Oversubscription Right").
> In the event that the Company's stockholders, other than Gunther Partners LLC, do not
> subscribe for and purchase all 16,000,000 of the Offered Shares, Gunther Partners LLC
> will subscribe for and purchase from the Company in the Rights Offering a number of
> shares equal to 16,000,000 less the number of shares subscribed for stockholders other
> than Gunther Partners LLC, up to a maximum of 14,000,000 shares. The net proceeds of
> the Rights Offering (a minimum of $7 million less offering expenses), will be used to
> repay in full the notes payable to Gunther Partners LLC ($4.5 million) and a stockholder
> and director ($500,000), to purchase all notes payable to the Estate for a total of $500,000
> and to purchase 919,568 shares of the Company's Common Stock held by the Estate for
> $137,935 (or $0.15 per share). The balance of the net proceeds from the Rights Offering

will be used for general working capital purposes. *(Source: Gunther International Ltd 10-KSB/A 7/30/2001)*

1. How much of the net proceeds from the rights offering will likely be available for general working capital purposes?
2. Compare the terms of the rights offering to the warrants embedded in the earlier financing arrangement. Why do you believe a rights offering approach is being pursued rather than a shelf registration targeting new shareholders?
3. What disclosures would you recommend be made by the company related to its financing, liquidity, and capital resources?

Directed Self-Study

What happened to Gunther International on December 4, 2003? [Access sec.gov for the answer.]

Key Terms and Glossary

balloon payment a large final payment on a loan that is repaid in installments.

collateral assets that agreement gives the creditor the right to repossess and/or to convert into cash if the borrower defaults on the lending arrangement; also referred to as security for a loan, leading to the terminology of secured debt

compound interest distinguished from simple interest by reinvesting each interest payment in order to earn more interest

continuous compounding assumes continuous compounding of interest rather than compounding at fixed intervals

cum rights with rights or rights on, distinguished from *ex rights*

deficit arises in retained earnings when the cumulation of all prior years' net income or losses, less dividends declared, is negative

ex rights purchase of shares not entitled to the rights to buy shares in the company's rights issue

exercise price the price at which the holder of a warrant or similar instrument is permitted to buy the stock or other instrument to which it is convertible or is transferable

funded debt matures after more than one year

guarantor that individual or entity promising to pay should the borrower default

line of credit a credit arrangement that permits a borrower to obtain funds up to a certain amount with prespecified terms, and an associated cost for the unused line of credit

maturity that date at which an agreement comes to an end, such as a bond, reaching that date on which repayment is demanded in the absence of a renewal

promissory note a written agreement specifying the terms of the debt

restatement adjustment of past reported financial statements

restructuring when applied to debt, refers to the renegotiation of terms that could include extension of the due date of principal and interest payments, reduction in the rate of interest on existing debt, and/or forgiveness by creditors of a portion of principal or accrued interest; also applied to changes in strategy and operations of a company (e.g., downsizing)

rights offering the issue of securities to current stockholders that is sometimes referred to as a privileged subscription issue

secured debt refers to obligations that if defaulted upon, lead to a first claim on specified assets

subordination refers to the rights of a party being legally set behind another's, such as subordination of debt meaning that claims would not be fulfilled until unsubordinated debt commitments were met; subordinated debt is often called junior debt, receiving payment only after senior debt has been paid in full

warrant instrument permitting the purchase of a specified number of shares at a specified dollar amount

working capital current assets less current liabilities (i.e., net working capital)

Further Readings

Adut, Davit, William H. Cready, Thomas J. Lopez. 2003. "Restructuring charges and CEO cash compensation: A reexamination." *The Accounting Review* (78, 1, January), pp. 169–192.

Beatty, Anne, K. Ramesh, and Joseph Weber. 2002. "The importance of accounting changes in debt contracts: The cost of flexibility in covenant calculations." *Journal of Accounting and Economics* (33, 2, June), pp. 205–227.

Beatty, Anne, and Joseph Weber. 2003. "The effects of debt contracting on voluntary accounting method changes." *The Accounting Review* (78, 1, January), pp. 119–142.

Beneish, Messod D., and Eric Press. 1993. "Costs of technical violation of accounting-based covenants." *The Accounting Review* (68, 2, April), pp. 233–257.

Benston, G.J., and L.D. Wall. 2005. "How should banks account for loan losses?" *Journal of Accounting and Public Policy* (24, 2, March/April), pp. 81–100.

Berger, A., and G. Udell. 1995. "Relationship lending and lines of credit in small firm finance." *Journal of Business* (68, July), pp. 351–381.

Berle, A., and G. Means. 1932. *The Modern Corporation and Private Property*. New York: McMillian.

Bitler, M., A. Robb, and J. Wolken. 2001. "Financial services used by small businesses: Evidence from the 1998 survey of small business finances." *Federal Reserve Bulletin* (April), pp. 183–205.

Black, B. 1992. "Institutional investors and corporate governance: The case for institutional voice." *Journal of Applied Corporate Finance* (5), pp. 19–32.

Cravens, Karen S., and Wanda A. Wallace. 2001. "A framework for determining the influence of the corporate board of directors in accounting studies." *Corporate Governance: An International Review* (9, 1, January), pp. 2–24 (Oxford: Blackwell Publishers).

Cravens, K. S., and W. A. Wallace. 1999. "Blue ribbon plan requires more disclosure to work." *Accounting Today* (July 26–August 8), pp. 14, 17, 40, 41.

Diamond, D. 1991. "Monitoring the reputation: The choice between bank loans and directly placed debt." *Journal of Political Economy* (99, 4), pp. 689–721.

Duru, A., S. A. Manis and D. M. Reeb. 2005. "Earnings-based bonus plans and the agency costs of debt." *Journal of Accounting and Public Policy* (24, 5, September/October), pp. 431–447.

Guenther, D., and M. Willenborg. 1999. "Capital gains tax rates and the cost of capital for small business: Evidence from the IPO market." *Journal of Financial Economics* (53), pp. 385–408.

Gul, Ferdinand A. and Sidney Leung. 2004. "Board leadership, outside directors' expertise and voluntary corporate disclosures." *Journal of Accounting and*

change to the LLP organization of audit firms." *Auditing: A Journal of Practice and Theory* (23, 1, March), pp. 53–67.

Opler, Tim C. 1993. "Controlling financial distress costs in leveraged buyouts with financial innovations." *Financial Management* (Financial Distress Special Issue, September), pp. 79–93.

Petersen, M., and R. Rajan. 1994. "The benefits of lending relationships: Evidence from small business data." *Journal of Finance* (49, March), pp. 3–37.

Press, E., and J. Weintrop. 1991. "Financial statement disclosure of accounting-based debt covenants." *Accounting Horizons* (March), p. 70.

Reilly, David. 2006. "No more 'stealth restating'—SEC forces companies to highlight earnings changes, not just tack them on to their newest filings." *Wall Street Journal* (September 21), pp. C1, C3.

Shleifer, A., and R. W. Vishny. 1997. "A survey of corporate governance." *Journal of Finance* (52, 2), pp. 737–783.

The Sarbanes-Oxley Act of 2002. Pub. L. No. 107–204 (July 30) 116 Stat. 745. H.R. 3763. 15 USC 7201 note.

Scott, Jr., J. H. 1979. "Bankruptcy, secured debt, and optimal capital structure: reply." *Journal of Finance* (March), pp. 254–260.

SEC. *Final Rule: Improper Influence on Conduct of Audits* Securities and Exchange Commission 17 CFR Part 240. 2003. [Release Nos. 34–47890, IC-26050; FR-71; File No. S7-39-02] RIN 3235-AI67 (June 26).

Sheikh, Aamer, and Wanda A. Wallace. 2005. "Certification in the presence of uncertainty." *Accounting Today* (19, 2, January 24–February 6), pp. 36, 37.

Sheikh, Aamer, and Wanda A. Wallace. 2005. "The Sarbanes-Oxley certification requirement: Analyzing the comments." *The CPA Journal, Special Auditing Issue, "Innovations in Auditing"—Constructing the Future* (November), pp. 36–42.

Smith, Jr., C. W., and J. B. Warner. 1979. "Bankruptcy, secured debt, and optimal capital structure: Comment." *Journal of Finance* (March), pp. 247–251.

Smith, Jr., C. W., and J. B. Warner. 1979. "On financial contracting: An analysis of bond covenants." *Journal of Financial Economics* (June), pp. 117–161.

Wallace, Wanda A. 2005. "Auditor changes and restatements: An analysis of recent history." *CPA Journal* (LXXV, 3, March), pp. 30–33.

Wallace, Wanda A. 2004. "Auditor rotation: A bad governance idea," Guest Column. *Directors & Boards* (28, 3, Spring), p. 14 [Also included in *E-Briefing* (1, 2, June 2004 online newsletter)]

Wallace, Wanda A. 2004. *Risk Assessment by Internal Auditors Using Past Research on Bankruptcy: Applying Bankruptcy Models*. Altamonte Springs, FL: The

Public Policy (23, 5, September/October), pp. 351–379.

Jones, Denise A., and Wanda A. Wallace. 2005. "Existing disclosure challenges of IPO allocations: A research report." *Research in Accounting Regulation* (18), pp. 107–126.

Lee, Edward, Konstantinos Stathopoulos, and Mark Hon. 2006. "Investigating the return predictability of changes in corporate borrowing." *Accounting and Business Research* (36, 2), pp. 93–107.

Leftwich, R. 1983. "Accounting information in private markets: Evidence from private lending agreements." *Accounting Review* (January), pp. 23–42.

Moehrle, Stephen R. 2002. "Do firms use restructuring charge reversals to meet earnings targets?" *The Accounting Review* (77, 2, April), pp. 397–413.

Muzatko, Steven R., Karla M. Johnstone, Brian W. Mayhew, and Larry E. Rittenberg. 2004. "An empirical investigation of IPO underpricing and the Institute of Internal Auditors Research Foundation.) [.PDF file and linked EXCEL worksheets available at: http://www.theiia.org/iia/index.cfm?doc_id=4619.]

Wilkinson, B. R, and C. E. Clements. 2006. "Corporate governance mechanisms and the early-filing of CEO certification." *Journal of Accounting and Public Policy* (25, 2, March/April), pp. 121–139.

Williamson, O. E. 1985. *The Economic Institution of Capitalism: Firms, Markets and Relational Contracting.* New York: Free Press.

Williamson, O. E. 1984. "Corporate governance." *Yale Law Journal* (93), pp. 1197–1230.

Williamson, O. E. 1979. "Transaction-cost economics. The governance of contractual relations." *Journal of Law and Economics* (22,2), pp. 233–261.

Wyatt, Anne. 2005. "Accounting recognition of intangible assets: Theory and evidence on economic determinants." *Accounting Review* (80, 3, July), pp. 967–1003.

"The creditors are a superstitious sect, great observers of set days and times. Blessed is he that expects nothing for he shall never be disappointed.

—*Benjamin Franklin*, **Poor Richard's Almanac**

CASE 2

Microsoft: Does Income Statement Classification Matter?

CASE TOPICS OUTLINE
1. Microsoft Disclosure
   A. Primary Business Alignment
   B. Direct Cost Recording

2. Consistency of Presentation

Microsoft filed its 10-K on September 28, 1999, and disclosed the following:

> Reclassifications. The Company changed the way it reports revenue and costs associated with product support, consulting, MSN Internet access, and certification and training of system integrators. Amounts received from customers for these activities have been classified as revenue in a manner more consistent with Microsoft's primary businesses. Direct costs of these activities are classified as cost of revenue. Prior financial statements have been reclassified for consistent presentation. Certain other reclassifications have also been made for consistent presentation. (*Source: 10-K filed 9/28/99*)

The financial statements for 1999 and 1998, as originally reported and as reclassified, are reported in Table 5.2-1.

Requirement: Disclosure and Strategy-Related Considerations

You are a personal financial advisor to a number of clients, one of whom is a sophisticated investor in Microsoft. The client, who just received the September 1999 10-K filing is perplexed as to the meaning of the reclassifications, reflected in Table 5.2-1. Moreover, given the earnings per share effects are zero, the client does not understand why the disclosure was made at all.

1. Explain why Microsoft has provided the detail evidenced in Table 5.2-1. Support your explanation with appropriate citations from FARS.
2. Do you believe that the type of disclosure provided by Microsoft was essential in order for the corporation to comply with GAAP? Why or why not?

Table 5.2-1   Reclassified Historical Income Statements by Year*

Microsoft Corporation Reclassified Income Statements (in millions; unaudited)	Reported 1999	Reclassified 1999	Reported 1998	Reclassified 1998
Revenue Operating expenses:	$13,222	$13,983	$14,484	$15,262
Cost of revenue	1,090	2,145	1,197	2,460
Research and development	1,889	2,030	2,502	2,601
Acquired in-process technology	0	0	296	296
Sales and marketing	2,766	2,331	3,412	2,828
General and administrative	392	392	433	433
Other expenses	60	60	230	230
Total operating expenses	6,197	6,958	8,070	8,848
Operating income	7,025	7,025	6,414	6,414
Investment income	1,318	1,318	703	703
Gain on sale	160	160	0	0
Income before income taxes	8,503	8,503	7,117	7,117
Provision for income taxes	2,920	2,920	2,627	2,627
Net income	$5,583	$5,583	$4,490	$4,490
Earnings per share:				
Basic	$ 1.11	$ 1.11	$ 0.92	$ 0.92
Diluted	$ 1.02	$ 1.02	$ 0.84	$ 0.84

*1997 Fiscal Year Reclassifications are likewise presented as reported and reclassified in the Microsoft filing.

3. Should business strategy influence the classification of revenue and associated costs in an information system? Give an example of how classification of revenue and associated costs might differ between two companies that provide services associated with system design, software development, Internet sites, and other products analogous to those of Microsoft.

Directed Self-Study

Access the June 30, 2006 annual report for Microsoft at sec.gov and determine if it contains any indication of reclassifications on the income statement. Compare and contrast the nature of any disclosures found to those profiled in the case.

Do Dell's Woes Relate to Classification?

On February 2, 2007, the *Wall Street Journal* reported "Dell's Woes Mount as Investors File Improper Accounting Suit" (by Don Clark, Christopher Lawton and John R. Wilke, p . A4). Do the allegations involve classification issues? Explain. Use FARS to evaluate each of the allegations.

Key Terms and Glossary

consistency comparability across time of generally accepted accounting principles' application

direct costs those costs that fluctuate directly with the product, such as raw materials and direct labor used to create physical products

reclassifications changes in the account used to record or present a transaction, event, or estimate

Further Readings

Alexander, David. 1999. "A benchmark for the adequacy of published financial statements." *Accounting and Business Research* (29, 3), pp. 239–253.

Bell, Timothy, Frank Marrs, Ira Solomon, and Howard Thomas. 1997. *Auditing Organizations Through a Strategic-Systems Lens.* KPMG Peat Marwick LLP.

Cato, Sid. 1988. "Manager's Journal: When preparing annual reports, less is definitely not more." *Wall Street Journal* (August 22), 1988 WL-WSJ 454421.

Doyle, Robert K., and F. Gordon Spoor. 1999. "How to start an investment advisory practice." *Journal of Accountancy* (187, 1, January).

Golub, Steven J., and Robert J. Kueppers. 1983. *Summary Reporting of Financial Information: Moving Toward More Readable Annual Reports* (A Research Study Prepared for Financial Executives Research Foundation).

Jacobs, Sanford L. 1988. "Annual reports in short form fail to catch on." *Wall Street Journal* (April 14), 1988-WL-WSJ 468976.

Littleton, A. C. 1953. *Structure of Accounting Theory.* American Accounting Association Monograph No. 5. Sarasota, FL: American Accounting Association, pp. 39–40, 44.

Price, Reneé, and Wanda A. Wallace. 2001. *Shades of Materiality* (The Canadian Certified General Accountants' Research Foundation, Research Monograph 24 published on CD-ROM).

Price, Reneé, and Wanda A. Wallace. 1996–1997. "Too many shades of materiality only serve to confuse." Audit & Accounting Forum. *Accounting Today* (December 16– January 5), p. 61.

SEC. 2003. "Frequently asked questions regarding the use of non-GAAP financial measures." Prepared by staff members in the Division of Corporation Finance. Washington, DC: U.S. SEC, (June 13).

SEC. 2003. SAB No. 103, Codification of Staff Accounting Bulletins (as posted May) — Topic 1: Financial Statements; Topic 2: Business Combinations; Topic 3: Senior Securities; Topic 4: Equity Accounts; Topic 5: Miscellaneous Accounting; Topic 6: Interpretations of Accounting Series Releases and Financial Reporting Releases; Topic 7: Real Estate Companies; Topic 8: Retail Companies; Topic 9: Finance Companies; Topic 10: Utility Companies; Topic 11: Miscellaneous Disclosure; Topic 12: Oil and Gas Producing Activities; Topic 13: Revenue Recognition.

SEC. 1995. WL 385858 (SEC Release No.) 59 SEC Docket 1556, Release No. 33–7183, Release No. 34-35893, Release No. IC-21, 166. "Use of abbreviated financial statements in documents delivered to investors pursuant to the Securities Act of 1933 and Securities Exchange Act of 1934." File No. S7-13-95, RIN 3235-AG49, (June 27).

Visvanathan, Gnanakumar. 2006. "An empirical investigation of 'closeness to cash' as a determinant of earnings response coefficients." *Accounting and Business Research* (36, 2), pp. 109–120.

Wallace, Wanda A. 2003. "Analyzing non-GAAP line items in income statements." *CPA Journal* (LXXIII, 6, June), pp. 38–47.

Make the scheme of accounts conform with the operating organization of the enterprise, because accounting data can thus be made to reveal the results of management's use of its opportunities.

—**A.C. Littleton**

[Source: <u>Structure of Accounting Theory</u>, American Accounting Association Monograph No. 5 (Sarasota, FL: American Accounting Association, 1966), p. 191]

CASE 3

Charitable Contributions and Debt: A Comparison of St. Jude Children's Research Hospital/ALSAC and Universal Health Services

CASE TOPICS OUTLINE

1. St. Jude Children's Research Hospital/ALSAC
   A. Primary Objective
   B. Sources of Capital
   C. Reporting Practices

2. Universal Health Services
   A. Investor-Owned Hospital
   B. Debt Including Leases
3. Comparison

Hospitals are an industry in which both not-for-profits and investor-owned facilities operate. The sources of capital available to the not-for-profits include charitable contributions and debt offerings—unless they are governmental, in which case, higher taxes are also an alternative. Debt availability is always, in part, a function of performance, and just as failures have arisen in both sectors, about one-third of the investor-owned hospitals have been described as losing money. Of interest is how can one effectively evaluate such an industry, with this type of diversity in organizational forms and capital availability? A necessary prerequisite to such an evaluation is to have a firm understanding of how charitable contributions are presented.

St. Jude Children's Research Hospital/ALSAC has the mission of finding cures for children with catastrophic diseases through research and treatment. For the fiscal year 1999, this entity reported total assets of $221,664,232 and income of $177,071,890. A Web site at http://www.stjude.org, as well as Guidestar's listing, references a Form 990 (Return of Organization Exempt from Income Tax) filing, availability of audited financial statements upon request, and information that the hospital has 2,100 employees and 350 volunteers. Founded in 1962, the organization seeks funds from contributions and grants for unrestricted operating expenses, specific projects, buildings, and endowments. More than 4,000 patients are seen annually, with a hospital maintaining 56 beds. The Form 990, Part III states that the hospital provided 15,231 inpatient days of care during the fiscal year and patients made 40,982 clinic visits. ALSAC is the American Lebanese Syrian Associated Charities, Inc., the fund-raising arm of St. Jude Children's Research Hospital. It reported 1999 total assets of $1,007,699,320 and income of $274,123,399. This organization reports the number of employees as 565 and the number of volunteers as 800,000. With its sole focus on the hospital, ALSAC's self-description explains that no child has ever been turned away due to an inability to pay for treatment and explains key accomplishments in the research area achieved by St. Jude's research and treatment of children with catastrophic diseases. What is borne out by the example of St. Jude is the fact that a review of the Form 990 filed for the fiscal year ending 6/30/99 indicates in Part VI the names of related organizations: ALSAC and St. Jude Hospital Foundation, both of which are tax exempt. To gain a sense of capital availability to a not-for-profit entity, affiliated entities must be considered. In addition, the role of volunteers is a source of human capital not effectively captured within the framework of financial statements for not-for-profits, as reflected in the Form 990 for the fiscal year ending 6/30/99 for ALSAC, which states in Part VI:

> Unpaid volunteers have made significant contributions of their time, principally in fund-raising activities. The value of these services is not recognized in the financial statements since it is not susceptible to an objective measurement or valuation and because the activities of these volunteers are not subject to the operating supervision and control present in an employer/employee relationship.

Hence, as one evaluates capital sources and uses by not-for-profits, care is needed to consider affiliated organizations' role, total contributions, and the effect of volunteerism on the comparability between not-for-profit and investor-owned operations.

Universal Health Services, Inc. filed its 10-K on March 28, 2001, for the calendar year 2000, which includes comparative information for 1999. Analysts have described the company as the most aggressive company in the industry over the 1999–2001 time frame in making acquisitions, particularly of not-for-profit operations and investor-owned operations experiencing losses. The company is praised for it high operating leverage, the relatively small number of shareholders relative to the magnitude of total revenue, and stock price as a multiple of earnings. The company operates 59 hospitals and, as of 1999, had an average number of licensed beds of 4,806 at acute care hospitals and 1,976 at behavioral health centers, with patient days of 963,842 and 444,632, respectively. Of interest is a commentary on the competition found in the company's filing:

> Competition
>
> In all geographical areas in which the Company operates, there are other hospitals which provide services comparable to those offered by the Company's hospitals, some of which are owned by governmental agencies and supported by tax revenues, and others of which are owned by nonprofit corporations and may be supported to a large extent by endowments and charitable contributions. Such support is not available to the Company's hospitals. Certain of the Company's competitors have greater financial resources, are better equipped and offer a broader range of services than the Company. Outpatient treatment and diagnostic facilities, outpatient surgical centers and freestanding ambulatory surgical centers also impact the healthcare marketplace. In recent years, competition

among healthcare providers for patients has intensified as hospital occupancy rates in the United States have declined due to, among other things, regulatory and technological changes, increasing use of managed care payment systems, cost containment pressures, a shift toward outpatient treatment and an increasing supply of physicians. The Company's strategies are designed, and management believes that its facilities are positioned, to be competitive under these changing circumstances. *(Source: 10-K filed 3/28/2001)*

Financial information is provided in Tables 5.3-1 and 5.3-2 for both the not-for-profit and the investor-owned hospitals.

Table 5.3-1   Financial Comparisons of the Not-for-Profit Entities

Fiscal Year Ended 1999	*St. Jude Children's Research Hospital Form 990**	*American Lebanese Syrian Associated Charities, Inc. (ALSAC) Form 990**
Contributions, gifts, grants and similar amounts received: Direct public support	$91,978,426	$231,793,748
Indirect public support		2,906,934
Government contributions (grants)	31,469,447	
Program service revenue, including government fees and contracts (i.e., health insurance revenue)	46,034,710	
Accounts receivable	24,217,029	4,230,764
Pledges receivable		23,604,748
Allowance for doubtful accounts	9,363,328	
Program service expenses		99,282,906
Program service expenses: Research	87,225,830	
Program service expenses: Education and training	5,471,186	
Program service expenses: Medical Services	93,735,602	
Reconciliation of revenue, gains, and other support to audited numbers: net unrealized gains on investments	−4,023,815	65,891,269
Deferred grant revenue	1,857,628 (Statement 5)	
Support from American Lebanese Syrian Associated Charities, Inc.	91,978,426 (Statement 7)	91,978,426 (paid per Statements 4, 6)
Excluded contributions		2,746,295 (Statement 1)
Excess or (deficit) for the year	−10,933,191	120,521,982

Fiscal Year Ended 1999	St. Jude Children's Research Hospital Form 990*	American Lebanese Syrian Associated Charities, Inc. (ALSAC) Form 990*
Net assets or fund balances at end of year	199,707,440	994,501,910
Temporarily restricted		15,715,890
Permanently restricted	14,000,000	247,147,826
Total liabilities	21,956,792	7,017,192
Schedule of deferred debits & credits by contract (FAS 116 adjustment noted to result in this deferred revenue)	157,628	

*The GuideStar.org Web site (http://www.guidestar.org) provides access to Forms 990 in .PDF format.

Table 5.3-2 Universal Health Services, Inc.'s Financial Excerpts*

Income Statements (in thousands)	Reported 1999 Calendar Year
Net revenues	$2,042,380
Operating charges	1,913,346
Components:	
Salaries, wages, and benefits	793,529
Provision for doubtful accounts	166,139
Lease and rental expense	49,029
Interest expense, net	26,872
Net income	77,775
Total assets	1,497,973
Total liabilities	856,362
Total retained earnings	482,960
Capital stock	306
Paid-in capital in excess of par	158,345

*The 10-K filing as of 3/28/2001 at EDGAR (http://www.sec.gov/edgar.shtml) provides financial statement information for 2000 and 1999.

Requirement A: Recording Revenue

1. What is meant by the reference in Table 5.3-1 to an FAS 116 adjustment?
2. How are contributions recorded? Is there a distinction between pledges receivable and accounts receivable?

3. Are there circumstances when financial statements can quantify volunteers' services?
4. Can financial statement users of not-for-profit hospitals' financial statements expect to be fully informed regarding affiliated parties, such as the linkages between St. Jude Children's Research Hospital, ALSAC, and the foundation cited? Explain.

Requirement B: Revenue Mix (Strategy-Related Considerations)

The 10-K filing of Universal Health Services, Inc. describes the mix of revenue sources, as depicted in Table 5.3-3.

Table 5.3-3   Patient Revenue Mix

	PERCENTAGE OF NET PATIENT REVENUES				
	2000	*1999*	*1998*	*1997*	*1996*
Third Party Payors					
Medicare...	32.3%	33.5%	34.3%	35.6%	35.6%
Medicaid...	11.5%	12.6%	11.3%	14.5%	15.3%
Managed Care (HMOs and PPOs)...	34.5%	31.5%	27.2%	19.1%	N/A
Other Sources.................................	21.7%	22.4%	27.2%	30.8%	49.1%
Total...	100%	100%	100%	100%	100%

N/A-Not available *(Source: 10-K filed 3/28/2001)*

1. How does this revenue mix compare with the revenue blend of the not-for-profit entity, St. Jude Children's Research Hospital (ALSAC)? Access the latest SEC filing and compare the reported revenue mix; has it changed?
2. What does that imply as to the strategies of investor-owned hospitals in managing risk and ensuring adequate capital relative to not-for-profit entities? An opportunity exists to explore the greater social and political questions that are frequently debated about the compatibility of profit-oriented entities and quality of health care, relative to not-for-profit entities. As background, identify what the latest SEC filings report concerning charity care.

Directed Self-Study

Access the 10-Q (from sec.gov) for the quarterly period ended June 30, 2006 and explain how Hurricane Katrina affected Universal Health Services. The same 10-Q reports on a funding commitment the company has made to the alma mater of the Chairman of the Board of Directors and Chief Executive Officer. Describe the disclosure and explain why the event is an "Other Related Party Transaction." [Download the 10-Q in text format and apply the Find capability in your word processor. Also access FARS and identify the guidance relevant to each event.]

Health Insurance, Public Policy, and Backdating

A key factor in the health care industry is health insurance. Public policy has debated universal health care, changes to governmental programs such as Medicare, adjustment of tax policy regarding employers' and employees' deduction for premiums, and alternative approaches to this sector of the economy. State and local governments, under a new accounting rule, have recently estimated their total retiree health bill to be about $1.1 trillion. Over the past decade, some governmental units used pension funds to help pay for double-digit growth in health care for retired public workers. Explain how accounting interacts with public policy. Use FARS as a resource, according particular attention to FAS 158.

Health insurer UnitedHealth has been the focus of media coverage involving what is known as the "options backdating scandal". UnitedHealth's internal probe estimates its past decade exposure at half a billion dollars ("UnitedHealth Faces Formal Probe," *Wall Street Journal*, December 27, 2006, p. B8). Is there a relationship between the magnitude of the restatement and the nature of the health care sector of the economy? Explain. The SEC's Division of Corporation Finance shared a "Sample Letter Sent in Response to Inquiries Related to Filing Restated Financial Statements for Errors in Accounting for Stock Option Grants" dated January 2007 (http://www.sec.gov/divisions/corpfin/guidance/oilgasltr012007.htm.) How helpful do you find such guidance?

Key Terms and Glossary

fund balance "refers . . . to a common group of assets and related liabilities within a not-for-profit organization and to the net amount of those assets and liabilities. . . . While some not-for-profit organizations may choose to classify assets and liabilities into fund groups, information about those groupings is not a necessary part of general purpose external financial reporting" (CON6, Footnote 45); fund balances may refer to such fund groups as operating, plant, endowment, and other funds (FAS 117, Par. 98).

permanent restriction "A donor-imposed restriction that stipulates that resources be maintained permanently but permits the organization to use up or expend part or all of the income (or other economic benefits) derived from the donated assets" (FAS 117, Par. 168). Information about permanent restrictions is useful in determining the extent to which an organization's net assets are not a source of cash for payments to present or prospective lenders, suppliers, or employees and thus are not expected to be directly available for providing services or paying creditors (FAS 117, Par. 98).

pledges receipts of promises to give

temporary restriction "A donor-imposed restriction that permits the donee organization to use up or expend the donated assets as specified and is satisfied either by the passage of time or by actions of the organization" (FAS 117, Par. 168). Separate line items may be reported within temporarily restricted net assets or in notes to financial statements to distinguish between temporary restrictions for (a) support of particular operating activities, (b) investment for a specified term, (c) use in a specified future period, or (d) acquisition of long-lived assets. Donors' temporary restrictions may require that resources be used in a later period or after a specified date (time restrictions), or that resources be used for a specified purpose (purpose restrictions), or both. For example, gifts of cash and other assets with stipulations that they be invested to provide a source of income for a specified term and that the income be used for a specified purpose are both time and purpose restricted. Those gifts often are called *term endowments* (FAS 117, Par. 15).

Further Readings

Baber, William R., Patricia L. Daniel, and Andrea A.
Roberts. 2002. "Compensation to managers of
charitable organizations: An empirical study of the role
of accounting measures of program activities."
Accounting Review (77, 3, July), pp. 679–693.

The Comprehensive Report of the Special Committee on
Financial Reporting. American Institute of Certified
Public Accountants. 1994. *Improving Business
Reporting—A Customer Focus.* New York: AICPA.

Council of Better Business Bureaus (CBBB). 2001. Web
site for the Philanthropic Advisory Service reports.
Available at: www.bbb.org/pas/reports.

Governmental Accounting Standards Board. 1990. *Service
Efforts and Accomplishments Reporting: Its Time Has
Come—An Overview.* Washington, DC: GASB.

Guidestar. 2001. Web site that reports Form 990, Return
of Organization Exempt from Income Tax, information
for charities. Available at: http://www.guidestar.org.

Houle, C. O. 1989. *Governing Boards: Their Nature and
Nurture.* (Washington, DC: Jossey-Bass and National
Center for Nonprofit Boards).

Joos, Peter, and George A. Plesko. 2005. "Valuing loss
firms." *Accounting Review* (80, 3, July), pp. 847–870.

Laswad, Fawzi, Richard Fisher, and Peter Oyelere. 2005.
"Determinants of voluntary Internet financial reporting

by local government authorities." *Journal of
Accounting and Public Policy* (24, 2, March/April),
pp. 101–121.

Parry, Robert W., Florence Sharp, Jannet Vreeland, and
Wanda A. Wallace. 1994. "The role of service efforts
and accomplishments reporting in total quality
management: Implications for accountants."
Accounting Horizons (8, 2, June), pp. 25–43.

Peebles, Laura. 2001. "The right philanthropic vehicle."
Journal of Accountancy (July), pp. 22–27.

Ripperger, Matt. 2001. "Analyst [A director with Warburg
Dillon Read's Healthcare Research Group] interview:
Hospital management services." *Wall Street Journal
Transcript* (February 7), Document # LAQ901.

Wallace, Wanda A. 2006. "Financial management in
government entails evaluating nonprofits: Are you
ready for the next natural disaster?" *Journal of
Government Financial Management* (55, 1, Spring),
pp. 44–57.

Wallace, Wanda A. 2003. "Avoiding the downfall of
windfalls." *Journal of Government Financial
Management* (52, 3, Fall), pp. 18–30.

Wallace, Wanda A. 2001. "How accountable are charities
for their performance?" *Accounting Today* (June
18–July 1), pp. 18, 20.

**Accounting deals with a system which is a human creation, designed to satisfy
human needs, and which must therefore, above all, be useful. The accounting
environment is prone to many influences of a nondeterministic nature, influences
related not only to long-term legal, cultural and political traditions, but also to
short-term movements of mass psychology. . . . The subject matter is of such
diversity and changing complexity that attempts to make predictions in accounting
are akin to the difficulties of predicting the conditions of turbulence inside a tornado
or the problem of "forecasting" next month's weather.**

**In principle it is possible for meteorologists to predict the weather at noon in
Chicago on January 1, 1981, just as it is possible in principle to predict an eclipse of
the sun a thousand years hence. In practice, weather predictions (unlike
astronomical predictions) are unreliable over the space of a month let alone a
millennium. Accountants, like meteorologists, are also faced with a complex world of
many interacting bodies. Nevertheless, they might be able to adopt the pure scientific
method, and perhaps enjoy as much success with it as meteorologists,
if—like—meteorologists—they only had to deal with the behavior of inhuman
molecules. But in contrast, the accountant's "molecules" think and feel, they have
traditions and cultures, they are governed by laws, act sometimes rationally and
often irrationally, and are susceptible to an enormous variety of psychological, social,
economic, cultural, and political influences. . . . Accountancy . . . deals with problems**

involving equity and balance and the resolution of conflict between different groups of human beings with widely varying interest and objectives.

—Edward Stamp

[Source: "Why Can Accounting Not Become a Science Like Physics?" <u>ABACUS</u> (Vol. 17, No. 1, 1981), p. 21]

CASE 4

Clarus Corporation: Recurring Revenue Recognition

CASE TOPICS OUTLINE

Clarus Corporation announced a change in its business strategy to support a broader range of software licensing arrangements. This meant definitionally that the company would move from the up-front license fee revenue model that had been used toward a subscription-based licensing arrangement that would require a ratable revenue recognition approach. The company understood that as a result of this change in policy, historical and future financial statement figures might not be comparable. Clarus Corporation issued a press release on December 15, 2000, excerpts from which follow:

> Clarus Expands Business Strategy and Model; Clarus Announces Initiatives To Serve the Growing Large to Mid-Sized Enterprise Market
> Clarus (NASDAQ:CLRS), a leading business-to-business (B2B) e-commerce solution provider, today announced its strategy to meet the growing demand in the large to mid-size enterprise (LME) market. This expansion of its market strategy is designed to accelerate adoption and results in a business model with a greater emphasis on recurring revenue.
>
> Clarus has focused on the LME market and has established itself as a leader in B2B e-commerce solutions. . . . Industry experts . . . report the LME market is entering a period of accelerated adoption. The Clarus solutions are designed to meet the needs of this target market by offering lower cost of ownership and speed of deployment advantages. As Clarus intensifies its focus on the needs of the LME market it will leverage key strategic partners . . . to deliver "turnkey" packages and fixed-fee offerings.
>
> "Global market adoption of electronic procurement solutions is less than one percent and even lower in the LME space," said Steve Jeffery, president and CEO of Clarus. "Clarus is positioned to meet this market opportunity with the right mix of products, services, partnerships and pricing."

Key to meeting the demand in this market will be breaking down the barriers to widespread adoption by reducing the risks and costs associated with traditional licensing and implementation of software. Clarus will move to a business model that will provide its customers greater flexibility to choose the way in which they procure their e-commerce solutions. Under this model, Clarus will recognize revenue from the sale of its products over a fixed period of time, reducing the upfront revenue recorded as compared with its traditional model, while generating an increase in the amount of sales backlog.

"This business model and strategy is an evolution of Clarus' longtime focus on the LME market," stated Jeffery. "We believe this shift will not only allow us to drive rapid customer adoption through directly addressing the needs of this target market, but will also provide a more stable and predictable financial model."

In order to meet the unique needs of the LME market, the majority of future Clarus contracts with customers will not meet the criteria for immediate revenue recognition. Instead, a recurring, predictable revenue stream will be recognized over an estimated 12 to 24 month period. Clarus anticipates that approximately 90 percent of its license business will be contracted under agreements requiring ratable revenue recognition.

Clarus also provided guidance for fourth quarter 2000 and for its fiscal year 2001 and 2002. Under the ratable revenue recognition model, the company expects fourth quarter 2000 revenue to be in the range of $4 million to $4.5 million, with an operating loss per share, excluding non-cash charges, of approximately $1.40. For fiscal year 2001, the company expects revenue to be in the range of $45 million to $50 million, and EPS, excluding non-cash charges, of ($2.14). Fiscal year 2002 projections are for revenues in the range of $115 million to $120 million, and EPS, excluding non-cash charges, of $1.08. The company plans to reach breakeven on a cash basis in the first quarter 2002, with profitability on a cash basis projected for the second quarter 2002. . . .

Clarus will host an investor conference call to discuss this announcement today. . . .

About Clarus Corp.

Atlanta-based Clarus Corporation (www.claruscorp.com; NASDAQ: CLRS), a leader in business-to-business (B2B) e-commerce, provides B2B procurement software and trading services that exploit the global marketplace of the Internet to manage corporate purchasing and enable digital marketplaces. . . . provides a comprehensive range of critical trading services such as payment settlement, supplier enablement, auctions, integration, and analytics. Designed to provide unprecedented interoperability. . . THIS PRESS RELEASE CONTAINS FORWARD-LOOKING STATEMENTS WITHIN THE MEANING OF SECTION 27A OF THE SECURITIES ACT OF 1933 AND SECTION 21E OF THE EXCHANGE ACT. ACTUAL RESULTS COULD DIFFER MATERIALLY FROM THOSE PROJECTED IN THE FORWARD-LOOKING STATEMENTS AS A RESULT OF CERTAIN RISKS INCLUDING THAT THE BENEFITS EXPECTED BY THE COMPANY AS A RESULT OF THIS ANNOUNCEMENT MAY NOT OCCUR. . . . *(Source: Press Release on 12/15/2000)*

Analysts describe Clarus as a company providing e-business solutions that enable procurement, supply-chain management, customer-and-supplier relationship management, and demand management processes of various enterprises—citing such competitors as Global Sources, Commerce One, FreeMarkets, and Ariba. In evaluating Clarus, the analysts compare a trading price in mid-2001 around $6 as low relative to a so-called cash per share value estimate from $7 to $10. The analysts point out that revenue growth is not evidenced in the financial statements because of a change in revenue recognition from what they refer to as a traditional license model and an up-front license model, toward a recurring revenue recognition model. As a result, quarter-to-quarter revenue comparisons witness a large decline from September to December. An interesting point is that the increased backlogs are essentially sources of future revenue.

In its annual filing with the SEC, Clarus Corporation described its revenue stream and relevant accounting principles as follows:

Sources of Revenue

The Company's revenue consists of license fees and services fees. License fees are generated from the licensing of the Company's suite of products. Services fees are generated from consulting, implementation, training, content aggregation and maintenance support services.

Revenue Recognition

The Company recognizes revenue from two primary sources, software licenses and services. Revenue from software licensing and services fees is recognized in accordance with Statement of Position ("SOP") 97-2, "Software Revenue Recognition", and SOP 98-9, "Software Revenue Recognition with Respect to Certain Transactions". Accordingly, the Company recognizes software license revenue when: (1) persuasive evidence of an arrangement exists; (2) delivery has occurred; (3) the fee is fixed or determinable; and (4) collectibility is probable.

SOP No. 97-2 generally requires revenue earned on software arrangements involving multiple elements to be allocated to each element based on the relative fair values of the elements. The fair value of an element must be based on evidence that is specific to the vendor. License fee revenue allocated to software products generally is recognized upon delivery of the products or deferred and recognized in future periods to the extent that an arrangement includes one or more elements to be delivered at a future date and for which fair values have not been established. Revenue allocated to maintenance is recognized ratably over the maintenance term, which is typically 12 months and revenue allocated to training and other service elements is recognized as the services are performed.

Under SOP No. 98-9, if evidence of fair value does not exist for all elements of a license agreement and post-contract customer support is the only undelivered element, then all revenue for the license arrangement is recognized ratably over the term of the agreement as license revenue. If evidence of fair value of all undelivered elements exists but evidence does not exist for one or more delivered elements, then revenue is recognized using the residual method. Under the residual method, the fair value of the undelivered elements is deferred and the remaining portion of the arrangement fee is recognized as revenue. Revenue from hosted software agreements are recognized ratably over the term of the hosting arrangements. *(Source: 10-K filed on 3/21/2001)*

Requirement A: Comparing Revenue Recognition Approaches

Clarus Corporation's 1999 and 2000 data divided between its previous human resources and financial software business (ERP) and the current e-commerce business, along with a few other pieces of financial information are reported in Table 5.4-1.

Table 5.4-1 Financial Information

Clarus Corporation Results of Operations* (in thousands)	Year Ended December 31, 2000	Year Ended December 31, 1999
Revenues: e-commerce		
License fees	$24,686	$9,969
Services fees	9,361	1,515
Total revenues development	34,047	11,484
Revenues: ERP		
License fees	0	5,132
Services fees	0	21,526
Total revenues	0	26,658
Cost of revenues: e-commerce		
License fees	154	400
Services fees	12,776	3,130
Total cost of revenues	12,930	3,530
Cost of revenues: ERP		
License fees	0	951
Services fees	0	11,387
Total cost of revenues	0	12,338
Total operating expenses	98,455	37,429
Operating loss	(77,338)	(15,155)

*Source: 10-K filing on 3/21/2001.

1. How does the described revenue recognition approach compare to other industry settings?
2. The analysts' reference to traditional license models in B2B (business-to-business) relate to up-front models in the "new economy," yet some would argue that tradition in accounting defers revenue to match the earnings process over time. In what sense has the new economy met tradition in the Clarus Company example? Explain, with support from FARS.
3. Do you concur that the recurring revenue recognition will enhance both visibility and predictability of financial results? Why or why not? (*Hint:* Access the Staff Accounting Bulletin (SAB) 101 on Revenue Recognition at http://www.sec.gov/interps/account/sab101.htm.)

Requirement B: Strategy-Related Considerations

Clarus Corporation accords attention to the fact that in October 1999, the Company sold its ERP business. Are there added complications of such an event for the evaluator of the company's financial performance? Explain.

Hindsight

Access Clarus Corporation's 10-Q for the quarterly period ended June 30, 2006 from sec.gov. Explain what has happened to the company subsequent to 2000. What is particularly unique about the income statement? Access the 10-K for the fiscal year ended December 31, 2005 to augment the information from the 10-Q and describe the entity's strategy going forward.

Directed Self-Study

Does Statement of Financial Accounting Standards No. 152 change revenue recognition practices in any manner? Use FARS to explore this question. [Access FASB-OP (amended), click on the Search toolbar, select the option Search Within a Single OP Document Title, type *fas 152* into the document title box and in the Query For: box type *revenue recognition*.]

Key Terms and Glossary

revenue recognition when revenue is recorded: revenue must be earned and realized or realizable before being recognized—two key criteria for recognition: (1) what constitutes substantive performance by a vendor [i.e., when is the earnings process substantially complete—SFAC No. 5, par. 83(b)]? and (2) how much assurance of collectibility is needed to justify recognition of revenue [i.e., when is revenue realized or realizable]?

subscription revenue an example might be revenues for a newspaper, which tend to be recorded as earned, pro rata, on a monthly basis, over the life of the subscriptions

"turnkey" packages reference to off-the-shelf product as distinguished from tailor-made software; the idea is to just "turn the key" to start the ready-made, standardized software

Further Readings

Altamuro, Jennifer, Anne L. Beatty, and Joseph Weber, 2005. "The effects of accelerated revenue recognition on earnings management and earnings informativeness: Evidence from SEC Staff Accounting Bulletin No. 101." *The Accounting Review* (80, 2, April), pp. 373–401.

Beaver, William H. 2002. "Perspectives on recent capital market research." *Accounting Review* (77, 2, April), pp. 453–474.

Berenson, Alex. 2001. "A software company runs out of tricks." *New York Times* (April 29).

Berenson, Alex. 2001. "Computer Associates officials defend accounting methods." *New York Times Company* (May 1).

Bonner, S. E., Z. Palmrose, and S. M. Young. 1998. "Fraud type and auditor litigation: An analysis of SEC accounting and auditing enforcement releases." *Accounting Review* (73, 4), pp. 503–532.

"News report: Financial reporting—Online financial reports show problems and promise." 2000. *Journal of Accountancy* (189, 2, February).

OECD Convention on Combating Bribery of Foreign Public Officials. 2000. "Financial transparency and accountability initiative: Overall observations" (April 17). Available at: http://www.transparency-usa.org.

Philipich, Kirk L., Michael L. Costigan, and Linda M. Lovata. 1994. "The corroborative relation between earnings and cash flow information." *Advances in Accounting* 12, pp. 31–50.

Phillips, Jr., Thomas J., Michael S. Luehlfing, Cynthia M. Daily. 2001. "Financial reporting/auditing—The right way to recognize revenue." *Journal of Accountancy* (191, 6, June).

Price, Jimmy. 2001. "Auditing e-business applications." *Internal Auditor* (August), pp. 21–23.

Schuetze, Walter P. 2005. "Statements of quality [editorial commentary]." *Barron's* (May 30), p. 39.

Bushee Brian J., Dawn A. Matsumoto, and Gregory S. Miller. 2004. "Managerial and investor responses to disclosure regulation: The case of reg FD and conference calls." *Accounting Review* (79, 3, July), pp. 617–643.

Davis, Angela K. 2002. "The value relevance of revenue for Internet firms: Does reporting grossed-up and barter revenue make a difference?" *Journal of Accounting Research* (40, 2), pp. 445–477.

Davis, A.K., R. Bowen, and S. Rajgopal. 2002. "Determinants of revenue recognition policies for Internet firms." *Contemporary Accounting Research* (19, 4), pp. 523–562.

Feroz, E. H., K. Park, and V. S. Pastena. 1991. "The financial and market effects of the SEC's accounting and auditing enforcement releases." *Journal of Accounting Research* (29, Supplement), pp. 107–142.

Guidera, Jerry. 2001. "Computer Associates posts quarterly loss of $410 million." *Wall Street Journal* (May 23), p. B6.

Henry, David. 2001. "The numbers game." *Business Week* (May 14), pp. 100–110.

Hudack, Lawrence R., and John P. McAllister. 1994. "An investigation of the FASB's application of its decision usefulness criteria." *Accounting Horizons* (8, 3), pp. 1–18.

Kimbrough, Michael D. 2005. "The effect of conference calls on analyst and market underreaction to earnings announcements." *The Accounting Review* (80, 1), pp. 189–219.

McNamee, David, and Sally Chan. 2001. "Understanding e-commerce risk." *Internal Auditor* (April), pp. 60–61.

Ness Joseph A., Michael J. Schroeck, Rick A. Letendre, and Willmar J. Doublas. 2001. "The role of ABM in measuring customer value, part one." *Strategic Finance* (March), pp. 32–37.

SEC. 2003. "Frequently asked questions regarding the use of non-GAAP financial measures." Prepared by staff members in the Division of Corporation Finance. Washington, DC: U.S. SEC (June 13).

SEC. 1999. "SEC Staff Accounting Bulletin (SAB): No. 101—Revenue Recognition in Financial Statements. 17 CFR Part 211.

Shridharani, Kaushik. 2001. "E-business applications." Analyst interview (CFA and Managing Director in equity research with Bear, Stearns & Co.). *Wall Street Journal transcript* (May 21).

"Special report, professional issues—COSO's new fraud study: What it means for CPAs." 1999. *Journal of Accountancy* (187, 5, May). [The Institute's Web site (www.aicpa.org) has an executive summary of the study.]

Thurm, Scott and Jonathan Weil. 2001. "Money & investing: Tech companies charge now, may profit later." *Wall Street Journal* (April 27).

Tie, Robert. 2001. "E-commerce: Get ready for the world of B2B." *Journal of Accountancy* (191, 6, June).

UBS Investment Research, Global Analyzer. 2003. *S&P 500 Accounting Quality Monitor, Bridging the Gap to GAAP EPS* (July 2), pp. 1–120.

Wallace, Wanda A. 2002. *Pro Forma Before and After the SEC's Warning: A Quantification of Reporting Variances from GAAP*. (Morristown, NJ: Financial Executives International (FEI) Research Foundation) (March): ISBN 1-885065-33-7.

Wallace, Wanda A. 2001. "EBITDA: Freedom of speech or freedom to confuse?" *Accounting Today* (15, 7, April 16–May 6), pp. 34, 35, 45.

Zarowin, Stanley. 2001. "Facing the future." *Journal of Accountancy* (April), pp. 26–31.

As we all know, profit figures are not reached by a formula. "Proper and appropriate" provisions may be necessary and in thus providing, prudent judgment is needed. It is when judgment is involved with a desire to reach a particular figure that "profit" becomes meaningless, and we are reminded of a company chairman who, in the days when accounts were not as clear as they are now, advised shareholders not to rely too much on the figures before them. Other figures, he said, could have been produced which would equally well have earned a clear [clean] certificate!

[Source: The Accountant (November 8, 1956), p. 571]

Indeed, this point was made before a senate subcommittee when one CPA reported an agency had made a profit of $5,226,000 when another reported a loss of $6,448,000. The dispute concerned the recognition of interest revenue.

[Source: "Two Accountants Disagree on RFC 'Profits,'" The Journal of Accountancy *(June 1950), p. 467]*

CASE 5

When Would Market to Book Be Less Than One? Does Acquisition by Stock Explain JDS Uniphase Corp.?

CASE TOPICS OUTLINE

1. JDS Uniphase Corp. 10-Q Filing
   A. Press Release and Media Commentary
   B. SEC Advice Sought and Results Noted
2. Revaluation

Market to book is a term applied to the ratio of a company's market value of equity (capitalization) to the book value of the equity of the company, and descriptive statistics in the literature for empirical samples of thousands of public companies over the past decades report medians (i.e., midway points within the sample, with half of the companies lying above and half lying below) of approximately 2. The 10-Q for March 31, 2001, filed on May 11, 2001, by JDS Uniphase Corp. included the following disclosures:

> The Company is currently evaluating the carrying value of certain long-lived assets and acquired equity method investments, consisting primarily of $56.2 billion of goodwill and the Company's $757 million equity method investment in ADVA (see Note 10) recorded on its balance sheet at March 31, 2001. Pursuant to accounting rules, the majority of the goodwill was recorded based on stock prices at the time merger agreements were executed and announced. The Company's policy is to assess enterprise level goodwill if the market capitalization of the Company is less than its net assets. Goodwill will be reduced to the extent that net assets are greater than market capitalization. At March 31, 2001, the value of the Company's net assets, including unamortized goodwill exceeded the Company's market capitalization by approximately $39.5 billion. The Company also examines the carrying value of equity method investments for recoverability on a regular basis, based on a number of factors including financial condition and business prospects of the investee

and the market value of the investee's common stock. Downturns in telecommunications equipment and financial markets have created unique circumstances with regard to the assessment of goodwill and equity method investments for recoverability, and the Company has sought the counsel of the Staff of the SEC on the interpretation of generally accepted accounting principles with regard to these matters. The Company anticipates recording additional charges to reduce the carrying value of the unamortized goodwill and acquired equity method investments and such adjustments could represent a substantial portion of their carrying value. Some of these charges may be recorded as an adjustment to the Company's financial statements at March 31, 2001 and should they be, the Company would restate its March 31, 2001 financial statements in subsequent SEC filings.

   ... Note 10. Equity Method of Accounting

   As of March 31, 2001, the Company had a 29 percent ownership stake in ADVA, a publicly traded German company that develops and manufactures fiber optic components and products and a 40 percent ownership stake in the Photonics Fund ("Photonics Fund"), LLP, a California limited liability partnership (the "Partnership"), which emphasizes privately negotiated venture capital equity investments. The Company accounts for its investments in ADVA and the Photonics Fund under the equity method. Due to the limited availability of timely data, the Company records the adjustments to its equity method investments in the subsequent quarter.

   For the three and nine months ended March 31, 2001, the Company recorded $44.5 million and $133.7 million, respectively, in amortization expense related to the difference between the cost of the investment and the underlying equity in the net assets of ADVA. At June 30, 2000, the Company's cost and estimated fair value of its investment in ADVA was $701.1 million. In the process of completing the E-TEK purchase accounting, the Company increased the cost and estimated fair value of its investment in ADVA to $931.5 million during the first fiscal quarter. The difference between the cost of the investment and the underlying equity in the net assets of ADVA is being amortized over a 5 year period. For the three and nine months ended March 31, 2001, the Company recorded a $0.6 million and $5.7 million net loss in ADVA relating to their three and six months ended December 30, 2000 financial results, respectfully. As of May 7, 2001, ADVA had not announced their financial results for the three months ended March 31, 2000. The Company will record its share of the income or loss of ADVA in the three months ended June 30, 2001.

   In the three and nine months ended March 31, 2001, the Company recorded a loss of $0.3 million and a gain of $0.6 million, which represented the Company's share of the earnings of the Photonics Fund Partnership for the three and six months ended December 30, 2000. The Company's share of the gain of the Partnership for the three months ended March 31, 2001 was approximately $0.8 million, which will be recorded by the Company during the three months ended June 30, 2001. *(Source: 10-Q filed 5/11/01)*

   The company later issued an 8-K that includes a press release containing the following related discussion:

Goodwill discussion

   As we announced in April and reported in our 10-Q, the Company has evaluated the carrying value of certain long-lived assets and acquired equity investments, consisting

primarily of goodwill and … our investment in ADVA. Pursuant to accounting rules, the
majority of the goodwill was recorded based on stock prices at the time merger
agreements were executed and announced. The Company's policy is to assess enterprise
level goodwill if the market capitalization of the Company is less than its net assets, with
goodwill being reduced to the extent net assets are greater than market capitalization.

Downturns in telecommunications equipment and financial markets have created
unique circumstances with regard to the assessment of long-lived assets, and we sought
the counsel of the Staff of the Securities and Exchange Commission on the interpretation
of generally accepted accounting principles with regard to this matter. We have had
communications with the Staff of the SEC, and we will amend our Quarterly Report on
Form 10-Q for the quarter ended March 31, 2001 to reduce the carrying value of goodwill
by $38.7 billion for that quarter. In addition, we recorded a $6.1 billion reduction for
goodwill in the quarter ended June 30 following further declines in our market
capitalization. Finally, approximately $300 million in certain amounts paid to SDL
executives in connection with the acquisition which were previously recorded as
acquisition costs in the quarter ended March 31, 2001 have been reclassified as a one-time
charge for that period and we also recorded a $715 million charge for that period to write
down the value of our equity investment in ADVA. Because of the significant industry
downturn we are in the process of performing a review of our long-lived assets in
accordance with GAAP, and this may result in further charges being recorded for the
fourth quarter of fiscal 2001 based on the value of such assets.

The largest portion of the Company's goodwill arose from the merger of JDS FITEL
and Uniphase and the subsequent acquisition of SDL, E-TEK, and OCLI. The businesses
associated with these business combinations remain significant operations within JDS
Uniphase notwithstanding the current business downturn and change in market valuations.

This significant reduction in our goodwill and other assets no doubt will result in
press reports or articles about a sizeable loss, so let me explain what it really means. This
goodwill resulted from our acquiring good companies when valuations were high. But
keep in mind that while we purchased highly valued shares, we were also in effect selling
highly valued shares at the same time as none of the transactions resulting in large
goodwill amounts were done for cash. Had these transactions been done at different times
when valuations were lower with exactly the same share exchange ratios, the goodwill
amounts would have been considerably smaller. Of course, these good companies likely
would have become parts of other companies and we would not have had the opportunity
to acquire them. So by avoiding goodwill we would have foregone many opportunities to
strengthen JDS Uniphase. And when you assess these charges, please keep in mind that
they were recorded at a time when our cash increased sharply, so these charges in no way
impaired our financial health or strength.

We are reporting a pro forma loss of $477 million or $0.36 per share for the fourth
quarter and net income of $67 million or $0.06 per share for the year ended June 30, 2001.
These results reflect the costs of the Global Realignment Program and charges for the
write-down of excess inventory and exclude the costs we have historically excluded,
primarily those related to merger and acquisition charges. *(Source: 8-K filed 7/26/01)*

The media discussed how the pro forma figure of $67.4 million for the fiscal year ended June 30,
2001, contrasted with the $50.6 billion full-year net loss for that period. It was observed that the pro

forma numbers excluded 98 percent of the company's $52 billion operating expenses, suggesting these were mainly write-offs of assets that had been purchased for inflated prices during the tech bubble. These charges are asserted by JDS to have not impaired either its financial health or strength because the company had purchased them with stock instead of cash. The analysts on Wall Street appear to have embraced the pro forma perspective of the company from the media coverage. Excerpts from the note in the quarterly filing that describes acquisitions completed during the first nine months of fiscal 2001, using the purchase method of accounting, are reported in Table 5.5-1.

Table 5.5-1   Acquisitions of JDS Uniphase Corp.

Note 9	Date	Purchase Price (in millions) (unaudited)	Purchased Intangibles	Net Tangible Assets	In Process Research & Development	Goodwill
SDL	February 2001	$41,514.8	$967.0	$617.4	$380.7	$39,549.7
OPA	January 2001	168.5	$5.6	$(4.6)	$3.0	$124.5
Iridian	October 2000	40.3	$ —	$2.3	$ —	$38.0
Epion*	September 2000	184.5	$14.6	$11.0	$8.9	$150.0
Other		10.2	$ —	$(0.3)	$ —	$10.5

*The purchase price includes the issuance of contingent consideration based on milestones reached during the nine months ended March 31, 2001, subsequent to the acquisition date. *(Source: JDS Uniphase Corporation 10-Q for the quarterly period ended 3/31/01, filed 5/11/01)*

Requirement A: Market-to-Book Ratio

1.   Why is the ratio of market to book an important consideration in evaluating a company's recorded values? Is it necessarily the case that market to book never drop below a value of 1.0? Why or why not?
2.   How important is the fact that the acquisitions were by stock instead of cash? Support your position with appropriate citations from FARS. Do you believe that the reported adjustments are sufficient to achieve a reasonable market to book? How often must goodwill be evaluated for impairment today?
3.   Is the equity method being applied acceptable? What seems distinctive about JDS Uniphase Corporation's practice?

Requirement B: Strategy-Related Considerations

Company management determines press-release content, and it is not restricted in the same manner as in 10-Q or 10-K filings, as long as nothing fraudulent is included.

1.   Do you believe JDS Uniphase was wise to emphasize a pro forma figure in the press release? Why or why not?
2.   Do you believe that actions should be taken by regulators to proscribe disclosures that fail to conform with GAAP in their press releases? Why or why not? Have any such actions been taken subsequent to the period described in the case?
3.   As an investor, how would you evaluate the company in light of the materials in this case, as well as subsequent evidence on the performance of JDS Uniphase?

Directed Self-Study

Many press releases have been observed to reference *EBITDA*. What does this term mean, and does FARS provide any related guidance? Be specific. [Open FASB-OP (amended) and query EBITDA. Then open EITF Abstracts and perform a similar search.]

Key Terms and Glossary

EBITDA　earnings before interest, taxes, depreciation and amortization is the general definition, but since this is not defined by GAAP, its application in practice has been observed to vary substantially, excluding a wide variety of costs—as examples, some companies exclude start-up costs, in-process research and development, merger-related costs, stock option compensation, and financing costs, among others

fair value　"the amount at which an asset (or liability) could be bought (or incurred) or sold (or settled) in a current transaction between willing parties, that is, other than in a forced or liquidation sale" (Appendix F Glossary, FAS 142) [See FAS 157.]

goodwill　"the excess of the cost of an acquired entity over the net of the amounts assigned to assets acquired and liabilities assumed" (Appendix F, FAS 142)

pro forma　historically referred to "as if" presentations, associated with two merging companies, to display comparative historical numbers as if the companies had been operating together for years; more recently, the term refers to disclosures in press releases that do not conform with a definition under GAAP but tend to be characterized as earnings without special or one-time charges, as well as charges management contends are unusual or unimportant, in order to communicate core earnings indicative of future operating earnings

Further Readings

Aboody, David, and Ron Kasznik. 2000. "CEO stock option awards and the timing of corporate voluntary disclosures." *Journal of Accounting & Economics* (29, February), pp. 73–100.

Arya, Anil, Jonathan C. Glover, and Shyam Sunder. 2003. "Are unmanaged earnings always better for shareholders?" *Accounting Horizons* (Supplement), pp. 111–116.

Baldenius, Tim, Nahum D. Melumad, and Stefan Reichelstein. 2004. "Integrating managerial and tax objectives in transfer pricing." *Accounting Review* (79, 3, July), pp. 591–615.

Bhattacharya, Nilabhra, Erin L. Black, Theodore E. Christensen, and Richard D. Mergenthaler. 2004. "Empirical evidence on recent trends in pro forma reporting." *Accounting Horizons* (18, 1, March), pp. 27–43.

Brown, Lawrence D., and Marcus L. Caylor. 2005. "A temporal analysis of quarterly earnings thresholds: Propensities and valuation consequences." *The Accounting Review* (80, 2), pp. 423–440.

Brown, Stephen, Kim Lo, and Thomas Lys. 1999. "Use of R^2 in accounting research: Measuring changes in value relevance over the last four decades." *Journal of Accounting & Economics* (28, December), pp. 83–115.

Financial Executives International and National Investor Relations. 2001. "Best practice" guidelines for earnings releases (April). Available at: http://www.fei.org.

Heflin, Frank, K. R. Subramanyam, and Yuan Zhang. 2003. "Regulation FD and the financial information environment: Early evidence." *Accounting Review* (78, 1, January), pp. 1–37.

Krull, Linda K. 2004. "Permanently reinvested foreign earnings, taxes, and earnings management." *Accounting Review* (79, 3, July), pp. 745–767.

Miller, Gregory S., and Douglas J. Skinner. 1998. "Determinants of the valuation allowance for deferred tax assets under SFAS No. 109." *Accounting Review* (73, 2, April), pp. 213–233.

Nichols, D. Craig, and James M. Wahlen. 2004. "How do earnings numbers relate to stock returns? A review of classic accounting research with updated evidence." *Accounting Horizons* (18, 4, December), pp. 263–286.

Price, Reneé, and Wanda A. Wallace. 2001. "Probability and materiality." *CPA Journal* (LXXI, 6, June), pp. 18–24.

Scherreik, Susan. 2001. "What the earnings reports don't tell you." *Business Week* (October 16), pp. 201–204.

Cheng, Qiang, and Terry D. Warfield. 2005. "Equity incentives and earnings management." *Accounting Review* (80, 2), pp. 441–476.

Demirakos, Efthimios G., Norman C. Strong, and Martin Walker. 2004. "What valuation models do analysts use?" *Accounting Horizons* (18, 4, December), pp. 221–240.

Elstein, Aaron. 2001. "Firms fatten up profit outlooks on FASB rule." Heard On The Street. *Wall Street Journal* (August 21), pp. C1–C2.

Erickson, Merle, and Shiing-wu Wang. 1999. "Earnings management by acquiring firms in stock for stock mergers." *Journal of Accounting & Economics* (27), pp. 149–176.

Financial Accounting Standards Board. 2001. "Financial Accounting Series, Statement of Financial Accounting Standards No. 142, Goodwill and Other Intangible Assets." (Norwalk, CT: FASB (June).

Shuping, Chen, Mark L. DeFond, and Chul W. Park. 2002. "Voluntary disclosure of balance sheet information in quarterly earnings announcements." *Journal of Accounting and Economics* (33, 2, June), pp. 229–251.

Teoh, Siew Hong, and T. J. Wong. 1993. "Perceived auditor quality and the earnings response coefficient." *Accounting Review* (68, 2, April), pp. 346–366.

Wallace, Wanda A. 2001. "EBITDA: Freedom of speech or freedom to confuse?" *Accounting Today* (15, 7, April 16–May 6), pp. 34, 35, 45.

Wallace, Wanda A. 2001. "Wording of earnings releases is a story in itself." *Accounting Today* (September 24–October 7), p. 69.

Weil, Jonathan. 2001. "Moving target: What's the P/E ratio? Well, depends on what is meant by earnings." *Wall Street Journal* (August 21), pp. A1, A8.

Accounting measurement which measures the economic performance of an entity is, therefore, not only a passive representative of real world phenomena, but is also an active agent affecting the real world through its influence upon the decision maker. Thus, we have a situation where two worlds, the real world and the informational world, mutually interact. One is not merely a shadow of the other. The importance of accounting in business should be analyzed within this dual framework.

—Yuji Ijiri

[Source: Theory of Accounting Measurement, Studies in Accounting Research, No. 10 (Sarasota, FL: American Accounting Association, 1975), p. 188]

CASE 6

UPS: The Tax Environment and Disclosure of Contingencies

A Tax Court case involves disputes between the Commissioner of Revenue and various taxpayers, including corporate entities. United Parcel Service was involved in such a case, the decision for which was filed on August 9, 1999. The case caption is: "UNITED PARCEL SERVICE OF AMERICA, INC. ON BEHALF OF ITSELF AND ITS CONSOLIDATED SUBSIDIARIES, Petitioner v. COMMISSIONER OF INTERNAL REVENUE, Respondent" No. 15993-95 UNITED STATES TAX COURT T.C. Memo 1999-268; 1999 Tax Ct. Memo LEXIS 304; 78 T.C.M. (CCH) 262; T.C.M. (RIA) 99268 August 9, 1999, Filed. Refer to Chapter 2 of this book for various locations in electronic databases or on the Internet where you can search to obtain a copy of the OPINION: MEMORANDUM FINDINGS OF FACT AND OPINION. Within Tax Court cases, deficiencies are first summarized, then findings of fact are detailed, and finally an opinion is expressed. The actual Tax Court case is 60 pages long; access that case and read it as the first step in completing this assignment. Remember that even if an electronic copy is unavailable, law libraries can be accessed to secure a hard copy of the Tax Court case whereby you can then read through the opinion.

It is useful to become acquainted with the manner in which tax disputes are evaluated and reported; as you review the case, consider the nature of the business, the allegations being analyzed, the defense of the taxpayer, and the position of the court. The background you obtain from reading the case will be used in analyzing the related accounting disclosures.

Note to Financial Statements

Access the 10-Q filed August 16, 1999 by United Parcel Service of America, Inc., and Subsidiaries from sec.gov. Particularly read through Note 4 to the unaudited consolidated financial statements.

That note describes its experiences associated with a Tax Court dispute and possible ramifications of the decision.

Requirement A: Interpreting the 10-Q Disclosures

You are an intern with the SEC for the summer. Assume that during the course of your internship, this quarterly filing was received from United Parcel Service (UPS), and you are asked to prepare an analysis of the conformance of the accounting treatment and disclosures that relate to the UPS tax environment—known to have been substantially affected by the recent Tax Court decision. Prepare an executive summary (one to two paragraphs) summarizing the tax court holdings. In addition, provide a detailed explanation of what is required by generally accepted accounting principles (GAAP) and compare those requirements to the disclosures reported by UPS. When differences are detected, explain why you believe UPS has provided the information in the filing, rather than the prescriptions by GAAP.

1. Would you propose that additional or different disclosures be requested from UPS? Why or why not?
2. In reading the 10-Q disclosures, you observed that the disclosures related to the tax litigation shown in Figure 5.6-1 seem quite different from the other litigation-related disclosures. Why is this the case, and are both in accordance with GAAP? Support your position with a flowchart that explains how, through consideration of guidance available in FARS, you arrive at your conclusion.

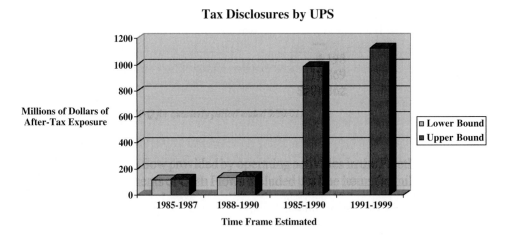

Figure 5.6-1 A number of estimates are disclosed in the 10-Q.

Requirement B: Cash Flow Implications—Strategy Choices

1. When UPS refers to cash equivalents in its 10-Q, to what is the company referring? The disclosure specifically refers to the company's ability to make a deposit with the IRS without affecting foreseeable operating expenses and budgeted capital expenditures. What information sources are relevant to evaluating this representation?

2. The disclosure indicates the company has a choice as to whether to make such a deposit. What other alternatives exist?
3. What strategy would you recommend to UPS regarding its handling of the 1999 tax environment faced by the company and what would be the related cash-flow implications of your suggestions? To facilitate your evaluation of UPS, refer to the Balance Sheet, Income Statement, and Cash Flow Statements, as well as the related Notes.

The Rest of the Story

In its December 31, 2000, 10-K, UPS detailed in its discussion of legal proceedings that it had appealed:

> In addition, during the first quarter of 1999, the IRS issued two Notices of Deficiency asserting that we are liable for additional tax for the 1985 through 1987 tax years, and the 1988 through 1990 tax years. The primary assertions by the IRS relate to the reinsurance of excess value package insurance, the issue raised for the 1984 tax year. The IRS has based its assertions on the same theories included in the 1983–1984 Notice of Deficiency.
>
> The IRS, in an issued report, has taken similar positions for tax years 1991 through 1994. We expect the IRS to take similar positions for tax years 1995 through 1999. Based on the Tax Court opinion, we currently estimate that our total after-tax exposure for the tax years 1984 through 1999 could be as high as $2.353 billion. We believe that a number of aspects of the Tax Court decision are incorrect, and we have appealed the decision to the U.S. Court of Appeals for the Eleventh Circuit. The Eleventh Circuit has heard oral arguments. We do not know when the court will render a decision. *(Source: 10-K for fiscal year ended 12/31/00)*

The company explains the basis for its estimates and its action to make deposits without making concessions:

> We determined the size of our reserve with respect to these matters in accordance with accounting principles generally accepted in the United States of America based on our estimate of our most likely liability. In making this determination, we concluded that it is more likely that we will be required to pay taxes on income reported by OPL and interest, but that it is not probable that we will be required to pay any penalties and penalty interest. If penalties and penalty interest ultimately are determined to be payable, we would have to record an additional charge of up to $681 million.
>
> On August 31, 1999, we deposited $1.349 billion, and on August 8, 2000, we deposited an additional $91 million, with the IRS related to these matters for the 1984 through 1994 tax years. We included the profit of the excess value package insurance program, using the IRS's methodology for calculating these amounts, for both 1998 and 1999 in filings we made with the IRS in 1999. In February 2000, we deposited $339 million with the IRS related to these matters for the 1995 through 1997 tax years. These deposits and filings were made in order to stop the accrual of interest, where applicable, on that amount of the IRS's claim, without conceding the IRS's positions or giving up our right to appeal the Tax Court's decision. *(Source: 10-K for fiscal year ended 12/31/00)*

The company's "new arrangement" referenced in August of 1999 is likewise described in more details—actions to eliminate the issues considered by the Tax Court post-1999:

> After the Tax Court decision, National Union Fire Insurance Company, a subsidiary of American International Group, Inc., notified OPL that effective September 30, 1999, it would terminate the five underlying policies that provide shippers' risk insurance for UPS customers. The termination of these policies triggered the immediate termination of the reinsurance agreement between National Union and OPL.
>
> UPS, on behalf of our customers, and National Union agreed on a restructuring of this program, which became effective October 1, 1999. Commencing on October 1, 1999, National Union issued five new policies that include coverage for UPS customers. Glenlake Insurance Agency, Inc., a licensed insurance agency formed in 1998 and a wholly owned subsidiary of UPS Capital Corporation, now offers excess value package insurance to be issued under the five new polices.
>
> UPS Re Ltd., a wholly owned subsidiary of UPS, has entered into a reinsurance agreement under which it will reinsure substantially all of the risks underwritten by National Union in exchange for substantially all of the premiums collected. UPS Re Ltd., is a licensed reinsurance company formed in 1999 to reinsure risks related to UPS and its subsidiaries. UPS Re Ltd., which is domiciled in Bermuda, has elected to be taxed on its income as part of UPS's consolidated income tax return for federal income tax purposes. This revised arrangement should eliminate the issues considered by the Tax Court in the Notices of Deficiency relating to OPL for the periods after September 1999. *(Source: 10-K for fiscal year ended 12/31/00)*

When It Rains It Pours

The IRS additional claims are described:

> The IRS has proposed adjustments, unrelated to the OPL matters discussed above, regarding the allowance of deductions and certain losses, the characterization of expenses as capital rather than ordinary, the treatment of certain income, and our entitlement to the investment tax credit and the research tax credit in the 1985 through 1990 tax years. The proposed adjustments would result in $15 million in additional income tax expense. Also, the IRS has issued a report taking a similar position with respect to some of these issues for each of the years from 1991 through 1994. This report proposes adjustments that would result in $155 million in additional income tax expense. For the 1985 through 1994 tax years, unpaid interest on these adjustments through 2000 could aggregate up to $368 million, after the benefit of related tax deductions. We expect that we will prevail on substantially all of these issues. Specifically, we believe that our practice of expensing the items that the IRS alleges should have been capitalized is consistent with the practices of other industry participants. The IRS may take similar positions with respect to some of these issues for each of the years 1995 through 2000. The IRS's proposed adjustments include penalties and penalty interest. We believe that the possibility that such penalties and penalty interest will be sustained is remote. We believe the eventual resolution of these issues will not result in a material adverse effect on our financial condition, results of operations or liquidity. *(Source: 10-K for fiscal year ended 12/31/00)*

In addition, the Tax Court decision has spawned related lawsuits:

> We have been named as a defendant in 23 lawsuits that seek to hold us (and, in certain cases, other defendants) liable for the collection of premiums for excess value package insurance in connection with package shipments since 1984 (or, in some of the cases, for shorter time periods). These cases generally claim that we acted as an insurer in violation of our shipping contract and without complying with state insurance laws and regulations, and that the price for excess value package insurance was excessive. Eighteen of these cases have been consolidated for pre-trial purposes in a multi-district litigation proceeding ("MDL Proceeding") before the United States District Court for the Southern District of New York. An amended consolidated complaint in the MDL Proceeding also alleges a violation of the federal RICO statute. Another complaint in the MDL Proceeding alleges violations of federal antitrust laws. We are in the process of seeking to have four of the remaining cases consolidated into the MDL Proceeding. The other remaining case was remanded from federal court to state court in Madison County, Illinois and is proceeding independent of the MDL Proceeding. No class has been certified in any of these cases. These actions all developed after the August 9, 1999 Tax Court opinion was rendered. We believe the allegations in these cases have no merit and intend to continue to defend them vigorously. The ultimate resolution of these matters cannot presently be determined. *(Source: 10-K for fiscal year ended 12/31/00)*

Appeals Court

On June 21, 2001, UPS filed Form 8-K containing the following press release:

> APPEALS COURT SUPPORTS UPS, REVERSES U.S. TAX COURT ATLANTA, (June 21, 2001)—The 11th U.S. Circuit Court of Appeals, in an important ruling, today overturned a 1999 decision that UPS had improperly tried to avoid federal income taxes when it restructured its program for providing extra package insurance to its customers.
>
> The appeals court said the IRS and Tax Court were wrong to brand UPS as attempting a "sham transaction" to avoid its tax obligations. After reversing the 1999 decision, the appellate court then remanded the case back to the U.S. Tax Court, saying any claims by the IRS should be analyzed under provisions of the Tax Code cited by UPS.
>
> "The sophistication (of the insurance revisions) does not change the fact that there was a real business that served the genuine need for customers to enjoy loss coverage and for UPS to lower its liability exposure," the court majority wrote in a 16-page opinion. "We therefore conclude that UPS's restructuring of its excess-value business had both real economic effects and a business purpose, and it therefore under our precedent had sufficient economic substance to merit respect in taxation."
>
> "For the foregoing reasons, we reverse the judgment against UPS and remand the action to the Tax Court. . . ."
>
> Based on the original Aug. 9, 1999, decision of a Tax Court judge that applied to the 1984 tax year, UPS estimated its potential liability at $1.8 billion for all subsequent years if his ruling were allowed to stand. The company then recorded a special tax assessment on its books of $1.786 billion, reducing its income for the second quarter of 1999 by a net $1.442 billion. Without conceding liability, UPS then paid $1.8 billion into a special

account with the IRS, pending a decision by the 11th Circuit Court of Appeals. The balance will remain in place pending further proceedings on remand.

"This case was much more to us than a dispute over tax regulations and Tax Code interpretations, because we hold nothing more sacred than our reputation," said UPS Chairman and CEO Jim Kelly. "So we are extremely pleased the original opinion has been reversed."

The case, known as *UPS vs. Commissioner of Internal Revenue*, was argued before the 11th Circuit on March 7. The case focused on the manner in which UPS decided to exit the excess value coverage business in 1984, creating a new, independent company known as Overseas Partners Ltd., or OPL. OPL subsequently based itself in Bermuda and over the years, grew into one of the largest re-insurance companies in the world.

Prior to 1984, UPS provided excess value coverage itself. After creating and spinning off OPL, UPS engaged another U.S. company, National Union Fire Insurance Co., to provide the insurance purchased by UPS shippers.

The IRS argued in 1997 that UPS had created OPL solely to avoid federal taxes and that UPS must pay federal taxes on OPL's income. UPS, for its part, adamantly and consistently disputed the IRS' position, saying it had followed all applicable laws and tax regulations in establishing OPL. The appeals court ruled today "that OPL is an independently taxable entity that is not under UPS's control."

Before and after the changes, UPS offered the lowest rates in the industry for excess value coverage. To this day, a package with a value of $300 can be insured at UPS for 70-cents, compared to $4 for the U.S. Postal Service, $2.50 for FedEx and $2.10 for DHL.

UPS is the world's largest express carrier and largest package delivery company, serving more than 200 countries and territories around the world. Headquartered in Atlanta, Ga., the company is located on the Web at www.ups.com. Earlier this year, UPS was recognized by *Fortune* magazine as "America's Most Admired" package and mail delivery company for the 18th consecutive year." *(Source: 8-K filed 6/21/01 Item 5. Other Events, Exhibit 99.1)*

Requirement C: Looking Back

Given the benefit of hindsight, how effective were the contingency-associated disclosures by UPS in 1999 and 2000? Explain. Access the most recent filing by UPS at sec.gov and determine whether the events in this case or related matters continue to be reflected and, if so, how. Describe how this case analysis would be affected had the events *followed* the issuance of FASB Interpretation (FIN) No. 48 *Accounting for Uncertainty in Income Taxes, an interpretation of FASB Statement No. 109*, issued June 2006.

Directed Self-Study

Did Statement of Financial Accounting Standards No. 154 entitled *Accounting Changes and Error Corrections* (issued in May 2005), replacing APB Opinion 20 *Accounting Changes* (issued in July 1971) alter the accounting treatment of a change in estimate? [Access FASB-OP (amended), click on Search in the Toolbar, and select Search Within a Single OP Document Title. Type *FAS 154* in the Document Title Box, and then in the Query For: box type *change in estimate*. The first hit will answer the question.]

Key Terms and Glossary

contingency "an existing condition, situation, or set of circumstances involving uncertainty as to possible gain (hereinafter a "gain contingency") or loss . . . (hereinafter a "loss contingency") to an enterprise that will ultimately be resolved when one or more future events occur or fail to occur" (FAS 5, par. 1).

Internal Revenue Service government agency charged with collection of taxes and enforcement of tax law

investment tax credit an offset to tax bills granted by Congress to encourage investment: The amount has been a function of the life of the asset acquired

probable "The future event or events are likely to occur" (FAS 5, par. 3). FAS 90, par. 45 observes: "some. . . respondents equated probable with certain. The Board notes that the term *probable* is defined in Statement 5 and is used in the same sense in this Statement. That definition is not synonymous with

certain, a term that connotes a much higher level of assurance than probable."

reasonably possible "The chance of the future event or events occurring is more than remote but less than likely" (FAS 5, par. 3). [Through analogy, FAS 69, par. 72 distinguishes proved, possible, and probable mineral interests granted by Congress to encourage investment: The amount has been a function of the life of the asset acquired.]

reinsurance the practice of insurance companies selling their insurance policies to another insurance company as a risk management arrangement

remote "The chance of the future event or events occurring is slight" (FAS 5, par. 4).

research tax credit an offset to tax bills granted by Congress to encourage spending on research

U.S. Tax Court specialized courts handling tax disputes

Further Readings

Beaver, William H. 1968. "Market prices, financial ratios, and the prediction of failure." *Journal of Accounting Research* (6, 2, Autumn), pp. 179–192.

Brazelton, J. K., and W. A. Wallace. 1999. "Taxes, inflation, and discount rates in damage computations." *CPA Expert* (Special Issue, AICPA Newsletter for Providers of Business Valuation & Litigation Services), pp. 1–5.

Brazelton, J. K., and W. A. Wallace. 1998. "How taxes are incorporated in evaluating investments: Implications for governmental financial management." *Research Supplement to Public Fund Digest.* (Washington, DC: International Consortium on Governmental Financial Management (I, 1, Winter), pp. 1–25.

Brazelton, J. K., and W. A. Wallace. 1997. "Audit and accounting forum: Effects of inflation, taxes and discount rates too often ignored in courts." *Accounting Today* (June 2–15), pp. 14, 16.

Buchman, Thomas A. 1985. "An effect of hindsight on predicting bankruptcy with accounting information." *Accounting, Organizations and Society* (10, 3), pp. 267–285.

"Business briefs: United Parcel Service Inc., Class-action suit is settled for $38.5 million in

cash flow measures." *Journal of Accounting, Auditing & Finance* (Fall), pp. 266–277.

Hodder, Leslie, Mary Lea McAnally, and Connie D. Weaver. 2003. "The influence of tax and nontax factors on banks' choice of organizational form." *Accounting Review* (78, 1, January), pp. 297–325.

Jensen, Michael. 1986. "Agency costs of free cash flow, corporate finance, and takeovers." *AER Papers and Proceedings* (76, 2), pp. 323–329.

Kochanek, R. F., and C. T. Norgaard. 1988. "Analyzing the components of operating cash flow: The Charter Company." *Accounting Horizons* (March), pp. 58–66.

Langley, M. 1986. "Generous juries: In awarding damages, panels have reasons for thinking very big." *Wall Street Journal* (May 28).

Largay, J. A., and C. P. Stickney. 1980. "Cash flows, ratio analysis and the W. T. Grant bankruptcy." *Financial Analysts Journal* (July-August), pp. 51–54.

Lev, B. 1969. "Industry averages as targets for financial ratios." *Journal of Accounting Research* (7), pp. 209–299.

McTague, Rachel 2005. "Nicolaisen says restatement needed when deal lacks business purpose." *Securities Regulation and Law Reporter* (May 9).

services." 2001. *Wall Street Journal* (August 7), p. A6.

Casey, C. J., and N. J. Barczak. 1984. "Cash flow—It's not the bottom line." *Harvard Business Review* (July–August), pp. 60–66.

Gentry, James A., Paul Newbold, and David T. Whitford. 1985. "Predicting bankruptcy: If cash flow's not the bottom line, what is?" *Financial Analysts Journal* (September–October), pp. 47–56.

Gleason, Cristi A., and Lillian F. Mills. 2002. Materiality and contingent tax liability reporting. *Accounting Review* (77, 2, April), pp. 317–342.

Gombola, M. J., and J. E. Ketz. 1983. "A caveat on measuring cash flow and solvency." *Financial Analysts Journal* (September–October), pp. 66–72.

Greenberg, R. R., G. L. Johnson, and K. Ramesh. 1986. "Earnings versus cash flow as a predictor of future

Plesko, George A. 2003. "An evaluation of alternative measures of corporate tax rates." *Journal of Accounting and Economics* (35), pp. 201–226.

Scholes, Myron S., and Mark A. Wolfson. 1992. *Taxes and Business Strategy: A Planning Approach.* Englewood Cliffs, NJ: Prentice-Hall, Inc.

Wallace, Wanda A. 2006. "Insights from preferability letters." *Business Horizons* (Kelley School of Business, Indiana University) (49, 5, September–October), pp. 403–414.

Wallace, Wanda A. 1989. "An early warning signal from the market: Its potential as an audit tool." *Advances in Accounting* (Supplement 1), pp. 205–231.

Wallace, W. A., and C. Wolfe. 1995. "Do expected audit procedures prompt more ethical behavior? Evidence on tax compliance rates." *Research on Accounting Ethics* (1), pp. 145–167.

"There's an unidentified growing object on the right-hand side of the balance sheet," representatives of Shell Oil told a Financial Accounting Standards Board (FASB) hearing panel in New York City on April 23, "and it's called 'deferred taxes.' That's the item these hearings are all about."

"Unidentified growing objects, UGO," mused FASB Chair Donald J. Kirk in response, "we're in danger of inventing a new acronym here."

[Source: "Spectre of UGOs Haunts FASB Hearing," <u>Tax Notes</u> (April 30, 1984), p. 456]

CASE 7

Embezzlement-Related Disclosures: Compliance with Guidance?

CASE TOPICS OUTLINE

Halifax Corporation provides installation, maintenance and training for computer, communications, and simulator systems. The corporation provides support to state and local governments as well as to commercial customers that include military bases, prisons, and office complexes. In addition, the company has offered Web site design services, on-site computer repair, and staff outsourcing. The 10-K for March 31, 2001, filed on June 28, 2001, by Halifax Corp. included the following disclosures:

> Embezzlement Matter
>
> On March 18, 1999, the Company announced that an internal investigation had revealed a material embezzlement by the former controller of one of the Company's subsidiaries. The embezzlement occurred over a four-year period and aggregated approximately $15.4 million of which approximately $15 million was embezzled from the Company and $400,000 prior to its acquisition by Halifax. After net recoveries through March 31, 2001, as discussed below, the cumulative net embezzlement loss to the Company was approximately $7.7 million.
>
>   The embezzlement had a material effect on the Company's financial statements. During the year ended March 31, 2001, the Company recovered $1,600,000 (net of recovery costs of $1,156,000). During the year ended March 31, 2000, the Company recovered $2,250,000 (net of recovery costs of $250,000) in conjunction with its embezzlement recovery activities. The specific terms and conditions associated with the payments, including the identity of the parties, are subjects of confidentiality agreements

that preclude disclosure. The embezzlement loss for fiscal 1999 was $6,093,000, offset by $3,500,000 in recoveries (net of recovery costs of $1,000,000), resulting in a net embezzlement loss for fiscal year 1999 of $2,593,000. . . .

Embezzlement Recovery

During the years ended March 31, 2001 and 2000, net embezzlement recoveries were $1.6 million and $2.25 million, respectively (net of recovery costs of $1,156,000 and $250,000, respectively).

The loss of approximately $2.6 million in 1999 was net of $3.5 million of total net recoveries realized from certain recovered assets (net of recovery costs) and insurance proceeds. For additional discussion see "Embezzlement Matter" in Item 1 and Note 2 of the consolidated financial statements.

Income Taxes

As a result of the Company's historical losses (principally from the embezzlement), the Company generated significant loss carryforwards (both federal and state). At March 31, 2001 and 2000, the Company had remaining net operating loss carryforwards amounting to approximately $8.6 million and $10.2 million, respectively. Due to the uncertainty of future realization, the Company has not recorded a net benefit for these operating loss carryforwards in its financial statements. . . .

Net income (loss) from Continuing Operations

The 2001 net loss of $840,000 from continuing operations was due primarily to higher operating expenses offset by embezzlement recoveries of $1.6 million.

The 2000 net income from continuing operations of $1.4 million was principally the result of embezzlement recoveries amounting to $2.25 million.

Net losses from continuing operations in 1999 of $5.3 million were the result of embezzlement losses of $3.6 million and operating loss, in the amount of $3.6 million. . . .

The Company believes that funds generated from operations, bank borrowings, embezzlement recoveries and investing activities should be sufficient to meet its current operating cash requirements through July 1, 2002, although there can be no assurances that all the aforementioned sources of cash can be realized. . . .

2. EMBEZZLEMENT MATTER . . . [same as first two paragraphs, prior page]

Recoveries relating to the embezzlement were as follows:

Fiscal 2001	$ 2,756,000
Fiscal 2000 and prior	7,000,000
Total recoveries	9,756,000
Recovery costs	(2,406,000)
Net recoveries	$ 7,350,000

The Company continues to pursue recovery activities from certain parties although no assurances can be given as to the timing or extent of such recoveries.

On January 9, 2001, the Securities & Exchange Commission issued a formal order of investigation of the Company and unnamed individuals concerning trading activity in the Company's securities, periodic reports filed by the Company with the SEC, certain accounting and financial matters and internal accounting controls. The Company is cooperating fully with the SEC. In addition, the Company has received an SEC subpoena for documents related to these matters. The staff of the SEC has advised that the inquiry is confidential and should not be construed as an indication by the Commission or its staff that any violation of law has occurred, or as an adverse reflection on any person, entity or security. The Company believes the investigation is primarily related to the previously reported embezzlement by one of the Company's former employees. *(Source: 10-K filed 6/28/2001)*

The company elsewhere in the 10-K filing states:

Certain statements in this Annual 10-K Report constitute "forward-looking statements" within the meaning of the United States Private Securities Litigation Reform Act of 1995. Such forward-looking statements involve known and unknown risks, uncertainties and other factors which may cause the actual results, performance or achievements of the Company, or industry results, to be materially different from any future results, performance, or achievements expressed or implied by such forward-looking statements. Such factors include, among others, the following: general economic and business conditions in the Company's market area, inflation, continuation of favorable banking arrangements, the availability of capital to finance operations and planned growth, ramifications of the embezzlement referenced herein, changes in government regulations, availability of skilled personnel and competition, which may, among other things impact on the ability of the Company to implement its business strategy.

The embezzlement matter did not involve or affect the Company's fulfillment of its Government contracts nor its accounting thereof, and it did not trigger any termination provisions under government contracts.

Item 3. Legal Proceedings. . . . There are no material pending legal proceedings to which the Company is a party. The Company is engaged in ordinary routine litigation incidental to the Company's business to which the Company is a party.

Item 9. Changes in and Disagreements with Accountants on Accounting and Financial Disclosure
Ernst & Young LLP (the "Former Accountants") resigned as the independent accountants for Halifax Corporation (the "Company") on October 19, 1999.

No report prepared by the Former Accountants on the consolidated financial position of Halifax Corporation at March 31, 1999 and 1998, and the consolidated results of operations and its cash flows of each of the three years in the period ended March 31, 1999, contained an adverse opinion or disclaimer of opinion, or was qualified or modified as to uncertainty, audit scope, or accounting principles.

In connection with the audit conducted by the Former Accountants for the fiscal year ended March 31, 1999, which was concluded on September 7, 1999, and which included the consolidated balance sheets of Halifax Corporation as of March 31, 1999 and 1998, and the related consolidated statements of operations, changes in stockholders' equity (deficit) and cash flows for each of the three years in the period ended March 31, 1999, there were no disagreements between the Company and Ernst & Young LLP on any matter of accounting principles or practices, financial statement disclosure, or auditing scope or procedure, which disagreements, if not resolved to the satisfaction of Ernst & Young LLP, would have caused them to make reference thereto in their report on the financial statements for those years.

The fiscal year 1999 audit was completed on September 7, 1999 with the issuance, by Ernst & Young LLP, of an unqualified opinion as presented in the Company's Form 10-K which was filed with the SEC on September 9, 1999. *(Source: 10-K filed 6/28/01)*

Halifax Corporation reported on its balance sheets total assets of $17,966,000 as of March 31, 2001, and $27,808,000 as of March 31, 2000. Excerpts from Management Discussion and Analysis are included in Tables 5.7-1 and 5.7-2.

Table 5.7-1   Excerpts from Results of Operations

Results of Operations for Years Ended [dollars in thousands, except per share amounts]	**March 31, 2001**	**March 31, 2000**	**Change**	**%**	**2000**	**1999**	**Change**	**%**
Revenues	$51,750	$53,530	$(1,780)	–3%	$53,530	$59,071	$(5,541)	–9%
Operating (loss) income	(1,417)	251	(1,668)	N/M*	251	(1,012)	1,263	N/M
% of Revenues	–3%	0%			0%	–2%		
Embezzlement (recovery) expense	(1,600)	(2,250)	(650)	–29%	(2,250)	2,593	(4,843)	NM
Income before taxes and discontinued operations	(817)	1,490	(2,307)	N/M	1,490	(5,428)	6,918	N/M
Net income	$1,098	$2,313	($1,215)	–53%	$2,313	$(5,299)	$7,612	N/M
Earnings (loss) per share—basic	$(.42)	$.70			$.70	$(2.64)		
Continuing								
Operations								

*N/M = not meaningful *(Source: 10-K as of 3/31/01, filed 6/28/01).*

Table 5.7-2   Factors that May Affect Future Results

Liqudity and Capital Resources	**2001**	**2000**	**1999**
Cash balance at March 31, 2001	$231,000	$1,800,000	$0
Working capital at March 31, 2001	$(102,000)	$3,481,000	$740,000
Net cash provided by operations before impact of embezzlement	$520,000	$1,641,000	$1,940,000
Net cash recovered (used) related to embezzlement	1,600,000	5,078,000	(5,421.000)
Net cash provided by (used in) operating activities	$2,120,000	$6,719,000	$(3,481,000)

(Source: 10-K as of 3/31/01, filed 6/28/01)

Halifax Corporation filed its 10-Q for the quarter ended September 30, 2001, on November 15, 2001, in which it discloses:

Embezzlement Recovery

Embezzlement recoveries (net of settlement costs) for the three and six months ended September 30, 2000 were $2.1 million and $1.8 million, respectively. There were no embezzlement recoveries for the three and six months ended September 30, 2001. . . .

Pursuant to the Company's credit facility the Company is required to satisfy two financial covenants; funded debt to EBITDA and fixed charge coverage ratio. The Company was not in compliance with the funded debt ratio as of September 30, 2001. The lender has waived the covenant violation at September 30, 2001. The Company and the lender have extended the original maturity date from August 31, 2002 to November 15, 2002. (See Note 4 to the condensed consolidated financial statements.). . .

Note 4-Debt

On December 8, 2000, the Company entered into a new revolving credit agreement with a financial institution which refinanced the Company's revolving credit line. Advances under the revolving agreement are collateralized by a first priority security interest on all the Company's assets as defined in the financing and security agreement.

The agreement also contains certain financial covenants and reporting covenants. Subsequent to September 30, 2001, the agreement, which originally matured on August 31, 2002, was extended to November 15, 2002.

The revolving credit agreement prohibits the payment of dividends or distributions as well as the payment of principal or interest on the Company's outstanding subordinated debt, which is owned by an affiliate. Interest expense on Subordinated Debt is accrued on a current basis. Pursuant to the terms of a subordination agreement related to the subordinated debt, concurrent with the extension of the revolving credit line discussed above, the due date of the subordinated debt was extended from July 1, 2002 to November 15, 2002.

The Company's credit facility requires it to satisfy two financial covenants; funded debt to earnings before interest, taxes, depreciation and amortization ("EBITDA"), and fixed charge coverage ratio. The Company was not in compliance with the funded debt to EBITDA ratio at September 30, 2001. Its lender has agreed to an amendment to waive the violations. It is the intention of the lender and the Company to restructure the covenants to assure that compliance can be achieved. *(Source: 10-Q as of 9/30/2001, filed on 11/15/2001)*

Of interest is a comparison of these disclosures to those made in the 10-Q filed as of September 9, 1999 for the period ended June 30, 1999 by Halifax Corp.:

Note 2—Embezzlement Matter and Restatement of Consolidated Financial Statements

On March 18, 1999, the Company announced that an internal investigation had revealed an apparent material embezzlement by the former controller of one of the Company's subsidiaries. The embezzlement occurred at, and was confined to, the Company's Richmond, VA based Halifax Technology Services Company ("HTSC"). At the time of the embezzlement, HTSC was a wholly owned subsidiary of Halifax Corporation, which resulted from a merger of CMSA (acquired by Halifax on April 1, 1996), and CCI (acquired by Halifax on November 25, 1996). On April 1, 1999, HTSC was merged into Halifax Corporation and is now a division of the Company.

The Company believes that a single individual, the former controller of HTSC, perpetrated the embezzlement. She was immediately terminated, has since been indicted, has pleaded guilty, and currently awaits sentencing. Under the terms of an agreement entered into with the Company, she is cooperating with the Company's recovery efforts.

The embezzlement occurred over a period of nearly four years and aggregated approximately $15.4 million, of which $15 million was embezzled from the Company and $400,000 from CMSA before it was acquired by Halifax. To conceal the embezzlement in the accounting records, the former controller made fraudulent adjustments totaling more than $21 million. Of the $21 million, the $15 million embezzled was recorded in the Company's statements of operations and balance sheets after the acquisition, approximately $2.2 million related to amounts reflected in the acquisition date balance sheet, and approximately $3.8 million related to other overstatements of operating results during the three-year period subsequent to the CMSA acquisition.

Under the terms of an agreement with the Company, the embezzler has transferred certain assets back to the Company. Some of the recovered assets have been converted into approximately $1.4 million in cash as of August 31, 1999. With an estimated $1.1 million of assets awaiting conversion to cash, the Company estimates approximately $2.5 million will ultimately be recovered from the embezzler. In addition, the full policy amount of $1 million from each of two separate theft insurance policies, or an aggregate of $2 million, has been received to date.

Therefore, from these sources, the Company expects a total recovery of $4.5 million (excluding recovery costs). The Company estimates that, net of recovery costs, approximately $3.5 million will be recovered. At March 31, 1999, the Company had received approximately $670,000 from its recovery efforts and recorded a $2.83 million recovery receivable to recognize its expectation of receiving the estimated $3.5 million of total net recoveries.

Due to the corresponding overstatement of taxable income, reported by the Company during the period of the embezzlement, the Company will file for a tax refund of approximately $808,000. The receivable is recorded in "Income Taxes Receivable" in the consolidated financial statements.

The embezzlement had a material effect on the Company's financial statements for fiscal years 1999, 1998 and 1997. In addition to the correction for overstated assets and understated liabilities, the Company recorded an embezzlement loss of approximately $2,593,000, $6,044,000, and $2,892,000 for the fiscal years ended March 31, 1999, 1998 and 1997, respectively. The embezzlement loss recorded in fiscal 1999 is net of the actual and projected net recoveries aggregating $3,500,000.

In addition to the notification and involvement of the appropriate authorities, and the intensive and ongoing investigative efforts, the Company has taken other important steps as a result of the embezzlement. The Board of Directors appointed a special committee of the Board to focus on the recovery of assets taken from the Company and minimization of the damages sustained as a result of the embezzlement.

The employment contract of the HTSC president was not renewed, and he is no longer employed by the Company. Furthermore, new executives have been hired to manage the technology services division and to consolidate the Company's financial and administrative activities. The Company has also transferred key accounting and cash management functions of HTSC to Company headquarters.

The Company's financial statements for the three months ended June 30, 1998 have been restated to reflect corrections due to the embezzlement. The effect of the restatement on results of operations for the three months ended June 30, 1998 is as follows:

	Three Months Ended June 30, 1998	
Statement of Operations	Previously Reported	Restated
Revenues	$17,264,000	$16,163,000
Cost of services	15,323,000	15,519,000
G&A expenses	1,306,000	865,000
Operating income	635,000	(221,000)
Interest expenses	355,000	355,000
Embezzlement loss	—	(1,798,000)
Income (loss) before taxes	280,000	(2,374,000)
Income taxes	129,000	(34,000)
Net income (loss)	$151,000	$(2,340,000)
Net income (loss) per share—basic	$.08	$(1.16)
Net income (loss) per share—diluted	$.07	$(1.16)

(Source: 10-Q as of 6/30/99, filed on 9/9/99)

Requirement A: Disclosure Practices

1. Do you find the disclosures in the 2001 10-K and 10-Q to be informative and sufficient as to the nature and extent of effect of the embezzlement matter? Why or why not?
2. What guidance exists to help you evaluate the sufficiency of the disclosures? Support your position with appropriate citations from FARS.
3. Reconcile the disclosures in the 1999 10-Q to those found in the 2001 filings. Do they compare reasonably? Explain.

Requirement B: Strategy-Related Considerations

1. What signals does Halifax Corp. include in its 1999 10-Q filing to indicate that it has treated the embezzlement matter seriously?
2. Do you believe this type of disclosure has particular importance to this company? Why?
3. Check the 10-Q for the quarter ended June 30, 2006 to see if any mention is made of the embezzlement. Describe what you find and its implications.

Directed Self-Study

Access sec.gov and select the full text search beta version of EDGAR that has two years of filings that can be searched as text. See if you can identify another public filing that discloses an embezzlement and how that disclosure compares and contrasts to the Halifax Corp. setting. [Access National Storm Management, Inc.'s Form 10-SB/A signed by the President and Chief Executive Officer on July

5, 2006, which includes the quarter ended March 31, 2006. Use the Find capability to locate the relevant discussion.]

Key Terms and Glossary

EBITDA earnings before interest, taxes, depreciation and amortization is the general definition, but since this is not defined by GAAP, its application in practice has been observed to vary substantially

involuntary conversions of nonmonetary assets FIN 30, Summary explains that: "Examples of such conversions are total or partial destruction or theft of insured nonmonetary assets and the condemnation of property in eminent domain proceedings."

nonreciprocal transfer "A transaction in which an entity incurs a liability or transfers an asset to another entity (or receives an asset or cancellation of a liability) without directly receiving (or giving) value in exchange" (FAS 116, par. 209). "In these transfers one of the two entities is often passive, a mere beneficiary or victim of the other's actions. Examples are gifts, dividends received, taxes, loss of a negligence lawsuit, imposition of fines, and theft" (superseded APS 4, par. 62).

risk "refers to any exposure to uncertainty in which the exposure has potential negative consequences" according to CON 7, Par. 64. The FASB describes various risks in FAS 133, par. 408: "The Board recognizes that entities are commonly exposed to a variety of risks in the course of their activities, including interest rate, foreign exchange, market price, credit, liquidity, theft, weather, health, catastrophe, competitive, and business cycle risks. The Exposure Draft did not propose detailed guidance on what risks could be designated as being hedged, other than to note in the basis for conclusions that special hedge accounting for certain risk management transactions, such as hedges of strategic risk, would be precluded. In redeliberating the issue of risk, the Board reaffirmed that hedge accounting cannot be provided for all possible risks and decided to be more specific about the risks for which hedge accounting is available."

Further Readings

Bellovary, J. L., D. E. Giacomino, and M. D. Akers. 2005. "Earnings quality: It's time to measure and report." *CPA Journal* (LXXV, 11, November), pp. 32–37.

Beneish, M. D., P. E. Hopkins, I. Ph. Jansen, and R. D. Martin. 2005. "Do auditor resignations reduce uncertainty about the quality of firms' financial reporting?" *Journal of Accounting and Public Policy* (24, 5, September/October), pp. 357–390.

Biggs, Stanley F., W. Robert Knechel, Norman R. Walker, Wanda A. Wallace, and John J. Willingham. 1995. "Analytical Procedures." *Auditing Practice, Research and Education: A Productive Collaboration.* Edited by Timothy B. Bell and Arnold M. Wright. New York: Published by the AICPA in Cooperation with the Auditing Section of the American Accounting Association, pp. 110–143.

Botosan, Christine A., and Marlene A. Plumlee. 2005. "Assessing alternative proxies for the expected risk premium." *Accounting Review* (80, 1, January), pp. 21–53.

Booz, Allen Hamilton. 2003. "Exclusive: The annual CEO turnover study" by Chuck Lucier, Rob Schuyt,

Morton, Sanford. 1993. "Strategic auditing for fraud." *Accounting Review* (68, 4), pp. 825–839.

National Commission of Fraudulent Financial Reporting (the Treadway Commission). 1987. *Report of the National Commission on Fraudulent Financial Reporting.* Washington, DC: U.S. Government Printing Office.

Palmrose, Zoe-Vonna. 1999. *Empirical Research in Auditor Litigation: Considerations and Data* (including a CD-ROM). Studies in Accounting Research #33. Sarasota, FL: American Accounting Association.

The Panel on Audit Effectiveness Report and Recommendations. 2000. Stamford, CT: Panel on Audit Effectiveness; The Public Oversight Board (August 31). Available at: www.pobauditpanel.org.

Report and Recommendations of the Blue Ribbon Committee on Improving the Effectiveness of Corporate Audit Committees. 1999. New York: NYSE and the National Association of Securities Dealers.

Ross, S. 1979. "Disclosure regulations in financial markets: Implications of modern finance theory and signaling theory." *Key Issues in Financial Regulation* (New York: McGraw-Hill), pp. 177–201.

and Eric Spiegel. CEO Succession 2002. *Strategy & Business* (31, Summer), pp. 31–45.

Byrne, J. 1996, 1997, and 2000. "The best and worst corporate boards." *Business Week* (November 25; December 8; and January 24).

Causey, Jr., Denzil Y., and Sandra A. Causey. 1999. *Duties and Liabilities of Public Accountants,* 6th ed. Starkville, MS: Accountants Press.

Chapman, Christy. 2003. "Sir Adrian Cadbury: Let there be light." *Internal Auditor* (LX, I, Februrary), pp. 38–45.

Cleary, Richard, and Jay C. Thibodeau. 2005. "Applying digital analysis using Benford's law to detect fraud: The dangers of type I errors." Research Note. *Auditing: A Journal of Practice and Theory* (24, 1, May), pp. 77–81.

Cohen, Jeffrey R., Laurie W. Pant, and David J. Sharp. 1993. "Culture-based ethical conflicts confronting multinational accounting firms." *Accounting Horizons* (7, 3), pp. 1–13.

Committee of Sponsoring Organizations (COSO). 2004. *Enterprise Risk Management—Integrated Framework* (September 29).

Committee of Sponsoring Organizations of the Treadway Commission (COSO). 1999. *Fraudulent Financial Reporting: 1987–1997*. New York: COSO.

Cravens, K. S., and Wallace, W. A. 2001. "A framework for determining the influence of the corporate board of directors in accounting studies." *Corporate Governance: An International Review* (9, 1, January), pp. 2–24.

Eilifsen, A., and W. F. Messier, Jr. 2000. "The incidence and detection of misstatements: A review and integration of archival research." *Journal of Accounting Literature* (19), pp. 1–43.

Erickson, Merle, Michelle Hanlon, and Edward L. Maydew. 2004. "How much will firms pay for earnings that do not exist? Evidence of taxes paid on allegedly fraudulent earnings." *Accounting Review* (79, 2, April), pp. 387–408.

Financial Executives International and National Investor Relations. 2001. "Best practice" guidelines for earnings releases (April). Available at: http://www.fei.org.

Finley, David R. 1994, "Game theoretic analysis of discovery sampling for internal fraud control auditing." *Contemporary Accounting Research* (11, 1), pp. 91–114.

Glass, Lewis & Co., LLC. 2004. "Auditor turnover—what investors should be watching" (January 28).

Glass, Lewis & Co. 2004. "Recently delayed annual filings." *Yellow Card Brief Alert* (March 17).

Healy, Paul M., and Krishna G. Palepu. 1993. "The

SEC. Speech by staff member: *Behind the Numbers of the SEC's Recent Financial Fraud Cases* by Richard H. Walker, Director, Division of Enforcement, U.S. SEC's 27th Annual National AICPA Conference on Current SEC Developments. 1999. (Dec. 7). Available at: sec.gov/news/speeches/spch334.htm.

SEC. Division of Corporation Finance Office of the Chief Accountant. 2005. Staff statement on management's report on internal control over financial reporting (May 16).

Turner, Lynn E., then-Chief Accountant of the SEC. 2000. Speech on *Audit Committees: A Call to Action* [Accounting Irregularities II: What's an Audit Committee To Do?] New York. (October 5).

UBS Investment Research. 2003. S&P 500 accounting quality monitor. Bridging the gap to GAAP EPS. *Global Analyzer* (July 2).

United States Department of Justice and United States Department of Commerce. 2002. *Foreign Corrupt Practices Act Antibribery Provisions* (March 15). Available at: http://www.usdoj.gov/criminal/fraud/fcpa/dojdocb.

U.S. Government Accountability Office. 2006. *Financial Restatements—Update of Public Company Trends, Market Impacts, and Regulatory Enforcement Activities.* Available at: www.gao.gov/cgi-bin/getrpt? GAO-06-678.

U.S. General Accounting Office (GAO, since renamed Government Accountability Office). 2003. *Financial Statement Restatement Database*. GAO-03-395R (January 17).

U.S. General Accounting Office. 2002. Report to the Chairman, Committee on Banking, Housing, and Urban Affairs, U.S. Senate. *Financial Statement Restatements—Trends, Market Impacts, Regulatory Responses, and Remaining Challenges* (October), GAO-03-138.

Walker, R. G., and S. P. Robinson. 1994. "Related party transactions: A case study of inter-organizational conflict over the 'development' of disclosure rules." *Abacus* (30, 1), pp. 18–43.

Wallace, Wanda A. 2005. *Internal Controls Guide,* 3rd ed. Chicago: CCH Inc. a WoltersKluwer Company.

Wallace, Wanda A. 2005. "Skinner's 'interpretation panel'—a means to balance 'power'." *Canadian Accounting Perspectives* (4, 2), pp. 301–20.

Wallace, Wanda A. 2004. *A Primer on Internal Controls and Auditing: Crucial to Government and the Economy.* (Alexandria, VA: Association of Government Accountants), (June). Available at: agacgfm.org/publications/wallace_order.aspx.

Wallace, Wanda A. 2004. "Auditor rotation: A bad governance idea." Guest Column. *Directors & Boards* (28, 3, Spring), p. 14.

effect of firms' financial disclosure strategies on stock prices." *Accounting Horizons* (7, 1), pp. 1–11.

Kinney, Jr., W. R., and R. D. Martin. 1994. "Does auditing reduce bias in financial reporting? A review of audit-related adjustment studies." *Auditing: A Journal of Practice and Theory* (13, 1, Spring), pp. 149–156.

Krishnan, J., H. Sami, and Y. Zhang. 2005. "Does the provision of nonaudit services affect investor perceptions of auditor independence?" *Auditing: A Journal of Practice and Theory* (24, 2), pp. 111–135.

Lattman, Peter, and Karen Richardson. 2006. "Hedge funds go after companies that file quarterly reports late." *Wall Street Journal* (August 29), pp. A1, A6.

Licata, Michael P., Wayne G. Bremser, and Theresa P. Rollins. 1997. "SEC enforcement actions against auditors: Auditing education linked to the pitfalls of audit practice." *Issues in Accounting Education* (12, 2, Fall), pp. 537–560.

Menon, Krishnagopal, and David D. Williams. 1994. "The insurance hypothesis and market prices." *Accounting Review* (69, 2), pp. 327–342.

Wallace, Wanda A. 2004. "To what extent are restatements associated with changes in boards?" *NACD-Directors Monthly*. National Association of Corporate Directors (NACD) (June), p. 19.

Wallace, Wanda A. 2002. "Assessing the quality of data used for benchmarking and decision-making." *Journal of Government Financial Management* (51, 3, Fall), pp. 16–23.

Wallace, Wanda A. 2000. "Reporting Practices: Potential Lessons From Cendant." *European Management Journal* (18, 3, June), pp. 328–333.

Wallace, Wanda A. 2000. "The value relevance of accounting: The rest of the story." *European Management Journal* (18, 6, December), pp. 675–682.

Wallace, Wanda A. 1980. *The Economic Role of the Audit in Free and Regulated Markets.* (New York: Touche Ross & Co. Aid to Accounting Education Program). Available at: http://raw.rutgers.edu/raw/wallace/homepage.html

Wright, Arnold, and Sally Wright. 1996. "The relationship between assessments of internal control strength and error occurrence, impact and cause." *Accounting and Business Research* (27, 1), pp. 58–71.

The hardest crossword puzzle to solve is the one in which we have penciled in a wrong word and are too stubborn or fixated to erase it; in much the same way, it is often easier to solve a problem when you are merely ignorant than when you are wrong.

—Sidney J. Harris

[Cited by George W. Downs and Patrick D. Larkey in The Search for Government Efficiency: From Hubris to Helplessness *(Philadelphia: Temple University Press, 1986), p. 49]*

CASE 8

What Constitutes a Subsequent Event? Related Gain Contingency Considerations

CASE TOPICS OUTLINE

1. Subsequent Event for Euronet Worldwide, Inc.
   A. Extinguishment of Debt
   B. Extraordinary Gain
2. Gain Contingency Considerations

Euronet Worldwide, Inc. provides both software and service solutions related to secure electronic financial transactions. A press release was issued by Euronet Worldwide, Inc. on September 10, 2001, in which it announced the appointment of Daniel R. Henry as President, in addition to his Chief Operating Officer (COO) role. The release elaborated on the fact that Mr. Henry co-founded the company with Michael Brown in 1994 and that Mr. Brown would continue as Chairman and Chief Executive Officer—no longer holding the title of President. This same release identifies the realization of a subsequent event reported in its Form 10-Q for the period ended June 30, 2001. Specifically, since that date, the company had exchanged senior discount notes for shares of its common stocks. The release quantifies implications of the exchange as of August 31, 2001 as decreasing the indebtedness since June 30, 2001, thereby resulting in an annual interest expense savings of approximately $2 million per year.

In its quarterly filing, Euronet Worldwide included the following notes among its disclosures:

EURONET WORLDWIDE, INC. AND SUBSIDIARIES
NOTES TO THE UNAUDITED CONSOLIDATED FINANCIAL STATEMENTS
SEPTEMBER 30, 2001 AND 2000

NOTE 1 — FINANCIAL POSITION AND BASIS OF PRESENTATION
The accompanying unaudited consolidated financial statements of Euronet
Worldwide, Inc. and subsidiaries (collectively, "Euronet" or the "Company") (formerly

Euronet Services Inc.), have been prepared from the records of the Company, pursuant to the rules and regulations of the Securities and Exchange Commission. In the opinion of management, such unaudited consolidated financial statements include all adjustments (consisting only of normal, recurring accruals) necessary to present fairly the financial position of the Company at September 30, 2001, the results of its operations for the three-month periods and nine-month periods ended September 30, 2001 and 2000 and cash flows for the nine-month periods ended September 30, 2001 and 2000.

The unaudited consolidated financial statements should be read in conjunction with the audited consolidated financial statements of Euronet Worldwide, Inc. and subsidiaries for the year ended December 31, 2000, including the notes thereto, set forth in the Company's Form 10-K.

The results of operations for the three-month and nine-month periods ended September 30, 2001 are not necessarily indicative of the results to be expected for the full year.

The Company generated an operating loss of $6.2 million for the nine months ended September 30, 2001 primarily due to the significant costs associated with the expansion of its ATM network and investment support and research and development in its software. In addition, the Company generated negative cash flows from operations of $0.3 million for the nine months ended September 30, 2001, as a result of these same factors. Based on the Company's current business plan and financial projections, the Company expects to reduce operating losses and net cash used in operating activities during the remainder of 2001. In the Processing Services Segment, the Company anticipates that increased transaction levels in its ATM network will result in additional revenues without a corresponding increase in expenses. In addition, the Company expects to further expand its ATM outsourcing services and offer new value-added services, which will provide continued revenue growth without significantly increasing direct operating expenses or capital investments. In the Software Solutions Segment, the Company expects to continue its strategic repositioning of its software business from direct software sales to software-only customers to more integrated solutions combining the strengths of the Company's electronic financial transaction network system with its software development strengths.

The Company has a $4.0 million credit facility under an unsecured revolving credit agreement (see Note 5). As of September 30, 2001, the Company had drawn $2.0 million against such credit agreement. In addition, the Company holds repurchased notes payable with a face value of DEM 139.7 million ($65.0 million) and a fair value at September 30, 2001 of $52.0 million. The Company believes that cash and cash equivalents at September 30, 2001, and the revolving credit agreement described above, will provide the Company with sufficient cash resources until it achieves positive cash flow. The Company nevertheless has a policy of assessing opportunities for additional debt and equity financing as they arise, and will pursue any such opportunities if the Company considers that they may contribute to fulfilling its financial and strategic business objectives.

Based on the above, management is confident that the Company will be able to continue as a going concern. Accordingly, these consolidated financial statements have been prepared on a going concern basis which contemplates the continuation and expansion of trading activities as well as the realization of assets and liquidation of liabilities in the ordinary course of business. . . .

NOTE 6—EXTINGUISHMENT OF DEBT

During the three months ending March 31, 2001, in a single transaction, the Company exchanged 8,750 Senior Discount Notes (principal face amount of DEM 8.75 million) of its Senior Discount Notes for two new Senior discount notes having an aggregate face amount of $2.9 million (the "New Notes"). The interest, repayment and other terms of the New Notes are identical to those of the Senior Discount Notes for which they were exchanged, except that (i) the principal amount was reduced as indicated in the previous sentence, (ii) the Company has the right to prepay the New Notes at any time at its option by paying the "Accreted Value" of the Notes, and (iii) the new notes are governed by a new Note Purchase Agreement rather than the indenture under which the Senior Discount Notes were issued and the New Notes therefore are not covered by any of the provisions of such indenture relating to action by the trustee, voting or maintenance of listing on a stock exchange. This exchange has been accounted for as an extinguishment of debt and issuance of new debt with a resulting $0.4 million (net of applicable income taxes of $0.3 million) recognized as an extraordinary gain on such extinguishment. The extinguishment gain (pre-tax) represents the difference between the allocated carrying value of the debt extinguished ($3.3 million) and the fair market value of the New Notes issued ($2.5 million), offset by the write-off of the allocated unamortized deferred financing costs ($0.1 million). This transaction was exempt from registration in accordance with Section 3(a)9 of the Act.

During the six months ending June 30, 2001, in eight separate transactions, the Company exchanged 48,600 units (principal amount of DEM 48.6 million) of its Senior Discount Notes and 145,800 warrants for 1,691,000 shares of its common stock, par value $0.02 per share. This exchange has been accounted for as an extinguishment of debt with a resulting $7.0 million (net of applicable income taxes of $1.0 million) recognized as an extraordinary gain on such extinguishment. The extinguishment gain (pre-tax) represents the difference between the allocated carrying value of the debt and any related warrants extinguished ($19.0 million) and the fair market value of the common stock issued ($10.5 million), offset by the write-off of the allocated unamortized deferred financing costs ($0.5 million). These transactions were exempt from registration in accordance with Section 3(a)9 of the Act.

During the three months ending September 30, 2001, in five separate transactions, the Company exchanged 34,000 units (principal amount of DEM 34.0 million) of its Senior Discount Notes and 102,000 warrants for 1,157,000 shares of its common stock, par value $0.02 per share. This exchange has been accounted for as an extinguishment of debt with a resulting $2.1 million (inclusive of an applicable income tax benefit of $1.0 million) recognized as an extraordinary gain on such extinguishment. The extinguishment gain (pre-tax) represents the difference between the allocated carrying value of the debt and any related warrants extinguished ($13.6 million) and the fair market value of the common stock issued ($12.2 million), offset by the write-off of the allocated unamortized deferred financing costs ($0.3 million). These transactions were exempt from registration in accordance with Section 3(a)9 of the Act.

The Senior Discount Notes that were acquired by the Company in the above exchanges have not been retired. The Company will consider additional repurchases of its Senior Discount Notes if opportunities arise to complete such transactions on favorable terms. . . .

NOTE 9—SUBSEQUENT EVENTS

As of November 9, 2001, in a single transaction, the Company exchanged an aggregate of face value DEM 3.0 million of its Senior Discount Notes for 79,500 shares of its common stock, par value $0.02 per share. This exchange will be accounted for as an extinguishment of debt with the resulting extraordinary gain on such extinguishment calculated as the difference between the allocated carrying value of the debt and any related warrants extinguished and the fair market value of the common stock issued, offset by the write-off of the allocated unamortized deferred financing costs. The transaction is exempt from registration in accordance with Section 3(a)9 of the Act. The Senior Discount Notes that were acquired by the Company in the above exchange have not been retired.

As of October 22, 2001, the Hungarian American Enterprise Fund exercised warrants to purchase a total of 102,500 shares of Euronet common stock, par value $0.02 per share, for an aggregate strike price of $598,500. The warrants had been issued under the Credit Agreement referred to in Note 5.

As of November 13, 2001, DST Systems, Inc. exercised warrants to purchase a total of 246,000 shares of Euronet common stock, par value $0.02 per share, for an aggregate strike price of $1,436,520. The warrants had been issued under the Credit Agreement referred to in Note 5.

Total proceeds to the Company of the above warrant exercises were $2,034,520.

(Source: 10-Q/A for the period ended 9/30/01, filed 11/21/01)

Elsewhere in the 10-Q/A filing, financial statements are presented, excerpts from which appear in Table 5.8-1 and Table 5.8-2.

Table 5.8-1   Liabilities and Stockholders' Deficit Excerpts from Consolidated Balance Sheet (Unaudited)

(In thousands of U.S. Dollars, except share and per share data)	*Sept. 30, 2001*	*Dec. 31, 2000*
LIABILITIES AND STOCKHOLDERS' DEFICIT		
Current liabilities:		
Trade accounts payable	$ 5,009	$ 5,223
Current installments of obligations under capital leases	4,295	3,466
Accrued expenses and other current liabilities	6,201	6,747
Short-term borrowings	531	—
Advance payments on contracts	1,838	2,155
Billings in excess of costs and estimated earnings on software Installation contracts	1,752	2,875
Total current liabilities	19,626	20,466
Obligations under capital leases, excluding current installments	7,624	8,034
Notes payable	46,217	77,191
Other long-term liabilities	2,000	—
Total liabilities	75,467	105,691

(In thousands of U.S. Dollars, except share and per share data)	*Sept. 30, 2001*	*Dec. 31, 2000*
Stockholders' deficit:		
Common stock, $0.02 par value. Authorized 60,000,000 shares; issued and outstanding 21,121,448 shares at September 30, 2001 and 17,814,910 at December 31, 2000	422	356
Additional paid in capital	105,924	81,327
Treasury stock	(145)	(140)
Employee loans for stock	(463)	(561)
Subscription receivable	—	(59)
Accumulated deficit	(122,566)	(123,811)
Restricted reserve	779	784
Accumulated other comprehensive loss	(2,906)	(2,697)
Total stockholders' deficit	(18,955)	(44,801)
Total liabilities and stockholders' deficit	$ 56,512	$ 60,890

(Source: 10-Q/A for the period ended 9/30/01, filed on 11/21/01)

Table 5.8-2   Excerpts from Euronet Worldwide, Inc. and Subsidiaries Consolidated Statements of Operations and Comprehensive Income/(Loss) (Unaudited)

(In thousands of U.S. Dollars, except share and per share data)	*Three Months Ended Sept. 30, 2001*	*Three Months Ended Sept. 30, 2000*
Total revenues	$ 15,681	$ 14,026
Total operating expenses	16,619	30,921
Operating loss	(938)	(16,895)
Other (expense)/income:		
Interest income	71	187
Interest expense	(2,063)	(2,505)
Foreign exchange gain/(loss), net	(3,560)	4,202
Loss before income taxes and extraordinary item	(6,490)	(15,011)
Income taxes	(1,015)	(767)
Loss before extraordinary item	(7,505)	(15,778)
Extraordinary gain on extinguishment of debt, net of applicable income taxes	2,097	—
Net income/(loss)	(5,408)	(15,778)
Other comprehensive loss:		
Translation adjustment	(3)	(65)
Comprehensive income/(loss)	($ 5,411)	($ 15,843)
Loss per share—basic and diluted: Loss before extraordinary item	$ (0.37)	$ (0.90)
Extraordinary gain on early retirement of debt	0.10	—
Net income/(loss)	$ (0.27)	$ (0.90)
Weighted average number of shares outstanding	20,426,648	17,541,079

(Source: 10-Q/A for the period ended 9/30/01, filed on 11/21/01)

Requirement A: Subsequent Events

1. Using FARS, identify guidance that might help a company such as Euronet Worldwide, Inc. determine whether something ought to be disclosed as a subsequent event.
2. Is there any relationship between subsequent event disclosures and gain contingencies? Support your position.
3. Today, would the extinguishment of debt be accounted for as an extraordinary gain? Explain.
4. Check the proxy statement that includes the notice of the Annual Meeting of Stockholders on May 18, 2006 and determine if any reference is made to early retirement of debt. Explain the implications of what you find. In addition, access the 10-K for the fiscal year ended December 31, 2005 from sec.gov and describe its presentations affected by early retirement of debt through year-end 2005.

Requirement B: Strategy-Related Considerations

Company management determines press-release content, which is not restricted in the same manner as either 10-Q or 10-K filings, as long as nothing fraudulent is included.

1. Do you find the disclosure in the press release of Euronet Worldwide, Inc. on September 10, 2001 regarding interest savings resulting from the subsequent event reported in the June 30, 2001 10-Q filing to be of assistance to capital market participants? Why or why not?
2. Should such consequences of subsequent events be included within the note to the financial statement itself? Why or why not? Is such a communication implicit in any case?

Directed Self-Study

What are the subsequent events reported by Microsoft Corporation in its 2006 10-K filing? Describe their implications. Evaluate their relationship to guidance in FARS. Identify other entities' reported Subsequent Events by using the full text search beta version of EDGAR. [Access sec.gov to locate the 10-K as well as to click on the beta version for the search process. Try the search phrase *Subsequent Events Item 304*. Then proceed to FARS, open FASB-OP (amended) and search the phrase *subsequent event* using Query. Perform the same query on *EITF Abstracts*.]

Does It Matter Where Guidance Is Located?

The FASB expects in early 2007 to deliberate on a project that plans to move guidance on subsequent events into GAAP (Attachment B, International Convergence–Status and Plans, Financial Accounting Standards Advisory Council, December 2006, Appendix 2, p. 12 – retrievable from fasb.org). Comparisons may be drawn to the developments in the area of defining the GAAP Hierarchy within the accounting literature rather than the auditing literature. Do you believe it matters where such guidance is located? Why or why not?

Key Terms and Glossary

Type I subsequent event "Those events that provide additional evidence with respect to conditions that existed at the date of the balance sheet and affect the estimates inherent in the process of preparing financial statements... The financial statements should be adjusted for any change in estimates resulting from the use of such evidence" (AU Section 560.06 of SAS No. 1).

Type II subsequent event "Those events that provide evidence with respect to conditions that did not exist at the date of the balance sheet being reported on but arose subsequent to that date. These events should not result in adjustment of the financial statements. Some of these events, however, may be of such a nature that disclosure of them is required to keep the financial statements from being misleading" (AU Section 560.06 of SAS No. 1).

Further Readings

American Institute of Certified Public Accountants (AICPA). 1998. *AICPA Professional Standards, Volume 1. U.S. Auditing Standards*. New York: AICPA – AU Section 561: "Subsequent discovery of facts existing at the date of the auditor's report" (June 1).

Botosan, Christine A., and Mary Stanford. 2005. "Managers' motives to withhold segment disclosures and the effect of SFAS No. 131 on analysts' information environment." *Accounting Review* (80, 3, July), pp. 751–771.

Dechow, P., A. Hutton, and R. Sloan. 1996. "Causes and consequences of earnings manipulation: An analysis of firms subject to enforcement actions by the SEC." *Contemporary Accounting Research* (13), pp. 1–36.

Ettredge, Michael L., Soo Young Kwon, David B. Smith, and Paul A. Zarowin. 2005. "The impact of SFAS No. 131 business segment data on the market's ability to anticipate future earnings." *Accounting Review* (80, 3, July), pp. 773–804.

Gigler, F. 1994. "Self-enforcing voluntary disclosures." *Journal of Accounting Research* (32), pp. 224–241.

Healy, Paul M., and Krishna G. Palepu. 2001. "Information asymmetry, corporate disclosure, and the capital markets: A review of the empirical disclosure literature." *Journal of Accounting and Economics* (31), pp. 405–440.

Skinner, D. 1994. "Why firms voluntarily disclose bad news." *Journal of Accounting Research* (32), pp. 38–61.

Wallace, Wanda A. 2004. "Darned if you do and darned if you don't." *Accounting Today* (18, 5, March 15–April 4), pp. 32, 33.

Wallace, Wanda A., and C. Kermit Littlefield. 1994. "What is the nature of subsequent event disclosures? Are good news and bad news symmetrically disclosed?" *Auditor's Report* (17, 3, Summer), pp. 12–14.

The basic difference between a technician and a professional person is that the former possess the know-how, while the latter, in addition to the know-how, understands why it should be done.

—Janusz Santocki

[Source: "Educating Tomorrow's Accountants," Management Accounting (January 1987), pp. 45–46]

CASE 9

Reconciling International Practices to Those of the FASB: Cash Flow

CASE TOPICS OUTLINE

1. Anglo American plc
   A. Differences in Terminology
   B. Press Release: Interim Results for 2001

2. Cash Flow Comparison

Anglo American plc is a global company, with an investor relations office in London, within the United Kingdom. The company operates in the mining and natural resource sectors—including gold, platinum, diamonds, coal, base and ferrous metals, industrial minerals, and forest products. Its operations are geographically diverse, with operations in Africa, Europe, South and North America, and Australia.

The language found in financial statements varies between the UK and the United States. This is evidenced in Table 5.9-1 which provides a comparison of certain basic terminology. Such financial statement terminology must be mastered to effectively read financial reports from each of these countries.

Table 5.9-1　Financial Statement Terminology

United Kingdom (UK)	United States (U.S.)
Turnover	Sales
Operating Costs	Operating Expenses
Provision for Depreciation	Depreciation Expense
Profit for the Year	Net Income
Profit and Loss Account	Retained Earnings
Depreciation	Accumulated Depreciation
Stocks	Inventory
Debtors	Accounts Receivable
Creditors Due in 1 Year	Accounts Payable
Other Creditors	Other Liabilities
Share Capital	Common Stock
Share Premium Account	Additional Paid-in Capital

Anglo American plc reports interim results for 2001 in a news release on September 7, 2001. Among the disclosures is mention of cash flow:

> Cash flow from operations was US$1,506 million compared with US$1,068 million in the prior period. This inflow was after a US$419 million increase in working capital. Purchases of tangible fixed assets amounted to US$772 million, an increase of US$168 million. Tax payments were US$347 million compared with US$180 million. The acquisition of businesses, primarily an additional small interest in Anglo Platinum, resulted in a cash outflow of US$154 million. *(Source: News Release on 9/7/2001)*

The Consolidated Cash Flow Statement for the six months ended 30 June 2001 is reported in Table 5.9-2. It is followed by the two notes referenced on the face of the statement. The news release indicates that the financial information was prepared in accordance with generally accepted accounting principles (GAAP) in the UK.

Table 5.9-2   Consolidated Cash Flow Statement for the Six Months Ended 30 June 2001

US$ million	Note	6 months ended 30.06.01
Net cash inflow from operating activities	8	1,506
Expenditure relating to fundamental reorganisations		(20)
Dividends from joint ventures and associates		223
Returns on investments and servicing of finance		
Interest received and other financial income		144
Interest paid		(254)
Dividends received from fixed asset investments		41
Dividends paid to minority shareholders		(281)
Net cash outflow from returns on investments and servicing of finance		(350)
Taxes paid		(347)
Capital expenditure and financial investment		
Payments for fixed assets		(772)
Proceeds from the sale of fixed assets		199
Payments for other financial assets (1)		(79)
Proceeds from the sale of other financial assets (1)		1,019
Net cash inflow/(outflow) for capital expenditure and financial investment		367
Acquisitions and disposals		
Acquisition of subsidiaries (2)		(154)
Disposal of subsidiaries		135
Investment in associates		(189)
Sale of interests in associates		(1,148)
Investment in proportionally consolidated joint arrangements		(51)
Investment in joint ventures		(22)
Net cash inflow/(outflow) from acquisitions and disposals		867
Equity dividends paid to Anglo American shareholders		(509)
Cash inflow/(outflow) before use of liquid resources and financing		1,737
Management of liquid resources (3)		(977)
Financing		(795)
Decrease in cash in the period	10	(35)

(1)   Disposal and acquisition of other financial assets included in fixed assets.
(2)   Net of assets resold of US$709 million in the second half of 2000 in respect of the acquisition of Tarmac plc.
(3)   Cash flows in respect of current asset investments.
(Source: Anglo American plc News Release 9/7/01)

Note 8 Reconciliation of group operating profit to net cash flow from operating activities

US$ million	6 months ended 30.06.01
Group operating profit–subsidiaries	1,326
Depreciation and amortisation charges	517
Decrease/(increase) in stocks	21
Increase in debtors	(302)
(Decrease)/increase in creditors	(138)
Other items	82
Net cash inflow from operating activities	1,506

Note 10 Reconciliation of net cash flow to movement in net (debt)/funds

US$ million	6 months ended 30.06.01
Decrease in cash in the period	(35)
Cash outflow/(inflow) from debt financing	824
Cash outflow/(inflow) from management of liquid resources	977
Change in net debt arising from cash flows	1,766
Loans and current asset investments acquired with subsidiaries	(42)
Loans and current asset investments disposed with subsidiaries	11
Currency translation differences	88
Movement in net funds/(debt)	1,823
Net (debt)/funds at start of the period	(3,590)
Net debt at the end of the period	(1,767)

Requirement A: Reconciliation to GAAP

1. Compare and contrast the presentation of cash flow information by this company operating in the United Kingdom to that required by GAAP in the United States. Specifically, access FAS No. 95 and compare and contrast the examples provided for presentation of cash flow to the contents of Table 5.9-2 and related notes.
2. Within the press release, mention is made of *working capital*. What is meant by this term and how does it relate, historically, to reporting practices in the United States?
3. Access the Web site for the company (www.angloamerican.co.uk) and download the most recent press release containing quarterly results. Locate the presentations analogous to those in this case and describe how they have changed, if at all. Compare them to the U.S. GAAP.

Requirement B: Strategy-Related Considerations

1. Do you find the content of cash flow-associated disclosures by Anglo American plc to be of more or less use in understanding the strategy of management when compared with the practices common in the U.S.? Explain.
2. The FASB 95 content includes the following phrasing:

Cash Flow per Share
FAS95, Par. 33
Financial statements shall not report an amount of cash flow per share. Neither cash flow nor any component of it is an alternative to net income as an indicator of an enterprise's performance, as reporting per share amounts might imply.

Do you believe this proscription is in the best interest of financial statement users? Why or why not?

Directed Self-Study

Statement of Financial Accounting Standards No. 123(R) entitled *Share-Based Payment* was issued in December 2004. Use FARS to describe how it affected the Statement of Cash Flows. In addition, explain why it is claimed to have resulted in greater international comparability. [Open FASB-OP (amended), click on the toolbar's Search option, and select Search Within a Single OP Title. Type *FAS 123r* in the Document Title Box and then click twice on the Heading menu, so that the full title appears in the Document Title Box. Move to Query For: and type the phrase *statement of cash flows*. Eleven hits will result, helping you discern the answer to the first question. For the second issue, follow the same steps but use the search phrase *international comparability*. This will be a basis for you to respond to the second query.]

An International Conundrum

The editorial page of the *Wall Street Journal* on August 28, 2006 (p. A12) describes a transaction between a foreign bank and a national bank in another country which led to the incarceration of the foreign bank's staff. Reportedly, legal transactions had resulted in a loss to the national bank, which led to a demand to be "made whole." What do such developments imply about accounting measurement, international harmonization, and comparability?

Key Terms and Glossary

cash   "cash includes not only currency on hand but demand deposits with banks or other financial institutions. Cash also includes other kinds of accounts that have the general characteristics of demand deposits in that the customer may deposit additional funds at any time and also effectively may withdraw funds at any time without prior notice or penalty. All charges and credits to those accounts are cash receipts or payments to both the entity owning the account and the bank holding it. For example, a bank's granting of a loan by crediting the proceeds to a customer's demand deposit account is a cash payment by the bank and a cash receipt of the customer when the entry is made." (FAS 95, par. 7, footnote 1).

cash equivalents   "cash equivalents are short-term, highly liquid investments that are both:
  a. Readily convertible to known amounts of cash
  b. So near their maturity that they present insignificant risk of changes in value because of changes in interest rates.
Generally, only investments with original maturities* of three months or less qualify under that definition.

financial flexibility   Concept Statement 5, footnote 13 states: "Financial flexibility is the ability of an entity to take effective actions to alter amounts and timing of cash flows so it can respond to unexpected needs and opportunities."

liquidity   Concept Statement 4, par. 54 states: "Financial reporting should provide information about how an organization obtains and spends cash or other liquid resources, about its borrowing and repayment of borrowing, and about other factors that may affect its liquidity. Information about those resource flows may be useful in understanding the operations of an enterprise, evaluating its financing activities, assessing its liquidity, or interpreting performance information provided. Information about performance and economic resources, obligations, and net resources also may be useful in assessing an enterprise's liquidity." Concept Statement 5, footnote 13 states: "Liquidity reflects an asset's or liability's nearness to cash."

working capital   current assets less current liabilities FAS 6, par. 20 notes that Chapter 3A of ARB No. 43, par. 7 defines current liabilities as those whose

*Original maturity means original maturity to the entity holding the investment. For example, both a three-month U.S. Treasury bill and a three-year Treasury note purchased three months from maturity qualify as cash equivalents. However, a Treasury note purchased three years ago does not become a cash equivalent when its remaining maturity is three months" (FAS 95, par. 8, including footnote 2).

liquidation "is reasonably expected to require the use of existing resources properly classified as current assets, or the creation of other current liabilities." That paragraph goes on to say that the current liabilities classification "is intended to include obligations for items which have entered into the operating cycle . . . and debts which arise from operations directly related to the operating cycle. . . ."

Further Readings

Casey, Cornelius J., and Norman J. Bartczak. 1984. "Cash flow—It's not the bottom line." *Harvard Business Review* (July–August), pp. 60–66.

Collins, W., E.S. Davies, and P. Weetman. 1992. "Management discussion and analysis: An evaluation of practice in UK and US companies." *Accounting and Business Research* (23, 90), pp. 123–137.

Cummins, J. David, Martin F. Grace, and Richard D. Phillips. 1999. "Regulatory solvency prediction in property-liability insurance: Risk-based capital, audit ratios, and cash flow simulation." *Journal of Risk and Insurance* (66, 3, September), pp. 417–458.

Dechow, Patricia M., and Ilia D. Dichev. 2003. "The quality of accruals and earnings: The role of accrual estimation errors." *Accounting Review* (Supplement), pp. 35–59.

Dhumale, Rahul. 1998. "Earnings retention as a specification mechanism in logistic bankruptcy models: A test of the free cash flow theory." *Journal of Business Finance and Accounting* (25, 7–8, September–October), pp. 1005–1024.

Doupnik, Timothy S., and Martin Richter. 2003. "Interpretation of uncertainty expressions: A cross-national study." *Accounting, Organizations and Society* (28), pp. 15–35.

Gentry, James A., Paul Newbold, and David T. Whitford. 1985. "Predicting bankruptcy: If cash flow's not the bottom line, what is?" *Financial Analysts Journal* (September–October), pp. 47–56.

Hanlon, Michelle. 2005. "The persistence and pricing of earnings, accruals, and cash flows when firms have large book-tax differences." *Accounting Review* (80, 1, January), pp. 137–166.

Jensen, Michael. 1986. "Agency costs of free cash flow, corporate finance, and takeovers." *AER Papers and Proceedings* (76, 2), pp. 323–329.

Kaplan, S. N., and R. S. Ruback. 1995. "The valuation of cash flow forecasts: An empirical analysis." *Journal of Finance* (50), pp. 1059–1093.

Kochanek, Richard F., and Corine T. Norgaard. 1988. "Analyzing the components of operating cash flow: The charter company." *Accounting Horizons* (2, 1), pp. 58–66.

Laitinen, Erkki K., and T. Laitinen. 1998. "Cash management behavior and failure prediction." *Journal of Business Finance and Accounting* (25, 7–8, September–October), pp. 893–920.

Ndubizu, G. A., and M. H. Sanchez. 2006. "The valuation properties of earnings and book value prepared under U.S. GAAP in Chile and IAS in Peru." *Journal of Accounting and Public Policy* (25, 2, March/April), pp. 140–170.

Nobes, C. W. 1992. *International Classification of Financial Reporting*, 2nd ed. London and New York: Routledge.

Nurnberg, Hugo. 1993. "Inconsistencies and ambiguities in Cash Flow Statements under FASB Statement No. 95." *Accounting Horizons* (7, 2), pp. 60–75.

Opler, Tim, and Sheridan Titman. 1993. "The determinants of leveraged buyout activity: Free cash flow vs. financial distress costs." *Journal of Finance* (48, 5, December), pp. 1985–1999.

Stephens, Ray G., and Vijay Govindarajan. 1990. "Small sample studies: On assessing a firm's cash generating ability." *Accounting Review* (65, 1 January), pp. 242–257.

Wallace, Wanda A. 2002. "Delay in accounting harmonization: Evidence on auditor selection and cost-of-capital effects, 1986–1990." *Research in Accounting Regulation* (15), pp. 39–68.

Wells, Brenda P., Larry A. Cox, and Kenneth M. Gaver. 1995. "Free cash flow in the life insurance industry." *Journal of Risk and Insurance* (62, 1, March), pp. 50–66.

"Out of sight, out of mind," when translated into Russian [by computer], then back again into English became "invisible maniac."

—Arthur Calder-Marshall

CASE 10

Is the Asset Impaired—or Perhaps a Big Bath?

On December 21, 2001, the *Connecticut Post* reported that a kitchen-sink quarter had been expected by analysts and that FleetBoston Financial indeed was providing such a cleanup of its balance sheet. On December 19, 2001, FleetBoston Financial Corp. filed an 8-K with the SEC which contained the following diclosures:

> FLEETBOSTON TO TAKE A SERIES OF ACTIONS TO STRENGTHEN
> BALANCE SHEET
> BOSTON, MA (December 19, 2001)—Recognizing the ongoing economic slowdown, FleetBoston Financial (FBF-NYSE) today announced a series of actions to strengthen the company's balance sheet. These actions will result in an after-tax charge of approximately $650 million ($.62 E.P.S.) to fourth quarter earnings. The Corporation expects to report a net profit of approximately $30 million ($.03 E.P.S.) in the fourth quarter inclusive of these actions and to release complete details of its fourth quarter results on January 16, 2002. "Our financial strength allows us to take actions now that will position FleetBoston to fully realize the benefits of the improved economic conditions we expect to see in the second half of 2002," said Chad Gifford, FleetBoston's president and chief operating officer. "It is our practice to address economic uncertainty up front and we are fortunate to have the financial capacity to take action now." The specific actions and estimated pre-tax charges are summarized as follows:
>
> - —ARGENTINA - A charge of approximately $150 million is being taken on our portfolio of Argentine government securities and loans. This brings to $200 million the total impairment charges taken against the Argentine portfolio this year, of which

$75 million will go to bolster loan loss reserves and $125 million relates to the recently announced government sponsored bond swap program. The Corporation has operated in Argentina for 85 years with great success and strong profitability. Its very experienced management team is well equipped to deal with the financial adjustment that is occurring in that country.

- —PRINCIPAL INVESTING - The Corporation has operated in this business for over 40 years and has generated strong returns over that period. The current environment is unprecedented in the confluence of negative factors affecting the principal investing industry. Write-downs of approximately $475 million will be taken to the carrying value of the portfolio in the fourth quarter, primarily in the technology and telecom sectors. This action follows a review of the portfolio in light of the pronounced weakness that has severely impacted market liquidity and the operating performance of the underlying investments, coupled with our intent to maintain a cautious stance on the economy. The principal investing portfolio of $3.6B is currently carried at a discount of approximately 25% of Fleet's original investment with discounts approaching 50% in the direct technology and telecom portfolio.

- —CREDIT ACTIONS - The current recessionary environment continues to strain a number of our domestic commercial and industrial customers. The Corporation continues to take an aggressive approach to recognizing these pressures and is committed to maintaining its established reserve strength. The Corporation expects to incur incremental credit costs of $175 million to strengthen the loan loss reserve to the $3 billion level and charges of $150 million related to the movement of approximately $350 million of problem credits to accelerated disposition status. During the quarter, write-downs were taken on a number of our larger troubled credits, including a well-publicized energy-related credit. As a result of these actions, the reserve-to-loans ratio is expected to rise to the range of 2.3% to 2.4% at year-end.

- —RESTRUCTURING CHARGE - The Corporation continues to be responsive to the current weak operating environment and wants to ensure that its expense base remains aligned with its revenue expectations, particularly in a weak capital markets environment. Approximately $100 million of charges are being taken to primarily cover severance and related costs for various businesses and is expected to further reduce staff by 700 individuals against our employee base of approximately 55,000 employees. Eugene M. McQuade, FleetBoston's vice chairman and chief financial officer stated: "The strength of our operating earnings as well as capital and reserves in excess of $20 billion afford us ample capacity to take these actions. We expect to end the year with healthy capital ratios of approximately 7.7% for Tier 1 capital and 6.5% for tangible common equity. Our expectation to achieve the analyst consensus estimate of $3.26 for 2002 earnings per share remains intact." Mr. Gifford further commented: "We have great confidence in the underlying strength of our franchise and we draw on that strength in taking these actions. Our greatest priority lies in seizing the potential of our extensive customer base and continuing the growth initiatives underway in our mainstream businesses."

- FleetBoston Financial is the seventh-largest financial holding company in the United States. A $200 billion diversified financial services company, it offers a comprehensive array of innovative financial solutions to 20 million customers in more than 20 countries and territories. FleetBoston Financial is headquartered in Boston and listed on the New York Stock Exchange (NYSE: FBF) and the Boston Stock Exchange (BSE: FBF).

- This release contains forward-looking statements that involve risks and uncertainties that could cause actual results to differ materially from estimates. These risks and uncertainties include, among other things, (1) changes in general political and economic conditions, either domestically or internationally, including the economic effects of the September 11, 2001 terrorist attacks against the United States and the response of the United States to those attacks, the continuing weakness in the Latin American economies, particularly Argentina, and a further deterioration in credit quality, including the resultant effect on the level of the Corporation's nonperforming assets and chargeoffs; (2) interest rate and currency fluctuations, equity and bond market fluctuations and perceptions, including continued weakness in the global capital markets and the impact of such weakness on the Corporation's Principal Investing and other capital markets businesses; (3) changes in the competitive environment for financial services organizations and the Corporation's ability to manage those changes; (4) legislative or regulatory developments, including changes in laws concerning taxes, banking, securities, insurance and other aspects of the financial services industry; (5) technological changes, including the impact of the Internet on the Corporation's businesses; (6) the ability of the Corporation to fully realize expected cost savings and realize those savings within the expected timeframes; and (7) the level of costs related to the integration of acquired businesses. For further information, please refer to the Corporation's reports filed with the SEC. *(Source: 8-K filed on 12/19/01)*

Earlier, the company had issued an 8-K/A that included a press release containing the following related discussion:

FLEETBOSTON REPORTS THIRD QUARTER EARNINGS OF $766 MILLION OR $.70 PER SHARE
COMMON DIVIDEND INCREASED BY 6%

Boston, MA (October 17, 2001)—FleetBoston Financial (FBF-NYSE) today reported third quarter earnings of $766 million, or $.70 per share, compared with $969 million, or $.87 per share in the third quarter of 2000. Earnings from the Corporation's primary capital markets units—Principal Investing, Robertson Stephens, and Quick & Reilly—fell by $239 million or $.22 per share from their level in the third quarter of last year reflecting continued slowness in the capital markets, exacerbated by the tragic events of September 11.

Offsetting these declines were earnings growth from several business lines including Retail Banking, Latin America, and Small Business; higher cash management fees; merger-related cost savings; and expense reductions from the corporate cost containment program. The current quarter's results included a gain on the sale of an equity investment, net of merger-related charges, totaling $60 million ($.05 per share), while the third quarter of 2000 included divestiture gains, net of merger related charges, totaling $59 million ($.05 per share).

Return on assets and return on equity for the quarter were 1.47% and 15.56%, respectively, compared with 1.78% and 21.6% a year ago. For the first nine months of

2001, earnings before strategic charges were $2.2 billion, or $1.96 per share, versus $3.02 billion, or $2.72 per share, in the first nine months of 2000.

FleetBoston also announced today a 6% increase in its quarterly common dividend to $.35 per share for shareholders of record on December 3, 2001.

Terrence Murray, Chairman and Chief Executive Officer of FleetBoston commented, "We have all been affected and, in many ways, transformed by the events of September 11. While Fleet was fortunate to not have lost any of our employees from this tragedy, we nonetheless grieve with the rest of the country over the many lives that were lost, including those of friends, relatives and business associates. During the past few weeks, I've spent quite a bit of time meeting with employees in many of our businesses, including those in and around New York City who were personally affected by the tragedy. It was truly inspiring to see first hand how incredibly well our employees in the area were handling the adversity and we can all learn a valuable lesson from their courage and determination to serve the customer."

Murray continued, "These are certainly difficult times for our economy and corporate America. An economic slowdown was well underway prior to September 11 and has now worsened. For Fleet, the biggest impact has been seen in our capital markets businesses, which continued weak throughout the third quarter. Despite the economy's performance of late, we remain very optimistic that our country will meet the economic challenges that we face and return to a period of growth and prosperity. We also remain enthusiastic about the future of FleetBoston as evidenced by our dividend increase. Our customer service efforts are gaining traction in our consumer businesses and in wholesale banking we are really beginning to leverage our lead relationships. These positive developments, coupled with our expense discipline and balance sheet strength, position us well to capitalize when economic conditions improve."

Chad Gifford, President and Chief Operating Officer said, "The Corporation moved ahead on a number of fronts during the third quarter. In an effort to support our country's financial markets and our shareholders in the wake of September 11, we announced a plan to repurchase up to $4 billion of our stock by December 31, 2002 and began executing on this program immediately. We also continued with our efforts to improve the customer experience. Specifically, we announced plans to open 28 new branches and 23 new ATMs in Massachusetts, while upgrading 27 other branches and ATM locations. In addition, we also opened an Investment Access Center in the MetLife building adjacent to Grand Central Station in New York City. This location not only provides our customers with traditional Fleet and Quick & Reilly products and services but also gives our customers self-service on-line access to their accounts. A milestone was reached with the recent enrollment of our two millionth HomeLink on-line banking customer. Finally, work continued during the third quarter on our announced acquisition of Liberty Financial's Asset Management unit and we expect to close shortly. We remain committed to our top priority of building shareholder value through strengthening our existing business lines and seizing the potential of our extensive customer base. We are intensely focused on execution and customer service-driven revenue growth.

Credit Quality/Balance Sheet

Nonperforming assets were $1.56 billion, or 1.22% of total loans, at September 30, 2001, up 12% from June 30, 2001. The provision for credit losses was $325 million in the current quarter, which matched net chargeoffs. In the third quarter of 2000, the provision was $325 million and net chargeoffs were $321 million. The reserve for credit losses was $2.73 billion at September 30, 2001, representing 2.14% of total loans and leases.

Total assets at September 30, 2001 were $202 billion, compared with $218 billion at September 30, 2000. The decline from a year ago is due, in part, to the sale/run-off of low-margin assets in connection with the Summit merger, and the sale of our mortgage company in June. Stockholders' equity amounted to $20 billion at September 30, 2001, with a common equity to assets ratio of 9.6%.

A detailed financial package containing supplemental information on the third quarter financial results can be found by accessing the Corporation's Web site (http://www.fleet.com). *(Source: 8-K/A filed on 10/17/01)*

The Company filed its 10-Q for the period ended September 30, 2001 on November 14, 2001, which contained the following observations:

Decreases in earnings from the prior year in both the three- and nine-month comparisons resulted from a significant drop in capital markets revenue due to the pronounced fallout experienced in U.S. capital markets which began in the second half of 2000. Declines in current-year revenues reflect the continued slowdown in these markets during 2001. These revenue declines were partly offset by improved results in Retail Banking and International Banking, as well as lower operating expenses resulting from a corporate-wide cost containment program and a drop in revenue-related compensation costs.

Although certain branch and other operations were affected by the September 11 terrorist attacks, and some employees were relocated from their New York locations to alternate sites in New Jersey following the attacks, FleetBoston's overall operations were only modestly impacted, and its consolidated results of operations for the third quarter and its overall financial condition were not materially impacted by these events. These events caused, and may continue to cause, additional weakness in the economy and in general business activities. FleetBoston continues to evaluate the effects of these events on the Corporation's fourth quarter and future results of operations.

Results for the three and nine months ended September 30, 2001 and 2000 included the following:

Three months ended September 30, 2001:

• Gain of $146 million ($91 million after-tax) from the sale of FleetBoston's investment in the NYCE Corporation.
• Summit merger-related costs of $52 million ($31 million after-tax), composed of $35 million of merger integration costs and $17 million of accelerated depreciation of assets to be disposed of at a later date.

Three months ended September 30, 2000:

• Branch divestiture gains of $164 million ($84 million after-tax) associated with the previously disclosed BankBoston merger.
• Merger integration costs of $40 million ($25 million after-tax) incurred in connection with the BankBoston merger.

Nine months ended September 30, 2001:

- Gains of $333 million ($204 million after-tax) from branch divestitures associated with the BankBoston merger and $146 million ($91 million after-tax) from the above-mentioned sale of the investment in the NYCE Corporation.
- Write-downs of $602 million ($370 million after-tax) taken against the carrying value of the Principal Investing portfolio.
- Summit merger-related costs of $863 million ($542 million after-tax), consisting of $463 million ($302 million after-tax) of merger- and restructuring-related charges, $135 million ($82 million after-tax) of merger integration costs and a $265 million ($158 million after-tax) loss from the sale of low-margin securities following the merger.
- Restructuring charges of $79 million ($50 million after-tax) primarily related to a reorganization of capital markets-related businesses.
- An aggregate loss of $428 million ($285 million after-tax) from the sale of the mortgage banking business. *(Source: 10-Q filed for the period ended 9/30/01 on 11/14/01)*

The Consolidated Statements of Income in the quarterly filing are reported in Table 5.10-1.

Table 5.10-1 FleetBoston Financial Corp. Consolidated Statements of Income (Unaudited)

Dollars in Millions (except per share amounts)	Three Months Ended September 30, 2001	Three Months Ended September 30, 2000	Nine Months Ended September 30, 2001	Nine Months Ended September 30, 2000
Interest income:				
Interest and fees on loans and leases	$2,601	$3,323	$8,517	$9,865
Interest on securities and trading assets	446	658	1,536	1,915
Other	302	128	781	508
Total interest income	3,349	4,109	10,834	12,288
Interest expense:				
Deposits of domestic offices	590	817	2,025	2,402
Deposits of international offices	274	332	849	926
Short-term borrowings	243	406	863	1,216
Long-term debt	363	558	1,300	1,535
Other	32	67	130	208
Total interest expense	1,502	2,180	5,167	6,287
Net interest income	1,847	1,929	5,667	6,001
Provision for credit losses	325	325	955	980

Dollars in Millions (except per share amounts)	Three Months Ended September 30, 2001	Three Months Ended September 30, 2000	Nine Months Ended September 30, 2001	Nine Months Ended September 30, 2000
Net interest income after provision for credit losses	1,522	1,604	4,712	5,021
Noninterest income:				
Capital markets revenue	460	752	455	2,632
Banking fees and commissions	406	400	1,201	1,207
Investment services revenue	348	423	1,099	1,399
Credit card revenue	193	186	520	529
Processing-related revenue	68	154	330	467
Gains on branch divestitures	—	164	353	843
Other	135	185	503	475
Total noninterest income	1,610	2,264	4,461	7,552
Noninterest expense:				
Employee compensation and benefits	979	1,178	3,008	3,995
Occupancy and equipment	283	294	847	903
Intangible asset amortization	96	97	294	291
Marketing and public relations	63	82	184	238
Legal and other professional	51	88	182	266
Merger- and restructuring-related charges	17	6	542	68
Loss on sale of mortgage banking business	—	—	428	—
Other	408	545	1,324	1,741
Total noninterest expense	1,897	2,290	6,809	7,502
Income before income taxes	1,235	1,578	2,364	5,071

Dollars in Millions (except per share amounts)	Three Months Ended September 30, 2001	Three Months Ended September 30, 2000	Nine Months Ended September 30, 2001	Nine Months Ended September 30, 2000
Applicable income taxes	469	609	926	2,055
Net income	$ 766	$ 969	$ 969	$ 3,016
Diluted weighted average common shares outstanding (in millions)	1,091.8	1,101.5	1,094.1	1,099.7
Net income applicable to common shares	$ 760	$ 959	$ 1,415	$ 2,987
Basic earnings per share	.70	.89	1.31	2.76
Diluted earnings per share	.70	.87	1.29	2.72
Dividends declared	.33	.30	.99	.90

See accompanying Condensed Notes to Consolidated Financial Statements; Note 6 is reported within this case.
(Source: FleetBoston Financial Corp. 10-Q for quarterly period ended 9/30/01)

NOTE 6. MERGER- AND RESTRUCTURING-RELATED CHARGES

In the first quarter of 2001, FleetBoston recorded aggregate merger- and restructuring-related charges of $487 million in connection with the Summit merger and a restructuring of its capital markets-related businesses. Of the $487 million, $408 million related to Summit and $79 million primarily related to capital markets. The $408 million charge was composed of $73 million of merger-related charges, $322 million of restructuring-related charges, and $13 million of accelerated depreciation of assets to be disposed of at a later date, which resulted from revisions to the estimated useful lives of assets currently in use that will be disposed when the Summit integration has been completed.

In addition to the merger- and restructuring-related charges, FleetBoston incurred $45 million of merger integration costs in the first quarter. These integration costs, which are expensed as incurred, include the costs of converting duplicate computer systems, training and relocation of employees and departments, consolidation of facilities and customer communications. During the second and third quarters of 2001, aggregate costs of $145 million, composed of $55 million and $90 million of additional accelerated depreciation and integration costs, respectively, were recorded.

In 1999, the Corporation recorded $467 million of restructuring charges in connection with the BankBoston merger. Additional information concerning these 1999 charges is included in Note 14 to the Consolidated Financial Statements included in the Corporation's Current Report on Form 8-K dated May 4, 2001. During the second quarter of 2001, $14 million of such charges were reversed, primarily related to severance and facilities accruals which were not fully utilized.

Restructuring-Related Charges

Summit

Of the $322 million restructuring-related charge, $150 million related to personnel, $96 million related to asset write-downs and contract cancellations, $60 million related to facilities and $16 million related to other restructuring expenses.

Personnel-related costs of $150 million included severance to be paid in a lump sum or over a defined period, benefit program changes and outplacement services for approximately 2,700 positions identified during the first quarter for elimination in connection with restructuring, principally as a result of the elimination of duplicate functions within the combined company. During the first nine months of 2001, approximately $89 million of personnel-related benefits were paid and approximately 2,500 employees were terminated and left the Corporation.

Asset write-downs and contract cancellation costs of $96 million related to costs to dispose of duplicate or obsolete equipment and computer software, and penalties incurred to cancel leases and other contracts. During the first nine months of 2001, $20 million of costs were paid and $51 million of write-downs were recorded.

Facilities-related charges of $60 million represented minimum lease payments related to duplicate branch and other facilities. During the first nine months of 2001, $1 million of facilities-related charges were paid and $8 million accrued for such charges, which were not fully utilized, was reversed. Other costs of $16 million included expenses and various other costs incurred to merge the two companies. During the first nine months of 2001, $9 million of other costs were paid.

Capital Markets

Of the $79 million charge, $52 million related to severance to be paid in a lump sum or over a defined period, benefit program changes and outplacement services for approximately 750 positions identified during the first quarter for elimination in connection with the restructuring; $23 million of costs related to future lease obligations and write-downs of capitalized assets; and $4 million of other restructuring expenses. During the first nine months of 2001, approximately 740 employees were terminated and left the Corporation, and $43 million of related benefits were paid.

The following table presents activity in restructuring-related accruals during the nine months ended September 30, 2001.

FleetBoston Financial Corp. Condensed Notes to Consolidated Financial Statements
September 30, 2001

Restructuring Accrual Activity

	Summit & Capital Markets	BankBoston
Balance at December 31, 2000	$ —	$146
Restructuring accrual	401	—
Restructuring reversal	(8)	(14)
Cash payments	(162)	(104)
Noncash write-downs	(51)	—
Balance at September 30, 2001	$180	$28

The $104 million of cash payments included in the table above related to the BankBoston merger consisted of $89 million of personnel benefits, $14 million in facilities charges, and $1 million of other restructuring expenses. The remaining accrual at September 30, 2001 is composed primarily of expected cash outlays related to severance and facilities obligations. *(Source: FleetBoston Financial Corp. 10-Q for quarterly period ended 9/30/01)*

The assets reported on the Consolidated Balance Sheets in the quarterly filing are itemized in Table 5.10-2.

Table 5.10-2   Excerpt from FleetBoston Financial Corp. Consolidated Balance Sheets (Unaudited)

Dollars in Millions, Except per Share Amounts	*September 30, 2001*	*December 31, 2000*
Assets		
Cash, due from banks and interest-bearing deposits	$ 15,001	$ 12,826
Federal funds sold and securities purchased under agreements to resell	7,500	1,959
Trading assets	6,663	7,108
Mortgages held for sale	539	2,138
Securities (market value: $22,255 and $34,932)	22,251	34,964
Loans and leases	127,820	134,834
Reserve for credit losses	(2,734)	(2,709)
Net loans and leases	125,086	132,125
Due from brokers/dealers	4,059	2,987
Premises and equipment	2,896	2,867
Mortgage servicing rights	—	2,695
Intangible assets	4,198	4,557
Other assets	13,669	14,859
Total assets	$201,862	$219,085

(Source: FleetBoston Financial Corp. 10-Q for quarterly period ended 9/30/01)

The derivation of net cash flow provided by operating activities in the FleetBoston Financial Corporation Consolidated Statements of Cash Flows included the line items (in millions): "Depreciation and amortization of premises and equipment" $445 and $437, "Merger- and restructuring-related charges" of $542 and $68, and "Write-downs of principal investing investments" in the amount of $602 and —, for the nine months ended September 30, 2001 and 2000, respectively.

Requirement A: Impairment of Assets and Write-downs

1. What accounting guidance applies to the determination of whether an asset is impaired? What guidance applies to quantifying the amount of a write-down, when it is deemed to be appropriate? Does the nature of the asset being written down influence such adjustments? How?

2. Using the disclosures by FleetBoston, write an executive summary as to the nature of the write-downs taken, and the likely implications of these actions for future periods. Provide the basis for your expectations in specific terms, detailing the types of accounts affected and estimated amounts. Support your position with appropriate citations from FARS.

Requirement B: Strategy-Related Considerations

Significant effects of write-offs in a single quarter have prompted the business press to dub such practices as "Rumpelstilzchen accounting" (i.e., turning future "straw" into "gold" by hitting current year's income with a large write-down) or "big bath accounting."

1. What are the circumstances in which company management may be more likely to take a write-down?
2. Should such a declaration be presumed to be a "big bath"? What differentiates the occasional write-off from a management strategy of a "big bath"?
3. Do you believe such practices result in effective financial reporting? Explain.
4. Access Staff Accounting Bulletin (SAB) 100 at sec.gov. Also find the article in the *Wall Street Journal* published August 28, 2006 (p. C1) that reports on how an international company's profit margin is affected by write-downs. In light of such regulation and media coverage, do you view accounting developments to date as leading to fewer or more "big baths"?

Directed Self-Study

Access sec.gov and describe what has happened to FleetBoston Financial Corporation since the events described in this case. What are the ramifications of what you find?

Key Terms and Glossary

big bath large write-downs of assets

capital market transactions hypothesis drawn from the theory that investors' perceptions of a firm are of importance to the corporate managers because they expect to issue public debt or equity or to make an acquisition of another company, especially when the latter involves a stock transaction

corporate control hypothesis is a theory motivated by empirical evidence that both boards of directors and investors hold managers accountable for current stock performance

impairment "the condition that exists when the carrying amount of a long-lived asset (asset group) exceeds its fair value" (FAS 144, par. 7)

"lemons" problem information problem that arises from differences in information and conflicts in the incentives between managers and capital providers; signaling is viewed as one approach to addressing the challenge of asymmetric information, whereby managers use voluntary disclosure practices and similar tools to inform the market participants of their expectations and accomplishments to date

Further Readings

Aboody, D., M. E. Barth, and R. Kasznik. 1999. "Revaluations of fixed assets and future firm performance." *Journal of Accounting and Economics* (26), pp. 149–178.

Ambrosini, Dana. 2001. "FleetBoston Financial cutting 700 jobs out of 55,000 workforce." *Connecticut Post.* Knight-Ridder/Tribune Business News (December 21). PITEM01355017, Infotrac Business Index.

Bartov, E. 1993. "The timing of asset sales and earnings manipulation." *Accounting Review* (68), pp. 840–855.

Beneish, M. D. 1999. "Incentives and penalties related to earnings overstatements that violate GAAP." *Accounting Review* (74), pp. 425–457.

Brown, P. D., H. Y. Izan, and A. L. Loh. 1992. "Fixed asset revaluations and managerial incentives." *Abacus* (28), pp. 36–57.

Dillon, G. J. 1979. "Corporate asset revaluations, 1925–1934." *Accounting Historians Journal* (6), pp. 1–15.

Easton, P. D., P. H. Eddey, and T. S. Harris 1993. "An investigation of revaluations of tangible long-lived assets." *Journal of Accounting Research* (31), pp. 1–38.

Gaver, J., and K. Gaver. 1998. "The relation between nonrecurring accounting transactions and CEO cash compensation." *Accounting Review* (73), pp. 235–253.

Gigler, F. 1994. "Self-enforcing voluntary disclosures." *Journal of Accounting Research* (32), pp. 224–241.

Healy, Paul. 1985. "The effect of bonus schemes on accounting decisions." *Journal of Accounting and Economics* (7, January 3), pp. 85–107.

Healy, Paul M., and Krishna G. Palepu. 2001. "Information asymmetry, corporate disclosure, and the capital markets: A review of the empirical disclosure literature." *Journal of Accounting and Economics* (31), pp. 405–440.

Holthausen, R. W., Larcker, D. F., and Sloan, R. G. 1995. "Annual bonus schemes and the manipulation of earnings." *Journal of Accounting and Economics* (19), pp. 29–74.

Johnston, D., and D. A. Jones. 2006. "How does accounting fit into a firm's political strategy?" *Journal of Accounting and Public Policy* (25, 2, March/April), pp. 195–228.

"Numbers game: Big bath? Or a little one." 1986. *Forbes* (October 6).

Ohlson, J. A. 1995. "Earnings, book values, and dividends in security valuation." *Contemporary Accounting Research* (11), pp. 161–182.

Rees, L., S. Gill, and R. Gore. 1996. "An investigation of asset write-downs and concurrent abnormal accruals." *Journal of Accounting Research* (34, Supplement), pp. 157–169.

Riedl, Edward J. 2004. "An examination of long-lived asset impairments." *Accounting Review* (79, 3, July), pp. 823–852.

Saito, S. 1983. "Asset revaluations and cost basis: Capital revaluation in corporate financial reports." *Accounting Historians Journal* (10), pp. 1–23.

SEC. 2004. Speech by staff member. Stephen M. Cutler, [Director, Division of Enforcement, U.S. Securities and Exchange Commission] Chicago, April 29. (24th Annual Ray Garrett Jr. Corporate & Securities Law Institute on the subject matter of how the SEC determines penalties.) Available at: http://www.sec.gov/news/speech/spch042904smc.htm.

SEC. 2003. Release No. 33-8216. *Filing Guidance Related to Conditions for Use of Non-GAAP Financial Measures; and Insider Trades During Pension Fund Blackout Periods.* Release Nos: 34-47583; IC-25983; FR-69; File Nos. S7-43-02 and S7-44-02 (March 28).

SEC. [Release No. 33-8040; 34-45149; FR-60]. 2001. Action: *Cautionary Advice Regarding Disclosure about Critical Accounting Policies* (December 12). Available at: http://www.sec.gov/rules/other/33-8040.htm).

SEC. 2000. Speech by SEC Chairman Arthur Levitt "The Public's Profession." (October 24). Available at: http://www.sec.gov/news/speech/spch410.htm

Skinner, D. 1994. "Why firms voluntarily disclose bad news." *Journal of Accounting Research* (32), pp. 38–61.

Strong, J., and J. Meyer. 1987. "Asset write-downs: Managerial incentives and security returns." *Journal of Finance* (42), pp. 643–661.

Walker, R. G. 1992. "The SEC's ban on upward asset revaluations and the disclosure of current values." *Abacus* (28), pp. 3–35.

Weberman, Ben. 1986. "Rumpelstilzchen accounting." *Forbes* (February 24), pp. 30–31.

Zijl, Tony van, and Geoffrey Whittington. 2006. "Deprival value and fair value: A reinterpretation and a reconciliation." *Accounting and Business Research* (36, 2), pp. 121–130.

Far better an approximate answer to the right question, is often vague, than an exact answer to the wrong question, which can always be made precise.

—John Tukey

[Source: Cited by George W. Downs and Patrick D. Larkey, <u>The Search for Government Efficiency: From Hubris to Helplessness</u> (Philadelphia: Temple University Press, 1986), p. 95]

CASE 11

Financial Instruments and Hedging: Measurement Challenges

On November 8, 2001, Enron Corp. filed an 8-K. Access that filing from sec.gov and read through its contents. The 8-K filing of November 8, 2001 by Enron Corp. also includes a press release dated November 8, 2001 regarding related party and off-balance sheet transactions and restatement of earnings. Review the content of that press release.

Moving backwards in time, consider a sample of the disclosures found in the year-end 10-K filing by Enron Corp. for 2000.

> In 2000 and 1999, Enron entered into various transactions with related parties, which resulted in an exchange of assets and an increase in common stock of $171 million in 2000. See Note 16.
>
> In 2000, a partnership in which Enron was a limited partner made a liquidating distribution to Enron resulting in a non-cash increase in current assets of $220 million, a decrease of $20 million in non-current assets and an increase in current liabilities of $160 million. . . .

9 UNCONSOLIDATED EQUITY AFFILIATES

Enron's investment in and advances to unconsolidated affiliates which are accounted for by the equity method is as follows:

(In millions)	Net Voting Interest(a)	December 31, 2000	1999
Azurix Corp.	34%	$ 325	$ 762
Bridgeline Holdings	40%	229	—
Citrus Corp.	50%	530	480
Dabhol Power Company	50%	693	466
Joint Energy Development Investments L.P. (JEDI)(b)	50%	399	211
Joint Energy Development Investments II L.P. (JEDI II)(b)	50%	220	162
SK - Enron Co. Ltd.	50%	258	269
Transportadora de Gas del Sur S.A.	35%	479	452
Whitewing Associates, L.P.(b)	50%	558	662
Other		1,603	1,572
		$5,294(c)	$5,036(c)

(a) Certain investments have income sharing ratios which differ from Enron's voting interests.

(b) JEDI and JEDI II account for their investments at fair value. Whitewing accounts for certain of its investments at fair value. These affiliates held fair value investments totaling $1,823 million and $1,128 million, respectively, at December 31, 2000 and 1999.

(c) At December 31, 2000 and 1999, the unamortized excess of Enron's investment in unconsolidated affiliates was $182 million and $179 million, respectively, which is being amortized over the expected lives of the investments.

Enron's equity in earnings (losses) of unconsolidated equity affiliates is as follows:

(In millions)	2000	1999	1998
Azurix Corp.(a)	$(428)	$ 23	$ 6
Citrus Corp.	50	25	23
Dabhol Power Company	51	30	—
Joint Energy Development Investments L.P.	197	11	(45)
Joint Energy Development Investments II, L.P.	58	92	(4)
TNPC, Inc. (The New Power Company)	(60)	—	—
Transportadora de Gas del Sur S.A.	38	32	36
Whitewing Associates, L.P.	58	9	—
Other	123	87	81
	$ 87	$ 309	$ 97

(a) During the fourth quarter of 2000, Azurix Corp. (Azurix) impaired the carrying value of its Argentine assets, resulting in a charge of approximately $470 million. Enron's portion of the charge was $326 million.

Summarized combined financial information of Enron's unconsolidated affiliates is presented below:

December 31, (In millions) Balance sheet	2000	1999
Current assets(a)	$ 5,884	$ 3,168
Property, plant and equipment, net	14,786	14,356
Other noncurrent assets	13,485	9,459
Current liabilities(a)	4,739	4,401
Long-term debt(a)	9,717	8,486
Other noncurrent liabilities	6,148	2,402
Owners' equity	13,551	11,694

(a) Includes $410 million and $327 million receivable from Enron and $302 million and $84 million payable to Enron at December 31, 2000 and 1999, respectively.

(In millions) Income statement(a)	2000	1999	1998
Operating revenues	$15,903	$11,568	$8,508
Operating expenses	14,710	9,449	7,244
Net income	586	1,857	142
Distributions paid to Enron	137	482	87

(a) Enron recognized revenues from transactions with unconsolidated equity affiliates of $510 million in 2000, $674 million in 1999 and $563 million in 1998.

In 2000 and 1999, Enron sold approximately $632 million and $192 million, respectively, of merchant investments and other assets to Whitewing. Enron recognized no gains or losses in connection with these transactions. Additionally, in 2000, ECT Merchant Investments Corp., a wholly-owned Enron subsidiary, contributed two pools of merchant investments to a limited partnership that is a subsidiary of Enron. Subsequent to the contributions, the partnership issued partnership interests representing 100% of the beneficial, economic interests in the two asset pools, and such interests were sold for a total of $545 million to a limited liability company that is a subsidiary of Whitewing. See Note 3. These entities are separate legal entities from Enron and have separate assets and liabilities. In 2000 and 1999, the Related Party, as described in Note 16, contributed $33 million and $15 million, respectively, of equity to Whitewing. In 2000, Whitewing contributed $7.1 million to a partnership formed by Enron, Whitewing and a third party. Subsequently, Enron sold a portion of its interest in the partnership through a securitization. See Note 3.

In 2000, The New Power Company sold warrants convertible into common stock of The New Power Company for $50 million to the Related Party (described in Note 16).

From time to time, Enron has entered into various administrative service, management, construction, supply and operating agreements with its unconsolidated equity affiliates. Enron's management believes that its existing agreements and transactions are reasonable compared to those which could have been obtained from third parties. . . .

Derivative Instruments. At December 31, 2000, Enron had derivative instruments (excluding amounts disclosed in Note 10) on 54.8 million shares of Enron common stock, of which approximately 12 million shares are with JEDI and 22.5 million shares are with related parties (see Note 16), at an average price of $67.92 per share on which Enron was a fixed price payor. Shares potentially deliverable to counterparties under the contracts are assumed to be outstanding in calculating diluted earnings per share unless they are antidilutive. At December 31, 2000, there were outstanding non-employee options to purchase 6.4 million shares of Enron common stock at an exercise price of $19.59 per share. . . .

16 RELATED PARTY TRANSACTIONS

In 2000 and 1999, Enron entered into transactions with limited partnerships (the Related Party) whose general partner's managing member is a senior officer of Enron. The limited partners of the Related Party are unrelated to Enron. Management believes that the terms of the transactions with the Related Party were reasonable compared to those which could have been negotiated with unrelated third parties.

In 2000, Enron entered into transactions with the Related Party to hedge certain merchant investments and other assets. As part of the transactions, Enron (i) contributed to newly-formed entities (the Entities) assets valued at approximately $1.2 billion, including $150 million in Enron notes payable, 3.7 million restricted shares of outstanding Enron common stock and the right to receive up to 18.0 million shares of outstanding Enron common stock in March 2003 (subject to certain conditions) and (ii) transferred to the Entities assets valued at approximately $309 million, including a $50 million note payable and an investment in an entity that indirectly holds warrants convertible into common stock of an Enron equity method investee. In return, Enron received economic interests in the Entities, $309 million in notes receivable, of which $259 million is recorded at Enron's carryover basis of zero, and a special distribution from the Entities in the form of $1.2 billion in notes receivable, subject to changes in the principal for amounts payable by Enron in connection with the execution of additional derivative instruments. Cash in these Entities of $172.6 million is invested in Enron demand notes. In addition, Enron paid $123 million to purchase share-settled options from the Entities on 21.7 million shares of Enron common stock. The Entities paid Enron $10.7 million to terminate the share-settled options on 14.6 million shares of Enron common stock outstanding. In late 2000, Enron entered into share-settled collar arrangements with the Entities on 15.4 million shares of Enron common stock. Such arrangements will be accounted for as equity transactions when settled.

In 2000, Enron entered into derivative transactions with the Entities with a combined notional amount of approximately $2.1 billion to hedge certain merchant investments and other assets. Enron's notes receivable balance was reduced by $36 million as a result of premiums owed on derivative transactions. Enron recognized revenues of approximately $500 million related to the subsequent change in the market value of these derivatives, which offset market value changes of certain merchant investments and price risk management activities. In addition, Enron recognized $44.5 million and $14.1 million of interest income and interest expense, respectively, on the notes receivable from and payable to the Entities.

In 1999, Enron entered into a series of transactions involving a third party and the Related Party. The effect of the transactions was (i) Enron and the third party amended certain forward contracts to purchase shares of Enron common stock, resulting in Enron having forward contracts to purchase Enron common shares at the market price on that day, (ii) the Related Party received 6.8 million shares of Enron common stock subject to certain restrictions and (iii) Enron received a note receivable, which was repaid in December 1999, and certain financial instruments hedging an investment held by Enron. Enron recorded the assets received and equity issued at estimated fair value. In connection with the transactions, the Related Party agreed that the senior officer of Enron would have no pecuniary interest in such Enron common shares and would be restricted from voting on matters related to such shares. In 2000, Enron and the Related Party entered into an agreement to terminate certain financial instruments that had been entered into during 1999. In connection with this agreement, Enron received approximately 3.1 million shares of Enron common stock held by the Related Party. A put option, which was originally entered into in the first quarter of 2000 and gave the Related Party the right to sell shares of Enron common stock to Enron at a strike price of $71.31 per share, was terminated under this agreement. In return, Enron paid approximately $26.8 million to the Related Party.

In 2000, Enron sold a portion of its dark fiber inventory to the Related Party in exchange for $30 million cash and a $70 million note receivable that was subsequently repaid. Enron recognized gross margin of $67 million on the sale.

In 2000, the Related Party acquired, through securitizations, approximately $35 million of merchant investments from Enron. In addition, Enron and the Related Party formed partnerships in which Enron contributed cash and assets and the Related Party contributed $17.5 million in cash. Subsequently, Enron sold a portion of its interests in the partnerships through securitizations. See Note 3. Also, Enron contributed a put option to a trust in which the Related Party and Whitewing hold equity and debt interests. At December 31, 2000, the fair value of the put option was a $36 million loss to Enron.

In 1999, the Related Party acquired approximately $371 million, merchant assets and investments and other assets from Enron. Enron recognized pre-tax gains of approximately $16 million related to these transactions. The Related Party also entered into an agreement to acquire Enron's interests in an unconsolidated equity affiliate for approximately $34 million. . . .

18 ACCOUNTING PRONOUNCEMENTS. . .

Recently Issued Accounting Pronouncements. In 1998, the Financial Accounting Standards Board (FASB) issued SFAS No. 133, "Accounting for Derivative Instruments and Hedging Activities," which was subsequently amended by SFAS No. 137 and SFAS No. 138. SFAS No. 133 must be applied to all derivative instruments and certain derivative instruments embedded in hybrid instruments and requires that such instruments be recorded in the balance sheet either as an asset or liability measured at its fair value through earnings, with special accounting allowed for certain qualifying hedges. Enron will adopt SFAS No. 133 as of January 1, 2001. Due to the adoption of SFAS No. 133, Enron will recognize an after-tax non-cash loss of approximately $5 million in earnings and an after-tax non-cash gain in "Other Comprehensive Income," a component of shareholders' equity, of approximately $22 million from the cumulative effect of a change in accounting principle. Enron will also reclassify $532 million from "Long-Term Debt" to "Other Liabilities" due to the adoption.

The total impact of Enron's adoption of SFAS No. 133 on earnings and on "Other Comprehensive Income" is dependent upon certain pending interpretations, which are currently under consideration, including those related to "normal purchases and normal sales" and inflation escalators included in certain contract payment provisions. The interpretations of these issues, and others, are currently under consideration by the FASB. While the ultimate conclusions reached on interpretations being considered by the FASB could impact the effects of Enron's adoption of SFAS No. 133, Enron does not believe that such conclusions would have a material effect on its current estimate of the impact of adoption. *(Source: Enron Corp. 10-K for 12/31/00, filed on 4/2/01)*

Requirement A: The Relationship of GAAP to Issues in the Restatement

1. Identify the guidance upon which Enron Corp. relies in its restatement. Using FARS, be specific as to the aspect of each pronouncement that ties to the key determinant of each restatement item.
2. The media noted that Enron's disclosures in mid-October first indicated a reduction in shareholder equity of $1.2 billion because the corporation had decided to unwind certain transactions with some limited partnerships with which it had done business. However, the elaboration on the situation led to the disclosure that the original accounting for the transactions was not in accordance with GAAP. The media has pointed out that the early 2000 issuance by Enron of shares of its own common stock to four "special-purpose entities" (SPEs) in exchange for a notes receivable would not qualify as an issuance of stock until cash was received. Explain why this is the case.
3. The media has discussed Enron Corp., pre-restatement, as being innovative in tailoring contracts, making new positions valued at over $4 billion each day. The point has been made that trading losses were not the focus of the bad news from the corporation, but rather that the erosion of the equity base of Enron Corp. through the restatement became the issue. Fears among trading partners arose as to Enron Corp.'s ability to finance its trading activity, since counterparties are expected to look to equity base for assurance. The reported rating downgrades—as they reached junk status, due to their below investment grade levels' effects on various transactions—were expected to force Enron to produce hundreds of millions of dollars in cash or stock. An estimated $3.9B of debt could come due, according to various media discussions, and Enron Corp. was not viewed as sufficiently liquid to meet such demands. Somewhat expected was the 8-K filed by Enron Corp., on December 2, 2001.

> ENRON FILES VOLUNTARY PETITIONS FOR CHAPTER 11
> REORGANIZATION; SUES DYNEGY FOR BREACH OF CONTRACT, SEEKING
> DAMAGES OF AT LEAST $10 BILLION
>
> FOR IMMEDIATE RELEASE: Sunday, December 2, 2001
> - Proceeds of Lawsuit Would Benefit Enron's Creditors
> - Company in Active Discussions to Receive Credit Support For, Recapitalize and Revitalize Its North American Wholesale Energy Trading Operations Under New Ownership Structure
> - Enron Will Downsize Operations and Continue Sales of Non-Core Assets
>
> HOUSTON—Enron Corp. (NYSE: ENE) announced today that it along with certain of its subsidiaries have filed voluntary petitions for Chapter 11 reorganization with the U.S. Bankruptcy Court for the Southern District of New York. As part of the reorganization process, Enron also filed suit against Dynegy Inc. (NYSE: DYN) in the same court, alleging breach of contract in connection with Dynegy's wrongful termination of its proposed merger with Enron and seeking damages of at least $10 billion. Enron's lawsuit also seeks the court's declaration that Dynegy is not entitled to exercise its option to

acquire an Enron subsidiary that indirectly owns Northern Natural Gas Pipeline. Proceeds from the lawsuit would benefit Enron's creditors.

In a related development aimed at preserving value in its North American wholesale energy trading business, Enron said that it is in active discussions with various leading financial institutions to provide credit support for, recapitalize and revitalize that business under a new ownership structure. It is anticipated that Enron would provide the new entity with traders, back office capabilities and technology from Enron's North American wholesale energy business, and that the new entity would conduct counterparty transactions through EnronOnline, the company's existing energy trading platform. Any such arrangement would be subject to the approval of the Bankruptcy Court.

In connection with the company's Chapter 11 filings, Enron is in active discussions with leading financial institutions for debtor-in-possession (DIP) financing and expects to complete these discussions shortly. Upon the completion and court approval of these arrangements, the new funding will be available immediately on an interim basis to supplement Enron's existing capital and help the company fulfill obligations associated with operating its business, including its employee payroll and payments to vendors for goods and services provided on or after today's filing.

Filings for Chapter 11 reorganization have been made for a total of 14 affiliated entities, including Enron Corp.; Enron North America Corp., the company's wholesale energy trading business; Enron Energy Services, the company's retail energy marketing operations; Enron Transportation Services, the holding company for Enron's pipeline operations; Enron Broadband Services, the company's bandwidth trading operation; and Enron Metals & Commodity Corp.

Enron-related entities not included in the Chapter 11 filing are not affected by the filing. These non-filing entities include Northern Natural Gas Pipeline, Transwestern Pipeline, Florida Gas Transmission, EOTT, Portland General Electric and numerous other Enron international entities.

To conserve capital, Enron will implement a comprehensive cost-saving program that will include substantial workforce reductions. These workforce reductions primarily will affect the company's operations in Houston, where Enron currently employs approximately 7,500 people.

In addition, the company will continue its accelerated program to divest or wind down non-core assets and operations. Details of the units to be affected will be communicated shortly.

The Dynegy Lawsuit

In its lawsuit filed today in U.S. Bankruptcy Court in New York, Enron alleges, among other things, that Dynegy breached its Merger Agreement with Enron by terminating the agreement when it had no contractual right to do so; and that Dynegy has no right to exercise its option to acquire the entity that indirectly owns the Northern Natural Gas pipeline because that option can only be triggered by a valid termination of the Merger Agreement.

The Chapter 11 Filings

In conjunction with today's petitions for Chapter 11 reorganization, Enron will ask the Bankruptcy Court to consider a variety of "first day motions" to support its employees, vendors, trading counterparties, customers and other constituents. These include motions seeking court permission to continue payments for employee payroll and health benefits;

obtain interim financing authority and maintain cash management programs; and retain legal, financial and other professionals to support the company's reorganization actions. In accordance with applicable law and court orders, vendors and suppliers who provided goods or services to Enron Corp. or the subsidiaries that have filed for Chapter 11 protection before today's filing may have pre-petition claims, which will be frozen pending court authorization of payment or consummation of a plan of reorganization.

The Wholesale Energy Trading Business

The discussions currently underway with various leading financial institutions are aimed at obtaining credit support for, recapitalizing and revitalizing Enron's North American wholesale energy trading operations under a new ownership structure in which Enron would continue to have a significant ownership interest.

"If these discussions are successful, they could result in the creation of a new trading entity with a strong and unencumbered balance sheet, the industry's finest trading team, and its leading technology platform, all backed by one or more of the world's leading financial institutions," said Greg Whalley, Enron president and chief operating officer. "We understand that it may take time for counterparties to resume normal trading levels with this entity, but we are confident that this business can be put back on a solid footing. Obviously, our potential partners share our confidence or they would not be at the table with us. We intend to take steps to retain employees who are key to the future success of our wholesale energy trading business and to regain the support and confidence of its trading counterparties."

Comment by Ken Lay

"From an operational standpoint, our energy businesses—including our pipelines and utilities—are conducting normal operations and will continue to do so, " said Kenneth L. Lay, chairman and CEO of Enron. "While uncertainty during the past few weeks has severely impacted the market's confidence in Enron and its trading operations, we are taking the steps announced today to help preserve capital, stabilize our businesses, restore the confidence of our trading counterparties, and enhance our ability to pay our creditors."

Enron's principal legal advisor with regard to the proposed merger with Dynegy, Enron's Chapter 11 filings, the Dynegy lawsuit, and related matters is Weil, Gotshal & Manges LLP. Enron's principal financial advisor with regard to its financial restructuring is The Blackstone Group.

About Enron Corp.

Enron Corp. markets electricity and natural gas, delivers energy and other physical commodities, and provides financial and risk management services to customers around the world. Enron's Internet address is www.enron.com.

Forward-looking Statements

This press release contains statements that are forward-looking within the meaning of Section 27A of the Securities Act of 1933 and Section 21E of the Securities Exchange Act of 1934. Investors are cautioned that any such forward-looking statements are not guarantees of future performance and that actual results could differ materially as a result of known and unknown risks and uncertainties, including: various regulatory issues, the outcome of the Chapter 11 process, the outcome of the litigation discussed above, the outcome of the discussions referred to above, general economic conditions, future trends, and other risks, uncertainties and factors disclosed in the Company's most recent reports on Forms 10-K, 10-Q and 8-K filed with the Securities and Exchange Commission.

(Source: 8-K filed by Enron Corp. on 12/2/01)

a. What is meant by the term "counterparty"?

b. Why would you expect counterparties to care about the equity of a company such as Enron?

c. What is meant by "unwinding," and how does this relate to the Enron Corp.'s filing of Chapter 11, if at all?

d. The partnerships attracting attention in the restatement were involved with derivative and hedging transactions. What is it about such transactions that makes the creation of partnerships as discussed in the 10-K of 2000 and in subsequent disclosures desirable? Do unique accounting implications for the recording of financial instrument and hedging transactions arise in this case setting? Explain.

e. The media has pointed out that a decade ago, 80 percent of Enron's revenues came from the regulated gas-pipeline business, and that by 2000, around 95 percent of its revenues and more than 80 percent of its profits came from trading energy and both buying and selling stakes in energy producers. Commodities trading in gas in 1989, moved to electrons in 1994, and to bandwidth in 1999. Pulp, paper, plastics, metal, and transportation were among its trading operations. Enron traded interest rates, credit risks, and even weather. EnronOnline's trading floor has been characterized as a sophisticated dot.com, engaged in commodity barter and arbitrage. At one point, Enron was trading at 55 times its earnings. Do these observations influence your analysis of the risk situation, both historical and future for Enron Corp. How?

f. In the 10-K disclosure on new accounting developments, mention is made of pending interpretations by the Financial Accounting Standards Board. Is this commonplace? Why or why not? What does it suggest about the accounting for derivatives and hedging? Explain.

Requirement B: Strategy-Related Considerations

The media has raised issues about the corporate governance structure and decisions made with regard to related party transactions by the Board of Directors. It has been alleged that there was insufficient transparency about potential conflicts of interest. The very idea that dealings with private partnerships run by its own officers may have created half of pretax earnings created questions as to the quality of earnings.

1. Why would a Board of Directors authorize transactions with a related party?
2. Did the Enron Board of Directors create any control structure relative to these transactions?
3. In the wake of the developments detailed in this case, and thereafter, how would you evaluate the actions of the directors?

Directed Self-Study

Many credit the Enron events as calling for particular attention to financial accounting and reporting for derivative instruments and special-purpose entities. Identify the standards that have been issued following the 2001 time frame that address issues involved in the debacle. What term has displaced "special-purpose entities" and why? [Go to the FARS Menu, click on Original Pronouncements, and then click on Statements of Financial Accounting Standards. Scroll down and click on FAS 133 to determine its issue date. That can be a reference point for exploring the evolution of standards. Open FASB-OP (amended) and do a query on the term *special-purpose entit** to assist in identifying relevant guidance. Be certain to consider all types of standards; remember to access the EITF infobase for a complete search.]

An Oxymoron: "Open Secrets"

The January 8, 2007 issue of the *New Yorker* published an article by Malcolm Gladwell entitled "Open Secrets – Enron, intelligence, and the perils of too much information." Read this article and prepare a position paper of your views on the disclosure practices of Enron, the role of GAAP and regulation, and the events since 2001 related to Enron. Also comment on the set of events that have unfolded for Arthur Andersen and its clients, including the verdict first received and that received on appeal. Be prepared to discuss your position.

Key Terms and Glossary

basis swaps "are derivative instruments that are used to modify the receipts or payments associated with a recognized, variable-rate asset or liability from one variable amount to another variable amount. They do not eliminate the variability of cash flows; instead, they change the basis or index of variability" (FAS 133, par. 391).

call options (or put options) on debt instruments can accelerate the repayment of principal on a debt instrument

contractually specified servicing fees "All amounts that, per contract, are due to the servicer in exchange for servicing the financial asset and would no longer be received by a servicer if the beneficial owners of the serviced assets (or their trustees or agents) were to exercise their actual or potential authority under the contract to shift the servicing to another servicer. Depending on the servicing contract, those fees may include some or all of the difference between the interest rate collectible on the asset being serviced and the rate to be paid to the beneficial owners of those assets" (FAS 140, par. 364).

credit risk the risk that counterparty will not pay what is owed (this can be reduced through use of exchange-traded futures, since the risk becomes distributed throughout the exchange, whereas in a contract, a counterparty's default or insolvency will result in delay or nonreceipt of the obligation); the risk of counterparty default is said to be more difficult to evaluate when it applies further into the future. The result of this difference in timing of payments is that the credit risk generally is greater for currency forwards than it is judged to be for rate swaps. Current credit risk of an interest rate swap is set at its replacement cost. Future credit risk rises and falls in proportion to the fluctuation in the instruments' values. A dome-shaped risk curve is typical, rising from origination and falling toward expiration. The idea underlying this shape is that at origination,

prevailing market price, a forecasted transaction does not give an entity any present rights to future benefits or a present obligation for future sacrifices" (FAS 133, par. 540).

forward-type derivative obligates one party to buy and a counterparty to sell something (i.e., a financial instrument, foreign currency, or commodity) at a future date at an agreed-on price

legal risk recognizes the possibility of legal responsibilities being altered due to legislative action; since derivatives markets are international, counterparties to the same contract may be expected to have different legal responsibilities toward one another, especially in the case of bankruptcy; this is more threatening due to the fact that many laws governing the over-the-counter (OTC) securities were written prior to the advent of OTC derivatives. In the late 1980s, the London borough of Hammersmith and Fulhan used interest-rate swaps to speculate on interest rates' direction, earning superior returns from volatile derivatives until interest turned against them. At that point, with big losses faced, the local officials declared that they were not allowed to invest in swaps and therefore should not have to bear the losses. The reality of legal risks was highlighted in 1990 when Britain's highest court, the House of Lords in the United Kingdom ruled for the municipalities, instantly transferring more than $150 million in losses from more than 70 local governments to the dealers. When the House of Lords nullified swap contracts that the municipality of Hammersmith and Fulham had opened, this action was reported to have destroyed contracts between 130 government entities and 75 of the largest banks in the world. Over half of all the realized derivative losses in 1991 were a direct result of this action by the House of Lords.

LIBOR swap rate "the fixed rate on a single-currency, constant-notional interest rate swap that has its floating-rate leg referenced to the London Interbank

interest rate uncertainty is an increasing function of the length of the forecast. Then, as time passes, the contract matures and fewer future payments remain at risk. Hence, the dome shape emerges. In contrast, the currency risk profiles are said to increase steadily, since the primary cash flow arises at the contract's end. Net arrangements and master agreements, increasingly common, help reduce credit risk. Regulators also have an influence on credit risk. As an example, the Central Banks of several countries including the U.S. Federal Reserve are on record warning that controls are essential before increasing credit. If global standards and policies emerge, the cooperation will no doubt lead to some reduction in both legal and settlement risks.

currency-sharing agreements divide foreign currency risk between two counterparties who may have long-term contracting arrangements, such as selling a component between manufacturers located in two different countries. Issues of whether to price in U.S. dollars or, for example, deutsche marks are common. The resolution can matter substantially in terms of the implications of foreign currency fluctuations. By sharing such risks, both parties effectively reduce risks.

derivative instrument "is a financial instrument or other contract with all three of the following characteristics:

    a. It has (1) one or more underlyings and (2) one or more notional amounts. . . or payment provisions or both. Those terms determine the amount of the settlement or settlements, and, in some cases, whether or not a settlement is required. . . .

    b. It requires no initial net investment or an initial net investment that is smaller than would be required for other types of contracts that would be expected to have a similar response to changes in market factors.

    c. Its terms require or permit net settlement, it can readily be settled net by a means outside the contract, or it provides for delivery of an asset that puts the recipient in a position not substantially different from net settlement" (FAS 133, par. 6).

derivatives transaction is a contract whose value depends on (or derives from) the value of an underlying asset, reference rate, or index.

embedded call "A call option held by the issuer of a financial instrument that is part of and trades with the underlying instrument. For example, a bond may allow the issuer to call it by posting a public notice well before its stated maturity that asks the current holder to submit it for early redemption and provides that interest ceases to accrue on the bond after the early redemption date. Rather than being an

Offered Rate (LIBOR) with no additional spread over LIBOR on that floating-rate leg. That fixed rate is the derived rate that would result in the swap having a zero fair value at inception because the present value of fixed cash flows, based on that rate, equate to the present value of the floating cash flows" (FAS 138, par. 40).

liquidity risk reduction of trades, perhaps stemming from turbulence in the markets, that reduces liquidity (i.e., the ability to convert into cash); reduction in liquidity can lead to more price volatility, less certainty, less trading, even less liquidity, continuing in a cycle

market risk any market-related factor that can change the value of the instrument; components that ought to be considered across the term structure include: absolute price or rate change (referred to as delta risk); convexity (gamma risk); change in price volatility (vega risk); time decay (theta); basis or correlation; and discount rate (rho); market risk management should take into account possible abnormal conditions and reduced liquidity

monetizing a financial concept of breaking economic markets into very small pieces that can be sold forward, hedged, borrowed against, and otherwise traded, as a tool for creating competitive markets

net arrangements and master agreements The Group of Thirty suggests a single master agreement rather than multiple master agreements, since the latter can permit "cherry-picking." In other words, a risk arises that the right to set off amounts due under different master agreements might be delayed. A master agreement should provide for full rather than limited two-way payments. This results in the net amount calculated through the netting provisions being due whether it is to, or from, the defaulting party. The benefits of increasing the certainty about the value of a net position under full two-way payments dominates alternative arrangements, based on the judgments of The Group of Thirty.

notional amount "a number of currency units, shares, bushels, pounds, or other units specified in a derivative instrument" (FAS 138, par. 40).

operating risk refers to losses stemming from inadequate risk management and internal controls by those firms that use derivatives; if there is incomplete involvement in or understanding of derivative portfolios by management, then operating risks increase. Operating risks involve inadequacies in documentation, credit controls, or position limits, as well as a lack of control over the use of leverage. Trading and exposure limits ought to be strictly applied, and leverage effects should be continuously monitored by considering liability exposures (analyzed by multiplying percentage changes in rates by the leverage factor to get one's hands around the entire exposure).

option contract provides one party with a right, but not an obligation, to buy or sell something at an agreed-on price on or before a set date, which presents one-sided

obligation of the initial purchaser of the bond, an embedded call trades with and diminishes the value of the underlying bond" (FAS 140, par. 364).

fair value "The amount at which an asset (liability) could be bought (incurred) or sold (settled) in a current transaction between willing parties, that is, other than in a forced or liquidation sale. Quoted market prices in active markets are the best evidence of fair value and should be used as the basis for the measurement, if available. If a quoted market price is available, the fair value is the product of the number of trading units times that market price. If a quoted market price is not available, the estimate of fair value should be based on the best information available in the circumstances. The estimate of fair value should consider prices for similar assets or similar liabilities and the results of valuation techniques to the extent available in the circumstances. Examples of valuation techniques include the present value of estimated expected future cash flows using discount rates commensurate with the risks involved, option-pricing models, matrix pricing, option-adjusted spread models, and fundamental analysis. Valuation techniques for measuring assets and liabilities should be consistent with the objective of measuring fair value. Those techniques should incorporate assumptions that market participants would use in their estimates of values, future revenues, and future expenses, including assumptions about interest rates, default, prepayment, and volatility. In measuring forward contracts, such as foreign currency forward contracts, at fair value by discounting estimated future cash flows, an entity should base the estimate of future cash flows on the changes in the forward rate (rather than the spot rate). In measuring financial liabilities and nonfinancial derivatives that are liabilities at fair value by discounting estimated future cash flows (or equivalent outflows of other assets), an objective is to use discount rates at which those liabilities could be settled in an arm's-length transaction" (FAS 138, par. 40). [See FAS 157.]

financial instrument "Cash, evidence of an ownership interest in an entity, or a contract that both:

  a. Imposes on one entity a contractual obligation*
    (1) to deliver cash or another financial instrument to a second entity or (2) to exchange other financial instruments on potentially unfavorable terms with the second entity.

  b. Conveys to that second entity a contractual right (1) to receive cash or another financial instrument from the first entity or (2) to exchange other financial instruments on potentially favorable terms with the first entity.

    *Contractual obligations encompass both those that are conditioned on the occurrence of a

risk. This is an important dimension of option-type instruments which is significant because the counterparty, the writer of the option, has only a potentially unfavorable outcome: at best, it retains the premium paid by the option holder while at worst, its losses could be virtually unlimited.

securitization "the process by which financial assets are transformed into securities" (FAS 140, par. 364)

settlement risk risk that arises when one party settles the contract before the other party does and the latter does not receive what is owed; this is referred to as Herstatt risk, with the namesake of Bank Herstatt which was a German bank closed by German regulators at the close of business on June 26, 1974—since U.S. banks paid the bank German marks specified in forward contracts before the other side of the contract was paid in U.S. dollars, losses resulted. Settlement risks can be sidestepped through the use of transfer agents and escrow agents or through a simple act of simultaneous transfers. Similarly, derivatives transactions such as rate swaps and other contracts that do not involve principal payments reduce Herstatt risk, as do master agreements and netting arrangements. If netting applies, current credit exposure is the sum of negative and positive exposures on transactions in the portfolio. However, for potential credit exposure, simulation of the entire portfolio is necessary because a summation will not effectively treat offsets or give credit for different timing of peak exposures, meaning that the exposure is overstated by a mere summation.

short sales (sales of borrowed securities) "Short sales typically involve the following activities:

  (1) Selling a security (by the short seller to the purchaser)

  (2) Borrowing a security (by the short seller from the lender)

  (3) Delivering the borrowed security (by the short seller to the purchaser)

  (4) Purchasing a security (by the short seller from the market)

  (5) Delivering the purchased security (by the short seller to the lender).

Those five activities involve three separate contracts. A contract that distinguishes a short sale involves activities (2) and (5), borrowing a security and replacing it by delivering an identical security" (FAS 133, par. 59).

systemic risk is the risk that any disruption will lead to widespread difficulties in firms, markets, or the financial system as a whole, such as a computer software problem within world financial markets and exchanges. Systemic risks in the derivatives market appear more problematic due to the domination of the market by a few large players; two U.S. banks accounted for 95 percent of the notional amount of derivatives in the U.S. banking system in 1992, whereas such domination is not at this

specified event and those that are not. All contractual obligations that are financial instruments meet the definition of liability set forth in Concepts Statement 6, although some may not be recognized as liabilities in financial statements—may be "off-balance-sheet"—because they fail to meet some other criterion for recognition. For some financial instruments, the obligation is owed to or by a group of entities rather than a single entity.

The use of the term *financial instrument* in this definition is recursive (because the term *financial instrument* is included in it), though it is not circular. The definition requires a chain of contractual obligations that ends with the delivery of cash or an ownership interest in an entity. Any number of obligations to deliver financial instruments can be links in a chain that qualifies a particular contract as a financial instrument. Contractual rights encompass both those that are conditioned on the occurrence of a specified event and those that are not. All contractual rights that are financial instruments meet the definition of asset set forth in Concepts Statement 6, although some may not be recognized as assets in financial statements— may be "off-balance-sheet"— because they fail to meet some other criterion for recognition. For some financial instruments, the right is held by or the obligation is due from a group of entities rather than a single entity" (FAS 138, par. 40).

firm commitment "agreement with an unrelated party, binding on both parties and usually legally enforceable, with the following characteristics:
  a. The agreement specifies all significant terms, including the quantity to be exchanged, the fixed price, and the timing of the transaction. The fixed price may be expressed as a specified amount of an entity's functional currency or of a foreign currency. It may also be expressed as a specified interest rate or specified effective yield.
  b. The agreement includes a disincentive for nonperformance that is sufficiently large to make performance probable" (FAS 138, par. 40).

floors, caps, and collars "Floors or caps (or collars, which are combinations of caps and floors) on interest rates and the interest rate on a debt instrument are considered to be clearly and closely related, provided the cap is at or above the current market price (or rate) and the floor is at or below the current market price (or rate) at issuance of the instrument" (FAS 133, par. 61). Also, an embedded derivative instrument in which the underlying is an interest rate or interest rate index—examples of which are interest rate cap or an

scale in most other markets. Since derivatives are growing and the market is beginning to get standard-setters' and regulators' attention, systemic risk is expected to decline.

take-or-pay contracts. "Under a take-or-pay contract, an entity agrees to pay a specified price for a specified quantity of a product whether or not it takes delivery" (FAS 133, par. 59).

The Group of Thirty, Consultative Group on International Economic & Monetary Affairs, Inc., 1990 M Street, N.W., Suite 450, Washington, DC 20036

transferee "An entity that receives a financial asset, a portion of a financial asset, or a group of financial assets from a transferor" (FAS 140, par. 364).

transferor "An entity that transfers a financial asset, a portion of a financial asset, or a group of financial assets that it controls to another entity" (FAS 140, par. 364).

underlying "a specified interest rate, security price, commodity price, foreign exchange rate, index of prices or rates, or other variable. An underlying may be a price or rate of an asset or liability but is not the asset or liability itself" (FAS 138, par. 40). "An underlying usually is one or a combination of the following:

  (1) A security price or security price index
  (2) A commodity price or commodity price index
  (3) An interest rate or interest rate index
  (4) A credit rating or credit index
  (5) An exchange rate or exchange rate index
  (6) An insurance index or catastrophe loss index
  (7) A climatic or geological condition (such as temperature, earthquake severity, or rainfall), another physical variable, or a related index" (FAS 133, par. 57).

undivided interest "Partial legal or beneficial ownership of an asset as a tenant in common with others. The proportion owned may be pro rata, for example, the right to receive 50 percent of all cash flows from a security, or non–pro rata, for example, the right to receive the interest from a security while another has the right to the principal" (FAS 140, par. 364).

unilateral ability "A capacity for action not dependent on the actions (or failure to act) of any other party" (FAS 140, par. 364).

value at risk is the most commonly recommended method for valuing portfolios. The idea is to determine a portfolio's change in value due to adverse market movements of any factor, such as volatility or price, for a specified period of time—preferably one day as the time frame for assessing change in value. The Group of Thirty contends that dealers should mark their derivatives positions to market on at least a daily basis for risk management purposes. Intraday or even real-time valuation is cited as potentially helpful in managing market risk of some option portfolios. The interest rate collar—that alters net interest payments that otherwise would be paid or received on an interest-bearing host contract.

forecasted transaction "A transaction that is expected to occur for which there is no firm commitment. Because no transaction or event has yet occurred and the transaction or event when it occurs will be at the

value-at-risk uses probability analysis based on common confidence intervals, such as 95% representing two standard deviations for a specified time horizon (e.g., a one-day exposure). The phrasing of the result of analysis might be at 95%, it can be determined that any change in portfolio value outside of a predicted range over one day from adverse market movement would be a specified amount.

Further Readings

"A tale of two banks: Events in Paris cast a fresh light on the drama in London." 1995. *The Economist* (March 11), p. 20.

Abken, Peter. 1994. "Over-the-counter financial derivatives: Risky business?" *Economic Review—Federal Reserve Bank of Atlanta* (March/April), p. 12.

Achenbach, Joel. 2001. "Enron, we hardly knew ye." *Washington Post* (December 6).

Adams, Jane B. 1995. "Simplifying accounting for derivative instruments, including those used for hedging." *Highlights of Financial Reporting Issues* (Financial Accounting Standards Board, January), pp. 1–7.

Ascarelli, Silvia, and Deborah Ball. 2001. "Behind shrinking deficits: Derivatives? Report suggests Italy used swaps to meet EU targets on budget." *Wall Street Journal* (November 6), p. A22.

Barrionuevo, Alexei, and Rebecca Smith. 2001. "Dynegy hits back at Enron with lawsuit: Claim is failed merger deal entitles concern to get Northern Natural Gas." *Wall Street Journal* (December 4), p. A10.

"Berardino Congressional Testimony." 2001. "Remarks of Joseph F. Berardino, Managing Partner, Chief Executive Officer, Andersen." U.S. House of Representatives, Committee on Financial Services (Chairman Oxley, Congressman LaFalce, Chairman Baker, Congressman Kanjorski, Chairwoman Kelly, Congressman Gutierrez) (December 12).

Berardino, Joe. 2001. "Enron: A wake-up call." *Wall Street Journal* (December 4), p. A18.

Bodily, Samuel, and Robert Bruner. 2001. "What Enron did right." *Wall Street Journal* (November 19), p. A20.

Brauchli, Marcus W., Nicholas Bray, and Michael R. Sesit. 1995. "Broken bank: Barings PLC officials may have been aware of trader's position: Investigators say firm knew extent of its exposure, but failed to respond—Leeson was 'hero' to some." *Wall Street Journal* (March 6), pp. A1, A7.

Breeden, Richard. The bankruptcy-court "corporate monitor" of MCI (formerly World.com) filed a report

Knecht, G. Bruce. 1994. "The lawyers' turn: Derivatives are going through crucial test: A wave of lawsuits." *Wall Street Journal* (Oct. 28), p. A1.

Lipin, Steven. 1994. "Gibson Greetings reaches accord in suit against bankers trust over derivatives." *Wall Street Journal* (November 25), p. A2.

Lowenstein, Roger. 1995. "Intrinsic value: As Orange County blames others, guess where latest report points." *Wall Street Journal* (September 7).

Lucas, Timothy S., and Janet Danola. 1993. "Improving disclosures about derivatives." *FASB Viewpoints* (December 31), pp. 1, 2.

Lucchetti, Aaron. 2001. "When bad stocks happen to good mutual funds: Enron could spark new attention to accounting." *Wall Street Journal* (December 13), pp. C1, C19.

McGee, Suzanne. 1995. "Farmers may be next victims of derivatives." *Wall Street Journal* (December 11), pp. C1, C14.

Mellino, Angelo, and Stuart Turnbull. 1995. "Misspecification and the pricing and hedging of long-term foreign currency options." *Journal of International Money and Finance* (June), pp. 373–393.

Melloan, George. 1995. "Leeson's law: Too much leverage can wreck a bank." *Wall Street Journal* (March 6), p. A15.

Michaels, Adrian. 2001. "Andersen chief calls for revamp of accounting system." *Financial Times* (December 4).

Mills, Mark, and Peter Huber. 2001. "Deregulation will survive Enron" [Editorial]. *Wall Street Journal* (December 6).

Molvar, Roger H.D., and James F. Green. 1995. "The question of derivatives." *Journal of Accountancy* (March), p. 55.

Nobes, Christopher W., Editor. 2001. *GAAP 2000: A Survey of National Accounting Rules in 53 Countries.* Arthur Andersen, BDO, Deloitte Touche Tohmatsu, Ernst & Young International, Grant Thornton, KPMG, and PricewaterhouseCoopers.

Pacelle, Mitchell, and Cassell Bryan-Low. 2001. "Enron's collapse roils insiders and Wall Street: Belfer Family is a big loser as stock dive." *Wall Street Journal* (December 5), pp. C1, C13.

in August 2003 that identified 78 reforms agreed to by MCI; these reforms involve accounting, cash flow reporting, dividend policy, internal audit, transparency policies, governance, and other topics. The report called "Restoring Trust" is available at: www.ragm.com/library/topics/Breeden_Restoring_Trust_Final-WorldCom082003.pdf.

Bryan-Low, Cassell, and Suzanne McGee. 2001. "Enron short seller detected red flags in regulatory filings." *Wall Street Journal* (November 5), p. C1.

Civil Action No. H-04–0284 (Harmon) First Amended Complaint by the United States Securities and Exchange Commission, Plaintiff, v. Jeffrey K. Skilling, Richard A. Causey, Defendants, United States District Court Southern District of Texas Houston Division, filed in February 2004. (See www.Findlaw.com.)

Conover, Teresa L., and Wanda A. Wallace. 2000. "Accounting hedges: Should we expect changes under SFAS No. 133?" *Advances in International Accounting*, Volume 13. Stamford, CT: JAI Press, pp. 119–132.

Craig, Suzanne, and Jonathan Weil. 2001. "Most analysts remain plugged in to Enron." *Wall Street Journal* (October 26), pp. C1, C2.

Credit Suisse Equity Research, First Boston, Research Team David Zion and Bill Carcache. 2003. Accounting & Tax. FIN 46, New Rule Could Surprise Investors (June 24), pp. 1–82.

Dhanani, Slpha, and Roger Groves. 2001. "The Management of strategic exchange risk: Evidence from corporate practices." *Accounting and Business Research* (31, 4, Autumn), pp. 275–290.

Edwards, Gerald, and Gregory Eller. 1995. "Overview of derivatives disclosures by major U.S. banks." *Federal Reserve Bulletin* (September), p. 820.

Emshwiller, John R. 2002. "Documents track Enron's partnerships: Top officers viewed deals as integral to ensuring growth in recent years." *Wall Street Journal* (January 2), pp. A3, A8.

Emshwiller, John R. 2001. "Enron transaction with entity run by executive raises questions." *Wall Street Journal* (November 5), p. A3.

Emshwiller, John R., and Rebecca Smith. 2001. "Corporate veil: Behind Enron's fall, a culture of operating outside public's view; hidden deals with officers and minimal disclosure finally cost it its trust; Chewco and JEDI warriors." *Wall Street Journal* (December 5), pp. A1, A10.

Emshwiller, John, and Rebecca Smith. 2001. "Dynegy's Enron deal faces uncertainties: Potential antitrust worries or new Enron liabilities could upset agreement." *Wall Street Journal* (November 12), pp. A3, A12.

Emshwiller, John R., and Rebecca Smith. 2001. "Enron did business with a second entity operated by another

Pacelle, Mitchell, Michael Schroeder, and John Emshwiller. 2001. "Enron would restructure around 'core.'" *Wall Street Journal* (December 13), pp. A3, A6.

Pinkston, Will. 2002. "TVA accounting is in dispute." *Wall Street Journal* (January 30), p. B9.

Pitt, Harvey L. 2001. "How to prevent future Enrons." *Wall Street Journal* (December 11), p. A18.

Pretzlik, Charles, and Gary Silverman. 2001. "Enron is regulators' nightmare come true. Banks on the hook. Companies & Finance: The collapse of Enron." *Financial Times* (November 30), p. 29.

Reilly, David. 2006. "FASB to issue retooled rule for valuing corporate assets—new method repeals limits spurred by Enron scandal; critics worry about abuses." *Wall Street Journal* (September 15), p. C3.

"Review & Outlook: What was Enron?" 2001. *Wall Street Journal* (December 12), p. A18.

Richardson, Karen. 2001. "Hong Kong may give investors broader reach to hedge funds." *Wall Street Journal* (December 13), p. C10.

Sapsford, Jathon, and Alexei Barrionuevo. 2001. "Reviving Enron requires return of old clients." *Wall Street Journal* (December 5), pp. A3, A10.

Schroeder, Michael. 2001. "Enron debacle spurs calls for controls." *Wall Street Journal* (December 14), p. A4.

Schroeder, Michael. 2001. "Enron debacle will test leadership of SEC's new chief: Harvey Pitt's handling of energy-trading firm's collapse to be watched closely." *Wall Street Journal* (December 31), p. A10.

Schroeder, Michael, and Greg Ip. 2001. "Out of reach: The Enron debacle spotlights huge void in financial regulation—energy firm lobbied hard to limit the oversight of its trading operations—keeping Ms. Born at bay." *Wall Street Journal* (December 13), pp. A1, A6.

SEC. 2003. Office of the Chief Accountant and Office of Economic Analysis. Study Pursuant to Section 108(d) of the Sarbanes-Oxley Act of 2002 on the Adoption by the United States Financial Reporting System of a Principles-Based Accounting System. Submitted to Committee on Banking, Housing, and Urban Affairs of the United States Senate and Committee on Financial Services of the U.S. Securities and Exchange Commission (Washington, DC: SEC).

SEC. 2001. "SEC issues financial disclosure cautionary advice:" "Action: cautionary advice regarding disclosure about critical accounting policies." 2001. Press Release No. 33–8040; 34–45149; FR 60 (December 12). Available at: http://www.sec.gov/pdf/33-8040.pdf.

Skinner, D. J. 1996. "Are disclosures about bank derivatives and employee stock options value-relevant?" *Journal of Accounting and Economics* (22), pp. 393–405.

Smith, Randall. 2001. "Lehman faced possible conflict as merger failed." *Wall Street Journal* (December 5), pp. C1, C11.

company official: No public disclosure was made of deals." *Wall Street Journal* (October 26), pp. C1, C14.

FASB. 2005. Exposure Draft Proposed Statement of Financial Accounting Standards. *The Hierarchy of Generally Accepted Accounting Principles* (Comment Deadline June 27, 2005). (Financial Accounting Series No. 1300–001 April 28).

FASB. 2002. *Proposal: Principles-Based Approach to U.S. Standard Setting* (Comment Deadline: January 3, 2003). (File Reference No. 1125–001 October 21).

"Five accounting firms issue statement on Enron." 2001. Joint Press Release (December 4) [Statement from Big Five CEOs Arthur Andersen, KPMG, Deloitte Touche, PricewaterhouseCoopers, Ernst & Young, Press Release Wires, FACTIVA].

Francis, Theo, and Ellen Schultz. 2001. "Enron faces suits by 401(K) plan participants." *Wall Street Journal* (November 23), pp. C1, C10.

French, Kenneth. 1988. "Pricing financial futures contracts: An introduction." *Financial Markets and Portfolio Management* (Spring).

Goldberg, Stephen, Charles Tritschler, and Joseph Godwin. 1995. "Financial reporting for foreign exchange derivatives." *Accounting Horizons* (June), pp. 1–15.

The Group of Thirty. 1994. *Defining the Roles of Accountants, Bankers and Regulators in the United States: A Study Group Report.* Washington, DC.

Herz, Robert. 1994. "Hedge accounting, derivatives, and synthetics: The FASB starts rethinking the rules." *Journal of Corporate Accounting and Finance* (Spring), pp. 323–333.

Hill, Andrew, and Peter Thal Larsen. 2001. "Enron promised dollars 1.5bn in emergency funding." *Financial Times* (December 4), p. 1.

Hill, Andrew, Sheila Mcnulty, and Elizabeth Wine. 2001. "A chaotic collapse: Enron's demise stems from a lethal combination of abundant financing and media hype. Investors' blind belief inflated an ultimately unsustainable bubble, says Andrew Hill." *Financial Times* (November 30), p. 20.

Jarrow, Robert, and Stuart Turnbull. 1995. "Pricing derivatives on financial securities subject to credit risk." *Journal of Finance* (March), pp. 53–85.

Jereski, Laura. 1994. "The wrong stuff: Good connections put hedge fund in business but a bad bet sank it—Manager David Weill, suave and impressive, drew in Europe's wealthy class—Adieu to a gilded world." *Wall Street Journal* (September 28), pp. A1, A8.

Kedrosky, Paul. 2001. "How Enron ran out of gas." *Wall Street Journal* (October 29), p. A22.

Kessler, Andy. 2001. "Lying is a capital crime." *Wall Street Journal* (November 30), p. A14.

Smith, Randall, and Steven Lipin. 1994. "Beleaguered giant: as derivatives losses rise, industry fights to avert regulation—stigma has already stalled 'exotic' end of business, where most of profit is—now a $35 trillion market." *Wall Street Journal* (August 25), pp. A1, A4.

U.S. Bankr. Southern District of N.Y. 2003. In re: Enron Corp., et al., Debtors, Chapter 11 Case No. 01–16034 (AJG) Jointly Administered. Third Interim Report of Newl Batson, Court-Appointed Examiner (June 30).

U.S. Bankr. Southern District of N.Y. 2003. In re: Worldcom, Inc., et al., Debtors, Chapter 11 Case No. 02-15533 (AJG) Jointly Administered, Second Interim Report of Dick Thornburgh, Bankr. Examiner (June 9).

Venkatachalam, M. 1996. "Value relevance of banks derivatives disclosures." *Journal of Accounting and Economics* 17, pp. 327–355.

Wallace, Wanda A. 2004. "Adding value through accounting signals." *California Management Review* (46, 4, Summer), pp. 120–137.

Wallace, Wanda. 1999–2000. "How important are thin-market considerations?" Assurance Forum. *Accounting Today* (13, 22, December 13–January 2), pp. 16, 68.

Wallace, Wanda A. 1999. *Performance Measurement and Risk Monitoring.* Boston, New York: Warren Gorham & Lamont, RIA Group.

Wallace, Wanda A. 1999. "Risk evaluation: Just who is minding the store?" Assurance Forum. *Accounting Today* (August 23–September 5), pp. 16, 45, 46.

Wallace, Wanda A. 1996. "FASB hedge accounting rule blurs fact." Audit & Accounting Forum. *Accounting Today* (June 3–16), pp. 16, 17, 20.

Weil, Jonathan. 2001. "After Enron, 'mark to market' accounting gets scrutiny." *Wall Street Journal* (December 4), pp. C1, C2.

Weil, Jonathan. 2001. "Arthur Andersen could face scrutiny on clarity of Enron financial reports." *Wall Street Journal* (November 5), p. C1.

Weil, Jonathan. 2001. "Basic principle of accounting tripped Enron." *Wall Street Journal* (November 12), pp. C1, C2.

Wilson, Arlette C. 1998. "The decision on derivatives (Accounting Standards for derivative instruments and hedging activities)." *Journal of Accountancy* (November).

Winograd, Barry N., and Robert H. Herz. 1995. "Derivatives: What's an auditor to do?" *Journal of Accountancy* (June), pp. 75–80.

Zuckerman, Gregory. 2001. "Hedge funds now frown upon anonymity." *Wall Street Journal* (December 13), pp. C1, C10.

If accounting is important and you change the accounting rules, then the play of the game changes.

— William R. Kinney, Jr.

[Source: Commentary on "The Relation of Accounting Research to Teaching and Practice: A 'Positive' View," <u>*Accounting Horizons*</u> *(March 1989), p. 123]*

CASE 12

Emerging Issues: The Agenda of FASB

CASE TOPICS OUTLINE

1. Priorities of the Financial Accounting Standards Board—Annual Survey of the Financial Accounting Standards Advisory Council
   A. Board Members' Rankings
   B. Your Rankings

2. Strategy-Related Considerations

The Financial Accounting Standards Board (FASB) evaluates potential agenda projects by considering the pervasiveness of the issue, alternative solutions, technical feasibility, cost-benefit relationship, and practical consequences. Annually, the Financial Accounting Standards Advisory Council (FASAC) administers a survey to solicit views of FASB members, council members, and their constituencies about future FASB agenda priorities and other matters. This survey is also sent to former members of FASAC. By accessing fasb.org, you can download both the survey form and the summary of responses for annual FASAC survey(s). In October 2005, the FASAC reported the results concerning priorities, future financial reporting issues, simplification, the right level of implementation guidance, and differential accounting standards for certain entities. The 2006 Annual FASAC Survey solicits constituents' views on the FASB's current priorities, future financial reporting issues, international convergence, and educational efforts.

Requirement A: Your Ranking

1. The five issues appearing most often as requiring attention on the FASB agenda are revenue recognition, pension accounting and related issues, the conceptual framework, financial performance reporting by business enterprises, and accounting for leases and other contractual obligations; see Section A of the downloadable Summary of Responses to the Annual FASAC Survey—Priorities of the Financial Accounting Standards Board (October 2005, FASAC). How would you rank-order these topics and why?

2. Compare and contrast your assessments relative to those reported for the FASB, as well as the examples of where the board members appear to differ from FASAC members. Do a similar analysis for other surveys available at fasb.org (2006 and later years).
3. Prepare your identification of issues and rankings, apart from the most recent survey results accessible at fasb.org. As background, review the survey results from prior years that are downloadable from the Web site and compare and contrast those with your assessments.

Requirement B: Strategy-Related Considerations

The FASB has its stated basis for setting priorities (see "Key terms and Glossary"). Apply those criteria to each topic and determine whether it is possible to assess which criteria took priority in setting the rankings.

Among the instructions to past surveys are reminders to respondents that the FASB always must consider the available resources in making agenda decisions and believes that it is not desirable to have projects on the agenda that are inactive for long periods of time. In addition, the board considers the opportunity to work jointly on projects with the International Accounting Standards Board (IASB) to meet the goal of achieving convergence. Thus, the instructions have advised that the council's views should be tempered by consideration of all of these factors. Do any of these considerations mitigate the effect of the key criteria set forth for the setting of FASB priorities? Do you believe such mitigation is appropriate and how should these additional considerations influence FASB standard setting, if at all?

Directed Self-Study

What was the primary reason the standard-setters issued Statement of Financial Accounting Standards No. 153 entitled *Exchanges of Nonmonetary Assets—an amendment of APB Opinion No. 29* in December 2004? [Access the FARS Menu, click on Original Pronouncements, click on Statements of Financial Accounting Standards, and then scroll down to FAS 153 and click again. Current standards contain a section within their summary that is entitled "Reasons for Issuing This Statement." Find that section.] Identify another pronouncement that was issued for similar reasons.

Are Accounting Rules to Blame?

The front page of the *Wall Street Journal* on January 20-21, 2007 (Sat/Sun edition) reported that Apple had cited accounting rules as the reason for imposing a fee to download a software enhancement. "Apple Gets a Bruise by Blaming a $1.99 Fee on Accounting Rules" by David Reilly is the companion story on page B3. Read the article, access Apple's web site to explore its press releases, and then search the media for other coverage of these events. Outline the various points made regarding GAAP and use FARS, as well as the sec.gov site, to evaluate whether accounting rules can indeed be blamed. What are the implications for standard setters and regulators? Explain.

Key Terms and Glossary

alternative solutions   FAS 89, par. 124 explains "The second factor considered is the potential for developing an alternative solution—whether one or more alternatives that will improve the relevance, reliability, and comparability of financial reporting are likely to be developed."

cost-benefit relationship   FAS 89, par. 117 elaborates on a setting in which this idea of relative costs and benefits is applied: "In addition to those views, the most frequently cited reason for discontinuing the supplementary disclosures was that the benefits derived from presenting that data had not been sufficient to justify the costs incurred." The Board notes an example of a disclosure considered in isolation as not being " unduly burdensome."

equity method of accounting   FAS 133, par. 455 states "Under the equity method of accounting, the investor generally records its share of the investee's earnings or losses from its investment. It does not account for changes in the price of the common stock. . . ".

going concern concept   FIN 39, par. 48 states "as a general rule, accounting should reflect what is expected to occur in the normal course of business and protection in bankruptcy is not pertinent when the probability of bankruptcy is remote."

pervasiveness of the issue   FAS 89, par. 123 explains "The first factor considered is the pervasiveness of the problem to be addressed. A determination is made concerning (a) the extent to which an issue is troublesome to users, preparers, auditors, or others, (b) the extent to which practice is diverse, and (c) the likely duration of the problem (that is, is it transitory or will it persist)."

practical consequences   FAS 89, par. 126 explains "The last factor considers practical consequences, namely, whether an improved accounting solution is likely to be generally acceptable and whether not addressing a particular subject might cause others to act, that is, the SEC or Congress."

technical feasibility   FAS 89, par. 125 explains "The third factor addresses the technical feasibility of a project, that is, the extent to which a technically sound solution can be developed or whether the project under consideration should await completion of other projects."

Further Readings

Beresford, Dennis R. 1993. "Frustrations of a standards setter." *Accounting Horizons* (7, 4), pp. 70–76.

Broadbent, Jane, and Richard Laughlin. 2005. "Government concerns and tensions in accounting standard-setting: The case of accounting for the Private Finance Initiative in the UK." *Accounting and Business Research* (35, 3), pp. 207–228.

The Economist. 2003. "True and fair is not hard and fast—the future of accounts" (367, 8321, 1, April 26).

Financial Executives International and National Investor Relations. 2001. "Best practice" guidelines for earnings releases (April). Available at: http://www.fei.org.

Flegm, Eugene H. 2005. "Accounting at a crossroad." *CPA Journal* (December).

Flegm, Eugene H. 2004. *Accounting: How to Meet the Challenges of Relevance and Regulation.* New York: Elsevier.

Griffin, Paul A. 1987. *Research Report: Usefulness to Investors and Creditors of Information Provided by Financial Reporting*, 2nd ed. Stamford, CT: FASB.

Herz, Robert H. 2003. "Commentary—a year of challenge and change for the FASB." *Accounting Horizons* (17, 3, September), pp. 247–255.

Holland, John. 2005. "A grounded theory of corporate

Schuetze, Walter P., and P.W. Wolnizer. 2004. *Mark-to-Market Accounting. "True North" in Financial Reporting.* New York: Routledge.

SEC. 2003. Release No. 33-8221; 34-47743; IC-26028; FR-70. Policy statement: Reaffirming the status of the FASB as a designated private-sector standard setter. (April 25).

Tandy, Paulette R., and Nancy L. Wilburn. 1992. "Constituent participation in standard-setting: The FASB's first 100 statements." *Accounting Horizons* (6, 2), pp. 47–58.

Upton Jr., Wayne S. 2001. Special Report: Business and Financial Reporting, Challenges from the New Economy. (April). Available at: fasb.org/new_economy/.

Wallace, Wanda A. 2005. "Skinner's 'interpretation panel'—a means to balance 'power' ". *Canadian Accounting Perspectives* (4, 2), pp. 301–320.

Wallace, Wanda A. 2004. "The economic role of the audit in free and regulated markets: A look back and a look forward." *Research in Accounting Regulation* (17), pp. 267–298.

Wallace, Wanda A. 2002. "Are there too many cooks in the kitchen?" *Accounting Today* (16, 19, Oct. 21–Nov. 3), p. 17.

Wallace, Wanda A. 2001. "Contrarians or soothsayers?" *CPA Journal* (LXXI, 12, December), pp. 34–41.

disclosure." *Accounting and Business Research* (35, 3), pp. 249–267.

Ijiri, Y. 2005. "U.S. accounting standards and their environment: A dualistic study of their 75 years of transition." *Journal of Accounting and Public Policy* (24, 4, July/August), pp. 255–279.

Krishnan, Rangani. 2005. "The effect of changes in regulation and competition on firms' demand for accounting information." *Accounting Review* (80, 1, January), pp. 269–287.

Leisenring, James J., and L. Todd Johnson. 1994. "Accounting research: On the relevance of research to practice." *Accounting Horizons* (8, 4), pp. 74–79.

May, Robert G., and Gary L. Sundem. 1976. "Research for accounting policy: An overview." *Accounting Review* (51, 4), pp. 747–763.

Ratcliffe, Thomas A. 2003. "OCBOA Financial Statements." *Journal of Accountancy* (196, 4, October), pp. 71–75.

Watts, Ross L. 2003. "Conservatism in accounting, part I: Explanations and implications." *Accounting Horizons* (17, 3, September), pp. 207–221.

Watts, Ross, and Jerold Zimmerman, 1986. *Positive Accounting.* Englewood Cliffs, NJ: Prentice-Hall.

Zeff, Stephen A. 2003. "How the U.S. accounting profession got where it is today: Part I." *Accounting Horizons* (17, 3, September), pp. 189–205.

Zeff, Stephen A. 1987. "Leaders of the accounting profession: 14 who made a difference," *Journal of Accountancy* (163, 5), pp. 46–71.

Zeff, Stephen A. 1986. "Big Eight firms and the accounting literature: The falloff in advocacy writing." *Journal of Accounting, Auditing and Finance* (1, New Series, 2), pp. 131–154.

Zeff, Stephen A. 1972. "Chronology of significant developments in the establishment of accounting principles in the United States 1926–1972." *Journal of Accounting Research* (10, 1), pp. 217–227.

'We should not lose the substance by grasping the shadow, but often the shadow helps us grasp the substance. The same may be said of the role of acounting in business. Just as culture affects and is affected by language, business affects and is affected by accounting. In his satirical article on clothes, "Sartor Resartus" (<u>trans</u>. "The Tailor Retailored"), Thomas Carlyle states, "Society is founded upon cloth," and ". . .Man's earthly interests, 'are all hooked and buttoned together, and held up, by clothes.'" [1834, p. 51]. Indeed, is it not true that business is founded upon accounting? Without accounting how could we hook and button our interests together?**

—Yuji Ijiri

[Source: <u>Theory of Accounting Measurement</u> Studies in Accounting Research No. 10 (Sarasota, FL.: American Accounting Association, 1975), p. 189; Ijiri cited Thomas Carlyle, <u>Sartor Resartus: The Life and Opinion of Herr Teufelsdrockh</u> (1834), edited by C. F. Harrold (Odyssey Press, 1937)]